McKenna Rhiannon,
Gwendolyn Morgan,
Seren Faye,
Ceara Roisín,
Áine Dorothy Maeve,
and Bree Evelyn Hope:
you are six of the best reasons
to write down Rory's stories.

And Liam, always.

to our Rock—
all other ground
is shifting sand

one

Abject humiliation. Utter despair. No eighth-grade graduation ceremony would be complete without them. Therefore it's necessary for some poor shlub to go belly-up on the gymnasium floor.

The recipe is perfect: take one crowded room of fidgety 14-year-olds (and a 15-year-old or two), make them balance square cardboard hats on their heads and wear hot, slithery, clumsy robes on top of fancy, uncomfortable clothes and awkward shoes—maybe even their first pair of heels—and then march them one by one up some wobbly stage stairs to collect a diploma (Which hand is for diploma grabbing? Which is for hand shaking? No one seems to remember!) and down some more wobbly stage stairs to the lure of freedom.

Do they at least spread gymnastics mats out at the bottom to catch the casualties? Nope—nothing there but beige rubber floor. I know it well.

With the right perspective, humiliation isn't entirely bad. We all need a serving of humble pie now and then. Even a public crash landing can be a blessing, especially if you fall clutching a diploma you weren't sure you'd even get. But that wasn't me, of course. I breezed through eighth grade.

(By breeze I mean more of a gale force wind. Blowing against me.)

No point reliving the whole year. Yes, there are some parts I like to replay over and over in my head...and then there are parts that keep replaying when I long to delete them. Though it would seem pretty sweet to scan life backwards, cut out the cruddy bits and just paste the good stuff together, the story wouldn't make much sense—and in my case, it would be pretty short. Weird how the bad stuff sometimes makes the good more real.

My junior high career had pretty much started out in the toilet, and I already knew eighth grade was going to be, to put it nicely, the big flush. Let's face it: three of my best friends (not much competition for that title, I'll admit) had gone on to high school and left me behind. Did I mention, left me behind with Jake Dean?

Jake wasn't in my homeroom class, but I almost wished he was. He got the teacher he wanted and never tired of gloating about it. I got Mrs. Palmer of the Perpetual Headache.

Honestly, how do people choose their careers? My sister, Sheelan, took some kind of career aptitude test in high school, and it informed her that she'd make a great meteorologist. She thought maybe they meant cosmetologist, so she took it again to be sure. The second result was food safety specialist. I think when Mrs. Palmer took that test, there was probably a question, *Does the mere presence of children cause you physical pain, particularly in the head and neck?* She answered yes, and it spit out her results: junior high schoolteacher. Only she never took it a second time, when it might have suggested game warden or bounty hunter.

I still had Mr. Behrens for English class. I even sat in the same seat as last year. But this year the eighth-grader sitting behind me wasn't Sam Newman. It was Jake's next-door neighbor, the new girl he'd been talking about half the summer, Bliss Hathaway.

Bliss defied all logic—one of those girls who comes in, knows nobody, but immediately has everyone scrambling to know her. No groveling at the bottom of the food chain, no pitiful attempts to wedge herself into established cliques. Bliss was a force unto herself. In some ways she reminded me of Shayne Svoboda: oblivious to labels, crossing all social lines with a smile. But there was something different about Bliss's smile, more mysterious and knowing.

The differences didn't stop with her smile. When she first walked into Whitestone Elementary in September, Jasmine Wee and I spotted her at the same time.

"Someone should tell her she missed the high school by about five blocks," Jasmine said.

Then I saw Jake scurry up to the girl, and it clicked. "No way."

"What?"

"She's the one who moved in next door to Jake," I said. "She's in his class."

"You can't be serious."

I just nodded while we watched her walk past with all the swerves and curves of a 17-year-old. Later I heard someone say that her boyfriend was a 17-year-old, but cafeteria gossip is about as trustworthy as cafeteria food.

"It's probably true," Jasmine decided later. She had chosen the macaroni and cheese over the grilled fish, a sure sign that all was not well. "Look—all the boys watching her? She's a magnet. Why not a 17-year-old boyfriend?"

I sighed. I doubted Jasmine was interested in those boys any more than I was, but I sympathized. Jasmine was built like a 10-year-old girl, and I was... Well, let's just say I may not have been interested in any of those boys, but the thought of being magnetic had its appeal.

Then Bliss passed my table. Our eyes met; for some reason, I smiled. Her eyebrows flicked upwards for a second, then she smiled back before she chose an empty table. Within thirty seconds, five other people had joined her.

"Where'd she move from?" Jasmine asked.

Jake had mentioned it, along with everything else he'd learned about this girl, like it was some earth-shattering discovery. "Idaho, or Colorado, maybe?" I said. "Something that ends with 'o'."

Jasmine nodded suspiciously. What she was suspicious of, I could only guess. "Figures," she said.

Bliss chose the seat behind me in English. Wherever she came from, it soon became clear that it was a place of far greater sophistication. Her accessories already suggested it, and her slightly mystified reaction to some of our primitive native customs (no yoga in gym class, for starters) reinforced it. She accepted the differences without comment—but we found ourselves commenting on our backward ways for her, suddenly dissatisfied with the smallness of our lives.

Sitting in front of Bliss in English class was the closest I ever expected to orbit her sphere, an unnoticed chunk of space rock caught in the outermost pull of her gravitation. Like Pluto: was it a planet or wasn't it? Did anyone care? I never for a second imagined that her gravity would pull me in, that she would learn my name, talk to me—actually stand up for me in a crushing moment when no one else made a move to stand up for me. I never dreamed she would call herself my friend. And if I had, I would've never in a decade of seconds dreamed that I wouldn't want any of it.

Kind of a long story.

I suppose it started in science. Bliss and Jake were both in the class with me, and Jasmine, too. It was Mr. Hayes's science class, the pinnacle of academics at Whitestone Elementary, the class that kids tolerated all the rest of eighth grade just to experience.

Mr. Dylan Hayes was an A+ Apple Award-winning teacher who obviously loved his job and hadn't been doing it long enough to lose his taste for it (he couldn't have been much over thirty). His passion for hands-on, down and dirty, explosive, bubbling, scream-inducing experiments earned him the instant devotion of all the boys; and his easygoing style, always with a ready laugh (and twinkling blue eyes) tended to gain the favor of the girls.

Not one to waste time, Mr. Hayes plunged right into a study of amphibians with the grisly grand finale of frog dissection. Dissection is a scientific term meaning to cut into a dead frog, probe around and discover various gruesome internal organs, and then spend the rest of the time taking cover while Kevin Sebeck and his friends flick tidbits of spleen and bile duct around the room, attempting to score points. Body shots were worth one point, face shots two, and anything that became embedded in a girl's hair was an automatic five-pointer.

My particular curly-ish, crazy-ish kind of hair traps flecks of frog guts like spider webs trap flies. Boys instinctively know these things.

Even so, I was morbidly fascinated by the idea of discovering Kermit's wee inner secrets. While the boys laid out their frog-gut battle plans, the girls were mostly deciding privately whether they would take the super-girly, squeamish approach to dead amphibians or put on a tough-girl show.

Since my lab partner turned out to be Jasmine—who was also fascinated but, like me, equally turned off by the idea—I planned to face the day with a who-cares sort of confidence I didn't feel. Jasmine chose the same attitude. We sorted casually through the wicked metal instruments laid out on our lab table, waiting for the tray with the splayed-out frog to arrive. When Mr. Hayes deposited it in front of us, I tried not to look as pale as I felt. Jasmine's eyes looked blacker than black in her own colorless face.

At the lab table in the back corner by the windows, Bliss Hathaway came to her feet. "Mr. Hayes," she said in a clear voice, "I have to object."

He finished tacking up a large frog-gut diagram before turning to her. "Do you, now?"

"I'm afraid so, sir." Somehow when she said 'sir', it didn't sound like kissing up. "The needless killing of animals goes against my deeply-held beliefs."

"The frogs are already dead, Bliss," Tiffany Klipfel whispered, in her own distinctive, clearly-audible raspy style. She was Bliss's lab partner and already looking a little wild around the eyes.

"But they were killed for this, and I can't support that with my participation. I believe we should respect life in all its forms."

Mr. Hayes was jotting something on a slip of paper. "Why didn't you say something before now, Bliss? You know you can come after school to discuss any concerns with me."

She smiled. "Thank you, Mr. Hayes. I hoped you would understand."

"There's at least one student every year who declines to participate in the dissection, though few of them do it with such eloquence. Come here."

By the time she reached the front of the classroom, her dimples were on full display. Mr. Hayes handed her the slip of paper. "This excuses you from class today and tomorrow, during which time you may go to the media center and begin researching your report on the life cycle of the frog—in all its forms."

"Thank you." She beamed at him.

"Never let it be said that I don't respect the deeply-held beliefs of my students." He watched her leave with a small shake of his head and the slightest smile.

I didn't give much thought to his words at the time. I was too busy staring Jasmine down. "Don't even think about it," I said.

"What?"

"Pulling a Bliss Hathaway and taking off."

"Please." She picked up the knife. As long as she wasn't required to eat the frog, Jasmine was okay with it.

It wasn't the first time Bliss would stand up for the rights of a weaker creature in science class. Only the next time, it got personal—I was her next frog on a platter.

Getting personal came naturally to Bliss. I never shared my seventh-grade story with her: the accident, my dad's death, my head injury and the visions of angels and demons. I had absolutely no desire to, or to talk about it with anyone outside of the four friends who already knew—Shayne, Allie, Sam and Jake—those of us who wore the white stones around our necks.

But I began to realize that Bliss knew things about me. Not everything, not all at once, but enough. She had ways of learning things—above and beyond the usual ways. Bliss's ways were unlike any I'd ever come in contact with. And I came in much closer contact than I ever should have.

I know I'm responsible, too. But I think it's fair to say that it's because of Bliss that a part of my life resurfaced that I had labeled as 'in the past' and filed neatly away. My angels came back. Only they weren't like I remembered them at all.

two

There was more to September than Mrs. Palmer's headaches, frog guts, and itchy school uniforms. Something actually had me looking forward to that month (so it had to be good): Teen Scene was starting up again.

Our youth group hadn't met since April, when Kellie Greene—the girls' fearless leader, as Shayne had called her—had suddenly died and left us all shell-shocked. We hadn't even finished up our series on the Armor of God. (We had never 'picked up' the Sword of the Spirit, but I guess you could say I'd had a little private lesson on the subject.)

I was anxious to know if Pastor Dan would pick up where we left off, or if it would be too weird without Kellie. She was a huge loss to the Front Street Temple, and to Whitestone Elementary. Art class had its paint and pencils, clay and paper maché, but it felt more like just another class now.

I can't say this was the only reason I couldn't wait for the Scene to resume. I had three other reasons: Shayne Svoboda, Allie

Rousseau, and Sam Newman. The three who had graduated and left me with Jake. I was ready to forgive them and be the fearsome fivesome again, to use Kellie's term.

I thought about it so much that I couldn't help talking about it. Jake had weaseled his way into the regulars at Bliss Hathaway's lunch table, and the other kids who had sometimes sat with Shayne and the rest last year had either graduated or migrated into different groups. So lunches generally involved me, Jasmine, and whoever else might be sitting close enough to join in a conversation if they wanted to. There wasn't a mad rush to join us, most days.

"Trying to break your personal record?" Jasmine asked me that Friday.

I stopped shoveling potato pucks into my mouth. "Hmm?"

"You're speed eating."

"Oh. Yeah." I swallowed. "I guess I want to get this day over with." Her look said, *and eating like a pig is going to accomplish this — how?* "I've been waiting for tomorrow forever."

"What's tomorrow?"

"Our first Scene meeting of the fall. You know, the church thing."

She nodded. It might have meant *Oh, that again.*

"I'll get to see Shayne and Allie."

Another nod, a down-then-up with a pause that definitely said, *And...*

"And Sam." I tossed it in there casually.

"But they graduated."

"The group's for teens, doesn't have to do with your grade really."

"You think they'll still come?"

My fork stopped halfway to my mouth. "Yeah. Why not?"

"Oh, you know." She shrugged. "Sometimes people get involved in different things once they're in high school."

"They'd never drop out of this. They've been waiting all summer, too."

"So you've kept in touch with them."

"Yep. Well, for most of the summer."

"Oh." She nibbled broccoli. "But not since school started."

"I guess not. No."

She nodded again.

And doubt began nibbling me like broccoli. They'd been at Whitestone High for weeks now. I remembered when Sheelan was a freshman, how she'd immediately joined everything but the chess club (they do have standards) and had extracurricular activities every day of the week and some on weekends. Allie and Shayne had been so excited, I could just imagine them doing the same. And Sam, well, he wasn't at Whitestone High at all. He was homeschooling. Who knew what that meant?

When I hadn't heard anything by noon on Saturday, I pretty much decided Jasmine was right. Either they weren't going to the Scene, or they were but I had to find my own way there. Either way, it would be humiliating to call Shayne now.

Since a little humiliation never stopped me before, I did park my sorry behind on the front steps at about the time Shayne and her older brother, Jeph, used to pick me up in the big brown Buick. Just in case.

Kingston Fisher opened his front door, right beside ours in the duplex but separated by an iron hand rail. He shuffled out with the usual grin. "Hey, Rory. Waiting for someone?"

"Yeah. No." I pushed the hair out of my face. "I don't know."

He sat down on the same step on his side of the rail, satisfied with my answer. "I can wait with you, if you want."

Kingston wasn't a bad person to wait around with, but right then I wasn't feeling like good company. I looked at him sitting there, though, and it reminded me of a time when we'd both sat in the same spot and he'd told me, *When in Rome, do what the Romans do*, and showed me a bunch of verses in the Book of Romans. And for the first time a whole lot of things had made sense to me, and I'd made the biggest decision of my life.

I gave him a smile, I couldn't help it. "How's school going, Kings?"

"Great. Mama let me put together my curriculum this year."

I shook my head. The Fishers were a revelation to me. They did things so differently, but it worked. Kings and I were the same age, but I knew he was doing stuff at home that I wouldn't see for years. Funny thing was, that didn't seem to even matter to them. They just liked being together as a family. I know, weird.

"Really?" I asked.

"Yep. I get to study Latin with another family. Medieval history, too."

"How's that work?"

"Hope and I go to their house twice a week for the Latin and history." His sister was twelve. "And twice a week we all do math and science here."

"Sounds pretty good." I think I sounded pretty distracted, because I was. My eyes were scanning every car that rounded the curve of Sweetnam Lane, but there was nothing promising. The Monstermobile was unmistakable even from a distance. You could almost feel it coming, like you feel a helicopter before you actually hear it. Still, I stared up the road, not even blinking.

"Do you know those people?" Kings asked, pointing. From the other direction, a small silver car was creeping along as if looking for a certain house number.

I hardly gave it a glance. "I don't think so." Then a double-take. "Hang on, I think that's Jeph. Yeah, and Shayne. It's them." I sprang up, yelled in the door to my mom that I was going, and scrambled down the front steps, flagging them down.

"Bye, Rory."

"Bye, Kings."

Jeph pulled into the driveway while Shayne rolled down her window and hung out of it. "We were trying to remember which house was yours. I wasn't even sure you were coming tonight."

"Sorry. I thought she'd called you," Allie said from the backseat. I hopped in to join her. "Should've known she'd lose your number."

"Hey, I had it in my organizer. I don't know why I couldn't find it."

"Maybe because your organizer is a shoebox filled with scraps of paper. Looks like a hamster nest."

"Hey, if the system works…"

"Obviously it doesn't—"

"It's okay," I interrupted. "I figured you'd show up." I saw Jeph looking at me in the rearview mirror, an unspoken question on his face. "Sheelan's not home," I told him.

He reversed out of the driveway. "She won't talk to me anyway."

"Well, you did ask her if you could call her, and then you never did," I said

"You did?" Shayne turned on him. "Ooh, bad move."

"It was right before Kellie… Before everything last April. Over five months ago. How long can she hold a grudge?"

"Don't ask," I said. I'd thought that he was better off without Sheelan back then, and nothing had happened to change my mind since. "But hey, what happened to the Monster—I mean the old Buick?"

"It's in the great demolition derby in the sky," he said, hand over his heart. "Or so I'm guessing. I traded it in for this."

"Nice."

"But it doesn't seat ten," Shayne said. "We can squeeze one more in here if we're lucky."

"Are we picking anyone else up?" I asked.

"Nope. Just us."

There wasn't much chance to look for Jake and Sam when we got there. The girls' group glommed together almost immediately and everyone talked at the same time—what happened over the summer, how high school was going, all that. I saw Mary Katherine, Caroline, other familiar faces. No one said anything about the smiling woman's face that was painfully missing, but it was a not saying that said a lot.

We were already entering the gym in our separate boy and girl lines when Jake sauntered over.

"Hello, ladies." His white stone pendant sat plainly on top of his black T-shirt. We all wore ours, but they were tucked out of sight. He noticed.

"Why are you hiding them?" he asked, dangling his.

"Hiding what?" Mary Katherine asked.

We all shot Jake a look, but he kept on talking. "Kellie gave all of us a necklace with a—"

"Jake," Allie said quietly.

"Who's 'all of us'?" Some other kids had gathered around.

The pastor saved us. "All right, everyone settle in and we'll get started," he called. Jake turned back to the boys' group, but Shayne grabbed his sleeve.

"Excuse me, Mr. Mouth," she whispered, "but I don't think Kellie meant for us to go around showing these off."

"Whatever." He tried to pull away, but she hung on.

"Where's Sam?" she asked.

Jake shrugged. "I thought you'd know."

"You're his best friend."

"I don't see him so much anymore." He snickered. "Sammy's a home boy now. Maybe home boys don't do youth groups."

"He's homeschooling, not a hermit," Allie said.

Jake shrugged again and left. Shayne turned to us. "Do you think he's right? Maybe Sam doesn't do any organized group things anymore?"

I said nothing. How could Jake and Shayne both be clueless about Sam? I couldn't process the fact. Why didn't they know? Why did I even care? Sam had his own life, he could do what he wanted. Maybe homeschoolers were too busy living outside the box to bother with run-of-the-mill church functions. He probably didn't even wear the white stone anymore. Too group-ish.

I was a rain cloud when pastor called us to order.

"Hello, all. I'm Dan d'Amico, youth pastor here at Front Street Temple, and the boys' group leader. It's great to see so many of you here tonight—familiar faces and new ones. Kellie would've been thrilled." There was a murmur of agreement at his words.

"She's with her King now, but we're still here to carry on the work she devoted her life to. A lot of you may already know Martina Thistlethwaite," and he gestured to a tall, slender woman standing against the wall, "but you might not know that she has generously volunteered to lead the girls' group this year."

Some of the girls around me, probably Front Streeters like Shayne and Allie, whispered to each other.

"We'll spend today getting acquainted with our groups, laying down the ground rules and all that, but next week we'll get right to the spiritual meat. And not to give anything away, but we'll be tackling that age-old question, *Why am I here?*"

The very question I'd asked myself the first time I'd come to the Scene. God hadn't wasted any time answering.

Martina made us sit in the inevitable getting-to-know-you circle on the floor. She perched on a stool. "I think Pastor was speaking philosophically when he asked, 'Why am I here?' But we'll use it as a way to introduce ourselves. I'll start." She smoothed a wisp of her pixie-cut black hair. Her fingernails were manicured and ruby red. "I'm Martina, I've been a member of the church here for four years, and I'm here because I admired Kellie's work and consider it an honor to continue it." She turned to the girl beside her, whose frozen-in-the-headlights stare marked her as a first-timer.

"Um, I'm Tess. I'm here because... Well, I know Mary Katherine from Holy Angels High School, and um..."

"She's here because I'm holding her lucky rabbit's foot hostage until she converts," Mary K said, dangling something furry and fuchsia over her head.

"Give me that," Tess said and grabbed it back with a laugh.

"So, Mary Katherine," Martina said, "you've brought a friend."

"A heathen friend who attaches animal parts to her keychain."

"I encourage all of you to bring friends whenever you like," Martina said. "If I'm not mistaken, Kellie had a tradition of celebrating the person who brought the most friends."

"A mountain bike," I said without thinking. The way I say a lot of things. The others looked at me as if I had ten heads. "The prize was a mountain bike..." I said less confidently.

"Um, no," Shayne said slowly. "It was a pizza party at her house."

The pizza party. We'd all been there: me, Allie, Shayne, Jake, Sam. That had been Shayne's prize? What about the bike—

Oh, yeah. Only Uri had said anything about a bike. Uri the supposed angel who turned out to be a lying devil—literally. Just one more way he'd tried to turn me against the people most able to help me. But they had stuck by me. Sure, they might have concluded that the psychiatrist was right, that it was all part of a mental break that happened to me after my dad died. Either way, it was okay.

But Sam. Sam had seen something different. He'd believed the angels and demons were real, even helped me to see the truth. Of all my friends, only he saw the big picture.

"What are you talking about, a mountain bike?" Shayne asked me.

"Just joking."

"Well, girls," Martina announced, "I admired Kellie, but you're going to find that I do things a bit differently."

Allie looked at Shayne and me, her eyebrows up.

On the way home she brought it up. "What do you suppose she meant by that?"

"She's just got other ideas about how to get new people to come," Shayne said.

"Setting traps, maybe," I said.

Shayne snorted. She picked at a little hole in the knee of her jeans.

"You're making that hole bigger." Allie pointed.

"I'm trying to. A little hole looks accidental. A big one looks like you meant it."

We reached my driveway too soon. It would be a whole week until we just got to hang out like this again. Unless we could get together during the week…

"See you next weekend?" Shayne asked.

So, a whole week. And even then, it might not be all of us at the Scene. I still looked forward to it, but maybe not quite as much.

three

You've got to love stores and shopping malls. One day, they're luring you in with offers of sunglasses, tanning cream and frosty beverages—then on the fifth of July, *whoosh*, they whip out the back-to-school displays. So we're home for a month, and you all can't wait to ship us off to school again? Summer, which just got rolling, is all of a sudden a downhill slide straight into polyester plaid and cinderblock walls.

Then by September 1st, the store aisles turn black and orange for Halloween. This I don't mind as much. But by the end of September, everyone's decided on their costumes and stuff and there's still a month to go. I know—fourteen-year-olds dressing up? Next they'll want to go trick-or-treating.

You better believe it. This was possibly the last year to get away with the begging-for-candy shtick, and I planned to go out with a bang.

I wasn't the only one with plans. At school the next week, the hot topic in the cafeteria, 'under the tree' (both Kellie's mural in the main hall and the real tree outside) and even in class when kids could get away with it, was Bliss Hathaway's Halloween party.

I doubt Bliss said more than five words about it. Jake took care of the rest. Every time I heard him talking, which was more than I cared to, he talked about the party. How huge it would be. How kick-butt the decorations would be. How much food there would be. The music, the people.

And the people wanted to know which people.

"Have you heard about Bliss Hathaway's Halloween party?" Tiffany Klipfel asked us at the lockers after school.

Jasmine rolled her eyes. "Would it be possible to hear about something else for a change?"

"Tell me about it. But everyone's saying that whoever's invited is instant 'elite.' And whoever's not—"

"Instant 'delete'," I said.

Jasmine snickered with me. "We'll survive somehow," she said. "Crushed, pitiful outcasts, but alive."

Not the reaction Tiffany hoped for. "But you know what else?" She looked over her shoulder; apparently the coast was clear. "I hear that Madi Swanson is planning a party the same night. Bigger and better, if she can help it—and she'll try to get more people to come to hers. It's going to be Halloween war."

"I don't know," I said. "Can you picture Bliss even caring about some scheme of the Mad Swan?" (Our occasional name for Madi. I'm not proud of it.) "She doesn't seem like the kind."

Tiffany shrugged skeptically. Turns out we were both half right.

Just like with the dead frog, Jasmine and I made a show of not caring much about parties. Yet we listened carefully to every overheard snippet of gossip about it and watched for any sign of invitations, any exultation or disappointment in the faces of our classmates. Not so much out of any hope of being invited—more to see who else wouldn't be invited. Whose company we would join, the ranks of the un-elite. The deleted.

Bliss said nothing, did nothing. And the furor grew.

Occasionally school pre-empted our obsession. Mrs. Palmer tried to drill the facts of early American history into our heads with dismal results. When we failed to get excited about regurgitating names and dates back at her, she warned us of the civics class waiting for us in our freshman year, and how passing its exam was required for high school graduation. But elementary school graduation seemed a lifetime away—threatening us with high school was like warning us about heart disease in our fifties because of what we ate today. Ancient history and distant future—both seemed pointless.

Then there was science class. Mr. Hayes also looked to the future, but he put a whole different spin on it. "Our next unit is one they don't expect you to begin studying until high school, at least not seriously. I suppose they think you're not ready for it." He plucked a piece of lint off his sweater. "I disagree."

"I'm with you, Mr. H.," Jake said.

"Well, I hope you're all with me on this," he said. "Because some people have a problem with it. As I've said before, I respect the fact that people have different beliefs. I have my own. But when I walk through that door, I step into the realm of science, pure and simple. Philosophy is for philosophy class, theology is for church. Here we're going to learn about scientific fact and sound scientific theory. We're going to learn about evolution."

Mr. Hayes's announcement was met with anticipation—not on the same level as Bliss's party, but pretty good for school. We were pretty impressed with ourselves, doing high school level work. And Mr. Hayes made us feel like we were part of something important—not a bad something, but slightly dangerous.

I'd never thought of science and religion together, or opposed to each other, but now that he had me thinking about it, he'd also reassured me. Mr. Hayes respected people's beliefs. No problem there.

Other things happened before I realized how wrong I was. Like later that week, when I stooped to pick up a book in front of my locker. My necklace slipped out from under my shirt and dangled in the air as I bent over. Even before I stood back up, a hand reached in and captured the white stone.

I straightened to find Bliss with the stone between her fingers.

"It's a talisman," she said. It wasn't a question.

A what? "Um, well…It's special," I said. "It was a gift."

She looked in my eyes. Hers were very light brown, like the lighter kind of brown sugar. "It has power," she informed me. "You can feel it if you know what to look for." Then she flipped it over. I wanted to stop her, but I couldn't without pulling it away and looking like a jerk. So she read my 'secret' name on the back of the stone.

"'Rejoiced over.'" She looked me right in the eye again. I expected her to ask me what it meant, imagined having to explain Zephaniah 3:14-17, why Kellie had chosen it, who Kellie was, what had happened to her. But she didn't ask me.

"I knew there was something about you," was all she said, setting the stone back on my shirt.

She smiled and walked away.

Thanks to the alphabet, Tiffany Klipfel's locker was on the other side of mine, and she had some kind of bionic ear anyway, so she would've heard the whole thing even if her last name had been Zipfel. "What was that all about?" she whispered.

"I have no idea," I said.

"She's going to invite you to her party. I can tell."

"She doesn't even know my name." Except the one on my stone, the one I wished I could take back from her.

"Just watch. You'll see."

I kept thinking about the whole weird exchange while I did my homework after school. I also listened to a prehistoric personal CD player that had once been my dad's. There was a risk that my answers to the history questions could have random song lyrics mixed in, but strangely enough, the music seemed to make the algebra go easier. Maybe the secret to algebra is not to think about it.

By the time I'd finished the math, my shirt was stained with a dribble of salsa, my hair was twisted into five crazy curls around my face—I had the habit of wrapping it around and around my finger while I worked—and I reached my favorite song on the CD. Perfect time to go out and 'check the mail' (get up and dance around like a fool).

I sang my way down the steps, bopping a little as I went. The mailbox was at the end of the driveway—a wasted trip because it was empty, not even the store ads or the missing persons postcard. I figured I'd make the most of it, though, singing louder than I dared to in the house where Sheelan would appear to critique my performance. There was no one around to hear me out here.

Dangerous assumption.

Halfway up the front steps, I felt the eyes on me. Then, in the shadowed half of the Fishers' steps, I detected a seated person. With 14-year-old-girl radar, I detected it was a boy. But not Kingston. The boy stood, pushing dark curly hair out of his face, revealing dark sparkly eyes.

My foot missed the next step. I lurched, caught myself, dropped the CD player. The headphones stayed on my head but the player shot off and cracked on the cement step.

"Hi, Rory," Sam said.

Hi, Sam, I said. Or I would've if I hadn't lost command of the English language. Instead I just let my mouth hang open a little.

"I knew you lived in one of these houses, but I couldn't remember which one."

"This one," I said. Stupidly. Pointing to my house. He'd come looking for my house?

But he didn't move off the Fishers' steps. He reached through the railing, picked up my CD player and examined it. "Wow, I haven't seen one of these in years. Looks okay." He popped it open, saw the disc. "It's the one I gave you."

"I meant to return it, but..."

"Yeah. It's been a while." He handed the player over. "But you like it?"

"Yeah, it's good." As in my-all-time-favorite good.

"Then keep it. I have it on my computer anyway." He pointed to his ear, suggesting my headphones. "Want to test and make sure it still works?"

I whipped the forgotten headphones off my head, feeling the ridiculous snakes I'd twisted into my hair while I did my homework—like Shirley Temple in dreadlocks. I scrubbed my hand through them. Now I probably looked like Albert Einstein. Then I remembered the salsa smear on my shirt, and I clutched the headphones to my chest to try to hide it.

As far as reunions went, this one wasn't going like I'd imagined it. Nevermind the specifics—let's just say in my imagination, my hair behaved and I didn't smell like onions.

"This one's my house," I said again, because saying something dumb rounded out the effect nicely. I just couldn't figure out why he was staying on the Fishers' steps.

The door swung open behind him, and Kingston popped his head out. "Y'okay out here, Sam?"

Mrs. Fisher was right behind him. "You sure you don't want to wait inside, honey?" Then she saw me. "Hello, baby girl."

Several things clicked at once.

"You're here to—" I said, pointing from Sam to the Fishers.

"You thought…" Sam started, then stopped.

Kings pointed from me to Sam. "You guys know each other?"

"From school," Mrs. Fisher guessed.

I pointed at Kings. "Math and science. You're trading math and science for Latin and history."

"Yep."

"You said 'they', not 'him'," I accused.

"Yeah, well, that's grammar, not math or history. I meant Sam. And his mom and dad."

And I'd actually had the idea that Sam had come around looking for my house. Embarrassing enough just in my own private head. But Sam knew it, too. My cheeks were red neon.

"Here's my ride," Sam said. The Newman's car rolled into the driveway, but the woman behind the wheel wasn't Sam's mom. "Got to go." He grabbed a beat-up guitar case I hadn't noticed behind him and jogged down the steps. "Thanks, Mrs. Fisher. Thanks, Kingston." He looked back for a second when he reached the car. "Bye, Rory." Strangely enough, his face seemed a bit red, too. Some things hadn't changed. We were still the Hot Face duo.

"See you Tuesday," he said.

four

I spent the next couple of hours—okay, days—trying to figure out if Sam's *See you Tuesday* was meant for me, the Fishers, or all of us. *Me*, I liked to think…until I thought it through and realized a 'see you Tuesday' spoken on Thursday would mean he didn't plan to go to the Scene on Saturday. So then I decided he was just talking to the Fishers.

I'd never even had a chance to ask him why he missed the last Scene. About all I'd had a chance to do was make a fool of myself. But that never takes long.

I didn't get the facts on Sam, but facts were flying fast and furious in science class that week. Coming at me so fast that I barely had time to scribble them in my notebook, let alone think about them much. Maybe that was the idea.

On Friday in Mr. Hayes's class, the dry erase board was emblazoned with the words **The FACT** *of Evolution*.

"Isn't it the Theory of Evolution, Mr. Hayes?" Tiffany asked as we took our seats.

He gestured towards the heavens with both hands. "That word. That word has been twisted, abused and misconstrued. *Theory* makes most people think, 'unproven'. Evolution—it's 'only' a theory. Could be wrong." He pulled out a marker and underlined **FACT** three times. "Let me set the record straight right here at the outset. Evolution is a fact. There are questions about the exact mechanisms of evolution—how it works—but whether it's by the mechanisms Charles Darwin described or some other, yet-to-be-discovered mechanisms, the fact of evolution is certain."

He scanned the classroom. "Let's make a pact right here and now. We'll agree not to toss the word *theory* around as if we can toss the whole concept out the window. Capiche?"

There was a general murmur of agreement across the room, and although we didn't actually understand what he was talking about, it intrigued us. All part of the lure of Mr. Hayes's Science Class—the man got fired up about this stuff.

I watched Tiffany, though. She hadn't meant to take the other side of a debate she never knew existed in the first place, but that's sort of what it looked like. And I'm sure that's definitely what it felt like. I could tell by her face that she probably wouldn't be asking any more questions that semester.

Opposite Mr. Hayes was not the place to be.

Under the triple-underlined **FACT** he began a list, each line drilled home by a pounded bullet-point.

"Fact." He spoke the words as he wrote them. "The earth, with water, is more than three-and-a-half billion years old."

"Fact: Cellular life has existed for at least half that time."

"Fact: Major life forms presently existing on earth were not all in existence in the past. Birds and mammals, for instance."

"Fact: Major life forms of the past are now no longer living. Dinosaurs, for instance."

"Fact: All living forms come from previous living forms, which at some point ancestrally were different than the present form."

He turned to face us. "If you disagree with any of this—in the face of all evidence—then I know of a club you might be interested in. It's called the Flat Earth Society."

We laughed.

Facts are what you get at school. Sometimes they trample over you too fast to see clearly, other times they dawdle on by while your eyes glaze over and drool dribbles onto your desk. But we were like buckets, and teachers had the stuff to fill us up. They'd dedicated their lives to it, given up all the possible glamorous jobs, or at least jobs that wouldn't stick them in a school for the rest of their lives. And they only wanted to teach us the truth.

Right?

I've had great teachers, teachers I've actually loved who obviously loved teaching us. But I had something important to learn about truth. I would learn it from the unlikeliest people—like Bliss. But that came later.

Friday night I holed myself up in my room with my ravioli from a can (a food that confesses its nutritional bankruptcy right there on the label, but what yummy bankruptcy it is). I wasn't hiding my ravioli, though. I was escaping Sheelan—her high-decibel phone conversations and her watchful eyes. I had plans I didn't want her to know about.

Actually, I planned to read my Bible. The last thing I needed was Sheelan cackling about me reading the Bible on a Friday night. I wasn't ashamed…just sick of Sheelan.

Ever since I woke up that morning in August with my dad's long-lost Bible in my arms, I tried to read it regularly. I wish I could say regularly was every day (it usually wasn't). But I hadn't forgotten the words of Micah, my angel-protector: "The *rhema* is your Sword. If you would wield your weapon well, you must learn it well."

The *rhema*, I had learned, was the active word of God. But the Sword of the Spirit often felt like it was sharpening me instead of the other way around. It wasn't always comfortable.

Today I wanted to go back to the start, so I flipped to Genesis.

In the beginning, God created the heavens and the earth.

Exactly what I thought it said. So whatever we learned in science class was going to describe *how* God created the heavens and the earth. Simple enough.

Then I noticed my dad's haphazard handwriting in the margin.

If monkeys → men, when did sin/death enter the picture?

Hard to say what he was getting at, there. I scanned for any other notes, then snapped the Bible closed. Sheelan's voice echoed in the hallway right outside my room.

"Why do you keep asking about Quentin? He's ancient history and you know it. Same as you and Tyler." There was a pause; she reached her room and shut the door, but I could hear her like she was in my room, or in my head. "Well, goody for him. I hope he and Emily are very happy together, getting fat on pretzels at the mall — no, I don't give a flip who he goes out with, because I don't give a flip about him."

A longer silence. I wasn't eavesdropping. I just happened to have ears that functioned. And our rooms happened to be connected by a heating duct, and sound traveled pretty well from vent to vent. We'd discovered this in our younger, more playful years.

"You're not making any sense, Tamika."

Quiet.

"Stop — no, you wait. Why don't you just come out and say it?" Something in Sheelan's room slammed. "I knew it! Tell me you're not serious. No way could you be back with Tyler… No way. You think I'll get back with Quentin just so we—"

Silence again. I ate my ravioli.

"Let me get this straight. You're asking me if it's okay for you to go out with Tyler—and Quentin and *Emily*—tomorrow night?" Sheelan asked, very calmly. (Bad sign.) "You know what, Tamika? I'm getting another call, and I'm taking it. Goodbye."

Her voice switched from steel gray to bubble-gum pink. "Hello? Speaking. Who's th…" The floorboards, creaking under her pacing feet, went quiet. "You have got to be kidding me. After five months, you decide to call now?"

I put my ravioli down and leaned closer to the heating vent.

"No, enough. Just stop right there. You know what? Sure. I'll go. Tomorrow, right? What time? Fine. Bye."

I put my fork down. Either I'd gotten a hold of some bad ravioli, or I'd just heard Sheelan agree to go to the Scene with Jeph Svoboda. I prayed I was wrong.

I suppose that made me a bad sister. I should've been praying that Sheelan would go to the Scene, and that she'd meet Jesus face-to-face, so to speak. That kind-hearted Jeph would gradually melt the Spiritual Ice Queen. But come on, the last time she went, she challenged the pastor and generally put on her unholier-than-thou attitude and paraded it around like a scary foreign supermodel. This was Sheelan—Miss 'God's either a wimp or a monster'. That's where she stood last I heard, anyway.

But there we were the next evening, Jeph driving his new compact car, Sheelan riding shotgun, and us other three squeezed in a backseat about the size of a lunchbox. Allie and Shayne kept giving me raised-eyebrow looks. I just rolled my eyes and shrugged.

"I can't believe she came," Shayne said once we'd entered the church gym and separated from Jeph and Sheelan.

"Yeah, how'd that happen?" Allie asked.

"A great cosmic accident," I said. I told them about Sheelan's phone calls.

"Sounds like a God thing to me," Shayne said.

Pastor Dan called for our attention. "We're going to try a different approach this year. Last year the girls and boys often had separate activities and different lessons, until our Armor of God study. It had a lot of impact, so we're going to join forces again. We'll still have separate discussion groups after the teaching, and we're keeping the gym open afterwards for basketball or just hanging out."

He approached a large, free-standing white screen. "You may notice some other changes. Like no more projecting my notes onto the wall. Thanks to the church's generosity and Martina's forward thinking, we're finally entering the computer age." He fiddled with a laptop on a small table, but the projection screen remained lifeless. "And obviously it's going to have to be one of you kids who gets us there."

A boy I remembered from last year, Silas, came up and with a few keystrokes had the first screen blazing overhead. It read: **WHY AM I HERE?**

I closed my eyes, waited for it. Very distinctly from the older teens' corner, I heard Sheelan's chilly laugh. Nobody missed the implications.

Mary K turned to me. "Isn't that your sister?" she asked, loud enough for everyone around us to hear. I let my face answer for me.

"Sam's missing again," Allie whispered.

"He said he might not make it," Shayne said.

I leaned in. "You talked to him?"

"IM'd him."

Pastor finished setting up, then told everyone to get comfortable. Jake joined us in the shuffle. "Talking about Sam?"

"Yeah. Do you know what's up? He told me he might not be able to come, but he didn't say why."

He shook his head. "He's been acting weird. Our home boy's just not the boy he used to be."

I didn't find Jake as clever as he found himself. "I saw him the other day, and he seemed alright."

"You guys have a date?"

"Funny. I saw him at my neighbors, the homeschooling family. They're doing some of their classes together. Turns out they met at a homeschooling support group or something."

"Hmm, small world," Allie said.

"Is this on?" Pastor's voice rang to the rafters and bounced off the back wall. "Sorry, folks. I'll tone it down a little." He fiddled with a microphone box at his waist.

"So, a question. THE question. The one everyone asks eventually. Even if we aren't aware of it, we live our lives either according to our perceived answer to this question, or in search of that answer. *Why am I here?*

"For some of you, it's a question of, 'For what purpose did God create me?' and you may already have some ideas. Right ones and wrong ones, if you're like most people. For others, though, it could be a question of, 'How did I come to be? Was it by chance? Do I have any purpose at all?'"

He picked up a Bible. "Now, I could go on for hours, days, about why this Book isn't just any book—all the evidence that points to its supernatural origin and why you can take it as God's Truth—and you know, that would be a brilliant topic for a future study. But for now, let's use as our launching pad the premise that this Book is true, reliable, and offers the answers to our questions."

I couldn't help it, I looked at Sheelan. Her face was a billboard that announced *Okay, I'm out. You just lost me.* She would never accept the Bible as a starting point.

"Right here in the God-breathed Word, the very first chapter of the very first book, we learn that we were created by Him for a purpose. Does anyone want to offer any suggestions about what that purpose might be?"

In an act of boldness—or because he was somehow oblivious to the stink of Sheelan's skepticism right beside him—Jeph spoke out. "To serve God?"

"Certainly," Pastor said. "Thanks, Jeph. To serve Him. Because He needs our help, right?" He chuckled. "Okay, maybe God doesn't *need* us to serve Him. Anyone who can create worlds out of nothing can probably handle things on His own just fine. But it is right for us to serve Him and seek His will. He is deserving of all that and more. Which leads us to another purpose..." He let the bait dangle, hoping for a few nibbles.

"To serve one another?"

"To take care of His creation?"

Pastor nodded. "Good, these are all good..."

I was fingering my white stone pendant, and a strange thought struck me. It came out of my mouth before I could shrink away from the thought of Sheelan's ridicule.

"To rejoice?" I asked.

Pastor Dan turned on me, finger pointing. "Rory's getting it. What are the angels around God's throne perpetually doing? To God be the..."

"Glory," various voices finished.

"Glory, folks." He fiddled with a remote and the big screen changed:

Give to the Lord the glory he deserves! Bring your offering and come to worship him. Psalms 96:8

"What would you say if you learned that your primary purpose for existing is to give glory to God—that it's what He created you for?"

There was murmuring in the back corner.

"Speak up, don't be shy. Was that you, Sheelan?"

I froze. Maybe Sheelan did, too. She wouldn't expect Pastor Dan to know her name. But she didn't sound frozen when she spoke—frosty, but not frozen.

"I was wondering what kind of being would create people just to glorify itself? Sounds like a massive ego to me."

I could wring Jeph's neck for ever thinking of inviting her.

"Doesn't it, though?" Pastor rolled up his sleeves. "And it would be massively egotistical if we were talking about a human being, wouldn't it? Then again, a human can't create galaxies, or quarks, or sunsets. Or people. Time for mind expansion, here. Toss out your picture of God as the Old Guy Upstairs. Imagine if you can—and you really can't, not with this limited earthly mind, but give it a shot—a Being completely *worthy* of everlasting praise, honor and glory. A Being that doesn't demand it but inspires it so that those in His presence cannot help but sing out *holy, holy, holy*. One that, if there were no mouths to sing His praise, the very rocks would have to cry out.

"When He gave you life, an eternal soul, and the possibility of spending forever in His presence loving Him and giving Him glory, He was giving *you* the indescribable gift, not Himself. Try to imagine.

"So, to serve and glorify Him. A wonderful purpose for your life. But these are general purposes, so to speak. Did you know God has a very specific plan and purpose for your individual life?"

I tried to scribble everything he said in my notebook as he went on. It was good stuff. And there was always the off chance that Sam might want to find out what he missed, and we could share our notes with him like they'd once done for me. I think I took even more notes than Allie.

"Okay, let's break apart into our groups to talk about this some more," Pastor Dan said after a while. When we gathered around Martina, she asked, "Why don't we go around and offer any ideas we might have about God's special purpose for our lives?"

"Come on," Shayne whispered. "I'm fourteen—like I have a clue."

"It's just an excuse for her to talk about herself," Mary K whispered back. "Watch, she'll volunteer to go first."

But she didn't. In fact, when each of us offered up our lame ideas or lack of them (except Caroline—she was rock-solid sure that God meant for her to be a nurse), Martina listened and said little. It wasn't exactly like she was privately rating our answers, but I had the impression she was assessing each of us. When it came around to her, she just offered to close with a prayer.

"You want to hang around a while?" Shayne asked us after Martina dismissed us. "Watch the guys play basketball?"

"Fine with me," Allie said. She was already watching the first free-throw practice shots. "But I'll play, not just watch."

Jeph came up to us. "Come on," he said.

"You're not staying?"

"It's time to go." We saw Sheelan already walking out the doors.

"We wanted—"

"You want a ride?"

"Alright, alright," Shayne said. "Sorry, guys."

I'm not sure why she was sorry, since it was clearly my charming sister's fault. But I wasn't really sorry. Hanging around didn't appeal to me so much, either. There was just something missing. And I had two days to kill between today and Tuesday.

five

Sunday and Monday proved to be virtually unkillable. Sunday began with a visit to the Super Everything Church in Westhaven.

It's technically the Believers Church, but some nicknames are just sticky, and the more we went, the more it reminded me of the huge discount mart that for years we'd called the Super Everything Store.

Not that you would call it cheesy. No, it oozed class. Well-dressed people, sparkling auditorium, gourmet coffee. I mean, Sheelan wouldn't settle for anything less, considering the whole religion thing was just something to endure for the sake of the social possibilities.

Mom and Sheelan didn't seem to detect the cheapness, the Super-Everythingness. Maybe I was wrong, but it felt to me like the church was peddling something precious like it was dime-store chintz.

We were still just visitors. We made it about twice a month, since Mom pulled some late Saturday nights waitressing. She stopped short of membership, saying that we were still 'church shopping', though we never went anywhere else. I secretly suspected that she only said this to cover for the Sundays when we didn't make it—people could just assume we were shopping elsewhere that week. It didn't matter too much if we joined or not; blending in with a crowd of lots of other visitors was Super Easy.

"You always seem so thoughtful after the service," Mom said to me as we filed past the pastry table, searching for the apple fritters.

"And that's bad?"

"Of course not. I just sometimes wonder what you're thinking about. You live a lot of your life in there." She tapped her temple.

"In your head?"

She gave me the *you know what I mean* look. "I hope you like it here at Believers. You're half of the reason we come, you know."

Yes, I knew. She reminded me whenever she detected the teensiest bit of reluctance or negativity from me. "What's the other half of the reason?" I asked.

She handed me a fritter and found one for herself. She was trying to think of the right answer. "Because it's the right thing to do. Your dad wanted it. You know that."

I nodded. "I like the music," I said, a peace offering. It was true. The music was the one part that got into me, and thanks to the words on the big screen and the sheer volume to drown my voice, I could also let it out of me. Some were just repetitive, but a lot of the songs, especially the older ones (back before 'worship music' when there were just 'hymns'), had some meat in them. The preacher's spectacular sermons usually just tasted like spiritual tofu.

Sheelan, the spiritual vegan, had no objections and used the time making eye contact with her growing network of church friends. Afterwards they broke away, drank coffee and laughed together.

This is where I'd love to say that those teens were snobby high-and-mighties, but I can't. Some of them would wave to me and smile, knowing I was Sheelan's sister, perfectly pleasant people. I just had to admit that Sheelan had a talent for making friends.

Me, I occasionally made eye contact with kids who looked about my age, and even ran into kids I recognized from school. It never amounted to much more than a 'hi' or a forced smile. I spent the rest of that Sunday questioning whether I had any talents at all.

I'd forgotten all about my true gift: publicly embarrassing myself. It only took half a day at school to remind me.

Mr. Hayes prowled the front of the classroom when we poured into science class on Monday. His oxford shirt hung over his jeans, the T-shirt beneath sporting some black-and-white bearded face I didn't recognize. Our backsides had barely hit the seats when he plunged in.

"Last week, you'll recall, we established some important facts. Namely that all life as we know it today once existed in some other form, and that over the course of millions of years, slow changes have wrought an evolution of species into the forms we know today. Agreed?"

"Yes," was the general response. I looked at my notes, and they agreed with Mr. Hayes. Not a shock, since they'd come from Mr. Hayes. I had no chance to give it any more thought. 'Had no chance', of course, might mean 'made no effort'.

"Excellent." He uncapped five or six different dry-erase markers and lined them up along the tray, ready for technicolor science action. "Then it's time to discuss the mechanism of this slow change. There may be room for differing theories here — remember, not whether evolution occurs, but how it occurs — but the overwhelming scientific consensus supports the idea of natural selection."

He wrote in red and talked as he went. "Natural selection: The process in nature by which, according to the theory of Charles Darwin, only the organisms best adapted to their environment tend to survive and transmit their genetic characteristics in increasing numbers to succeeding generations while those less adapted tend to be eliminated."

"In plain English—no, even better, in Play Putty." He reached under his desk and grabbed two heaping handfuls of squishy pink dough and smacked them down onto his desk. From his drawer he pulled a long strand of red licorice, snapped it into two pieces, and stuck one into each of the two blob creatures. "Merely by chance, Lumpy Creature X," he wagged Lumpy X's licorice, "grew a longer tongue than Lumpy Y. Turns out a longer tongue was an advantageous genetic mutation that allowed X to catch its prey more effectively." The tongue dove into Mr. Hayes's hand and came out with a marshmallow stuck on it. "X thrived, grew strong, and easily beat out puny Y when it came time to catch the eye of a healthy young Miss Lumpy."

Several boys whistled their approval of Lumpy X.

"So X got a mate, reproduced, and passed on his genetic advantage to another generation of Lumpies. Poor Y wasn't so lucky and never passed his genes along through offspring due to the fact that he was smaller, weaker and was eaten before he could." He flung Lumpy Y across the room where it stuck to the wall. "*Voila,* you have natural selection. Simplified, and just one example among untold possibilities, but multiply it over countless species and millions of years, and you can see the power of the mechanism."

We were pretty much hysterical with laughter by that point.

"Can I eat that licorice?" someone called out

"If you can guess what my next question will be," he said.

Mr. Hayes didn't care much whether we raised our hands or not, so someone from the other side of the room just called out his guess. "Is the purpose of evolution to develop stronger, better animals?"

Mr. Hayes took off his silver oval-rim glasses and flicked a booger of Play Putty off the lens. "No, that wasn't going to be my question, but I'd better address it. Let's see, where to begin? Simple answer: no. I won't go into the whole issue of 'better'—just consider that 'stronger' might not ensure survival. Perhaps weaker but faster is the advantageous adaptation.

"Nevermind that. The important thing to understand is that evolution doesn't have a *purpose*. Evolution is merely a random process by which organisms adapt to their environment. Where there is randomness, there cannot be purpose."

Now Jake spoke up. "So porcupines just sort of happened. Duck-billed platypuses, dung beetles…"

"Just sort of happened over millions of years of selection for traits and mutations that increased the odds of survival and the eventual weeding out of those that did not."

Jake finished his thought. "…people?"

Mr. Hayes shrugged—not an uncertain shrug but a *there you have it* sort.

I laughed.

When I did it, I expected to be one of several laughers. Obviously Mr. Hayes was baiting us, the way teachers do to test if you're paying attention. But I laughed alone. No problem—I guess no one else got it but me.

"Something amusing, Miss Joyce?"

"Well, it's just what you're saying…"

"Yes?"

"You're basically telling us that humans just sort of happened, by chance."

He gestured for me to continue.

"Which would mean we have no purpose for being here." I smiled, waiting for him to admit that I'd caught him, and to explain the truth of the matter. I'm not sure what I expected that truth to be, or what I expected him to think it was, but I didn't expect him to turn and pull down a chart that showed a parade of apes, each one slightly more erect, more humanlike, until the last and least hairy stretched upright and proudly led the others in a creepy primate parade.

"Ultimately," he said, "discussion of purpose belongs in a philosophy classroom. Not that I don't enjoy waxing philosophical—" he scruffed up his light brown hair and perched his glasses on the end of his nose in absent-minded professor style, "—but time and the board of education simply do not allow it here. I'm obliged to stick strictly to cold, hard science."

The class rippled with the fuzzy chuckling affection reserved especially for Mr. Hayes. My smile was still plastered on my face, so I must've blended right in. Meanwhile, my mind was trying to fix the jigsaw. But it was like the old puzzle you find at your grandma's house, some pieces missing and others there from some altogether different puzzle.

On the way out after class, Mr. Hayes motioned me over to his desk. "Why don't you come see me after school?"

I did, not knowing if he meant to make everything clear for me or if I was in trouble. Turns out it was neither. But the trouble would come around eventually.

"Right, Rory, come in," he said, shoving a stack of papers into a canvas briefcase. "So you're going to be my Deep Thinker this year?"

"I don't know about that…"

"Believe me, I appreciate a student who thinks and doesn't just write down everything I say exactly as I say it then spit it back out on the test. It's the thinkers who end up really getting it." He looked at me over his glasses, and his eyes were particularly blue. "Even if they disagree with me at first. I always win them over in the end." He smiled and wagged his eyebrows. "You know, people learn the truth best when they understand the objections to the truth, too."

By now the classroom was empty except for us, or so I thought. "It's not that I object—I mean, maybe, but I'm not even sure. I'm still trying to understand."

"You were one of Kellie Greene's disciples, weren't you?"

I flushed; I didn't know what to make of the question.

"I mean that in a good way, of course. Kellie was a fine lady. She was something of a mentor to you, right?"

I felt the white stone hanging around my neck like a lead brick. "I guess you could say that."

He nodded. "I guessed that your objection—or maybe I should say hesitation—with my teaching had a religious basis."

I straightened a little. Maybe Mr. Hayes understood. "Yeah, you know, it's funny because just the other day at our youth group we were talking about how God made us for a special purpose—"

"Rory, I'll say it again, I respect that my students have diverse beliefs and differences of opinion," he said. "And I just want you to know that there are plenty of good, thinking people out there who don't have any problem balancing their religious faith and the fact of evolution. Plenty of folks believe that God uses evolution as a means of creating. I can't go into all the nitty gritty of it, but I thought it might put your mind at ease and that maybe you would look into it yourself if you were interested. Theistic evolution, they call it."

"Okay, yeah. Right." That was simple. God and evolution, purpose and randomness, working together. It was a relief, actually. "Thanks, Mr. Hayes."

"Do you have any questions?"

"Nope. Well, just one. Why didn't you explain all that in class?" Surely there were others besides me who had this confusion. Surely I wasn't the Only Confused Person. Surely I just felt like it most of the time, but it wasn't true.

"Come on, Rory. You couldn't be a friend of Kellie Greene's and not know the answer to that."

Ah. "Because it's God stuff? You're not allowed to talk about religion at all?"

"I have to avoid any appearance of endorsing a particular religion. Separation of church and state. Public school means state school, my dear."

"The supply cabinet is all organized, Mr. Hayes," a voice said from the back of the room. I jerked around. Bliss Hathaway watched us from behind the gunmetal gray cabinet door.

"Excellent. Thank you, Bliss."

"Anything else I can do?"

"You can go and do your reading for tomorrow. That goes for both of you. I like it when my thinkers have something to say in class."

So we left together, Bliss and I, and it was obvious she'd heard everything. And not in the sense of 'overheard', unless you would also call my hovering over the heating vent to hear Sheelan's phone conversations overhearing. I couldn't shake the feeling that Bliss had purposely placed herself in that classroom to listen. What goes around comes around, I guess.

But when things come around in my life, they tend to come like a bullet train while I'm standing on the tracks, looking stupidly in the other direction.

six

Tuesday after school I was in and out of my locker and home in record time.

I flung aside my school uniform and climbed into some jeans and a seashell-pink sweater from Grandma Judy—normal human teenage clothes. The make-up and hair adjustment just followed naturally. No particular reason.

Math had all the appeal of a kick in the shins and history practically gave me the heaves, so checking the mail provided the perfect escape. I took my time on the way back from the curb: tied my shoe, pulled a weed. Nevermind that it started to drizzle. A little drizzle never hurt anyone. A little drizzle put some curl into my well-spritzed hair.

A lot of drizzle made it frizzle. Unfortunately, when you let the front door slam shut behind you but don't have your house key, a lot of drizzle is what you get. I stood there jiggling the knob as if it might show me mercy and unlock itself. I rang the doorbell.

Sheelan was upstairs. She'd take her time and then point out how lame I was, but she'd let me in.

I rang the bell again. Then I remembered: Sheelan had her music cranked. She wouldn't hear an air raid siren.

I investigated the alternate entrances. Garage, closed; side door, locked; back door, ditto. Throwing pebbles at Sheelan's window... No good, only a rock through the window would get her attention.

The mail grew moist in my hands, and I began reconsidering the rock idea. The drizzle became more of a sprinkle as I returned to the front door. In other circumstances, I would've already been at the Fishers', but now I had to take into account the doofus factor, because undoubtedly I looked like a doofus and while this would come as no surprise to the Fishers, there were perhaps certain non-Fishers present. Worse yet, it could look like I'd orchestrated the whole thing.

I'd just keep ringing our doorbell and hope to catch Sheelan in the three seconds of silence between songs. Intent on pressing the button every second or so, I didn't notice the two pairs of dark eyes watching me from behind the Fishers' glass storm door.

"What're you doing?" a high voice asked, muffled by the glass.

I nearly dropped the mail. "Oh, um... Hi, Charity."

"Tee-Tee."

"Right. Hi, Trinity. And hi, Charity."

"I'm Tee-Tee. She's just fooling."

"Well, hi both of you, whichever."

They looked me over, chewing on the colorful baubles that fastened the ends of their fuzzy black braids.

"What're you doing?"

"Getting the mail."

"Getting wet," Charity said, and the sisters giggled.

"Why don't you go in?" Trinity asked.

"Because I'm locked out—"

"MAMA!" Trinity (I think) was already heading back into their kitchen. "Rory got herself locked out again."

I sighed. The *again* was a nice touch, considering the last time I'd done this they were probably still in diapers.

Mrs. Fisher swung the door open, wooden spoon in hand. "Oh, baby girl, come on in here out of the wet."

I didn't exactly hurry up their steps. "Do you have our spare key by chance?" I asked. There wasn't much chance. My mom had never reached that level of neighborliness with the Fishers. Borrowing an egg, returning a newspaper thrown badly by the paper boy, but no key swapping.

"Sorry, we don't. But we have apple cobbler, still warm." The smell of it poured out of the doorway, and not for the first time I was lured into the Fisher home by a mouth-watering dessert. And it wasn't even Friday. "If the boys will clear the table, we can all sit and have some."

"We're almost done, Mama," Kingston said as I followed Mrs. Fisher into the kitchen.

"Wait, honey, don't add that all at once—"

But Kings was already pouring a powdery substance into a liquidy substance. I had a glimpse of his gleeful face and, beside him, Sam's, before a cloud of white foam expanded upwards and burst into flecks of wet confetti. It made sloppy smacking sounds as it hit the wall.

After a moment of quiet, the boys collapsed laughing. I wiped my face and wrinkled my nose at the splotches on my seashell-pink sweater.

"Vinegar?" I guessed.

"Boys," Mrs. Fisher said, sergeant-style, "what's the first rule of science experiments in this house?"

"Clean up after," they said together.

"The other rule."

"No digging holes in the backyard?" Kings guessed. This earned him a raised eyebrow from his mom.

"Um, measure as accurately as possible?" Sam guessed correctly. "Hi, Rory."

"Hi."

Mrs. Fisher was already dabbing at me with a towel. "This will wash right out. Come over here." She steered me towards the mirror in the front hall, which revealed mascara racooning around my eyes, victim of rain or science or both.

This is life as a fourteen-year-old. You aim for pleasing shades of pink and subtle beauty enhancements and you end up damp and smelling like a pickle.

The cobbler waiting on the freshly-wiped table was some consolation. I considered turning it down to demonstrate my dainty appetite, but who was I fooling? The boys fell on theirs like wolves. My use of a fork and napkin looked dainty enough.

"Remember to record your findings in your notebooks," Mrs. Fisher said. "And wipe yourselves off, both of you. You're a mess."

Sam rubbed a towel over his arms, and I noticed what had looked subtly different about him, aside from the longer hair. "How do you manage to get a tan in the fall?" I asked.

He held out an arm, as if noticing the tan for the first time. "My dad had a conference in Orlando."

Kings put his arm alongside Sam's. "That's not tan. Now this is tan."

"You have a certain advantage."

"We're like chocolate and caramel," Kings said (two of his favorite things).

I had the third. I pushed up my sleeve. "And here's the marshmallow."

"Naw, even you're not that white, Rory." Kings chuckled. "You're more like the nougat."

"So I'm chewy and a little nutty, is that it?"

"But sweet," Sam said, obviously without thinking it through. Then he realized how it sounded and grabbed his science notebook as a diversion. "Okay, record our findings... How do you spell *kersplowie*?"

They laughed some more, and the tan practically hid his reddened cheeks. Oh, to escape the curse of the Hot Face. I would never be so lucky. Tanning was not my genetic destiny.

"*K-e-r Splowie*," Sam spelled out loud. "I love science," he said. I must've rolled my eyes.

"Science woes?" Kings asked me. He used words like 'woes'.

"You could say that. Last month it was dissecting a frog."

"I had to do that, too. Pretty nasty," Sam said, clearly meaning 'nasty' in the boy sense, which was hugely positive.

"Yeah, and now we've moved on to evolution." Maybe I was trying to impress.

"Hmmph," Kings said around cinnamony apples. "They ought to teach that in folklore, not science." Sam snorted his agreement.

I didn't quite follow. "Yeah, well it's funny because it sort of goes along with—or against, I guess—what we've started talking about at the Scene, about being created for a purpose." I saw Sam stop chewing for a second. "Everyone's been wondering about you not being there," I told him.

"Yeah, I wanted to come, but—" When he paused, I knew I was either about to hear something important that he felt comfortable enough to share with me, or...not. "I couldn't," he finally said.

I sighed inside.

"But I told Shayne I wasn't coming. I IM'd her, anyway." Another pause. "Your IM's been inactive for a while."

He'd noticed? "Um, yeah, well. Yeah. My sister killed the dumb computer downloading a virus or something."

"Oh. It's probably not dead. Want me to look at it?"

I opened my mouth, but in usual style the intelligent words were unavailable. Sam, coming into my house, fixing my computer...so we could IM the way we had in the spring? Sam, coming into my house, with Sheelan home...so she could give us one of her meaningful looks, humiliating me and ensnaring him with an effortless quirk of her shimmery pink lips.

But my mom wasn't home, and there was the rule about boys when she wasn't home. Did that count with just-friend boys, or was it just for boyfriends?

"Um," I started. Then Trinity came alongside me, spraying a glob of aerosol whipped cream the size of her head on top of her cobbler.

"You can't go to Rory's house 'cause she locked herself out."

Thanks, Tee-Tee. Just in case anyone had forgotten my stupidity. But stupidity gave way to a flash of brilliance. The phone! Sheelan might not hear the doorbell, but she had a supernatural ability to hear the phone ring. I'd call and have her let me—and Sam?—in.

"Aw, that's okay," Kings said. "I'll help Rory later."

Kings had helped me with computer problems before. He was a whiz. And a good friend. I could've strangled him.

"And don't you have your guitar lesson today?" I asked to cover up my sudden violent urge.

"No. I do it whenever," Sam said. "I just had one Saturday night."

I didn't think about that until later on, in my own family room working on some science questions while Kingston resuscitated our computer. (Sheelan had answered my call on the second ring and opened the door for me with a roll of her aqua eyes.)

"There," Kings said, tapping one last key with satisfaction. "You're up and running: internet, email, instant messaging. Just be suspicious of email attachments from unknown sources."

"I'll tell Sheelan, not that it'll do any good." I barely looked up from my homework. That's when it hit me: Sam had said his guitar lesson was Saturday night.

Kingston read over my shoulder. "We've got some good books about evolution if you're interested. From the Bible point of view, know what I mean?"

"Yeah," I said distractedly. "My teacher told me there's plenty of people who believe in God and evolution." Sam had missed the Scene for a guitar lesson?

He gave his throaty laugh as he headed for the front door. "Anything works if you don't actually think about it too much."

I laughed, too, the *I don't get it but I don't want to think about it now* kind. So Sam really was giving up on the Scene.

Oddly enough, Bliss Hathaway put the whole evolution business back on my radar. Without warning, one day at lunch she slid her tray across from mine and sat down, utterly confusing her cafeteria fan club. They milled around their usual table and finally settled there, leaving a seat open for Bliss who completely ignored them.

"You've been thinking about what Mr. Hayes told you after class the other day," she said. It wasn't a question.

But it was true. I did a shrug-nod.

"I could tell." She nibbled a cracker then brushed crumbs off her school blouse—the one that looked like a flour sack on me but hugged her in all the strategic spots. "It's good. You notice how almost everyone just takes what he says as sacred truth? It doesn't even occur to them to question it. Just because he's a teacher, an adult—and cute. Me, I've learned to question authority."

Jasmine approached the table, found her usual seat taken, and took a spot a couple of spaces down. Her black hair and eyes flashed in the florescent light.

"Yeah," I said, hoping an all-purpose word would take care of my part of the conversation.

"I mean, that theistic evolution rubbish—who does he think he's fooling?"

Maybe he'd been fooling me. I did like the idea of having it both ways: keep your God, but safely separate from the cold, hard facts of science. "Well," I said, "it doesn't exactly mesh with my beliefs, but there's a lot I'm still learning…"

"Right, I know. Always seeking, always learning, it's the way to be." Her eyes were like caramel today. "But in private Hayes tells you that it's fine to believe in a God who caused it all, then in class…?" She shook her head, then scooped up her tray, apparently planning to rejoin her restless groupies. "Anyway, I thought you'd like to know you're not the only one bothered by it. I'll stand behind you on this one."

I can't say I wasn't warned. By now I should've known that Bliss didn't just say things because they sounded nice. When she said *stand behind you*, she meant it literally.

seven

Question: What's worse than a pop quiz on a Friday? Answer: A test you know is coming on Monday. Mr. Hayes told us to kiss our weekend goodbye with that choice bit of news. The quirk of his mouth as he made the announcement said *Yeah, but you love me anyway*.

My usual approach to a Monday test—staring vacantly at my notebook late Sunday night—probably wouldn't cut it for this one. So while Saturday afternoon unfolded like a sun-drenched marigold outside, I stayed inside with fascinating accounts of different-sized finch beaks on the Galapagos Islands and pictures of bones named *Archaeopteryx*, which I guess means 'suppose dinosaurs eventually became birds'.

By the time Shayne, Jeph and Allie picked me up for the Scene, I'd come to the uncomfortable conclusion that somehow evolution had to be true and God had to be true, too. I wasn't tortured by it—again, it's basically what Mr. Hayes had hinted at—but it fit like a pair of last year's shoes. And if you know anything about me, you know sometimes I can't even squeeze into last month's shoes.

Part of me hoped Pastor Dan wouldn't talk so much about that 'created for a purpose' stuff this week. I wanted to think about something else. When we walked in and saw **KINGDOM KIDS** illuminating the screen, I had a surge of hope. When we saw Sam standing in a group of boys, I had a surge of something else.

"Look who's here," Shayne said.

"I guess he didn't have his guitar lesson today," I said.

She scrunched up her face at me. "What?" Then she spotted Sam and smiled at me sidelong. "I wasn't talking about Sam." She pointed behind him.

Ericson Greene stood in the back of the gym talking to Pastor. I hadn't seen Kellie's husband since he'd given us the white stones at Sam, Shayne and Allie's graduation.

Jake came up beside us. "You see who came today?"

"I wonder how he's doing," Allie said.

"Ask Sam. I guess they've been hanging out together."

"Sam and Ericson? Really?"

"Oh, yeah, they're real pals now." He tilted his head and blinked his eyes girlishly. I couldn't tell if he was just being Jake or implying something meaner.

"I wonder why they don't include us," Allie said.

"Why would they?" Shayne asked.

"Because he and Kellie were going to start the teen thing at their house?"

"Oh, yeah!" Shayne pointed at each of us. "That would be sweet. We could make more pizza."

I cleared my throat. "Wasn't that more Kellie's thing?"

"No. Ericson made the pizza."

"I mean the group thing. He was obviously part of it, but…"

Shayne deflated. "I suppose it would just make him miss her even more."

"Doesn't matter," Jake said. "We weren't invited." Then his face and his whole posture changed, and I knew Sam had come up behind us. We split apart to let him into the circle. "And the fivesome is complete," Jake said in his movie-preview-man voice.

"Hi, guys," Sam said.

"Where've you been?" Shayne asked.

Allie flipped her blond hair back. She'd gotten it cut in a layered style that made her look five years older. I could only dream of having silky-straight, obedient hair. "Rory said you have guitar lessons on Saturday now?" she asked.

His eyes flicked to me then away again. "Sometimes. I had one today, but earlier. My teacher drove me here, actually."

"Oh. Well, I guess that's okay," Shayne said. "We'll let you away with it this time, Shaggy." She ruffled his loose, sloppy curls before he could duck out of the way.

"Take a seat, everyone." It was Pastor Dan, pecking at the laptop on the desk a bit more confidently this week. "Thanks for your patience."

We settled on the floor, the five of us together for the first time that fall. Allie beside me, Sam and Shayne in front of us, and Jake sprawled off to the side.

It didn't feel exactly like I'd expected.

Pastor Dan asked us, "What would you rather read: a historical novel or a history textbook?"

"Does anyone actually read textbooks?" Jake wondered.

"Stories," Pastor answered himself. "Something in us responds to stories. It's probably just the way God hard-wired us. So Jesus knew to communicate his messages in parables. They expressed big ideas in familiar terms, painted a picture in the mind—sure, a picture not everyone understood at the time, but we do have some advantages that Jesus' audience didn't," and he held up his Bible with its loads of commentary and notes.

"Matthew chapter thirteen has a lot of what we call Kingdom parables.

"But what Kingdom is Jesus talking about, exactly? Whose is it?"

"God's," several people called out.

"Okay, then where is it? When is it?"

"In heaven?" someone ventured.

"Sure. But not just in heaven. Go to verse 24. Toby, will you read?"

The boy sitting next to Silas read about how the Kingdom of Heaven was like a farmer who planted good seed, but his sneaky enemy came along and planted weeds alongside it. The farmer decided he should let the weeds and the wheat grow together until the harvest, when the weeds would be sorted out and burned. Jesus explained that he was the farmer, the good seed was the people of the Kingdom, and the weeds were those whose allegiance was with Satan. And the harvest workers—the reapers and sorters—would be the angels, at the end of the world. It gave me a shivery feeling.

"So," Pastor Dan went on, "the Kingdom. It's not just heaven, is it? The good seed is sown right here, in this world. God is sovereign over all, and He is eternal. He *rules*. But specifically, the Kingdom includes all created intelligent beings in heaven *and* earth who are *willingly subject* to Him. It's not a place so much as a spiritual fellowship with God, one that starts when we are born again, and it never ends. Jesus told the Pharisees that the Kingdom of God wasn't something they were going to observe, like an era or a physical phenomenon—it was something within a person, born of the Spirit. Yet it will be fully manifested on earth when Jesus returns."

He stopped his pacing. "Here we are, folks, all of us together. Believers and unbelievers. Kingdom people and not-Kingdom people, in a world that groans under a curse. But even though

Kingdom folks live in it, we don't really belong." He clicked at the keyboard and a new screen popped up:

IN the world not OF the world:
John 15:19
Philippians 3:20

"Jot these references down, read them on your own this week. Jesus himself says you don't belong to this world. Paul tells the Philippians that their citizenship is in heaven.

"So does that mean we hunker down and twiddle our thumbs and wait for Jesus to return?" No one answered, though judging by his tone the answer wasn't yes. "Let's focus now on what this Kingdom stuff is all about."

Focus, yes. That's what I needed to do. This kingdom talk reminded me very much of things told me by certain angels that a certain psychiatrist insisted (without actually saying so) didn't exist. Which I eventually believed until we were both proven way wrong. The angel Rafie had talked about Jesus as a Friend; to Micah, the warrior, He was more of a Commander-in-Chief. But Gabby had often spoken of Him as the King. She'd also gently showed me that I was not some generic 'child of God' just because I was born human, created by God. If, by the Holy Spirit, I believed in Him as my Father, and His Son as my Savior, then I was adopted into the family of heaven. A child of the King.

And the Kingdom, apparently. Maybe now I was supposed to actually learn what that meant.

Except that meant concentrating. Listening at the Scene was ten times easier than listening at school, but after a week of it, the 14-year-old brain suffers major burnout. It didn't help that Jake was firing little wads of paper at Allie's head and mine—until he discovered that when he hit Sam's head, the paper missiles stuck in the curls without Sam actually noticing. Sam was a bit distracted anyway. Shayne's elbow kept creeping up and nudging him in the ribs, as if they were sharing some sort of private joke.

I glanced at Allie—to see if she was taking notes that I might borrow later—but she was watching me watch Sam and Shayne. Her barely-there blond eyebrows went up, until a stray paper wad thwacked her between the eyes.

I scooped up a handful of paper bits and flung them back at Jake. Almost simultaneously, my eyes met those of Martina Thistlethwaite at the side of the gym. She pointed once at me, once at Jake, then at the door.

"Looks like we're in trouble," he said, not all that unhappy about it. My face was a steaming tomato by the time we reached the back of the gym. I felt Shayne and Allie and Sam—and everyone else, probably—watching. Martina walked us out into the foyer.

"If you two have come here to play, the swings and slides are out back," she said.

"Is there a merry-go-round?" Jake asked hopefully. He clamped his mouth shut when she turned her frosty blue eyes on him.

"You're distracting those who came here to listen and learn," she continued. "I had hoped that was your reason for being here, too."

My mouth opened and closed uselessly. The only question was, pummel Jake now or pummel him later? To my utter astonishment, he reached over and patted my arm. "Let Rory go back in," he said to Martina. "I'll explain everything."

She gave him the narrow eye but nodded at me. I wandered back into the gym as if stepping away from a Historic Moment. Jake, taking responsibility for his goofus actions? I might have told the others, who gave me sympathetic looks as I rejoined them, but they'd never believe it.

I shouldn't have, either. When Jake and Martina returned a minute or two later, it was time to break into our groups. Jake gave me a reassuring nod and went off with the boys while we sat in the girls' circle with Martina on her stool.

"I'm excited about today's topic," she said. "I grew up reading stories of adventure and romance, dreaming of knights and castles. The thought of some faraway kingdom with a noble, courageous king absolutely enchanted me. I hope at least some of you grew up reading similar stories and dreaming those dreams." No one said it, but some of us admitted it with a smile.

"It used to make me sad in a way, too—wistful—because I thought it was only a story. Not until I was an adult did I realize that there really was a mighty King, far more worthy of service and devotion than any fictional one, and a Kingdom in which I was invited to serve. I don't want you to go that long without realizing that the best Story is true. And God puts that yearning in our hearts so that it might lead us to Him. Let's talk about His Kingdom, and share some of our own thoughts.

"Oh, but before we do, I feel I should say something." She shifted her slender backside on the stool to get more comfortable (without more natural cushion, I doubted she ever would). She looked around but didn't make eye contact with me. The warning lights started spinning in my head.

"We have a relatively short time together here. Every moment is precious. When we waste them goofing off, we're disrespecting our neighbors, hurting ourselves, ultimately dishonoring God."

My tomato face returned, with a side of hot sauce.

"I remember being your age—it wasn't that long ago, really—and I understand what it's like. But this isn't an appropriate place to try to impress a boy, even if you're seriously crushing on him."

I didn't hear a single thing more about Kings or Kingdoms after that. My only awareness of the group around me was the occasional sly look one of them would give me. Other than that, my thoughts were totally fixed on Jake Dean.

After we prayed and broke apart for the night, I stalked right over to where he and Sam were having some sort of arm-punching contest. Shayne and Allie stuck right behind me.

"What did you tell her?" I demanded.

"Tell who?" Jake asked innocently. I shot eye-daggers at him until he continued. "Oh, Miss Thistle-Wait?" He pronounced her name right; it just somehow sounded all wrong. Not as wrong as his next words, nevermind that he was just joking. "I just told her that you have the hots for me. But I promised I wouldn't let it cause any more problems. Don't take it personally, but I might have to keep my distance for a few weeks."

eight

By Monday morning, I wasn't thinking about Jake as much. At least my hands weren't itching to wrap around his neck and squeeze quite as much. But I couldn't afford to think about him at all, since I had a science test sitting on the desk in front of me that needed all my brain power.

I forced my mind away from that revolting moment when Jake revealed my undying love for him—and worse, the looks of laughter and uncertainty on the faces of Shayne and Allie and Sam. They'd actually considered it possible! Only for a split second, but never was there a more horrible second. There was no escape: science test or no, my memory insisted on replaying the whole thing, then the conversation afterwards.

Sheelan hadn't graced us with her presence that week, so we could hang out for a while, shooting baskets and talking. (This would have been heavenly minus the Jake factor.) We finally got off the Rory-loves-Jake topic, but naturally the conversation then turned to school, where we were forced to spend an unnatural portion of our lives.

"I can't believe the amount of homework they expect us to do," Shayne said, taking a shot and missing the rim by a mile. "I mean, it's nothing like eighth grade. Enjoy yourselves, guys."

I knew she didn't mean to talk down to us, but still I found myself saying, "Yeah, well I just spent hours studying for the dumb evolution test we've got on Monday." I was impressed by how that sounded.

"Why?" Jake asked. "Watch, I'll just look through my notes Monday morning, and I bet I'll get a better grade than you."

My shot bounced off the rim and nearly smacked him on the back of the head. So close.

"I remember that unit," Allie said. "What a pain. I'm so glad we don't have to deal with evolution again until advanced biology."

"Yeah, maybe it'll make more sense then," Shayne said.

"Doubt it." Sam took a shot, and the basketball wobbled around the rim a few times, then fell out.

I hoped he would say more, but he and Jake chased after the rebound. So I tried. "Yeah," I said, "I've been trying to figure out how the stuff we've been talking about here and the stuff we've been learning in science can both be true."

Allie waved the very thought aside. "Don't bother. I figure it's one of those questions I'll ask God when I get to heaven. As far as I can see, it's not our job to understand how God made the world, just to believe that He did it." She took the free throw shot and made it.

"Yeah, that's what I think," Shayne said. "And why couldn't God use evolution as a way of creating everything?"

"That's what Mr. Hayes sort of hinted at when I talked to him after school," I said.

"I don't know," Sam started, then Jake tried to wrestle the ball from him.

"You guys think too much." Jake elbowed Sam and won the ball. "Whatever the teacher taught, write that on the test, get your grade, and move on. I mean, face it, science has all the facts and evidence on its side, and the Bible is just about whether you believe it or not. It's not like you can fight that battle. Mr. Hayes would have you for lunch."

Sam looked like he would say something, but Allie caught the ball and held it, looking over Sam's shoulder. We all turned and saw Ericson approaching.

"Hey, guys," he said.

"Hey," we answered. No one thought of anything better to say.

"Sam, I've got to go. Do you need a ride?"

"Thanks, but I can just go with Jake."

"You'd better come get your guitar out of the van, then."

"Sure. I'll be right there."

Ericson waved at us. "Good to see you guys."

"You, too. Bye."

We all turned to Sam.

"I thought you said you drove here with your guitar teacher," Shayne said. Clearly none of us were destined to become detectives. But a second later I pointed at Sam.

"Ericson's your guitar teacher?"

He nodded, scuffing a shoe across the floor.

"Hey, that's great."

"He plays guitar? Since when?" Jake asked.

"You know he's a music teacher," Sam said.

"I knew he was some sort of teacher. I figured it was art, like Kellie was. Hey, does he have an electric guitar? You should trade him. I can't figure out why any kid who gets to choose a guitar for his birthday would pick acoustic."

"You've been saying that for two years. Get over it, already."

"Hey, go get your guitar and play us something," Shayne said, pushing him towards the door.

"Yeah, like 'Kum-ba-yah' or 'Puff the Magic Dragon'." Jake rolled his eyes. "Acoustic. Please."

Sam escaped a command performance since Jake's ride showed up a few minutes later, and Jeph was ready to go right after that. But I kept replaying that conversation the next night when I should have been focused on my science notes. It didn't help that I was in the family room recliner and Sheelan and my mom were watching some marvelous makeover program where a plain-Jane, fashion-challenged soul was transformed into a flashy, plastic, smiling version of her former sad self. Sheelan told me I should forget the science and take notes on the TV show instead.

Since I was just a few feet away, I heard the quiet *ding* and noticed a small window pop up on the computer screen. It had been so long, I'd almost forgotten what the IM window looked like. I popped out of my chair.

samIam: *looks like you're back online*

I scrambled for something genius to say.

REJoyce316: *yep*
samIam: *you're the only one*

Naturally I read this as *there's no one else to talk to, guess I'll just talk to Rory.* My fingers, poised claw-like over the keyboard, sagged a bit. He blooped again.

samIam: *I hardly find anyone on anymore*
REJoyce316: *not even Jake?*
samIam: *he's usually gaming*

Jake did talk a lot about blowing aliens away online, come to think of it. Yawn.

> **REJoyce316:** *not your thing?*
> **samIam:** *I like the World War II games, but it eats up a lot of time. Jake stays up as late as he wants.*
> **REJoyce316:** *I was about to fall asleep studying*
> **samIam:** *science again?*
> **REJoyce316:** *sadly yes*
> **samIam:** *making sense now?*
> **REJoyce316:** *can't say it is*
> **samIam:** *good*
> **REJoyce316:** *????*
> **samIam:** *what they're teaching doesn't make sense*
> **REJoyce316:** *????*
> **samIam:** *not if you believe the Bible*
> **REJoyce316:** *but what about the people who say you can believe both?*
> **samIam:** *that God used evolution to create everything?*
> **REJoyce316:** *yeah*
> **samIam:** *doesn't work*
> **REJoyce316:** *why not?*
> **samIam:** *well, what's been bugging you about the stuff Mr. Hayes is teaching?*

I thought about it a minute.

> **REJoyce316:** *I guess the part about there being no purpose to it all*
> **samIam:** *right. that's the 'natural' part of naturalistic evolution*
> **REJoyce316:** *so what? Just disagree, say God used evolution, but He did have a purpose. Adam and Eve were the goal, and apes eventually got us there.*

> **samIam:** *but what about sin?*
> **REJoyce316:** *what about it?*
> **samIam:** *think about it. When did death come into the picture?*
> **REJoyce316:** *in the Bible, you mean?*
> **samIam:** *see, it's already different. In the Bible, death was a result of sin.*

I chewed on that. Something *dinged* in my brain, and I flew upstairs to grab my dad's Bible. Then I pounced on the keyboard again. Whatever complaints I had about Mrs. Palmer, her preference for printed essays and papers had already made me a faster typist.

> **REJoyce316:** *but with this natural evolution stuff, death was always part of the life cycle.*
> **samIam:** *so sin doesn't factor into it*
> **REJoyce316:** *this reminds me of something…*

I opened to Genesis and found my dad's writing in the margin. *If monkeys → men*, **when did sin/death enter the picture?**

> **REJoyce316:** *if what Mr. Hayes teaches is true, then people evolved from apes*
> **samIam:** *and*
> **REJoyce316:** *and death would have to be part of God's design, not a result of sin*
> **samIam:** *so*
> **REJoyce316:** *so that part of the Bible would have to be wrong*
> **samIam:** *not just that part*
> **REJoyce316:** *what do you mean?*
> **samIam:** *why would we need a Savior to defeat sin and death*
> **REJoyce316:** *if death was part of the plan from the beginning*
> **samIam:** *aha*

> **REJoyce316:** *and sin wasn't sin*
> **samIam:** *???*

I was on a roll now.

> **REJoyce316:** *think about it. There was no first man and woman, no fall in the Garden of Eden. Just chimps who started standing up straight, and millions of years, and survival. Behavior wasn't right or wrong, it was just something that helped you survive or didn't.*
> **samIam:** *hadn't thought about it like that*
> **REJoyce316:** *so basically, humans are just*
> **samIam:** *animals in pants*

For some reason my embarrassment radar went off, like I was walking on the fringe of something delicate. But when I probed, I couldn't find anything specific. Still, better to play it safe.

> **REJoyce316:** *it's good that we can have these lighthearted chats*
> **samIam:** *yeah, like what's on TV, the weather, the origin of humanity and sin*
> **REJoyce316:** *all that stuff*

I laughed but tried to smother it. No use—it came out as a giggle. Sheelan cast her suspicious eyes my way.

> **samIam:** *I blame you*
> **REJoyce316:** *how's that?*
> **samIam:** *it's not like I IM about this stuff with anyone else*
> **REJoyce316:** *no? then why do you seem to know all about it?*
> **samIam:** *I'm just a font of wisdom*
> **REJoyce316:** *ah*
> **samIam:** *actually, we talked about all this a little at the Fishers. And Ericson has some books about it*

REJoyce316: *really?*

samIam: *yeah, he reads a lot. I guess this is something he's interested in. You know, you should talk to him, maybe borrow some of the books*

REJoyce316: *sounds good to me, but it's not like I can just drop by for a visit or something*

samIam: *I guess not*

Then I had a flash of pure inspiration, or at least pure wishful thinking. What if I went to see Ericson Greene with Sam when he had his guitar lesson? I imagined the scenario, and it positively exploded with possibility. There were no IM *dings* for a minute or two, and I pictured Sam considering the same thing.

samIam: *I can just ask to borrow the books for you, and bring them to the Fishers'.*

So much for our great minds thinking alike.

REJoyce316: *great. doesn't help me with the test tomorrow, though*
samIam: *frustrating*
REJoyce316: *do you think Jake's right?*
samIam: *that he'll hardly study and get a better grade than you? He's dreaming.*
REJoyce316: *no, I mean about just writing the answers the teacher wants, getting the grade and moving on*
samIam: *I guess that's what most kids do*

Suddenly, being like 'most kids' didn't sound as appealing as it usually did to my 14-year-old self.

samIam: *I think that's what they're counting on*
REJoyce316: *???*

> **samIam:** *that we'll just spit back the "right" answers and not think about it too much*
> **REJoyce316:** *but it still sort of sticks in your brain*
> **samIam:** *right—after you hear it enough, it sounds like the truth. And if you don't hear the Truth, or anything else for that matter, you almost don't have a choice but to believe.*
> **REJoyce316:** *you make it sound like brainwashing*
> **samIam:** *scary, cause when you think about it, they won't listen to any other ideas. They just shut you down.*

There he went again, making me look at things through a bigger lens. Suddenly this wasn't just about a grade. It wasn't even about pleasing the most popular teacher in the school. It was about Truth.

It was easier when it was just about a grade.

> **samIam:** *I guess I should let you get back to studying*
> **REJoyce316:** *seems kind of pointless now*
> **samIam:** *there's got to be a reason you're wrestling with this now. It's good.*
> **REJoyce316:** *we'll see. I need to go since my sister is reading over my shoulder.*

"As if I don't have anything better to do," Sheelan said, huffy. Proving that she was reading over my shoulder. How dense can you get?

> **samIam:** *hello, Rory's sister*

I liked the fact that he at least pretended not to remember her name, even if I didn't believe it. Boys never forgot her name.

"Hey, Mom, Rory's chatting with her boyfriend online. Did you give her permission?"

"Really?" Mom put down her glass of wine and peered at the computer screen. "What's his name? It's not the Svoboda boy who drives you to the church thing, is it? He's too old for you, Rory."

"Don't worry, Mom. Jeph only has eyes for Sheelan."

"Please." Sheelan rolled her eyes.

REJoyce316: *it's getting crowded here*
samIam: *over and out, then*
REJoyce316: *later*
samIam: *one more thing—1 Corinthians 1:27.*

I winced. People who could throw out Bible verses off the top of their head intimidated me.

REJoyce316: *okay...*
samIam: *It's on the Fishers' kitchen wall. That verse, I mean.*
REJoyce316: *oh. Thanks!*
samIam: *l8r*

That had been the night before, but it felt like a year ago. Now I sat staring at the test in front of me, and the *scritchy scratch* of pencils whispered around me. *Just do it, Rory. Write the 'right' answers.*

Then Sam's words popped up in front of my eyes like I was looking at the IM screen again: *I think that's what they're counting on... that's we'll just spit back the "right" answers and not think about it too much.*

My hyperactive teenage sense of injustice flared up like a hammered thumb. It wasn't just that this stuff probably wasn't even the truth. It went totally against the Truth. Did I have my Belt on?

Then I heard another whispery voice, more like my own, remembering the verse I had read before I went to bed that night, and again when I woke up. 1 Corinthians 1:27. *But God has chosen the foolish things of the world to put to shame the wise…*

I took a deep breath and began filling out the test paper. I knew it was a risk, but I failed to realize that the course of my entire life could be determined by my answers. It was a foolish thing.

nine

The rest of the week was uneventful. Deceptively uneventful. The calm before the storm, the deep breath before the plunge.

True to his word, Sam brought me a few books he borrowed from Ericson. But Tuesday it poured rain, so there was no chance encounter on the front steps. He left the books with Kingston, who brought them to me the next day. They were pretty meaty (lots of words, not many pictures), but just looking through the chapter headings gave me confidence that I'd done the right thing on the Monday test.

The feeling didn't last.

In class on Thursday, Mr. Hayes gave me a certain look. He didn't say anything, but I knew all in an instant that he'd been grading our tests, and he'd gotten to mine. By the time I walked home from school that afternoon, I was kicking myself. What had I been thinking?

The day didn't give a care about my mental struggle. It was one of those early October, Indian summer days when the sky is insanely aqua blue and the changing leaves glow like thousands of orange paper lanterns. The breeze smelled good enough to eat, or maybe it was the fragrance of baking bread that poured from the open windows and screen door of the Fisher house.

"We studied the chemistry of bread baking in science today," Kingston said. He stepped out with a steaming, buttered slice for me when I climbed the steps. "Yeast is freaky stuff."

"Freaky delicious," I said, sinking my teeth in. "Mmnn, this is even better than Grandma Judy's." Which until that moment I didn't think was possible.

"Sam made it. He's pretty good."

I tried to picture that. "Tell him it's great." I peeked behind Kingston.

"He already left. Something happened at home and he had to go before the bread was done baking." He shook his head with deep regret.

So it was that I faced Friday, test-return day, without the pep talk I'd hoped to get from Sam. And who else would understand what I'd done? Come to think of it, I wasn't even sure I understood what I'd done.

Mr. Hayes returned our test booklets in the usual way, placing each one face-down on the desk in front of us. He began his usual speech. "Your grade is your own business. It's not a class ranking system. It's a measurement of your understanding of the material and whether you need to revisit it and better learn it. It means something only to you and to me."

By this point, I was barely taking in oxygen. There were only three or four left in his hands. The others were peeking inside the front cover of their own booklets, where I glimpsed red marks. Beside me, Jasmine opened her booklet in plain view, then gave me a *do you mind?* look when I saw the big red A. I got the feeling she didn't mind too much.

Then Mr. Hayes laid mine down, his fingertips pressing on top of it for a second or two before he moved on. My palms were sweating when I lifted it and peeked inside. No marks on the first page. Looking around to make sure no one was watching, I flipped through the other pages. Nothing. Not a single red mark, no grade, no comments.

"Overall, you guys did a passable job on the multiple choice. Some of your essay answers were very creative. Creative is fine, up to a point. When you crossed the border into the realm of the ludicrously mistaken, I deducted points." There was some laughter at this, probably from the relieved people who scored higher than they expected. "I think I was pretty generous, since some of this is higher-level science than you're expected to learn at this grade level. Almost all of you received a passing grade."

He sat on the edge of his desk and made a teepee with his hands, pressing the point against his mouth. "One of you didn't receive a grade at all."

Everyone glanced around curiously, as if the ungraded person might have a neon arrow pointing down at her head. I looked around, too, shrugging when Jasmine caught my eye. Her eyes dropped to my test book, safely closed under my hand.

"This person shall remain anonymous," Mr. Hayes went on, his eyes roving the class but not settling on anyone. Still, I felt his glance pass over me like a flamethrower. "I understand that this individual's test results are the result of some confusion and personal conflict, and not some attempt to be 'smart'. Because of this—" he stopped and placed a hand over his heart, "—and because I'm a compassionate fellow who believes in second chances, I will offer one now."

He stood and walked behind his desk, taking a seat. He hardly ever sat during class. It had the feeling of a judge sitting at his podium. His next words hit me like the banging gavel.

"Next Wednesday, an hour before school starts, I will be here. There will be another test waiting on the desk in the back corner. The anonymous student, should he or she choose, may come then and retake the test, and that will be the score that counts towards their final grade at the end of the semester."

"What about anyone who just wants to try for a better grade?" Jake asked. "Not me, of course," he added.

Mr. Hayes shook his head.

"Aw, where's the compassion?" Jake lifted a dramatic hand.

Jasmine leaned over and whispered in my ear. "Why should only one person get a second chance? It's not fair."

"You've got nothing to worry about. You got an A," I said.

"Maybe, but what if I wanted to try for a perfect score? Technically I should be offered the chance, if this other confused person gets one."

If I had something intelligent to say to that, I forgot it when Bliss Hathaway turned in her seat and looked directly at me. Then she raised her hand.

"Yes, Bliss?"

"What will happen to this person if they decide not to retake the test?"

Why was she asking that? It made it look like she was Miss Anonymous. Not that I minded if people thought it was her. She was the kind of person who could pull that off and look good. I would just look like a dope.

"Then they'll be choosing to take an Incomplete mark in the grade book."

I wasn't sure what that meant, but it didn't sound good. Enough said. I'd made my point, right? Now it was time to get practical, and thankfully I was getting a chance to do it.

"I'm not sure that's fair, Mr. Hayes."

Really, Bliss, it's fine.

"You're right in a way, Bliss. If I were being totally fair, I would just give the person a failing grade. I'm being unreasonably reasonable in this case."

"But if the person answered the questions according to her deeply-held beliefs, why should you expect those to change by next Wednesday?"

I couldn't believe she'd said *'her* deeply-held beliefs'. Anonymous, Bliss. Anonymous. Without it, this became the humiliation of the century. Of the decade, at least. And did she have to keep throwing me those little side looks?

Mr. Hayes leaned back in his chair, folding his arms behind his head in an effort to relax. "I thought I'd made it clear that this class is strictly about science—about deeply true facts, not beliefs. But because it seems I wasn't as crystal-clear as I believed, I'm giving this person a chance to shift gears from beliefs to true science."

Message received. By me, anyway. So why was Bliss standing up? Don't stand up, Bliss. Don't look right at me like that, Bliss.

"I think I have to object," she said, crossing her arms, her light brown eyes lit up. "What Rory did was very brave."

Had she actually said my name?

People were turning to look at me. She'd said my name.

"She stood up for what she believes in."

I'm not standing, Bliss. You're standing.

By now all eyes had turned from Bliss to me. I felt myself shrinking—but sadly, not enough to disappear.

"I'm standing with her."

ten

According to the Amazing Nature channel—located snugly beside the Retro Sitcom channel—a coral reef is an astounding, delicate balance of life. Change the temperature or chemistry of the water ever-so-slightly, introduce or eliminate certain microscopic critters, and you upset the entire mix and doom it to destruction. A coral reef is a lot like junior high.

Bliss had done what amounted to dumping a barrel of barracudas into a goldfish pond. I was still trying to figure out if I was a barracuda or a goldfish. Mostly I felt like algae.

Jasmine didn't exactly move away when I sat down across from her at lunchtime, but her body language shrieked confusion. Did she want to be seen with me? Had I actually done anything wrong? Was I just the weird girl who had God issues and couldn't cope with the idea of evolution? Was I any weirder than I had been the day before, or the year before, when we'd started doing lunch? Did she want to be seen with me? (Major issue, worth repeating.)

Oddly enough, there was similar trouble at the Bliss Hathaway table. Bliss was usually the last to arrive, and there was usually a shuffle for every seat but hers. This time no one seemed able to make up their mind. Was the Bliss table still The Table? If they chose a different one, would someone else swoop in and claim their seat, when it turned out Bliss was still cool and this was still The Table after all? I watched the general milling around, for the first time realizing that I wasn't the only one who might suffer from Bliss's revelation in science class.

Suffering was probably too strong a word. Bliss breezed into the cafeteria with a sack lunch and, without so much as a glance at her usual table, sat down beside me. This caused a shocked stillness at The Table. Shocked stillness could also describe Jasmine for a few seconds. Then her body language started shrieking a whole new confusion.

"Hey," Bliss said.

"Hey," I said.

"Do you do egg salad? My sister made the lunches this morning, and she gave me egg salad—even though she knows I've gone vegan."

My eyes flicked to Jasmine, who was a vegetarian. I had a feeling that vegan trumped vegetarian on the scale of dietary righteousness; judging my Jasmine's cold eyes, I was right.

"Um, yeah. I eat egg salad." The only way I liked it was in Grandma Judy's egg-and-tuna-salad combo.

"Good, because I see you picked the pasta today. I checked and it's totally vegan. Let's trade."

She wasn't exactly asking, so I couldn't exactly refuse. "Um, I did eat some of it."

"So? I'm not afraid to catch Rory germs." She laughed. "Ooh, I might start thinking for myself and questioning authority! Oh, wait—I've already got that disease. I'm safe." She lifted the plate of steamy spaghetti and sauce off my tray and plopped a foil-wrapped square in its place. "Honestly, can you believe that Hayes? I thought he was different, you know? Well, maybe it's too soon to judge him, but I can smell a closed mind a mile away. Still think he's cute, though."

I took a bite of Bliss's sandwich to avoid speech. Speech might have been a better option. All at once, I knew with utter certainty that Bliss's sister hated her.

"Listen," she said, ignoring the gestures of Jake and one or two others at her usual table. "I know it was a bit awkward in class."

I bit back the *well, duh* and swallowed it with a mouthful of the awfulest stuff that ever called itself egg salad. I gave her a gracious half-shrug since she was about to apologize and all.

She said, "And I'm guessing you still feel kind of weird about it, so I just want to say forget it. You don't have to thank me or anything."

The egg salad seemed to stiffen like drying concrete in my mouth. Concrete was quite possibly one of the ingredients.

"Wherever this thing goes," she said, "I'm behind you on it."

Like a runaway go-cart, perhaps? And how was she behind me? She wasn't any more behind than she had been standing *with* me in class. From where I sat, it looked like she was in front and standing alone.

"I'm glad to do it, just for the principle of it. But out of friendship, too." She dove hungrily into my spaghetti. Just like that she had claimed my lunch and my allegiance, both without actually asking.

"Oh. Well…" I tried. Jasmine lifted a black eyebrow at me. "Thanks, I guess."

"Come on, I just said you don't have to thank me. But you know what you can do instead?" Since I couldn't begin to guess, she enlightened me. "You can help me plan my Halloween party."

"Me?"

"Sure. I haven't even decided if I'm going to invite a whole bunch of people or just a handful. But you know everyone here way better than I do, so you can help me pick."

I didn't even have to look Jasmine's way to know she'd heard every word. I could feel the exclamation points shooting off of her like poisoned darts.

"Oh, and I have to decide on my costume. I've got this fantastic catalog. Let's say you come over after school next week, and we can start planning."

I knew she wasn't waiting for my answer. It was a done deal.

"Wow. I can't believe you did that."

It was Sam speaking; it was Saturday, shooting hoops after the Scene. And it would've been sort of sweet, mostly funny—if he hadn't already said it maybe five times.

"Dumb," Jake said, probably the tenth time.

"It took guts," Shayne said, shooting and missing for the sixth time. "Rory's got hoopspa."

"I think you mean *chutzpah*," Sam said.

"Does that mean guts?"

"Sort of."

"Then she's got that."

Allie shot and made it for the fourth time. "Did Mr. Hayes give you an F?"

"No, an Incomplete."

Shayne said, "That doesn't sound too bad. Better than an F," she added, nibbling on the ends of her hair. That worried me; she reserved hair nibbling for moments of deep concern.

"I'm not so sure," Allie said, worrying me more.

"Wow." Sam again. I gave him a look. He sort of shrugged helplessly. I knew what he was thinking: *Did I convince her to do this?*

Yeah, pretty much, I answered with my eyes. "Well, what would you have done?" I asked, meaning it for him but knowing the others would include themselves. Then I rethought the question. "No, I mean what did you do? You all took the same test."

"I already told you," Jake said with his Patient Kindergarten Teacher voice. "Plus I told you *before* the test, not that it did any good. Write what the teacher teaches, get the grade, done."

"And what grade did your master plan get you?" Allie asked.

"A passing one, which is better than a noble and stupid Incomplete." He endured everyone's hard stares with total lack of concern. "Okay, so what did you guys write on the test?"

The other three looked at each other.

Jake nodded knowingly. "Just as I thought."

"I decided that even though I didn't really understand it all, and I couldn't agree with it all, it didn't matter as long as I still believed what was important," Allie said in her own defense.

"You mean you didn't want to risk getting anything less than an A and losing the race for class valedictorian," Jake said. "Which you ended up losing anyway."

Allie passed him the ball. Or you might say she tried to cream him with it.

"I hardly even remember that test," Shayne admitted. "It was way at the beginning of the school year. That was the one with the creepy monkeys, right? You know, the stages where the monkeys gradually turn into a human?"

"Technically, apes," Allie said.

"What about you, Sam?" Jake asked, all sweetness.

He started polishing his glasses, but his almost-black eyes flicked up and met mine for a second. "Well, I did tell Mr. Hayes I had serious doubts." He sighed and put the glasses back on. "But I wrote the answers he wanted on the test." Then to me he said, "I didn't realize you were going to challenge all his 'facts' right there on the test."

I fought the mighty urge to pound him.

Then he said, "If I'd known then what I know now—not that it's much more, but it's a bit... Well, now I kind of wish I'd done what Rory did."

And I forgave him all at once.

"Rory got something good out of it, anyway," Jake said.

"What's that?" a few of us asked, including me.

"An alliance with Bliss Hathaway."

"What's a 'bless halfway'?" Shayne asked.

"You mean, *who's* a Bliss Hathaway," Jake said. "Come on, I told you about her. My next-door neighbor—and the one girl everyone in the eighth grade wants to hang with."

Allie turned to me. "Bliss? That's her name?"

I shrugged, hands up. "Apparently."

"And she saved Rory from total humiliation by standing up for her in class."

"She totally blew my cover, you mean. No one knew I was the one with the Incomplete until she 'stood up' for me."

"She launched you from nothingness to royalty, and you know it."

"I think you're exaggerating a bit, Jake."

Allie cut in. "But what's going to happen with the test?"

Jake waved it off. "She gets to take it again next week and totally save her own behind."

"Mr. Hayes is giving you a second chance?" Shayne asked. "He was always pretty cool."

"Even a bad grade is better than an Incomplete," Allie agreed.

"I suppose," I said. After the incident in class, my thoughts had turned from principles to practical. Now, as I caught Sam watching me, I realized that underneath I still had a squirmy feeling about the whole thing. "I don't know," I finished weakly.

Jake tucked the basketball under his arm and stared me down. "Oh, I see. You want to take it to the next level."

"What level would that be?" Shayne asked.

"Rory's had a taste of fame, and she likes it. I bet she stands her ground and doesn't retake the test. And milks this for all it's worth."

Allie knocked the ball away from him. "Give it a rest, Jake. Maybe that's what you would do, but Rory's not like you."

"Yeah, right. Humble little Rory, never ever concerned about what people think of her, or whether they notice her at all. We'll see." He ducked as the ball sailed right where his head had been. "Hey, I wouldn't blame you, Rory. You've got a sweet thing going. Ride it to the end of the line, I say."

Sam leaned against the cinderblock wall. "You're missing the point."

"So, what is the point, All-Knowing One?"

"Well, what makes next week any different than this week? I mean, if Rory thought it was wrong to write the 'acceptable' answers on the test last week, what's happened to change that now?"

Good old Sam. You could always count on him to put into words the uncomfortable truth you were desperately trying to avoid.

"How about the threat of failing science class?" Shayne asked.

"Really," Allie put in, "Rory made her point, didn't she? Mr. Hayes knows how she feels—maybe the whole class. Mission accomplished. Now she can complete the test, get a good grade, and everyone's happy."

Jake made a free throw. "What was the mission exactly?" he asked me. "Because all you accomplished was to make Hayes think you're a loony, or just plain obnoxious. The whole class would, too, if it weren't for Bliss taking your side. Just another Jesus freak kicking up a stink."

"So I give Christianity a bad name?" I asked him.

"You said it, not me," he said. It was amazing what you could get away with when no one ever took you seriously.

"What about what Pastor Dan talked about today?" Shayne asked. "All that salt and light stuff. I wonder if this is kind of about all that."

"I fail to see the connection," Jake said.

"Probably because you failed to pay attention," Allie said.

"No, I heard him loud and clear," he said. "Christians are supposed to be bright and shiny people in the world, sprinkling tasty flavor wherever we go. Can't see how Rory accomplished that by annoying the teacher and making the other kids think she's a pain."

"I don't think that's what the salt and light thing means," Sam said.

"Sam's right," Allie said. "Salt wasn't just a seasoning back in Jesus' time. It was a preservative. They didn't have refrigerators, you know."

"Really?" Jake asked in his Idiot voice.

Sam spoke up. "Salt kept food, like meat, from rotting. Christians are supposed to help stop the rot in the world."

"Gross," Shayne said, then she pointed at Sam. "You mean that by standing up for the truth, Rory is sort of fighting the rot of evolution?"

"Oh, I'm sure Mr. Hayes would appreciate you calling his class rot."

Sam looked vaguely troubled. "Well, it's hard for any of us to take on a teacher, since they're in authority." Then he asked me, "Did you start any of those books from Ericson?"

"I looked through them. Haven't had time to *read* read."

"One is about how the problem isn't the idea of evolution, exactly. Everyone agrees that creatures change over time, and Darwin explains one way that can happen. What they're not mentioning is that Darwin can't explain how everything came to be in the first place. They want to believe he does, but the evidence just isn't there."

"Oooh...it's a conspiracy," Jake said, waggling his fingers at us. "Come on. Why would they want to teach us wrong science? You're paranoid."

"Maybe Rory can lend you the books when she'd done."

Jake made a show of barely-restrained excitement.

"I'd be interested in reading them," Allie said, not one to be less informed than her friends. "You say you got them from Ericson?"

Sam nodded. "He knows a lot about it."

"I bet he could explain it a lot better than the books do," Shayne said. "It'd be great if we could all go over there sometime. Books like that put me to sleep."

"And pizza at Ericson's keeps you awake," Jake guessed.

"We can't just invade Ericson's house like that," Allie said. "Things are different now."

But I could see the faraway look in Sam's eyes. An idea was cooking.

eleven

Wednesday—test re-take day—loomed over me like that two-ton weight that falls on unsuspecting cartoon characters. Except I doubted that, once squashed, I would pop right back into shape.

The only good thing about that Wednesday was that Tuesday came first, and on Tuesday there was a chance I'd see Sam at the Fishers. I could say that I wanted him to boost my confidence, assure me that I was doing the right thing by not giving in to Mr. Hayes's pressure. But I was planning to give in to Mr. Hayes's pressure.

Yep, I was playing it safe. Like Allie had said: I'd made my point, now it was time to cover my butt. It sounded more reasonable every day. Unfortunately, I also remembered what Sam had said. Now I needed him to tell me that, no matter what he'd said, taking the test was still okay.

Then Monday after school, Bliss came up to my locker. "Think you can find my house?" she asked.

I wished Tiffany's locker wasn't right next to mine, where she could watch and take notes on my every move. "I guess," I answered Bliss. I'd only been to Jake's a couple of times, just driveway drop-offs, but the houses on that end of the subdivision were pretty memorable—unlike my block of cookie-cutter duplexes. "Next to Jake's, on Windham Lane, right?"

"Come over after school tomorrow," she said.

Bliss's tactic of not actually asking questions eliminated her need to wait for answers. So on my walk home the next day, I turned away from Sweetnam Lane—away from home, the Fishers' house, and my chance of getting Sam's blessing for chickening out and taking the science test the next day.

If our subdivision was a large open mouth full of spaghetti (stay with me here), Sweetnam lane would be the curving row of smaller bottom teeth, and Windham Lane the rainbowing arc of gleaming upper teeth. In between, the jumble of shorter, intersecting streets and cul-de-sacs. Windham Lane crowned them all, a brick-and-stone-encrusted sweep of ever-larger homes. I could pick out Jake's red-brick-and-white-column house without much trouble. On the left was a white brick monstrosity that looked like a little museum, right down to the stone lions on either side of the steps. A small, dark woman in a rose-colored sari was at the mailbox. I didn't think Bliss looked even part Indian, so I concluded the house on the other side must be hers.

It was frame and stone, with a cottage feel. An enormous, expensive cottage, one that would've felt more at home on a forested mountainside. My finger lifted to ring the doorbell, but then my eyes dropped to the welcome mat: *LeVey*.

I stood there, puzzling over whether Bliss Hathaway was more likely to live with an Indian woman or someone named LeVey. As I puzzled, the door opened. A girl stood there—familiar, but not Bliss—and just watched me.

"Is this the Hathaway house?" I asked, trying to figure out where I knew her from.

She pointed at the welcome mat with *duh* written all over her face.

"I'm looking for Bliss Hathaway's house," I said. "Is it the white one on the other side there?"

She shook her head, then continued to just watch me with her pale gray eyes, half-hidden by a fringe of black hair—the kind of blue-black that only comes from a bottle.

I kept trying. "You go to Whitestone Elementary, right?"

She nodded.

"Do you know where Bliss lives?"

Another nod. "Here, unfortunately." She pointed behind me, and I saw a shiny black car pull up to the curb. Bliss hopped out and said something to a driver I couldn't see, then the car sped off. She smiled as she came up the steps.

"I didn't think you'd get here before me. You walk fast," she said. "So, you've met Journey."

A light came on in my brain. That name: Journey LeVey. She was in my English class—a seventh-grader in Mr. Behrens combined seventh/eighth-grade class, just like I'd been last year.

"You're in our English class," I told her, and she didn't disagree. "Why are you at Bliss's house?"

Bliss opened the door and breezed past Journey, motioning for me to follow. "Because she's my sister," she answered my question.

"Half sister," Journey corrected instantly.

I glanced at them for the brief moment they were beside each other. Bliss with her thick, shiny nut-brown hair, streaked with shades of caramel, and her smooth golden skin and unexplainable late-high-school curves; then Journey, all paleness and bottle-blackness, the slouchy kind of posture that Grandma Judy poked me in the ribs to correct, and eyes that sliced right into you.

Whatever parent they shared, they must've taken after their Then I had a thought, and it came out of my mouth without thinking. "You made the egg salad sandwich," I said.

Those gray eyes drilled into me. "You ate that?"

"Bliss and I traded lunches."

Journey gave Bliss a look of disbelief, then stalked up the curving staircase without a word.

Bliss hardly spared her a glance. "She's always trying to get me, but I'm always one step ahead of her," she said. She didn't say that she'd known the sandwich was tampered with when she gave it to me—but she didn't say that she hadn't, either. I followed her past a living room that was all creamy white, from the flimsy drapes to the poofy furniture to the spotless carpet. On a table in the corner stood a marble statue of a woman, glowing like an ancient goddess under a soft light that came from a source I couldn't see.

Then we were in the kitchen, three times the size of my mom's, gleaming with stainless steel and dark granite. Bliss pulled a glass pitcher from the fridge. "Green tea?" she asked.

"Sure," I said. Nevermind that I wasn't a huge fan of tea, hot or cold. This was just the kind of kitchen where you drank chilled green tea. Even the ice that clinked into the glasses looked more sparkly and pure than the cloudy hunks we pried out of the plastic trays at home. I took a sip and discovered it was unsweetened. And I'd always thought the primary purpose of a cold beverage was to deliver high fructose corn syrup to my bloodstream.

"This way," Bliss said. I followed her down a few steps into a rec room with a hardwood floor and suede furniture, sipping my purposeless drink. She spoke again. "Hi, Tam."

"Hi, Bliss. Who's your friend?"

I nearly spilled tea over myself. On a giant floor pillow in the dim corner sat a cross-legged girl playing with a deck of cards.

She flipped one onto the floor beside some others, studied them, then carefully placed them back into the deck before finally looking up, smiling.

"This is Rory. She's in my class. Rory, this is Tam."

Tam stood, and as she moved into the light I saw that she wasn't a girl, just a petite woman, middle-aged. (My mom complained that I called everyone from twenty-eight to forty-five middle-aged. She didn't know what was worse, that I considered the upper twenties to be old, or that soon she wouldn't even qualify as middle-aged anymore, and what would that make her? Older, I told her.)

Tam reached out to shake my hand, but she stopped after one pump. "Do you feel that, Bliss?"

I extracted my hand.

"Yeah, I thought I did," Bliss said.

"You mean you knew you did. You're so sensitive to those things."

Feel what? I can't say I was any more graceful socially than I was physically, but because it was better than standing there in silence while Tam examined me, I said, "It's nice to meet you."

"And you, too," she said. Her eyes roamed, sort of half-focused, as if it was also nice to meet the air around my head. And what, exactly, was she looking for? I wondered.

"Tam, I'm looking for that costume catalog."

"Right. Check in the office. I think your mom ordered 'Empress of the Night' for herself."

Bliss beckoned and I followed her into a back room with plum-colored walls and an L-shaped glass desk. A woman sat there under a window. The light of a bright, pearly-gray, overcast day lit her hair and skin like marble, washing out the color. She smiled at us but held up a finger for quiet. The other hand was at her ear.

"Yes, any day after the fifteenth of the month should work for you. Correct. Certainly. You're most welcome." Then she snapped a wafer-thin cell phone shut and stood, walking around the desk to meet us. Even when she moved out of the colorless sunlight, she hardly looked less pale and elegant. Her skin was only a shade darker than her platinum blond hair, smooth and flawless, the hair swept up into a twist.

"Rory," she said, "I'm glad you came."

"Um, thanks," I said, then added, "Mrs. Hath—um, Mrs. LeVey."

She smiled, white teeth. "Sylvie Rhaynes."

"Oh. Sorry—I just…"

"I know, the welcome mat. It may not be my name anymore, but it's still Journey's."

Bliss gave a little snorty laugh. "And she'd probably never find her way home if her name weren't on the front step."

Her mom raised one eyebrow. "Removing it would symbolize something to her that I don't intend. Anyway, it's just to wipe our feet on, so I don't mind it at all." She played with a string of pearls peeking from her silky blouse. Her skirt was slim and she wore high heels like she was at work. Judging by the room, she was at work.

"You came for this, I assume." She swept a catalog off the desk and handed it to Bliss. Then her phone chirped. She looked at it. "Mr. Anton. He can't seem to make a move these days without calling me first. I'd better take the call." She smiled, and it said *goodbye and shut the door behind you* without a word.

Bliss did shut the door, rolling her eyes, which said *give me a break* without a word. I made a face that showed I got the joke. I didn't, but no self-respecting fourteen-year-old is going to admit they don't get the joke.

We settled onto a suede sofa, and she asked, "So, have you thought about how you'll dress for Halloween?"

"Oh, yeah." For over a year. My dad and I had planned to rig up a hilarious costume last Halloween, but then he'd had to take some overtime and somehow we never got the chance. I ended up being a pirate chick like five other seventh graders, only mine wasn't as cool. But not this year—this year I'd be the piggyback baby, for Dad.

I described it to Bliss, the baby "body" on the back of my shirt so that my head looked like the baby's head, and a fake head below mine so it looked like I was riding on someone's back.

She laughed, her mouth twisted to one side. "Hilarious. Good one, Rory. But seriously, have you thought of a real costume? Have a look at some of these."

I took the catalog she pressed into my hands, but I didn't even see the first few pages I flipped past. I kept seeing my dad's face when he told me he had another weekend job he had to take, he was sorry.

My eyes finally focused on a page filled with women in French maid costumes, vampiress costumes, naughty schoolgirl costumes… "What…?"

"No, towards the back," Bliss said, flipping the pages for me. "Those are the adult costumes. Here—the teen section."

The girls did look a little younger, but the costumes weren't all that different. Not as many plunging necklines, but making up for it with a lot of short skirts and exposed belly buttons.

"I'm loving the 'Queen of the Undead', here," and she pointed at a shadowy-eyed girl with a glossy black wig and a glossy black satin dress with slits from here to Indonesia and fishnet stockings. "But there's also the 'Bad Fairy'. Too sweet." The Bad Fairy wore a scanty, tattered little black-and-purple number with wicked black bat wings and butt-stomping knee-high combat boots. "Which do you think?"

I groped for the neutral position. "Um, I think Jake Dean said something about going as lord of the undead."

"Jake? So what?"

"So you don't want to be, like, the queen to his king, do you?"

"So you think I should invite Jake."

I blinked. "I just figured you would."

"I hadn't really thought about it." She shrugged. "It's up to you, I guess."

Up to me. I drew in a breath, a long one that tasted like pure power. I had Jake's Halloween fate in the palm of my hand. How simple it would be to exact my revenge. I examined the Bad Fairy, her spiky hair and sassy pout, her little sneer that looked suddenly appealing. She wouldn't hesitate to cast Jake into the pit of the uninvited, the unelite—the deleted.

And be kind to one another, tenderhearted, forgiving one another, even as God in Christ forgave you.

I looked over my shoulder, as if the voice came from someone else, but it was in my head. Still, it sounded a bit familiar, almost like Kellie Greene's, or maybe Gabby's. It didn't matter; I knew what it was—God's Word. Probably from Ephesians. I'd read that the most since the whole Armor of God thing. I knew this was a chance to put the Word into action.

But I was weak. This was *Jake*. I should've said, *Yeah, I think you should invite him—he's really looking forward to it.* Instead I said, "He's right next door. You know he's going to come whether you invite him or not."

She gave a little snort. "I'm sure. Yeah, we'll invite him, whatever."

So Jake made the list. Part of me still relished the idea that I could always change that.

"What do you think of that one?" Bliss pointed to another fairy costume, this one all green and ivy-ish, more innocent than the black-and-purple one but still showing plenty of leg and completely bare arms.

"It's great."

"That's it, then. I'm the wicked fairy and you're the good one. It'll be perfect."

I guess so, if perfect meant me looking perfectly ridiculous. A five-foot-eight-inch fairy with huge feet. "I'm not sure…"

"You like the bad fairy better? We could switch, but honestly I think you'll look much better in the green, with your hair. Plus I already have boots like the bad fairy's wearing. Size seven."

She did? Who actually owned boots like that? "No, I like the green one fine—"

"That's that, then. Let's order them today, express shipping."

"I just don't know if… It'll fit me."

She gave me the caramel-colored eye. "That's why you order it in your size, genius." She would've laughed, but then her face shifted. "Don't worry about the price—we'll just use my mom's credit card."

"Really?" I hadn't actually moved beyond worrying about humiliating myself to worrying about the cost of humiliating myself, but another glance revealed the costume price of $39.95. Forty bucks? But I could humiliate myself for free. "I wouldn't expect your mom to do that," I tried.

"She doesn't care." Her voice was sort of flat. "Anyway, this is our party, right? We've got to have the best costumes." She folded the page to mark it, then tossed it aside. "I'll order online tonight. Now we should work on the guest list, figure out the food… Tam's doing the decorations, but I have to pick them. This could take a while."

Somehow when I wasn't looking, this had become 'our' party. Maybe that was a good thing—I hadn't decided—but one thing was sure: I didn't have all afternoon to spend on it. I had to study for my make-up test first thing in the morning. I told Bliss.

She laughed and gave me a little shove on the shoulder. I'd never known how hilarious I was. "You crack me up," she said.

"As if you'd ever take that total cop-out 'I'm sorry I stood up for my beliefs, I'll never do it again' test."

"Heh heh… Yeah."

"That's what I like about you, Rory—it's what makes you different from those other youngsters. Well, one of two things, really. But I could tell straight off that you weren't afraid to go against the flow."

So when I'd walked into Bliss's house, I was: 1) glad to be one of the kids invited to her party; and 2) planning to go home soon and study for my test. When I left her house two hours later I was one of the kids hosting the party and a go-against-the-flow girl who wouldn't dream of abandoning my principles and taking that test.

I wondered who I would've been if I'd just gone home and talked to Sam.

twelve

So here's the part where I describe my intestinal fortitude (guts) and how I bravely refused take the make-up test. Because I did refuse to take it.

Except now it didn't feel like I was standing up for my principles, the Truth, or even for Sam Newman's principles and Truth. Now it felt like I was caving in to Bliss Hathaway's truth.

Since by this point everyone knew I was the not-so-anonymous-non-test-taker, they all knew immediately when I became the ever-so-unanonymous-non-make-up-test-taker.

"Are you nuts?" Jasmine asked, speaking for 50% of my classmates. According to Tiffany Klipfel's unofficial class poll, 45% thought what I did was pretty cool, while 5% (a boy named Ronnie who fell asleep a lot) didn't know what was going on and didn't much care.

"Come on," I said, trying to win Jasmine over to the 45% camp to be my swing vote. "I couldn't just pretend like I believe all that Darwin junk—"

"No, don't even start with that 'deeply-held beliefs' rubbish. You're like Bliss's pet parrot."

Harsh. "You don't even know what I believe," I shot back.

"Nobody does, Rory. Do you even know?"

Those words still rattled in my skull at the Scene that Saturday. Great fun, having Jasmine in your head for days on end. They were the only words I had from her all week—we didn't even speak at lunchtime. I took advantage of the situation and chose every deep-fried and/or meat-based product on the menu. By Friday (aka Deep Fry-day), my chicken thingers, french fries and fried mozzarella sticks drove her to another table completely. And I had a new grease-induced pimple.

It didn't matter too much what Jasmine did, because on Wednesday Bliss sat with me and a few others joined us; by Thursday it was pretty much the entire Bliss Table relocated to mine; and on Friday Bliss was absent for reasons unknown, but the rest of the kids still sat at my table. It was a pretty good feeling. I had myself pretty much convinced that God was rewarding me for standing up for His truth, but somehow I wasn't quite able to hold my head so high when I walked into Mr. Hayes's classroom and saw the look on his face. He hadn't said a word about it.

And yes, there was Jasmine's comment. It replayed in my memory as I listened to Pastor Dan talk about salt again that Saturday.

"Ahoy, ye salty dawgs," he greeted us in his best (worst) pirate voice. We groaned.

"If he says 'aargh', I'm outta here," I whispered to Mary Katherine, sitting in front of me. Sam happened to be sitting beside her. He bared his teeth at me, pirate-style.

"Were you a salty Christian this week?" Pastor asked, thankfully in his normal voice. "Maybe you're not sure. Here's one way I test myself—I ask myself, did I glide through the week, mostly smiling, pleasing everyone, all comfy-cozy?" He scratched at his chin, now as bare as the rest of his head. "I shaved for my wife, and that pleased her. My head feels naked, but she's happy."

He waited for the bald jokes to quiet. "But seriously, that's not what I mean. And I don't mean to suggest that you should be out there purposely making waves, either. But how many times are we faced with the temptation to nod and smile and make people like us when inside the little alarms are going off because we know what they're doing or saying isn't true or God-honoring?"

You know how you can be so busy noticing other people's reactions—to see if the message speaks to them—that you don't let it speak to you?

"How many times do we let the chance slip by? The chance, not to confront or accuse people, but to engage them in a meaningful dialogue. It's not your job to change people's minds and hearts. That belongs to the Holy Spirit. But it is our job to speak the truth in love. Expose them to some new ideas, maybe get them thinking a little.

"Or do you think any differently from the non-believers around you?"

He let that one hang for a minute. Then he pressed his little clicker and the screen lit up.

> *Then we will no longer be like children, forever changing our minds about what we believe because someone has told us something different or because someone has cleverly lied to us and made the lie sound like the truth. Instead, we will hold to the truth in love, becoming more and more in every way like Christ, who is the head of his body, the church. Ephesians 4:14-15*

I read the words and understood them. I didn't think they applied to me.

When we gathered with Martina, she asked if anyone knew Proverbs 4:23 off the top of their head. Our consolation for not knowing it is that no one else did, either.

Except Allie ruined this. "Oh, I know! 'Guard your heart, for it is the wellspring of life.' Right?" Martina nodded, and we congratulated Allie with dirty looks. She smiled in the face of our disapproval. "Hey, my Grammy taught me to cross-stitch with that verse."

"So our hearts are the wellspring of life," Martina cut in. "Any ideas on what this means?"

Caroline's hand crept up like a gopher peeking from its burrow. "Well, your heart pumps all the blood through your body. I guess you should guard your vital organs."

Martina was already shaking her head. "But when the Bible talks about our hearts, is it really referring to the organ? Shayne?"

"My dad always says our heart is the place where we connect with God."

"Or fail to connect, as the case may be."

The conversation whisked onwards, and no one else paid much attention to Caroline, stampeded over and left in Martina's dust. I could imagine how Kellie would've responded instead.

"Answered like a future nurse," I whispered to Caroline, for Kellie as much as for her. She smiled shyly.

"Rory, if you have something to share with the group, please say it so we can all hear."

Caroline's eyes begged me not to draw attention to her. Somehow, something sensible came out of my mouth, maybe because I was thinking about not embarrassing someone else instead of not embarrassing myself for a change. "I was just thinking that guarding your heart might be about making sure you're not soaking up all the stuff the world wants you to believe, because, you know, garbage in, garbage out."

Martina's glacier-blue eyes locked onto me for a few moments. I figured she was trying to find something wrong with what I said. "And that's the wellspring, isn't it? Or as another version puts it, out of your heart are 'the issues of life'. If you soak up the culture indiscriminately, it changes your worldview, and it pours back out of you. You will become indistinguishable from the rest of the world. Jesus didn't call us on a covert operation. We're not supposed to camouflage with the unbelieving world. Salt and *light*, ladies.

"So to guard our hearts... Do we withdraw from the world, like hermits?"

"No," came the common answer.

"We're *in* the world, just not *of* the world," Mary K said, with a nod and smirk that said *yeah, I was listening to that part, don't I look good?*

Martina had the frosty eye on Mary K now, who somehow missed the warning. "So we don't withdraw. But do you feel you're equipped to counter all the wrong ideas out there?"

"I do what I can," Mary K said with a show of humility. "Salt and light, like you say."

"So you'll shut out all the evil influences of the world? You'll know them when you see them? Or do you even think that way when you're outside these walls?"

"Um, sure. I guess?"

Martina flicked her thumbnails against the other shiny, pink fingernails on each hand. She was clearly unconvinced. "I want this to be the verse you meditate on this week." She reached into a stylish tote bag and pulled out a stack of narrow strips, each with a silky red tassel but obviously lacking the candy bar that Kellie liked to include with her verses. "I made you these Scripture bookmarks. Tuck them right inside your Bibles. Hopefully that means you'll see them every day." She gave us a meaningful look.

"You need to ask yourselves: Am I really prepared to shine Light into dark places? Am I even plugged into the Power Source? Do I act one way when I'm here," she gestured around them, "but another way when I'm out there? And if so, why?"

A better question might have been, *Is your brain still here with me, or is it over there where the boys are starting to play basketball?* But I wouldn't have answered anyway because my brain was over there where the boys were starting to play basketball.

When our group dispersed, most of us wandered over towards the basketball nets in that casual way that suggested it had nothing to do with the boys, just the random leading of our feet. And, just as randomly (or so I like to think), a stray ball shot straight at my face.

The *smack* wasn't the sound of my nose or my dignity being flattened. It was the ball meeting Allie's capable hands. She plucked it from the air an inch from my nose and took the shot.

"Three points," she said.

"And one face saved," I said, letting out my breath. "Thanks."

Jake dribbled past. "I didn't think you cared about saving face, Rory," he said.

"What's that supposed to mean?" Shayne asked.

"You mean you didn't tell them that you refused to take Hayes's make-up test?"

They all looked at me, including Sam, who had just joined us. "Seriously?" he asked, his eyes all big and innocent-looking with those dark eyelashes, like the eyes of someone who hadn't all but told me I shouldn't take the make-up test. But I couldn't blame him, because I wasn't sure he was the reason I hadn't taken it.

"Rory, such a rebel," Shayne teased.

Allie didn't look so amused. "I guess you have to do what you think is right, but…"

"But…?" I asked.

"Now you have to take an Incomplete, right?"

"I guess so. I suppose my science grades will be pretty sad this semester." I shrugged. Not that this didn't bother me, but it would never bother me as much as it would Allie.

She seemed to hesitate. "You might want to talk to Mr. Hayes about it," was all she said. For the first time I had the thought that this might have consequences beyond a blot on my report card.

Jake snorted. "Allie's just miffed that your shot at fame worked so much better than hers." He rolled his eyes at our puzzled looks. "Oh, come on. Allie tried for grade-fame, but she got beat out for valedictorian and just ended up a wanna-be, a Number Two. Rory tossed her grades in the garbage and ended up Little Miss Popularity."

"Really?" Shayne asked me, smiling. "How bizarre."

"Well, if you can call following Bliss Hathaway around like a puppy 'popularity'," Jake added.

I gaped at him. Me, the puppy? The only thing he hadn't done was chew on Bliss's shoes. "Sorry if I stole some of her attention from you, Jake." *Maybe if you sit up and whine and beg, she'll notice you.*

"Please. I'm her neighbor, the first person she met in this town. Like you could compete with that."

"I don't think I have to compete for anything, Jakey-boy. Where were you when Bliss and I were planning her Halloween party?" *Certainly not on the invite list, except that I took pity on you.*

"A party?" Shayne asked. "What, with costumes and stuff?"

"Yep. We ordered our costumes from this cool catalog." A catalog I would've been embarrassed to show them. Why had I even mentioned it? "We're going to decorate, too — you should see all the stuff you can get online. The house is going to look like a graveyard. We're going to spend that Friday night decorating, and I guess part of Saturday if we need to — "

"Ooh, you're on the stage crew," Jake said. "You act like you have the lead role."

So maybe I was bragging a little. "Well, it's Bliss's party. But she did say she wouldn't do it without me." I said it to shut him up, and it worked. It was Sam who spoke.

"What day?"

I turned to him. "That's the best part. Halloween's on a Saturday this year. So we're having the party on the actual day." Did I imagine that his face fell a little? "Oh, but I won't have to miss the Scene. I promised her I'd come right after."

"Hey, that means we'll be here on your birthday, Sam," Shayne said.

"Yep."

"Sweet."

"You mean," I said, "your birthday's…?"

"On Halloween. Yeah."

"Every year," Jake told me helpfully.

"I bet you had some pretty good birthday parties as a kid," I said.

"Not Halloweeny ones, if that's what you mean."

Jake snickered. "He said 'Halloweenie'."

Sam ignored him. "My mom never went for the whole Halloween thing. I always got a birthday party instead. A few times we did costumes."

"I remember! You were Peter Pan." Jake doubled over in a fit of laughing.

Sam got a bit of the hot face. "Yeah, but weren't you a kitten?"

"Please! It was the Cowardly Lion."

"Looked like a kitten."

We all meowed at Jake. He grabbed a stray ball that bounced our way, took a shot, and sank it.

"Nothing but net, Peter Pan."

"Nice shot, Kitty."

Allie cut in. "So are we doing the usual this year, Sammy?"

"That's the plan."

I had to know what 'the usual' was, but if I asked, it would look like I was fishing for an invitation. Allie must've seen my desperation. "The traditional pig-out at Sam's for his birthday."

"Can I pick the movie?" Shayne asked.

"You did last year, and there wasn't a single explosion or car chase," Sam pointed out.

"That's because it was set in medieval times. I thought you liked that stuff."

"Yeah, the castle sieges and duels and all that. Not the fainting maidens."

She giggled. "Sounds like the name of a band. The Fainting Maidens."

"So when will the maidens be fainting this year, Sam?" Allie asked.

"My mom and dad said Saturday night would work. You can all come after the Scene, if you want." He didn't look at me.

Allie and Shayne did. "Rory, I guess you can't come," Allie said.

"Bummer."

That was Jake. He didn't bother to hide his smirk.

thirteen

I'd bragged myself into a corner.

Yet another reminder that I suffer from Big Yap Syndrome. This is when your lips flap and the worst choice of words comes out at the worst possible moment.

If I hadn't gone on and on about Bliss's party, I might've played it off: *Oh, that? Yeah, I guess I'm invited. But so are a lot of people. She won't miss me if I can't make it.* But no, instead I set myself up to be the lynchpin of the whole operation. Now if I even hinted at the possibility of not going, I'd look like a complete jerk.

So the days following were an exercise in self-torment. The thrill of self-importance, the attraction of a swanky, no-expense-spared, everyone-wants-to-be-there party with the best music, food, costumes, and decorations began to shrivel beside the alternative: a few of my favorite people—some more favorite than others—hanging out and laughing, watching movies, plundering Sam's secret stash of snack foods in the den.

Mostly I blamed Jake, whose obnoxious behavior had triggered my big yap moment. And when I thought of him and

Allie and Shayne going to Sam's without me, I started to blame all of them. Why hadn't Shayne insisted that I forget the other party and just come with them to complete the fearsome fivesome? Where was Allie with her reasoning that I'd been friends with Sam for almost a year (okay, more like 8 months) but I'd only known Bliss for a few weeks?

I blamed Sam, too. Not because he hadn't tried to convince me to come—he couldn't do that any more than I could just come out and admit I'd rather go to his party than Bliss's. No, I blamed him for something far stupider, for having a birthday on Halloween.

By Friday the 30th, life was a mess in general. Somehow the rumor spread that I was solely responsible for the invite list. Nevermind that it was basically true—I just resented the fact that it was common knowledge. I blamed Jasmine for that, since she'd been there when Bliss gave me the job; only much later did it occur to me that Bliss might've leaked the information herself. Now I had half the eighth grade ticked off at me, since Bliss couldn't invite them all. Except Madi Swanson and her clique—they were mad at me because I was fraternizing with the enemy. Not that they'd ever shown interest in being my friend.

That night I stayed way too late at Bliss's house helping with the decorations, which were pretty wicked. I was supposed to try on my costume, too, which had been backordered but promised to arrive that day. It was a no-show.

"Maybe I'd better get home and throw a different costume together. Anyway, I'm supposed to be home by 10:00," I told Bliss at 9:30. I was actually supposed to be home at 9:30, but somehow 10:00 sounded so much more adult.

"I thought you said your mom was working late," Bliss said.

"Yeah…"

She shrugged and gave me a puzzled look that said, *So what's the problem? She'll never know.* "Don't worry about the costume—I'll handle it."

"And you can't go before you test my witches' brew," Tam called, coming from the kitchen with two glasses of a frighteningly green beverage. Not green like cafeteria gelatin or kiddie juice. Green like pond scum. "If you approve, I'll make a whole cauldron of it tomorrow."

I took a barely-wet-your-lips sissy sip. It was sweet, so an improvement over the green tea, and there was a hint of fizz. But mostly it tasted like grass.

"I used wheatgrass to get that marvelous color."

I nodded, which was enough encouragement for her. Bliss laughed after Tam had returned to the kitchen. "She's such a happy little witch."

"Watch it, or she'll add eye of newt or something."

"Don't worry. She'd take it as a compliment. She's a Wiccan." She saw my blank look, which she must've taken for surprise. "Oh, yeah. That's not just a soap and lotion shop she's running in Westhaven. She's got a special room in the back for the 'initiated'. And her little sisterhood meets here sometimes, because her apartment's too small. Lately she's into communicating with the spirits and all that. Remember the first day you came here? She thought she could feel them around you."

I felt a little prickle of goose bumps, up one arm and down one leg. "She thought you could, too."

"Yeah. She thinks I've got natural talent or something. But I don't really go in for all that spiritual stuff. I'm more on the agnostic side of the scale."

Agnostic. I repeated the word in my head so I could remember it and look it up in the dictionary when I got home. I sensed it wasn't a church denomination. "So your 'deeply-held beliefs'…"

"Are just as deeply held as yours. You know, one of the reasons I liked you right away is because you're not like some of the other Christian kids I've known. You have your beliefs, but you respect that mine are different."

Because she of course hadn't phrased any of that as a question, I wasn't forced to answer. And yes, the fact that it had been delivered as a gooey, delicious compliment made it almost possible to ignore the hard, bitter little nugget in the center.

But the nugget wormed its way out in my dreams that night. I was walking that path again, the one that was barely wide enough for a single traveler, but somehow when you came upon another person on the path, it became wide enough for both of you. I saw someone ahead, vaguely familiar, and I tried to catch up. My feet were bare and a little sore, and I had some sort of heavy hat on that kept slipping down low on my forehead, almost over my eyes. Add to that a wide belt that was obviously a few sizes too big and wanted to ride around my thighs instead of my hips, and you can see why catching up took a lot of effort.

Just as I came alongside the person, we reached the top of a hill. The trees opened up, and the path became broader, paved with cheerful little bricks that glowed warmly in the sunshine. There were many more people on the road ahead, and it all had a feeling of going to a picnic. I thought of brownies, fruit salad, turkey sandwiches and cheese curls, lemonade. I smiled up at the person beside me. He smiled down at me and my blood nearly curdled in my veins.

Familiar—as in blue-eyed, windswept, drop-dead gorgeous, horribly familiar.

A hand gripped my shoulder and jerked me in the other direction. A different pair of blue eyes, crackling electric blue, burned into mine. "Not that way," he said, deep and stern.

Now I faced a side path, or what I'd thought was a side path, hardly a bunny trail. It was rocky and climbed at an uninviting angle. But considering the alternative... I looked back. No one there but me. Then I woke up.

You'd probably expect that I thought long and hard about the dream and what it meant, and I appreciate the vote of confidence but I'm afraid the truth is disappointing. I ate two bowls of cereal and promptly forgot about it. The feeling of it hung around me all day, though, like a smell—the kind when you can't decide if it's sweet or slightly stinky.

I spent the morning digging around for something that could pass as a costume and wouldn't make me the laughingstock of the town. I'd just about settled for either a Greek goddess or a Charlie Brown-style ghost (either of which could be devised from an old white bed sheet) when Sheelan appeared, shoving the phone in my face.

"Do you know who this is? Because they've beeped into my conversation like three times, and it's getting a little annoying."

I read the caller ID. *Rhaynes, S.*

"Yeah, that's for me." I grabbed for it.

"Not so fast." She turned away and started talking again. "I have to go. When are you picking me up? How about nine?" She laughed at whatever the other person said.

"Sheelan, I'm gonna miss the call—"

Her eyes snapped blue-greenishly at me, but she still had her sweet phone voice on. It must've been a boy.

"Okay, I'll see you then." Giggle. "Bye." Pause. "Hang up." Giggle. "No, you hang up."

I grabbed the phone. "Here, let me help." I mashed the buttons.

"Hello?" I tried, while Sheelan shouldered past me, with extra shoulder but no fists or elbows. She was clearly in a good mood, no doubt because she had a Halloween date.

Amazingly, Bliss was still on the line. "Rory, I called the costume people, and they're guaranteeing that yours will arrive by 4:00 today."

"Oh. Great." I had warmed up to the idea of hiding under a bed sheet. Now I'd be in what was hardly more than a leotard with a few leaves attached.

"So what time can you get here?"

"Well, the youth group thing I told you about should end around—"

"No way. You've got to get here before that. You haven't even tried on your costume, plus there's the makeup. Without it you'll look like a third-grader."

A five-foot-eight-inch third grader?

"Tam's taking care of the food and everything, but the DJ's coming early to set up, so we can pick out all the songs we like. You have to be here at 4:00. 5:00 at the very latest. My mom wants me to stay home—says she's got some sort of surprise for me. But Tam can pick you up."

This was where, as my dad used to say, the rubber met the road. The right choice seems so obvious, doesn't it?

"Yeah, okay," I said.

You know, if it was Shayne on the phone saying I couldn't go to the Halloween party, I had to go to the Scene, I would've said 'yeah, okay' to her. Which is pretty much admitting that I'm spineless. But it wasn't Shayne on the phone, and I was spineless.

I reasoned that other kids would probably miss the Scene tonight, though I now knew some of them didn't even celebrate Halloween, for reasons I only partly understood. I reasoned that seeing Shayne, Allie, Jake and Sam leave together afterwards would make me feel even worse than not seeing them at all. I reasoned that it wasn't my fault that between the two of us, Bliss had all the backbone.

I hate reason.

And now that I'd caved in like a soggy ice cream cone, I had to call Shayne and let her know not to pick me up for the Scene. Except I didn't call. I sent her a vague email instead, telling her I couldn't make it without really explaining why (she probably wouldn't think to wonder why until Allie asked her later). Shayne wasn't the kind of person to check her email multiple times daily, so I just sort of hoped she'd get it in time. If she didn't, I wouldn't be home when they showed up, and I felt bad about that, in a relieved sort of way. She'd find the email eventually and it would show that I'd tried to let her know ahead of time. My gutlessness knows no limits.

Tam showed up around quarter to five in a lime green doodlebug car. Here's where my mom might've stepped outside and done the mom thing, checking out just who I was riding off with, who was going to be at the party, and all that. But she was running late for her waitressing shift and only had time to glance out the window.

"Your friend's mom?" she asked.

"No. Her mom's best friend."

"And the house is up on Windham Lane?"

I told her the address.

"Nice neighborhood. You helped quite a bit with the party, didn't you?"

"Mm-hmm."

"So I can trust that it's all on the up-and-up?" My quizzical look said plenty. "Clean, decent fun?"

"Mom, it's a costume party."

"And what's your costume again?"

"A woodland fairy."

"How cute."

"Mom, Tam's waiting."

"You call adults by their first names now?"

"Only when I don't know their last names."

"You could find out, you know."

"Mom." Two syllables.

"Okay, go ahead. Have fun. Do you have a ride home?"

"Yeah." I silently willed her to say nothing else.

"9:30."

I groaned. "The party starts at 8:00! It's Halloween—"

"10:30, final."

I ran with it. "Bye!"

"Be careful, be smart," she called after me.

It was good advice. I should've taken it.

Tam was smiling when I climbed in the passenger seat. She was also already in costume—at least I hoped it was her costume. She looked like she was ready for the Renaissance Fest. Her short, spiky hair didn't exactly match the medieval clothes, but it did show off the big silver stud in the top of her ear.

She saw me noticing. "Like it? I just got it done last night."

Wasn't she, like, forty or fifty? "Did it hurt?" It looked sore.

"Sure. But the pain is part of the whole experience. It can lead you into uncharted territory, if you know what I mean."

I didn't. To me, pain was like an unsweetened beverage, to be avoided at all cost.

At the stop sign she looked at me, that same foggy sort of searching glance I'd seen before. "Does this day have a special significance for you?" she asked.

"Well…" I said. "It is Halloween."

"Hmm, that might be it. Spirits are on the move this night. But I mean the date, the 31st. Were you born on a 31st? Or maybe it's the numbers three and one."

What was she on about? "No, I was born on the 16th. Of March."

"Well, that's a three and a one—and a six. Hmm. Oh, I should just leave the numbers up to Sylvie. That's her business."

I figured that meant Sylvie was an accountant or something. Since I didn't know what we were talking about, anyway, I decided to change the subject. Grandma Judy once gave me this conversation advice: when in doubt, stick to the weather. "It's almost dark already."

"Now that Daylight Savings Time is ended," she said. "You'll get to see the front yard decorations to best effect. And better yet, inside I have a smoke machine. I'm with the Quarry County Drama Group, and they let me borrow it. Some of them even came over to help set up."

"Was that the surprise Bliss was talking about?"

"Oh, no." A mysterious little smile crept over her face. "That's something much better. And if I'm not mistaken, that's Sylvie's car in the driveway, which means she's already home with the 'surprise'. Bliss'll be over the moon."

Tam parked on the street so I could get the full view of the front yard. In the cold, colorless dusk, the fake gravestones looked disturbingly real. Tam hadn't chosen the silly kind with names like 'Frank N. Stein' and 'Ima Goner'. They were nameless, anonymous little slabs, suggesting people whose memory had died with them. One of the stones sat in the remains of the flowerbed, and the soil was turned to look like a fresh grave. A fake hand thrust out of the dirt, a stiff claw.

Tam went into the garage and flipped a switch; purple lights hidden among the stones cast a ghastly glow and threw freakish shadows over the black-looking grass. I had thought this stuff was pretty cool when I saw it in the catalog. I wasn't sure why my feelings had changed. I tried to shake it off.

"So?" Tam asked.

"Wicked," I said.

"Wait 'til you see inside." We went in through the garage.

"Thanks for the ride, T—" I remembered my mom's words. "I mean, Mrs.… or Miss…?"

"It's Tamsyn Tomas. Mistress Tamsyn, if you wish to be proper." She swished her long velvet skirts and curtsied before opening the door to the house.

There in the middle of the living room, caught in the most gruesome case of lip-lock I'd ever had to witness at point-blank range (even including Sheelan and her ex-boyfriend Quentin), were Bliss and some guy I'd never seen before.

Mistress Tamsyn shot me a sly smile. "Looks like Bliss found her surprise."

fourteen

If only the surprises had stopped with Bliss. But no. I was also surprised to learn that Nico, her boyfriend from Colorado or Idaho or wherever, had not been exaggerated up to age seventeen by the Whitestone Elementary rumor mill. He was not only all of seventeen, but he'd even reached eighteen in their months apart. He looked twenty-four.

Bliss pried herself off of him long enough to introduce us. "Rory, this is Nico. Can you believe it? My mom flew him in for the weekend to surprise me."

"Chow," he said to me. I thought he was hungry, until he turned back to Bliss and said, "Chow bella," and I detected the Italian accent. Then I detected more kissing about to happen, so I mumbled some excuse, ducked into the bathroom and shut the door quickly behind me.

I turned to discover that either Sylvie Rhaynes' sleek, L-shaped desk was now in the bathroom, or I'd missed it by one door. She smiled at me, held up a finger, and proceeded with her phone call.

"Yes, but you cannot deny the power of six for you, Leslie. Your entire life vibrates with it. Good and bad—your capacity to love is tremendous, but you have to take responsibility for your choices, and watch out for your tendency towards meddling and jealousy." She drummed her French manicure on the shiny desk surface. "That's right. Next month in particular, the eleventh month. Especially on the fourth and the fifteenth. Watch for the chart, I'm emailing it now. Oh, don't mention it. Goodbye."

She snapped the cell phone shut with a sigh. "People are curious creatures, aren't they? They come to me for guidance, and when I give it, they're as likely as not to resist it. At first." She laughed and smoothed a lock of platinum blonde hair behind her ear. "The numbers don't lie, Rory. They reveal, they instruct without judging, but they do not lie."

I now began to suspect that Sylvie Rhaynes wasn't an accountant. She gestured for me to have a seat across the desk from her. I did, feeling more like a client than her daughter's friend.

She went on. "The numbers led me to Whitestone, and one day they will lead somewhere else again. Where might they lead you, do you think?"

"I'm not sure I..."

"Have you experienced the phenomenon of a repeating number?"

Ordinarily I might've had no clue what she was talking about, but it just so happened that not long ago a certain number had popped up a lot. "Actually, yeah. For a while I kept seeing three-sixteen—"

"Your birthday? March sixteenth, or maybe June thirteenth?"

Freaky. "Mm-hmn, March sixteenth."

"That's not uncommon. You'd see in on the clock a lot, the page where you stopped in a book, that sort of thing? Hotel room number?"

Hospital room number. "All those sorts of things. What does it mean?"

She leaned forward. "It can mean many different things, or you might say, apply to many situations. But they are always significant. You may think of them as messages you send yourself, a sort of higher consciousness communicating to you in present time. A reminder, a warning, a mental pat on the back."

Lots of words making little sense. But wasn't that how I felt when I read the Bible sometimes? Yes…and no. When I read the Bible and didn't understand, it felt like walking on solid ground with my eyes closed. I couldn't see, but my feet were firmly planted and I could trust that my eyes would open sooner or later. Sylvie's talk felt more like a dazzling web that caught all sorts of light but swung over a void.

"Messages you send yourself?" a voice asked behind me, making me jump. "Or messages from someone or something else out there?"

Tam had entered the room silently. I imagined she had materialized right behind me, witchy-poo style. I had Halloween on the brain.

She was sharing a meaningful smile with Sylvie. "We often debate this point."

"It's not that I deny the spirit world or the potential for outside guidance," Sylvie said. "I simply believe that we have an inner font of wisdom, and some of us are more attuned to it and tap into it, sometimes without even knowing it."

"The spirit without and the spirit within," Tam said. "I sense that Rory knows something of this."

I chewed my bottom lip. My own encounter with the spirit world had been abrupt, astonishing, and sometimes violent. But it had worked together for good, even the scary parts.

They were waiting for me to say something. "I know about the Holy Spirit, inside me."

They exchanged a knowing glance. "The God-Spirit," Sylvie said, nodding. "Called by different names, but it all comes down to the god within us."

That sounded okay. Maybe?

"What about her numbers?" Tam asked.

"Three, one and six equal ten, which is also one."

"Ah," Tam said, nodding at me. "Auspicious."

Did that mean it was good? Should I even care?

"But your birthday, the sixteenth, is really a seven. Do you like drawing and writing?"

"Yeah, I do."

"And you're a procrastinator, I'll bet."

"Um…"

She laughed. "That's okay, you don't have to admit it. But I happen to know that you haven't even tried on your Halloween costume yet."

"Well, that wasn't really my fault. I planned to try it out yesterday, but the guys didn't deliver it until today."

Sylvie looked at Tam. "Sevens hate any interference with their plans."

I felt my face crinkle up skeptically. "You can tell all of that from the day I was born?"

"The date, yes. It doesn't all apply to everyone. But if you're a typical seven, you're something of a homebody. Yes? And you live a lot of your life in here." She tapped her head.

This was a little freaky. "My mom tells me that sometimes."

"And I'm guessing that your tendency to overanalyze things can complicate your life at times." She laughed. "No, no, don't start analyzing that. You have a date with a Halloween costume and some makeup, and I have a sneaking suspicion that Bliss might be too busy to help you."

"I'll help you out, and then you can help me in the kitchen," Tam said. The doorbell rang. "And I bet that's the DJ. We'd better get cracking, Rory."

Sylvie rose and held her hand out to me. I clumsily moved to shake it then saw she was offering a business card. "Call me if you're interested," she said.

Sylvie Rhaynes, it said. *Numerology consultant*. Beneath her phone numbers were the words, *Numbers, the Universal Language*. It was the quality kind of card, with raised glossy letters.

"I waive my fees for Bliss's friends."

Bliss seemed to have forgotten she had friends. I spent the next hour trying to make three square inches of stretchy green fabric cover all of my square inches, plus the round inches. Strategically placed leaves made the leotard a bit more modest, but the designer hadn't been nearly strategic enough for my taste. I did like the tights, which had what looked like ivy climbing up each leg, but I managed to poke my thumb through them in my epic battle to get them onto my legs. I think the only way to get those things on was to use one of those machines that stuffs the sausage meat into the casing. I hoped the gauzy leaf skirt would disguise the tear.

I strapped on the crowning piece, delicate butterfly wings in shades of green, blue and brown. The mirror in the spare bedroom was small, but as far as I could tell, I looked pretty good.

Then I discovered the horror hidden in the bathroom: two full length mirrors. One on the wall and the other on the door, together they provided an unmerciful view of my front and back. It was then I gained a new understanding of God's merciful nature. He puts our backsides behind us for a reason.

A tap on the door. I hoped it was Bliss, Bliss in her own costume, Bliss just as insecure about it as me. "I brought my makeup kit," Tam's voice said.

When we emerged twenty minutes later, I was virtually unrecognizable and glad of it. Maybe I'd be that party guest that everyone treats politely but keeps their distance, because no one can remember her name.

Except I was feeling more like the hostess than a guest. Bliss and Nico had vanished, and there I was arranging finger foods with Tam, selecting music with the DJ, lighting candles and testing the smoke machine. When I had to peel frozen grapes so we could add "eyeballs" to the witches-brew punch, I began muttering about uncooperative fruit and disappearing friends.

Tam only laughed. "There's no point in trying to rein in Bliss Hathaway. She was born to be original, free-thinking and independent. Mostly we just stand aside and let her blaze her own trail." She plopped a handful of grape eyeballs into the brew. "I'd follow her anywhere."

The ringing doorbell kept me from chewing on that last, odd statement. And suddenly Bliss was breezing past me in full costume, gesturing for me to follow. "Let's see who's the first to arrive," she said through glittery purple-black lips. Her wings flounced behind her like a bat with attitude; her boots offered stompings to anyone who got in her way. She had become the bad fairy; she and the costume were made for each other, even more than the catalog model. Next to her, I looked…

The door opened to reveal Jasmine Wee. Of course I'd made sure her name was on the list—out of equal parts friendship and fear. And of course she was the first to arrive. I sensed that it didn't score her any points with Bliss. You were supposed to want to be there, but not in a desperate way.

She shrugged off her coat and revealed her costume.

"Let me guess," I said, a little embarrassed for her. "You're a sleepwalker."

There they were—the cold eyes. "These aren't pajamas, Rory. They're scrubs."

I made an exaggerated sigh of relief. "I thought maybe you were having the pajama dream, only for real. You know, the one where you get somewhere and you take off your—"

"Note the stethoscope? I'm an intern. That's a doctor," she added in case I was an idiot, which clearly was what she thought of anyone who didn't know what an intern was (which I did—a split second after I saw the stethoscope).

"Yeah, it's great," I said. Good thing I'd jumped in there to save her from embarrassment. "And I'm a—"

"Tree. Yes, I can see that."

"A woodland fairy, actually." I knew the leaf crown had been a mistake. But Tam had braided it so tightly into my hair, it was possibly permanent.

"You look depraved," she said to Bliss, as a compliment. "Oooh!" She had just noticed the mist creeping up from downstairs. "Check this out." And she proceeded into the house to do just that. Bliss followed, leaving me to answer the next ding-dong. That ding-dong was Tiffany Klipfel.

Then I had what's known as a paradigm shift (pronounced 'pair-a-dime', leaving lots of room for such Dad jokes as 'What's a paradigm?'/'Twenty cents! Har har har.'). This is when you're suddenly forced to scrap the rules you thought the world operated under as you realize there's a whole different set of rules. I had, as usual, been obsessing about how to get through this night in this costume with this standard to live up to (Bliss) without completely embarrassing myself. With the arrival of Jasmine and Tiffany, my planets screeched to a halt in their orbits and started barreling in the other direction.

I had pretty much invited most of the guests. That meant their behavior, their costumes, their everything reflected back on me. I went from fear of doing something embarrassing to fear of everyone else doing something embarrassing. The planets reversed in orbit, but you'll notice the pitiful sun they revolved around was still the same.

The music started chugging, and in singles and groups the majority of our class showed up—zombies, vampires, werewolves and even an evil Raggedy Ann—joined Bliss downstairs where the fog was lit by green lights that made the food table look like a scientific experiment gone wrong. I stole the occasional peek as I passed back and forth, hanging people's coats in the back entryway.

It was better to keep busy. Then I wouldn't keep looking at the clock and wondering. But my internal clock kept right on ticking, telling me that by now Sam, Allie, Shayne and Jake would be at Sam's house. And I kept right on wondering if they felt like someone was missing, or if it was just like old times again, the four of them.

Everyone who was invited had arrived—everyone but Madi Swanson and her following. I'd had the idea to invite them, too, and Bliss had agreed because she thought it was delightfully devious. I'd meant it more as a peace treaty in the Halloween Party War.

Instead of joining them, I flounced upstairs (stupid wings) to use the bathroom in a more private area of the house, since I had to practically undress to do it. I stared at myself in the mirror as I washed my hands, and I didn't look like me. Funny thing was, it wasn't the makeup or the costume. I just had this feeling that even without all of that, I still wouldn't quite know that face looking back at me.

Finally I sighed and opened the door. A creature of the night stood there, staring at me from behind her veil of black hair.

Journey LeVey, in her regular clothes. One day out of the year, she blended in.

We just looked at each other for a few long seconds. "Hi," I said.

"Not exactly in a huge hurry to join the party," she observed.

Sad part was, she was right. When had that happened, exactly? Better question, when had I ever really wanted to be at this party? "You coming down?" I asked.

She rolled her eyes. "Please." The doorbell rang. "You'll be expected to get that," she said, a cool mocking look in her gray eye.

I clomped down the stairs, trying to think of who still hadn't shown up. Hadn't everyone on the list arrived? I might've known I was in for another surprise. I opened the door.

Perfectly at home amid the gravestones and eerie purple light of the front yard stood a dark-cloaked figure with blackened eyes and gray cheeks. His rusted iron crown marked him as a king of the undead.

"Hey," Jake said. "Did I miss anything?"

fifteen

I stared at Jake while my brain tried to add things up. Math and puzzling situations—both tend to make my mouth hang open.

"Stop looking so intelligent and let me in," he said, pushing past me. "Sounds like you started without me. What'd I miss?"

Oh, I don't know, I wanted to yell, *maybe Sam's party for starters?* "What are you doing here? I thought you'd be at Sam's."

"Yeah, I know you did, which I guess is why you guys never gave me my invitation. But did you really think I'd miss this?"

"What about Sam's party?"

"That's not a party. That's just more of the usual. Anyway, he's a big boy. He can always do it another night." He looked around, gyrating to the music. "Now this is a party. Man, check out the smoke and the lights—and did you see the front yard? This whole place looks like a set at a professional theater. I'm going downstairs. How's the food?"

I battled the urge to rip off his rusty crown and ram it down his throat. "But...you can't just ditch Sam on his birthday."

"Why not? You did."

Ouch. "You're his best friend."

He shrugged as if that were a matter of debate. "A friend will understand that there's no way anyone should have to miss this." The music got louder. We practically had to shout.

"So now it's just Sam, Shayne and Allie?"

"No."

"Who else?"

"No, I mean Allie couldn't make it. Wasn't at the Scene, either. Her Grammy's sick."

This just kept getting better. "So just Sam and Shayne?"

"Yeah, see? Maybe I'm doing Sammy a favor. Now, do you mind?" He swept his cloak around himself and glided Dracula-style down the stairs to the family room/dance floor.

"You're not even dressed as a vampire," I muttered after him. He wouldn't have heard me even if I screamed it, because someone had cranked the music up again.

I wandered into the kitchen and grabbed a cup of the vile green punch with the grape eyeballs. It was no more than I deserved. Paradigm shift number two (PS#2, you might say): it's not all about me.

If we're honest with ourselves, we'll admit that life is pretty much all about *me*—maybe until we have kids of our own, who believe it's all about *them* and force us to rethink matters. It's a vicious cycle until someone finally realizes it's not about me or you or them. It's about *Him*, the capital-H Him.

I can't say I'd made that huge of a leap just yet, but at least I got over the *me* stuff a little bit. Oh-so worried about how I'd look or what everyone would think of me, how bummed *I* was to miss Sam's party, I didn't give much thought to what Sam might be feeling. Maybe I wasn't indispensable to the success of his party, but here were two of the four people he invited, choosing to go somewhere else. Then a third person can't make it, and what's he left with?

A date with Shayne, maybe.

Jake had made it sound like Sam might not be unhappy about that arrangement. I thought of all the little signs I thought I'd seen, all my moments of suspicion, and I had to admit Jake might be right.

When I trudged into the family room, I probably looked more like Jake's undead twin than a sprightly fairy. One look at him and I was sure of it. He looked like he'd been beaten with the proverbial ugly stick, followed by the lesser-known misery stick. I tracked his gaze and saw Bliss and Nico dancing in a way that left no doubt about their feelings for each other. It also left no stomach unturned, or so I thought.

Tam came up between us and put an arm around each of our shoulders. "Hello, friends and neighbors." She also watched the happy couple but without our disgust. "Aren't they sweet? You know, Bliss didn't speak to Sylvie for a month when she heard we were moving out here, separating her and Nico. Sylvie still feels badly about it." Just then Bliss shot Tam a look that put the Jasmine Wee Cold Eyes to shame. "Oh, I forgot." Tam chuckled. "I'm under strict orders to stay in the kitchen unless I'm bringing more food out. M'lord and m'lady." She curtsied and swished out of the room, whistling a tune that was drowned by the Richter-8-level music.

I shot Jake a testing glance, to see if he was safe to talk to. "That's a bit weird," I said. He heard me, only because a slower, softer song had started.

"What, that this twit's the only one without a costume?"

"Maybe he's dressed as a hunky Italian boyfriend," I tried. No laugh from Jake. "Anyway, I meant Tam. Lady Tamsyn."

"Sure she's weird. She tries hard enough."

"I mean, she's way older than Bliss—she's her mom's friend—but she almost acts like…"

"Like she thinks Bliss is the boss of her? Yeah, I know."

"So why do you suppose she acts that way?"

"Because she thinks Bliss is the boss of her." He copied my *I don't understand* look and added a twist of *duh*. He knew more than me and was enjoying it. "She thinks that in a past life she was some kind of priestess, and that Bliss was like her high priestess or something. Some wise, all-knowing one." He waggled his fingers in mystical motions. "Bliss thinks it's a crock of hooey, but she totally plays it to her advantage." Admiration crept into his voice before he remembered his annoyance with Bliss. "It's all stupid," he added, to cover it up.

I was just sticking with weird at the moment. No doubt about it, the Rhaynes/Hathaway/LeVey house was unique. I supposed we all seemed dull and small-minded to them.

Tiffany Klipfel scurried up to us in her black cat costume. "You won't believe this," she whisper-shouted, leaning in close to my ear. "Bliss's boyfriend isn't seventeen. He's eighteen! And he hardly speaks any English, just Spanish."

"Italian," I corrected, not caring much.

"And did you know that Kate Zyskowski came with Ronnie Plowman? They came together."

I didn't mean to be rude, but my head was like an overflowing sock drawer, and most of my thoughts were mismatched or had holes in the toes. There just wasn't room for the unlikely pair of Katie Zyskowski and Ronnie Plowman.

Tiffany saw she was getting nowhere. She searched the room for something fresh and irresistible, and wouldn't you know, she found it. "You…have…GOT…to be kidding," she said, all breathy. "Is that…?" She gasped. "It is! Look over there, talking to the DJ. Make that flirting with the DJ."

I did. "Looks like Courtney and Britnee," I said dully. I didn't remember letting them in.

"Exactly." She pursed her painted pink lips, and the whisker dots on her cheeks quivered.

Then I got it. Courtney and Britnee were Madi Swanson's henchmen. Henchwomen, whatever. They should be at her party. Bliss may have done more than win a battle with this party. She may have won the whole war. "That's unexpected," I said.

Tiffany Telegraph had already left to spread the news. Jake and I stood by the food table and ate without tasting. I paid no attention to the amount of guacamole I was eating. I would find out how much a little later.

"Slow down or you'll pop those tights," he told me.

"Shut up, Jake." I didn't have the energy to think of a good comeback.

"What are you supposed to be, anyway? That guy on the can of vegetables? The Jolly Green Giant?"

"Yes, Jake. That's who I am. The Jolly Green Giant. And you're the Count from Sesame Street, right?"

He let that one go. "Where'd Bliss go?"

"I don't know."

The party carried on for some time without any sign of her glossy bat wings or glittery purple and black gear. Nico was also conspicuously absent, but neither of us mentioned it. Jasmine joined us, enjoying a large cup of grassy green beverage while I fiddled and tweaked and adjusted my itchy costume. It offered me no relief. I thought about the piggyback baby costume with a slightly sick, melancholy feeling in my stomach. One of those out-of-the-blue, sideswipe miss-my-dad moments.

The dancing stopped when the music shifted from rhythm-driven to something more mystical, with voices chanting softly in an unfamiliar language and strange eastern-sounding instruments droning. Definitely not one of the songs I'd chosen with the DJ earlier. Britnee, who had come dressed as a belly dancer, shimmied and spun to the appreciation of the boys and the rolled eyes of most of the girls.

"Come check this out," Tiffany called over the music, and Britnee lost her audience as most of us made our way through the kitchen into the white living room. The lights were off, but dozens of candles were burning, their little amber tongues tasting the air as we passed. The room still seemed colorless, except for the gold and scarlet of Miss Tamsyn's gown. She stood behind a table set with a game board.

"A little diversion, young ones?" she asked. "Bliss, I was hoping you would lead."

We turned and saw that Bliss had rejoined us, though Nico was nowhere to be seen. "You can do it just fine yourself," she said.

"But you are the best. The spirits respond to you."

I shot a look at Jasmine. "Spirits? To play Scrabble?"

She snorted. "It's a ouija board, Rory."

"Oh." I'd never actually seen one, but I knew people asked it questions and supposedly the answers were spelled out for them. I figured it had all the sophistication of a Magic 8-Ball.

"Circle 'round, friends," Tam urged. "Take a candle."

Everyone did. It was Halloween, when playing dress-up was acceptable and you didn't have to worry about whether the game might be lame or not. Still, I wasn't sure. I thought of those kids from the Scene who didn't celebrate Halloween. I thought of Sam. What was it they objected to? Was this the sort of thing they'd have a problem with? I looked uncertainly at Jake. He was choosing a candle, a black one that gave off a musky smell.

"Should we?" I whispered, hoping he understood me.

He gave me the half-open-eye roll. "It's a ouija board. Come on, you can buy these at ToyMart."

As it was, the circle was forming on either side of me, and I was in it whether or not I meant to be. Tam moved around the circle, switching some people's candles with others, as if somehow it mattered which one we held. She came to me and her lips pressed together, her eyes searching. Then she nodded and strode over to a candle on a table in the farthest corner and brought it back to me. It was fat and squatty and a deep brownish red, resting in a cup made of some sort of scratchy, pitted stone. The melted wax pooled around the wick, liquid and quivering in my hands.

"I don't really believe in…" I tried. She shook her head and winked.

"Open your mind," she said to everyone, but I felt like she meant it for me. "Close your eyes. Empty yourself."

There were giggles and a few impatient sighs, but everyone closed their eyes. The exotic music still wailed softly in the other room; I also heard light puffs of breath and smelled the sharp hot smell of smoke.

"Observe complete silence." When we were still, "Open your eyes."

At first we blinked against the dazzling candlelight. Then I could tell that the room was actually darker than before. Only the candles we held in our hands were lit, creating a ring of fire around the table where Bliss sat alone, her hands resting palms upward on either side of the board. We watched her while she did nothing—or nothing that we could see. Her eyes were closed. Minutes passed. Even the soft music had stopped, and there was only quiet. Oddly, no one giggled or coughed.

Then Bliss opened her eyes and nodded at Tam. The woman was flushed. "The spirits are summoned?"

Jasmine looked up at me, rolled her eyes.

"I didn't have to summon anything. They were already here."

Murmurs, quiet laughs. This was theater, a parlor game.

"Bliss will require three of you to join her at the table, where you will place a single finger upon the planchette. The lightest touch is all that is needed. The spirits will direct your movements."

"Yeah, right," Jasmine whispered. "Everyone knows the people move it themselves."

Tam had chosen Ronnie and Courtney, and now she approached us. Her hand settled on Jasmine's shoulder. "I always include a skeptic," she said softly.

Jasmine shrugged and took a seat at the table. Tam raised her hands and spoke a string of words in some solemn language I didn't understand. It felt like a prayer. This wasn't comforting.

The liquid wax trembled in the top of my candle. What in the world was I doing? *For we are not contending against flesh and blood.* The words zipped across my mind like a shooting star, there and gone before you're sure of it.

Tam stood behind Bliss and laid her hands on her shoulders. Bliss shrugged them off irritably. "If any would speak, speak now," Bliss said in a low voice.

Nothing happened. *I should speak,* I thought. A*gainst the principalities, against the powers, against the world rulers of this present darkness, against the spiritual hosts of wickedness in the heavenly places.* My tongue sat like a hunk of raw meat in my mouth.

Then the widget-thingy — the planchette — moved across the board. There were a few gasps, including from some of those seated at the table. I couldn't see Jasmine's face. But I did see the little wooden triangle slide completely off the board. Bliss looked at Tam and shook her head.

"Try again."

Bliss closed her eyes for a full minute, then spoke in a flat voice. "How many are you?"

Again a long pause. The planchette crept down towards the numbers at the bottom of the board. Then it swiftly slid over to the number 3.

"There are three ghosts in the room with us?" Tiffany squeaked.

"Shh."

After another pause, the thing moved to the number 1. Then nothing. I drew in a breath. Thirty-one, it was October 31st, blah blah blah. Just a game.

It moved to the 6.

"Three hundred and sixteen?" Jake asked. "Man, it's crowded in here."

Tam silenced him with a gesture. "The numbers are separate: three, one, and six." Her eyes met mine before I could look away. Yes, I got the point. Three sixteen. Whatever she and Bliss were up to, they meant it for me. I suppose they thought they were paying me a compliment.

"Are you good spirits?" Courtney blurted.

"Silence, please. Leave the questioning to Bliss."

But maybe because Courtney was touching the planchette, it responded. It didn't move to the 'yes' or 'no'. It slid back to the 3.

"Three are good," Bliss said, again in that strange, expressionless voice. "What about the one, and the six?"

Silence and stillness. A minute passed. No answer came.

Very quietly, Jake hummed scary movie music beside me. The musky smell of his candle and the spicy scent of mine mixed and filled up my head, thick and aching.

Then Bliss asked, "Are you the one?"

The planchette crept over to the 'yes'.

This sounded… I scrunched up my face and tried to push the thickness out of my head. I had to think. Three good and one…questionable? It was almost like—

"Are you linked to this house? Or a person present here?" Bliss asked.

The wooden planchette shot off the board. Jasmine and Courtney let out a little scream. Ronnie looked more awake than I'd ever seen him in class. In the circle, the other kids exchanged looks of uncertainty or that certain mix of fright-delight, or both.

Tam set the planchette back on the board. "Continue."

Bliss let out a breath that sounded tired. Not bored tired, just used up. "Are you linked—"

Before she could finish, the thing started to move.

R

Don't do this, Bliss, I wished I could say. This isn't my idea of fun.

E

I had a moment of relief. It wasn't spelling R-O-R-Y. Then it moved a final time.

J

"There's no one here named Rej," someone said.

"How about initials?" Tam suggested softly, already knowing.

Not everyone knew my middle name, but I was the only R first name with a J last name. All eyes turned to me. Their faces were lit from beneath; even those without masks or makeup looked ghoulish. And suddenly it all clicked. Only a few people knew about my angel experience earlier that year—three good angels and one fallen—and one of those people was standing right next to me. Jake didn't know much, and what I had described to him he thought of as just some kind of schizophrenic episode, but that apparently didn't matter. He'd been desperate to score points with Bliss from the beginning. Apparently he'd told her everything he knew about my angels, and now she was using it to put on this creep show.

She was looking at me. I watched her glittery dark lips move. "Are you with Rory Erin Joyce?" she asked the 'spirit'.

In the hall, the front door opened, a figure in fluttering black swept in. Several girls stifled screams (a couple of guys, too). It was just Sylvie, Empress of the Night. With her came a gust of wind, blowing out all the candles.

All but mine. Everyone stared.

I swallowed. Okay, hard to explain how they'd arranged that. I grew angry because it felt better than scared. But I knew how to end it. There was one thing they couldn't know. Surely I'd never told another living soul—at least not another human being.

"What's its name?" I asked.

Tam stepped forward. "Wait. A name is a powerful thing…"

Exactly. It had the power to put this sick game to rest.

"I wouldn't advise—"

Her advice didn't seem to matter, because the planchette was already moving. None of the pauses, the creepy crawling. With an audible scrape it slid. Someone pulled me close to the table, and the light of my candle illuminated the first letter. Unlike my initials, no one said it out loud.

U

My hands twitched. A drip of hot wax ran painfully over my fingers.

R

I

The candle tipped, and in the instant before the liquid wax doused the flame, I could see it pouring down my hands, dark red like blood.

Then I was on my knees, retching. When someone found the light switch and flicked it, it revealed me on the creamy white carpet beside a small puddle of blood red and a large puddle of guacamole green.

sixteen

"You like avocados, don't you?"

I pushed the bowl back towards Grandma Judy like it had bit me. "Gran, I got sick on guacamole Saturday night."

She shook her head, picking the pale green chunks out of the salad. "I hope you're not permanently turned off avocados. They're a super food. Packed with nutrition."

I poked at the salad. It was Monday, I was home sick from school, and Gran had come over with food. But no homemade cookies, no banana bread, not even zucchini bread. Gran was on a health kick, and that meant she was kicking out the three 'white poisons': sugar, salt, and bleached flour. In other words, the staples of my diet.

"Eat that, now. Your mom says you didn't touch a bite yesterday. And half of what you put in your mouth most days isn't even real food. But this, this is fuel. It'll get you back on your feet."

"So would a Snickers bar." She gave me a look; I ate the salad.

I guess it was pretty good. Not Snickers-bar good, but at least there were hard boiled eggs and bacon pieces in it. Still, I was in no hurry to get back on my feet. Gran didn't know that it wasn't really bad guacamole that had knocked me off them in the first place.

I hadn't eaten on Sunday (besides a secret bowl of cereal) because then it looked like I had food poisoning or the stomach flu, and then I could stay home from school on Monday. I told myself it was to give everyone a day to talk about my puke-fest at Bliss's party, and then by Tuesday it wouldn't be breaking news anymore. Still bad, but not Monday-morning bad.

It's weird. I didn't think about it as much more than that, that I'd been sick in front of half the eighth grade. I didn't think about what had made my stomach twist so violently. When I started to, I would tell myself that it was just a stupid thing that happened because of all the ooky-spooky Halloween hype, and because Jake Dean had a big mouth. I made it about Jake and guacamole.

Even with Gran Judy there, I pushed the other thoughts away. One of the few people on earth I could possibly talk to about this stuff, and instead I talked about how some candy bars might be classified as health food.

Sometimes in the quieter moments I had a ticklish feeling, like a whisper urging me to do something important. I even had a light bulb moment when I tripped over my Bible, which had somehow ended up on the middle of my bedroom floor. But when I picked it up and read, the words just rustled like dry leaves and blew away. I didn't think to pray.

Something fell out of my Bible. I picked up the tasseled bookmark that Martina had given us at the Scene. *A prudent person foresees the danger ahead and takes precautions. The simpleton goes blindly on and suffers the consequences. Proverbs 27:12.*

That was our meditation verse? Leave it to Martina. A bookmark from Kellie Greene would've said something about

God's Word being a lamp unto my feet, or cutting like a two-edged sword. Martina, blindness and suffering.

The thing about spiritual blindness is that you can't always see it. I know, *duh*. Here's a clue, though: if you're constantly being blindsided by stuff, you might have this problem.

Tuesday blindsided me. I knew to expect some teasing, unwanted attention, and all that—and as I dragged my feet to school I began to question the wisdom of staying home on Monday, which had just delayed the inevitable and made me more conspicuous. So the glances and whispers as I wove through the hall to my locker weren't surprising. But the sheet of paper taped to my locker door caught me off guard.

It would seem that someone not only had a camera handy during the drama at Bliss's party, but they'd also had the perfect timing to catch me in mid-spew. There I was in full color (possibly enhanced color…surely it hadn't been *that* green), and underneath were printed words calling me a name I didn't even understand. I snatched it off, but my hot face had instantly gone from Defcon 3 to Defcon 1.

"Everyone knows." Tiffany stood beside me, pretending to search for something in her locker. "You're a celebrity. Half the kids think it's gross, half think it's pretty cool."

"Who did this?" I crumpled the paper. "I don't even know what it means."

"I'm not sure who took the picture. But you know that old movie about the demon-possessed girl who puked up green stuff? That's why they're calling you—"

"Fine, whatever. I get it." I slammed my locker, held my stack of books in front of me like a shield, and stalked off straight to Mrs. Palmer's room.

My dad and I always used to talk about what power we'd want if we were superheroes. Mine was different every time the subject came up. Dad considered lots of options but always came back to the same one—indestructibility. (I thought about that a lot after the car accident.) More and more lately, I'd been liking the idea of invisibility.

Clearly God and I didn't see eye-to-eye on this issue. I wanted to go unnoticed; He gave me reddish hair and made me one of the tallest kids in the class. Mrs. Palmer spotted me instantly and called me to her desk while the other kids made their way to their seats.

"Here, Rory." She handed me an open-ended envelope, then removed her glasses—which only made her owlish eyes look even bigger—and rubbed the side of her head with her middle finger. Bad sign: she didn't usually start the temple massage until after lunch. Late morning on a bad day.

"The first-quarter report cards came out yesterday. You need to take it home for your mom to sign, and return it by Friday."

"Okay." I started to slip it out of the envelope, then hesitated. She gave me a go-ahead nod. I saw the usual Bs with a smattering of As. B- in math, but I wasn't going to argue about that. Then my eye snagged on something. In science I had an 'I'.

Now you have to take an Incomplete, right?

I heard Allie's voice in my memory. So 'I' was for Incomplete. It wasn't as scary-ugly as an F, but it sat there glaring up at me like a little…evil 'I'.

Mrs. Palmer noticed me noticing. "Yes. Mr. Hayes alerted me to the situation. This needs to be sorted out."

Something about her seriousness made my mouth go dry. That on top of the embarrassment at my locker made me suddenly want to tear around the room, knocking over desks and breaking the points off pencils. I hated school!

Somehow my voice, when it came out, sounded cucumber-cool. "Yeah, I guess I'll just have to bust my behind getting As in science for the rest of the year. To make up for a cruddy first quarter."

She graduated from temple-rubbing to the bridge-of-the-nose massage. I braced myself. "It's more complicated than that, Rory. Technically, an Incomplete mark prevents you from advancing to the next grade."

"You mean…"

"An Incomplete means you won't graduate."

I wish I could report that this was the low moment of my day, but it was only a brief rest stop on the way to rock-bottom. I mulled over the rest of the emotional mudslide as I walked home from school. What a mess my life had become. Bliss, meanwhile, glided through it all as breezy-clean as a fabric softener commercial.

Her advice? "Don't even worry about it," she'd said.

My Defining Grade School Moment was green projectile vomiting, and I wasn't supposed to worry about it?

"You're building something priceless," she'd said.

"Like what, exactly?" I'd asked.

"A reputation."

I stared at her, but she didn't seem to be joking. "Wouldn't a good reputation be preferable?" I asked.

She shrugged. "Doesn't matter much. Sometimes bad is better." The half-smile she gave me had more than a little Bad Fairy in it.

I tried to push it all out of my mind: the satisfied smirks of the kids I hadn't invited to the party (ever-so-sorry for me and my guacamole/evil spirit incident); the unsure-I-want-to-be-seen-with-you look on Jasmine's face at lunch; the unsure-I-have-any-real-friends sensation I experienced as a result.

A smells-like-chocolate-chip sensation at the Fisher's front door would've been a bright spot in a dark day, but home-ec Friday was ages away, so the chances were slim. Still, when I rounded the curve of Sweetnam Lane, I spotted something on the

Fisher's front steps that made my heart do that clumsy sort of dance called hope. It looked like a curly-wurly dark head bent over a guitar.

My whole body felt like a sigh. *Thank you, God.* A friend.

Sam must not have heard me coming. His fingers moved from one position to another on the frets of the guitar; I knew from the sound and my distant days of piano that he was practicing chords. Then the fingers of the strumming hand began picking out quick notes, stumbled, tried again, stumbled again. He let out a puff of breath that made the hair hanging in front of his face flick up. That's when he spotted me.

"Hey," he said, lowering the guitar.

"Hi." I let my backpack rest on my bottom step. "Sorry to interrupt."

"You weren't. I was just waiting."

For a second I was sure he was going to add *for you*, but he stopped short of it. There was one of those moments of full of waiting, what Mr. Behrens would call a 'pregnant pause'. Then I blurted out, "You're pretty good."

"At this?" He set the guitar aside. "Not really."

"Seriously. That song—"

"You recognized it?"

"Um, it did sound familiar."

"If I were any good, you would've recognized it." He laughed, but it wasn't the usual Sam laugh that sort of erased any embarrassment or discomfort that might've come before it. After this laugh, there was still something in the air.

Either I'm clueless or super-perceptive, because my conversation generator leapt onto the subject of the parties and decided that was the way to go. "Did you have a good birthday?"

"Pretty good, yeah." He scuffed his shoes along the concrete steps. I doubted his mom would appreciate that, but I don't think he was aware he was doing it. "Not as exciting as your party, from what I hear," he said.

I got stiff. What had he heard? "Well, there's good exciting, and then there's just...bizarre." He just gave a sort of sideways nod and picked at the threads of a loose button on his shirt. "When Bliss is involved," I went on, "it's bound to be a little strange."

"Yeah? What's she all about, then?"

"I don't know. How do you mean?"

"You've been hanging out with her, right?"

"I guess so."

"So what's her story?"

"You mean Jake hasn't filled you in on her life history?" I asked.

He half-smiled. "Yeah, well, just the kind of stuff he's interested in. I don't think he knows her very well."

"Probably not. She's the mysterious type. But she backed me up in class when I disagreed with the whole Darwin-evolution thing. I guess I kind of assumed she believed in God, at least."

"Does she?"

"I'm not sure, exactly." I'd looked up *agnostic*. It sort of meant that she had no opinion about God one way or another, because she didn't think there was any way to know for sure if He was real. "She says she's agnostic. Sometimes I just think she's a little obnoxious."

His head came up; he couldn't help himself. He nodded wisely. "She's agnoxious."

Then our eyes met and at the exact same moment we both said it.

"Obnostic."

We laughed. It was a good moment. Shame it didn't last.

"So," he said. "Are you trying to be a good influence on her or something?"

I laughed again, partly because once you're already laughing it's easy to keep doing it. But mostly because the idea of me influencing Bliss was like an umbrella influencing a thunderstorm. "Not much chance of that. Even her mom just seems to step out of her way. Her mom's friend, Tamsyn, treats her like she owns the place."

"Does she tell you what to do, too?"

The emotional equivalent of a prickly pufferfish swelled up in me. "Hardly." He said nothing, which felt like doubt. "If she ever does, it's in the friendship way. You know how sometimes there's the friend with all the ideas and the take-charge sort of personality, and then there's the one who goes along for the ride."

"So where do you plan to get off?"

I stared at Sam. Was it Sam, or someone more abrasive, cleverly disguised as easygoing Sam? "What do you mean?"

"I mean, how far down that road do you go? Like, some people might've stopped before the séance."

"Séance?"

"That's what you call it when you try to summon spirits, Rory."

"I never—" but I stopped because I knew the fact that I'd mostly just stood there and done nothing wasn't a very solid defense. "I didn't know that kind of thing was going to happen."

"The decorative graves in the front yard might've been a clue."

"It wasn't just me, you know. Jake was right there, too." Then it dawned on me. "Is that what this is about? Look, I'm sorry I couldn't come to your party. I didn't have much choice." That fell flat, because half-truths are like half-inflated balloons. I hurried on. "I can't say the same for Jake, who wasn't even officially invited to Bliss's, but showed up anyway."

This is the time-honored (or at least age-old) technique of deflecting attention away from your own crime by pointing to your neighbor's worse one. What a smooth operator I am.

"Jake did come to my party. Late, and he didn't stay long. But long enough."

My stomach flopped. "He went from Bliss's party straight to yours?"

"I guess hers ended earlier than planned."

I said nothing.

"What were you thinking, Rory?"

"What?" Denial. Not just a river in Egypt.

"A ouija board? That's spiritism."

"It's just a dumb board game."

"Really."

"It was just a bunch of kids messing around on Halloween."

"But do those kids have a clue about the battle, the Armor—or that there's even an actual spirit world? They're just dumb kids who think they're playing with matches, but you know they're playing with a nuclear detonator. And you don't just watch, you join them?"

A wave of heat surged up my face and down my arms and legs. Still, I tried to laugh it off. "Oh, and I suppose I should've stood on the coffee table and shouted, 'Beware the Board Game from Hell!' or something like that? Besides, Bliss seems to know plenty about spirits, and her mom and Tamsyn, too."

"Which makes me wonder what you were doing there in the first place." He locked his guitar in its case with a sharp snap, snap, snap.

I thought I saw the curtain twitch in the Fisher's front window; I couldn't see anyone, but I lowered my voice. "It almost sounds like you're saying I shouldn't hang out with Bliss because I'm a Christian. I must be wrong, though, because didn't Pastor Dan say we can't keep the salt in the shaker and the light under the bushel? We can't just stay in the holy huddle and avoid the rest of the world?"

"I'm not—you're just—" He let out an explosive breath, raked his hands through his hair. With the glasses, he looked like Boy Einstein. "I'm not talking about what a generic Christian should do. I'm talking about Rory Joyce, who ought to know better than to mess around with the spirit realm like it's some game."

"It WAS a game. I mean, it came in a box, you can buy it at ToyMart—"

"Then what about Uri?"

All that heat in my face and limbs drained away. "How...?"

"U-R-I. Uri is his name, isn't it? The one who—"

"Stop it!" I turned away, sick all over again, but without the belly full of guacamole to make me throw up. I fell over my backpack instead and scraped my hands on the crumbling edge of the concrete step. "Don't ever say that name!"

Sam was on his feet. "Wait—"

But I didn't wait. I reacted as if he'd slapped me across the face. "No. It all makes sense now. I wondered how Jake knew that name—I was sure I hadn't ever told him. But obviously I must've told you. Thanks for keeping it to yourself. I suppose gossip is just fine, as long as it's among your fellow Christians."

"I don't know what y—"

"Enough! I get it. I'm supposed to be some Prudence McPrissypants now, who only hangs out with other goody-goodies, baking muffins and embroidering Bible verses on handkerchiefs." (Where'd that come from?) "Well, I'm sorry, Sam, but I have to live in the real world and spend all day with real people who believe different things than I do."

He kept his mouth shut. I wasn't so smart.

"I don't have the luxury of hiding in my house with my mama and being oh-so-sure of what I believe in because I don't have to actually come in contact with anyone who disagrees with me."

Even as I said it, I wished I could suck the words back in, chew them and swallow so only I would have to taste them. The color drained from his face, and thanks to me I also got to watch as behind those thick eyelashes the coffee-brown of his eyes flattened almost to black. He slung his messenger bag over his shoulder and lifted the guitar case in his other hand.

"I guess I didn't see it that way," he said.

"Well, maybe now you do," I muttered to his back. He was already halfway to the sidewalk. I fumbled with my keys, but my hand was stiff, and the scrape had started to sting and bleed. I refused to watch Sam walk away.

seventeen

The week lingered on like a bad smell. When a bad smell won't go away, you have to consider the possibility that it might be coming from you.

I stunk, and I knew it. The more I knew it, the more crud I threw on the stinky garbage pile of my anger towards Sam, because it's always easier to blame the other guy. It never helps the situation, but it's easier.

I did have a few things to help keep my mind off my battle with the *SS Newman*. Things like the new behind-my-back nickname at school, Demon Puker. And other things, like the possibility of not graduating in the spring. I told myself that I didn't want to graduate with a bunch of kids who called me Demon Puker anyway. Better to stay behind and join a whole different class. Yeah, then I could be sixteen when I graduated eighth grade, and that would be just nifty.

Otherwise, I had no problem with the seventh graders. It seemed dumb to get all superior on them when mere months ago I'd been one of them, slightly fearful of the eighth graders. When I got yet another uncertain look from Jasmine in the cafeteria—despite the fact that I'd picked the vegetarian entrée—I even went so far as to sit with a seventh grader.

Journey LeVey peered through her veil of hair when I sat across from her. There were others at the table, but no one near enough to suggest a lunch buddy.

"If you're looking for Bliss, she's AWOL today," she said.

I definitely wasn't looking for Bliss. She'd hardly been at school all week. "Where's she been?"

Journey said *who knows, who cares,* all with a twitch of her nose. "Somewhere with Nico, I'm guessing."

"He's still around?"

"Until Sunday." Obviously she was counting the minutes. "It's been just a peachy week."

"Tell the Demon Puker all about it."

Now the corner of her mouth twitched, maybe her version of a smile. "Excellent performance Saturday night."

"Yeah, apparently a lot of people enjoyed it. It's my claim to fame now."

With a flick of her hand she said *Who cares what people think?* "That's what's bothering you? Big deal. That kind of stuff is my life."

"Yeah, well I also got in a huge fight with one of my best friends." That sounded strange. Best friends? I'd never used those words for Sam before, at least not out loud. Now that I had, it didn't sound wrong. Sam was one of my best friends. Until I'd gone and ruined it. (No, wait—he'd ruined it, when he'd blabbed all my secrets to Jake Dean. This was Sam's fault. That was my story and I was sticking to it.)

"You've got friends?" Journey asked, in a way that suggested it automatically disqualified me from complaining.

"Plus I found out that I might not graduate just because I refused to write answers I didn't believe on a test."

Maybe I was trying to impress her. It didn't seem to work. "Sounds like something Bliss put you up to," she guessed.

"I can't remember why I did it anymore. I might as well just give them what they want and get on with my life."

"Or not," she said. "They're bluffing, you know. They want you to graduate as much as you do. Otherwise they all look bad. They'll give you a way out. Just ask Bliss. She's always refusing to do stuff and getting away with it."

"Like the frog she wouldn't dissect."

"Let me guess: the Deeply-Held Beliefs speech?"

I blinked. "You mean she doesn't…"

"Fight for the rights of frogs everywhere? Hardly."

"Have deeply-held beliefs, I mean."

She swirled a bread stick in her tomato soup. "Bliss believes in getting what Bliss wants. You might say she's the high priestess of getting what she wants." She bit the end off the bread stick. "And you get to be her disciple."

I'd only ever heard that word used about the guys who followed Jesus. It didn't give me a comfortable feeling to hear it used with Bliss—and me. "Please," I said, to brush it off.

She shrugged with one shoulder. It said, *just watch and see.*

That was Thursday, and I hurried up the steps when I got home to avoid any possible encounter with Sam. It was all very unnecessary since (as I later came to realize) he was avoiding me like a flesh-eating virus.

That Friday was unremarkable except that Bliss's long absence now had an official excuse: "the flu" (absolutely necessary to do the "finger quotation marks" for that one). Everyone joked about the new outbreak of the Italian Flu. Myself, I couldn't figure out how she got away with it.

Friday was also the day I got the big assignment. I hadn't even begun to work up the courage to get face-to-face with Mr. Hayes and ask for a way out of my Incompleteness. Surprisingly enough, Mrs. Palmer had done it for me.

She beckoned me to her desk when I returned from lunch, still smelling of fish thingers and ketchup. She smelled like garlic and spearmint. She slipped a roll of mints back into her top drawer and slid it shut, but not before I saw the row of headache medicines. I almost suggested that she might save a lot of money on aspirin if she just didn't pull her hair back so tight that it made her eyes bug out. I decided against it.

"I just spoke with Mr. Hayes," she said.

"Oh." I pictured them in the teachers' lounge. I'd always imagined it as a sanctuary of gleaming crumb-free tables, comfy chairs and carpet, with a fridge full of good stuff and all the appliances necessary to make good stuff even better. Teachers lounging, laughing, and students strictly forbidden. But somehow I couldn't see Mr. Hayes and Mrs. Palmer chit-chatting, trading his gourmet croissant for her buttered scones. I wondered if teachers had cliques and designated tables just like us in the noisy, smelly, florescent-lit cavern of the cafeteria.

"It seems he's perfectly willing to saddle you with that Incomplete mark. Permanently," she said. She sounded rather willing to let him.

But saddle? Wrong. Saddles suggested riding, escape, freedom. I'd be shackled. Shackled to Whitestone Elementary for another year, probably to the very same desk in Mr. Hayes' science class, facing that evolution test again. Like a repeating nightmare. Journey was wrong—they didn't care if I graduated or not.

Mrs. Palmer went on. "He says he offered you a second chance on the test, but you ignored it."

"I wouldn't say ignored…"

"He doesn't plan to offer you a third chance."

I sighed. Graduation at age sixteen. My mom was going to kill me. Sheelan would have ammunition to verbally shoot me down for the next…oh, eighty years or so. Until I died.

"I suggested a report, instead."

I hardly heard her. I was busy thinking about next year, when I'd have to stand up for truth and refuse to take the test again. Graduation at sixteen began to look almost appealing next to graduation *never*.

"He said he would accept no less than ten pages, and that he would name the topic."

I stared at her, empty-headed, until my brain finally jogged up and hopped back inside. "A ten-page report? You mean, instead of the test?"

"Yes, and I suggest you take him up on the offer."

Mrs. Palmer had plea-bargained for me? "No more Incomplete?"

She nodded. "He'll give you the details of what he expects." And just like that, she opened her planner and called class to order.

I slid into my seat. Journey was right—they really did want me to graduate.

The fragrance of baked wonderfulness wrapped around me when I got home. Things were definitely looking up. Of course it came from the Fishers' house and not mine, but Kings was waiting for me.

"Try this," he said, handing me a napkin. Nestled inside was a warm, rolled-up pastry bursting with sticky, chocolaty, nutty fruity goodness. "They're still kind of hot, but we couldn't wait. Sorry if it's messy."

I sank my teeth into it with a sigh. "I forgive you." We ate in happy silence for a bit. "What is it, anyway?"

"It's called rugelach."

"Auntie Camille's recipe?" I doubted I could get my arms all the way around his Auntie Camille, but at that moment I was ready to try.

"Nah, one of Sam's. Or his mama's, maybe. It's Jewish."

My swallow went down hard. "Sam's here?"

"Not today. Too bad, 'cause the rugelach turned out great. You can tell him next time he's here."

I crammed the sticky napkin in my coat pocket. "Yeah…I don't know about that."

"Don't know about what?"

"I don't know if Sam wants to talk to me."

He chewed slowly. "Tee-Tee told me you guys were arguing out here a few days ago. I thought she was making it up. She's very dramatic."

I shrugged.

"That explains why he left in such a hurry, I guess." The wind curled around the bottom of the steps, blowing yellow and brown leaves in a crazy circle. "Is he mad at you?"

"Probably," I said, wrapping my coat a bit tighter. I wasn't about to repeat the idiotic things I'd said to Sam. The bad taste of them was still in my mouth, competing with the nutty sweetness of the pastry. "I think maybe he was ticked off because Jake and I couldn't come to his birthday party."

"Really? He didn't seem ticked off. I'm sure he wanted you guys there and all, but don't feel all bad about it, Rory. We had a great time."

I blinked. "You were there?"

"Yeah, sure I was. A few other people, too."

Really. "Shayne Svoboda…"

"Yeah, she's great. Funny." He hesitated, and he might have blushed a little, but it was hard to tell with his brown cheeks.

"Who else?"

"A kid named Silas."

Silas from the Scene. He and Sam would shoot baskets together sometimes.

"And another girl."

"Allie made it? I thought she had to take care of her Grammy."

"Allie? No, not Allie. Her name was Tali." The way he said it, it didn't rhyme with Allie—more like collie. I pictured a girl with fluffy brown and white hair and a pointy nose.

"Who's Tali?"

"Sam's cousin, I think. Her mom was visiting Sam's mom."

"His Aunt Bekah?"

"No, that's his Dad's sister. They're American. But Tali and her mom have the same accent as Mrs. Newman."

"So Tali's mom is Mrs. Newman's sister."

He scrunched up his face. "I don't think so."

"But if Tali's his cousin, and she's not from the American side..." I don't know why it mattered so much to me.

"I think she's like a distant cousin. Or maybe they're just good friends and he calls her mom 'Auntie' like we do with Auntie Camille. Oh, hang on a minute." He rambled back inside, probably for more rugelach. I was digesting the fact that Auntie Camille wasn't actually Kingston's aunt, and deciding whether I'd wait in the cold wind in hopes of more pastry or just go in my own house, when Kings finally came back. He had a digital camera.

"I've got pictures from Saturday," he said. His sturdy fingers flicked over the tiny buttons, surprisingly nimble. "Here's the start." I leaned over the rail as he scrolled through each shot. The first were some rather distorted close-ups of Kingston's face. He laughed his rolling chuckle. "I took those myself. Here, look at this one of Sam. That's a real Norman helmet he's wearing. His dad got it from some guy in England, but he's going to give it to a museum."

I didn't know what a Norman was, but the helmet fit Sam surprisingly well, even if the dark curls poking out the bottom took the edge off its fierceness. It coordinated well with his long-sleeved T-shirt, which also had a helmeted knight on it. The knight seemed to be missing his limbs, though. The words *It's just a flesh wound* suggested some hilarious inside joke I was outside of.

The next several pictures involved Shayne, Silas and some cheese doodles. Then I saw a pair of cinnamon-brown eyes in a golden face, the kind of eyes with the naturally dark lashes that left eyeliner and mascara to the less fortunate girls. Wavy brown hair down to her elbows.

"That's Tali," Kings said, as if I hadn't figured that out. She was smiling in the next picture. Now I understood what fancy-pants poets meant when they compared women's teeth to a string of pearls.

"It was a little hard to understand her at first. They're from Israel."

In the next picture she was beside Sam, and they were laughing, her warm eyes dancing. Her hand on his arm.

"How nice," I said.

eighteen

I spent all Saturday morning choosing what attitude I'd wear to the Scene that night.

There's the Hey, Nothing's Wrong Here approach, the one where you go in like it's no big deal, everything's cool. This one makes you look bulletproof—if you can pull it off. If you can't and actually reveal that you do have feelings, then you end up looking like a big faker or a baby.

Then there's the I've Been Wronged approach. This involves immediately finding potential allies to your cause and convincing them how awful the other person has been to you. Very important to catch them before they hear both sides of the story.

And yes, there's always the What Would Jesus Do? approach. I did consider this one, but I have trouble with it. Whenever I ask myself what Jesus would do if he were in my situation, I'm always left thinking *Jesus never would've gotten himself into this dumb situation*. Besides, the Jesus way usually involves being humble, being sorry for what you did wrong, forgiving people for what they did wrong, and all that sort of really hard stuff. Which, yes, is probably why it actually works, but did I mention that it's really hard?

So no WWJD. I was planning to try Approach #1, but if it fizzled fast I'd leap on Option #2 and run with it. I was pretty sure I could get Shayne and Allie on my side, just by playing the girls vs. boys angle.

None of it mattered, because Sam didn't come.

Shayne and Allie didn't seem to notice. Jake didn't say anything, either. They must've known why he wasn't there, or they'd be looking for him. But if I asked them, they'd know I didn't know, and they'd want to know why I didn't know. Then I'd have to tell them that Sam wasn't talking to me. Unless *that* was the reason why Sam wasn't there—to avoid me—in which case, if they already knew why he wasn't there, they already knew he wasn't speaking to me.

I squeezed my eyes shut, in case this would help me to become someone else, or at least think like someone else. No use — it was too hard and Pastor Dan's voice was too distracting. A person couldn't even think with all that talking.

"Is your Belt slipping a little lately?" he was asking.

That again? Did every lesson have to boil down to a wardrobe malfunction? But there was something vaguely familiar about that image; I had a foggy memory of trying to walk with a belt slipping around my knees. Like that could've happened. I hardly ever wore belts.

"Remember? The Belt of Truth: the foundation of our spiritual armor? A soldier keeps his armor in top shape—his life depends on it. So how do we perform a diagnostic on our own Belt? What are the signs of…" And he zapped the big screen with his little remote. Two words popped up, white on black: **TRUTH DECAY**

"…Truth Decay," he finished, ignoring the groans as usual. "How can we diagnose it? How do we know it's happening to us?"

One of the older boys raised a hand. "If your life doesn't look any different from unbelievers," he said.

Pastor Dan scrubbed his chin, where the goatee was already growing back. Apparently the billiard-ball look hadn't suited him. "Yes, but we have to be careful not to fall into an 'us and them' mindset. The only difference between me, a sinner with Christ, and that guy out there, a sinner without Christ, is that God in His inexplicable grace has brought me to a knowledge of the truth.

"It's not because I'm especially clever or good. It's ALL grace. And in humility and gratitude, I want to try to live in a way that pleases God and might cause that other guy to want to know more about this gift of grace. So don't any of you go feeling all superior to your unbelieving neighbors. Got it?"

"Got it," we answered. Feeling superior...Not exactly a struggle for me.

"Anyway, comparing ourselves to the people around us doesn't cut it. That's where we fall into the trap of *I'm basically a good person*—that attitude that we're doing pretty well on our own strength. After all, I don't do all the stuff those other kids are doing..." He looked around the room. "Sound familiar? That's a Christian who knows he or she needs a Savior, but maybe just a little Savior."

Pastor Dan dragged up a stool and sat. I couldn't remember ever seeing him sit down. "Imagine you're in a room like this one," he said. "Okay, right, you are in a room like this one. Imagine it's full of people, all standing up. Some of you are like me, on the short end of the scale, but say some of you are NBA height. Hey, since we're imagining, let's just say some of you are NBA superstars—in fact, let's say *I'm* an NBA superstar, seven feet tall. Now, we're going to start jumping, to see how high we can jump. Do any of us have an advantage?"

Our reaction was *duh*, but the respectful, meant-for-authority-figures variety of *duh*.

"Okay, so us seven-footers are going to jump the highest. But what if I tell you that our goal is to jump and touch the ceiling of this gymnasium?"

We all looked up at the 30-foot-high steel rafters.

"That advantage suddenly doesn't seem so impressive. Now, imagine the ceiling is as high as, say, the moon. Or the far end of the solar system, or the known universe. Will all the jumping practice in the world, the best shoes—the space shuttle—make a difference now?

"Well, neither will all the good things you do in your life. Trying to work your way into heaven by being a good little Christian is like trying to jump and touch the farthest star—the distance created between you and God by a single sin is incomprehensible."

A single sin. The words made me cold. Uri had said something like that, that one little sin was all it took to keep you out of heaven.

"So don't believe the lie that you're do-gooding your way up to heaven, with a little boost from a grateful Jesus. We ALL need a Savior who can reach all the way across eternity, reach all the way down and lift us out of the bottomless pit—every one of us needs the same Savior.

"The biggest objection to Christianity that I've heard from people your age is that those of us who call ourselves Christians tend to act like we've got it all figured out, we're above it all, we're so very good—while all the time our lives tell a different story."

Someone made a comment about 'walking the talk,' Pastor Dan went on about hypocrisy, and the rest of the discussion hopped down that bunny trail. But there was no escape—Martina had a sheet for each of us with 5 SIGNS OF TRUTH DECAY.

"I need five of you to look up verses," she told us as we took our papers and sat. "You all brought your Bibles?"

Allie waved hers. "Thanks for the bookmark, Martina." She pulled it out, and I saw she had the Proverbs verse about the heart being the wellspring of life.

Next to me, Caroline ran the silky red tassel through her fingers. I saw she had the same 'guard your heart' verse from Proverbs. Finally I pulled Shayne's out of her Bible.

"Hey, you lost my place," she said. "Didn't you get one? I'm sure Marina has more."

"No, here." I handed the bookmark back. Proverbs 4:23. They all had the same. Only mine was different. Mine, about blindness, danger, and consequences. Lucky me. "I must've left mine at home," I said.

Martina was assigning verses. "Okay, the first sign of Truth Decay: Immaturity. Shayne, will you look up Ephesians 4:14 for us? It should be familiar to you."

Shayne's eyebrows wagged. "Immaturity? Wonder why she chose that one for me," she whispered.

"Mary Katherine, you take Immorality. Ephesians 4:19."

Mary K just nodded with a knowing look at all of us.

"Tess, do you have a Bible? Great. You look up the verse for Injustice, Isaiah 59:14. And Caroline, Illegality. Proverbs 29:18."

It was warm in the gymnasium, but I couldn't take off my sweater because the shirt underneath was too tight to wear alone. I blinked hard, but my eyes wanted to be dozy.

"Rory, that leaves you with Unreality."

"Figures," I thought—out loud.

Her icy blue eye glittered at me. "Second Thessalonians 2:12, Rory."

I was still searching for it when Shayne read her verse and they began talking about immaturity. Second Thessalonians, I discovered, was a whole two pages long. The old flip-and-find method doesn't work well for these little ones. Didn't matter much, anyway, since the verse didn't make any sense when I did find it.

I half-listened to the talk around me, wondering if the heat was making my face pink, wondering how long it would be before we could play basketball, wondering if I'd find out any more about Sam, wondering why I cared about Sam, spiller of secrets. Wondering how many times Martina had said my name before I finally heard her.

"Welcome back, Rory. Deep in thought about your verse?"

"Well, I don't get it. It starts in the middle of a sentence."

"Read it."

I cleared my throat. "…that they all may be condemned who did not believe the truth but had pleasure in unrighteousness."

"Okay. They who?"

"Exactly."

"Did you read back a verse or two? Ladies, if you're unsure about meaning, always look to the context. Go back a bit and you'll see that Paul is talking about Satan's trickery: '—with all power, signs, and lying wonders, and with all unrighteous deception among those who perish, because they did not receive the love of the truth, that they might be saved. And for this reason God will send them strong delusion, that they should believe the lie, that they all many be condemned who did not believe the truth but had pleasure in unrighteousness.'

"This is tough stuff, girls. We could talk for weeks about God choosing you to receive the love of the truth—His choice, not yours—but let's look at the two sides of the coin here. Either you believe the lie, or you receive the truth. Either you have pleasure in unrighteousness, or you love…what? The Truth. If you find yourself caught up in something that God condemns, you'd better take a long hard look at yourself. Whose camp are you in?"

Just what was she suggesting, here? I mean, it was a pretty safe bet that everyone in our circle was a believer. (I couldn't say for sure with Tess; she was still 'just visiting'.) Why the suggestion that we still had to choose a side? Didn't accepting Christ kind of put the period at the end of that sentence? Done deal.

Martina told us to do this, that, and the other during the week, then finally it was time to play basketball. Jake, Mary K, Tess, Silas, and a couple of other kids joined in our game of Horse, so it hardly mattered that Sam wasn't there. No one even asked about him. It was obviously perfectly acceptable to everyone that he wasn't there.

It was obvious that everyone knew why he wasn't there. Obviously, the reason was me.

You've probably heard the expression, *the less said, the better*. Well, my mouth apparently never heard that one. Probably because it was too busy yapping.

"No Sam again, huh?" I observed to no one in particular.

A few grunts, nods. Oh yeah, they definitely knew about our fight. So why keep on talking about him?

Because I'm hopelessly lame. "Maybe he's getting bored with the sermons," I said.

"What do you mean?" It was Silas who asked. I don't believe I'd ever spoken directly to Silas before, though he seemed like a nice enough guy. Kind of reminded me of a slightly older Sam, if Sam were black.

"Oh, you know," I said. "'The Belt of Truth slipping' and all that. We've kind of been there, done that." I missed my shot—and not in the basketball game (okay, I missed that one, too).

"Pastor Dan's just trying to teach us how to live out our faith in the world and not get sucked into worldly things."

"Right, I know. And he wants everyone to get the point, so he keeps repeating stuff for the people who've missed a Saturday."

Mary K waved and I tossed her the ball. "What are you talking about? Every week's been a new topic. Wake up and smell the PowerPoint presentation."

This conversation had careened off the tracks. I needed a do-over. "Well, I don't know, maybe I'm just missing Kellie." There, I couldn't go wrong with that. "Martina's fine and all, but I'm just not..." I made the universal sign for 'getting much out of it'.

No one seemed to recognize the sign.

"You know, she's not exactly..."

No one jumped in to finish my thought. Instead, Allie said, "Just because Martina's not Kellie doesn't mean she won't be good. I think you need to cut her some slack." She took aim and sunk a 3-pointer. Because she was always sinking those stupid 3-pointers. I bet she could dribble and do a lay-up, too.

"Shh," Shayne said. She passed me the ball, which I tossed to Jake, who happened to be on the other team. He did an obnoxious little dance for my benefit, shaking his dumb shaggy haircut. "Martina's looking over here," Shayne added. "I think she can hear us."

"Oh well," I said. "So it's one more person ticked off at me, so what? She can get in line behind Sam."

"What?"

"You don't have to pretend you don't know. He's all annoyed and probably doesn't want to be in the same room with me. Though I'm actually the one who's mad at him — I'm guessing he didn't tell you that side of the story. So that's why he's not here."

Shayne scrunched up her eyebrows and wrinkled her nose. "Um, no... I don't think so. He said something about a family thing he had to go to."

"A big party for his Aunt Sabra who's visiting from Israel," Allie supplied. "Though your theory sounds very interesting." She tucked the ball under her arm. "Go on, we're listening."

"Yes, we could tell you had something on your mind," said Mary K. "Tell us all about your fight with Sammy, dear. Was it tempestuous?"

By sheer force of will, I held the hot away from my face. Time for a diversion. "That is definitely not what's been on my mind. I've got bigger problems, like the 10-page report I have to do for Mr. Hayes to make up for the test I didn't take."

They took the bait. Just like that, we were talking about *Fact vs. Faith* and they were giving advice and offering to help me do the research (mostly Allie on that). My mouth carried on with the new conversation, but the whole time I was thinking about Sam's family party for his Aunt Sabra.

I could imagine who else would be there—one pearly-toothed not-really-a-cousin in particular. I could imagine them all eating rugelach and pasta salad, sharing stories and laughing, fiddling and dancing in their stupid circles…holding hands.

Sam Newman was now officially on my blacklist.

nineteen

for those who would like to point out how unfair it was for me in particular to get ticked off at Sam for skipping the Scene to go to a party, let me respond with one of my dad's favorites: Who Ever Said Life Was Fair?

Anyone who cares to suggest that jealousy had something to do with my ticked-off state, I'd like to introduce you to five reasons to change your mind. (Please imagine my five fingers clenched in a threatening fist... Yeah, I know. That was more convincing when my dad used to do it.)

A bad mood, when you coddle it long enough, grows into a big, fat bad attitude faster than a larvae grows into a pupa. I knew that, now that we were studying insects in science. Yippee.

Where I live, November is a good month for a bad attitude. The October air, crisp and sweet like apples, goes cold and flat and smells more like the refrigerator vegetable drawer that needs to be cleaned out. The trees are naked, but they're all pointing their fingers at you, like you're the one who ought to be ashamed of yourself. The rain is impossibly cold but refuses to be snow.

To top it off, my mom dropped some delightful news on us.

"I may have to work on Thanksgiving," she told us on one of the rare nights when we all ate together.

I slapped my burrito back onto my plate. "What? You said your office is closed for the four-day weekend."

"I'm not talking about Reinbolt's. Rocky's."

Sheelan didn't look up from her magazine when she spoke. "You said you were going to quit waitressing."

"I said I want to quit. But I can't afford to."

"Who eats at a restaurant on Thanksgiving?" I demanded to know. Whoever they were, I deeply resented them and their need for a waitress.

"People who don't want to cook. Listen, I know it's lousy, but I owe Ruthie a favor and I can't really say no—"

"Sure you can. You just say it. You tell her you've got—" I stopped. *A family.* That's what I was going to say. Then it hit me: Mom seemed sorry about all this, but not... *sorry* sorry. Mom was avoiding Thanksgiving because of the big gaping hole in our family.

"Grandma Judy will have you over. She's a better cook anyway, right?" she asked brightly, as if it were about the food. "Listen, I'm sorry it has to be this way, but it won't be for much longer. The office manager position at Reinbolt's is opening up early next year, and I'm almost guaranteed to get it. That means more money and no more waitressing But for right now, I can use all the extra cash I can get. With Christmas coming, you know."

"If you don't work on Christmas, you mean." I said it because I was disappointed. Why is it that when you're feeling rotten, you want to go and make everyone else feel rotten, too? It's not as if being surrounded by cranky people improves the situation.

I know she heard me, because she got still for a second. Then she went on eating like I hadn't said it. Sheelan started talking like she hadn't heard it, probably because she hadn't. I'm mostly a buzzing sound in her ears, like a mosquito.

"It's okay, Mom. I might have another invitation, anyway." She didn't say more, but the way her strawberry-blonde curls bounced around her face spoke for her. They said, *It's with a boy—don't you wish you were me?*

And I was so right. When I found out which boy, I got carpet burn on my chin from my jaw hitting the floor. But that wasn't until Saturday.

Meanwhile, things were getting interesting at school. My first clue—no, my first clue was when Courtney and Britnee had showed up at Bliss's party instead of Madi's—so my second clue was the cafeteria seating shake-up. All of a sudden, the Madi Swanson table was no more. The Kevin Sebeck table was no more. There seemed to be a power struggle as Courtney and Britnee competed for the remnant of Madi's followers, while the boys took advantage of the confusion and started to divide and conquer the girls. But where was Madi?

I must've asked it out loud, because Tiffany slid her tray next to mine as we made our lunch selections and answered my question. "Madi's gone. She moved to Toronto or Canada or someplace. Can you believe it?"

"And look," I said, still fascinated by the confusion at the tables.

"What, Courtney and Britnee? Yeah, real BFFs, right? They must've known Madi was leaving—that's why they went to Bliss's party instead. Now they're jockeying for Madi's position."

I kept watching as the ex-Swansonites and the Sebeckians finally settled into a restless configuration of girls and boys intermixed. "They're like frightened cattle without a herder," I said, almost feeling sorry for them. As sorry as you can feel for people who would skip out on their best friend's last party before she moved out of the country.

Tiffany had followed me to a table, sitting across from me. "Oh, let them worry about their precious cafeteria seats. I've got my eyes on a bigger prize." I glanced at her, which she interpreted as intense interest. She leaned in. Beside her, Jasmine was pretending to read a historical novel and eavesdropping. "Student council president," Tiffany whispered.

Of course. By some evil chance, Tiffany had been placed in the same class as Madi since second grade. And every year, Madi had beaten her out of some exalted position: teacher's pet, after-school board eraser, bathroom line monitor, class secretary, whatever. This year it had been the penultimate position: student council president, second only to the crowning glory of valedictorian. After a week of campaign posters and heartfelt, meaningless speeches, a landslide vote had declared Madi the winner.

Now, by default (and lack of any other takers), Tiffany could finally ascend to the position she'd probably dreamed of since her attempt to be the official hamster feeder in kindergarten.

Two days later, Bliss Hathaway was giving her acceptance speech as the new student council president. She met me at my locker after school, maybe looking for a pat on the back, I don't know.

"Congrats," I said, painfully aware that Tiffany was at her locker behind me.

"Thanks for voting for me," Bliss said, not seeming to care where Tiffany was, or to consider the possibility that I hadn't voted for her. And I hadn't. But it wasn't the sort of thing you just told someone—even if you very badly wanted the person at their locker behind you to know it—so I didn't.

"I didn't even know you were interested in student government," I said instead.

She shrugged. "I can take it or leave it. I was bored, so I figured why not?"

Tiffany's locker door slammed behind me, and I heard her stomp away.

"Come home with me, you can see one of Tam's 'gatherings'. She's having her spaz sisterhood meeting at our house tonight."

"Um, thanks. I don't want to…you know, intrude."

"No, Tam and my mom love you. They think you're all…" And she made some finger-waggling gesture that I had no clue how to interpret.

"I would, but I've got to get started on this stupid paper."

"*Fact vs. Faith*, huh?" She laughed. I wondered how she knew the title of my paper. "How do you even start a report like that?"

I smiled, the kind that moves your lips and nothing else. "At the library, I guess."

"Don't tell me you plan to do your research in books. It's all internet. I mean, you could go out there and grab a paragraph here, a paragraph there, and you'd have your 'report' in an hour."

"Yeah, I plan to search the internet. The computers at the library are faster than mine at home."

She stared with those caramel sundae eyes. "You've got to be kidding. Yours must be ancient if you think the ones at the library are fast. Come and use my laptop. It rips."

I might've had to say yes since I couldn't think of a good reason to say no, but Bliss's pocket began to play music. She slipped out a phone no thicker than a thin mint cookie, flipped it open and began talking into it.

"Nico," she sighed, and I made a quick escape. I don't think she noticed.

When I walked home, wondering if it were possible for your face to freeze and break off the front of your head entirely, I saw a car pull up into the Fisher's driveway. A huge army-green coat with legs on the bottom and a rusty orange knit cap on top came down the steps. I wasn't close enough to see his face, but I felt him look down the street and spot me. He hopped into the car and it drove off in the other direction.

It took two cups of cocoa to thaw me out, but all the marshmallows in the world wouldn't have made it taste sweet.

I dawdled around on the internet but couldn't get anywhere useful, so I checked my email. There, almost buried in the junk, was a little gem: an email from a real person I actually knew. My thrill fizzled when I saw it was from Martina Thistlethwaite.

Ladies,
Remember your assignment for the week. See you Saturday.

It had all the warmth of an overdue notice from the library (the only mail I ever got in the regular mailbox). Just what assignment was she talking about? Like we didn't get enough assignments at school. I vaguely remembered sticking a piece of paper into my Bible at the Scene last Saturday. That was probably Martina's homework. I'd get to it later.

I said the same thing about *Fact vs. Faith* and settled down in front of the TV with a bag of cheese popcorn and my algebra homework. I kept the algebra tucked safely away in its folder so as not to besmirch it with cheesy fingerprints. But it made a good lap tray for the popcorn.

And so there I was the next day at lunch, scrambling to finish the math homework, five minutes before math class started. Jasmine watched me with a look of disgust. Then again, she was eating the Special of the Day: Turkfu (tofu turkey).

Bliss slid in beside me. Judging by her Maggie Jo's Coffee Shop cup, she'd gone out for lunch. She did this sometimes; I never saw who drove her. "Trouble with your math?" she asked.

"I didn't realize Palmer gave us a hundred problems to do. I've been wasting my whole lunch hour." Have I mentioned that our lunch 'hour' is forty-five minutes long?

"Well, here." She plopped her notebook beside mine. All the answers, problems one to twenty-two (in algebra, twenty-two might as well equal a hundred).

"Um, thanks. But I can do the problems—"

"In three minutes?"

"It's not that I don't get them."

"Exactly. You know how to do them, so what's the big deal? Just write down the answers and let's go."

Jasmine was watching me. I cringe to remember it. Not because of the cold eyes—as a matter of fact, they weren't cold at all. Just watching.

The school bell dinged the two-minute warning. I grabbed Bliss's notebook and started copying. Jasmine walked away.

I ended up at Bliss's house after school. I pretty much had to when she gave me her cell phone.

"Here, you want this?" she asked me after the dismissal bell. She'd just come from Mr. Hayes' class, and it was in her pocket, which was against school rules.

I looked at the thin mint phone, not understanding. "Thanks, but I don't need to make any calls right now."

She'd already gotten it into my hand. "No, I mean you can have it. I got a new one. Check it out." She pulled out a glossy little screen and began tapping it here and there while it blazed color and sound under her fingertip. "Music, phone, internet, everything."

"Nice. But you might still want this one—"

"It's yours, I don't want it."

"Do I have to buy minutes, or what?"

"No, just use it."

I flipped it open, and it gave a little chirp. Coolness.

"Come to my house, use my laptop for your research."

"Yeah, okay." Couldn't exactly say no, when she'd just given me an obviously-expensive phone. Part of me had that Christmas feeling, after you open a great gift but you're already wondering what else there might be.

The feeling lasted all of five minutes. That's how long it took for our ride to show up. Bliss decided it was far too cold to walk the half-mile, so her fingers danced over her funky new phone, and she summoned help. Not Tam, as I expected, but a neighbor boy, a high-school senior who drove a black car with tinted windows and a practically nonexistent back seat—where I was crammed—and drove it way too fast.

When he tore up to the curb in front of her house, he tried to kiss her. She laughed and hopped out. "As if, Cody." I climbed out awkwardly after her, and he peeled off almost before I had both feet on the ground. I saw him swing into a driveway eight or nine houses down. When he got out of the car he raised his hand in what might've been a wave or possibly an obscene salute.

"Nice," I said.

There was no sign of adults inside. Journey exited the kitchen as we entered, her gray eyes pinned on me with a look not unlike pity in them.

To compare Bliss's laptop with our PC at home would be something like placing Disneyworld beside the coin-operated carousel in front of the supermarket. It did rip; it ripped with ferocious style. If we had spent fifteen or twenty minutes searching for material for my paper, we probably would've found enough for a 50-page report. But when she powered the thing on, the start-up page was her personal profile in the latest hot online community.

"Hey, I can't believe I haven't friended you on InterFace yet," she said.

"Um," I hesitated, not wanting to admit I didn't have an InterFace account. "Well, I used to do *ePeople*…"

"Hopeless. I had so many losers bugging me on *ePeople*. You seriously don't InterFace? We have to get you set up. You'll be in my network." And we spent the next two hours creating my profile, complete with a photo of me in my woodland fairy get-up—the only picture of me she had, and one that she thought was perfect—plus a whole bunch of all-about-me surveys, quizzes, decorations and other mostly useless information.

Other than the embarrassing fairy photo, it was great fun. Until it was time for me to go home, that is. Mrs. Rhaynes and Tam were still gone, and when I called home, I got bumped into our voice mail, which meant Sheelan was on the other line ignoring the call. It probably didn't even matter, since Mom was sure to be working on a Friday night and had the car anyway.

It was daylight-savings dark outside, and blowingly, bitingly cold.

"I can call Cody," Bliss said. "He's a jerk, but he'll basically do whatever I tell him."

"No, it's fine. I'll walk," I said with a casual courage I didn't feel. She said goodbye at the door with a casualness she apparently did feel. The cold sunk its claws into me instantly. I had gloves, but I'd forgotten my hat at home.

Home. I measured the distance by lampposts, a feeble glow at the bottom of each driveway. Each pale puddle of light was separated by a long stretch of dark. Long enough for dark thoughts to creep in. By the time I turned onto Sweetnam Lane, I was walking so fast it might as well be called jogging. No passing cars, no people in garages or doorways. I could've been the only human alive.

I had the key in my hand a quarter mile from home, but my frozen legs stumbled up the steps, my fingers fumbled thickly at the lock. Then I was inside, closing the door behind me with my entire body.

No amount of chicken soup (Grandma Judy must've been there; I'd missed her), no number of blankets seemed to warm me. Later I slipped my flannel-clad legs under flannel bedsheets and still shivered. I dreamed of a dark road that stretched on and on before me. The lanterns along the way grew dimmer and farther apart, the darkness between them blacker, the farther it went. I walked on, regardless.

twenty

Sheelan came to the Scene the next day. Need I say more?

Maybe I do. Because it wasn't like you'd imagine it. First of all, she traipsed out to Jeph's car as if she were...well, maybe not excited about going, but perfectly willing. Crammed in the back seat with Shayne and Allie, watching her laugh at Jeph's jokes, swat him playfully on the arm, and all that other sickening flirty stuff, something fascinating and awful occurred to me.

One look at Shayne confirmed it. Jeph was Sheelan's new boyfriend.

In true Sheelan style, she did a complete 180º turn. Jeph's friends at the Scene, so recently worthy of little more than a cold glance and a sniff—if they were visible to her at all—now smiled under showers of Sheelan sunshine. When Pastor Dan welcomed her back, she gave her perky thanks and showed her dimples.

The poor fools thought they were winning her over. It was like a train wreck; I couldn't look away. I might've watched her the entire time if not for the sudden appearance of Sam Newman.

He came in behind Ericson Greene. The sight of Ericson caught my full attention, so when Sam stepped out from behind him, I was already staring right at him. Like synchronized swimmers, our eyes met with a splash and then jerked away. With our hot faces and obsession with looking at anything but each other, we must've looked pretty silly. Again, like synchronized swimmers.

Allie looked from Sam to me with one eyebrow raised. I was saved by Pastor Dan's voice.

"Come in, everyone. Let's get right to it. Find a seat and settle in." He waited until we had, then after a short prayer, said, "I have a question. A show of hands, please. Who here would say that worldly things—like money, power, sensuality—can become idols? And for our purposes today, let's define 'idol' as anything we make more important than our relationship with God."

A forest of hands bristled across the room.

"Okay," he said. "Now, as bad as that might be, who here would say that it would be much worse to, say, worship Satan?"

No-brainer. Most of our hands flew up again. The few people who hesitated squirmed under our withering stares. *Hello, what could be worse than Satan worship?*

Pastor waited a few moments, let us put our hands down and get comfortable before he said it.

"What if I told you they can amount to the same thing?"

Mostly we laughed—not the belly-clutching kind, but the as-if kind. Until we noticed he wasn't laughing with us.

"No, I'm not saying…" and he chewed on it for a moment, "…that spending more time watching TV than reading your Bible makes you a Satanist. But let's root out some of his lies right now, shall we? First, what do you picture when you hear 'Satanist'?"

Our answers would've made any low-budget horror movie director rub his hands with glee: black robes, sinister symbols, bloody altars. I'd seen my share of those kinds of movies, and I could've gotten caught up in the same sense of dark theater except for the single image that leapt into my mind. A knife of dull, pitted stone, its pores dark with ancient, unspeakable acts. I kept quiet.

Pastor Dan listened for a while, walking back and forth. Finally he interrupted the devilish brainstorming. "All in all, it sounds like a lot of drama. Very obvious stuff. If you walked into a place where the Enemy was worshipped, you'd know it instantly, right? If you were involved in some sort of activity and the devil showed up, you'd know it immediately."

There was a general mumble of agreement.

He sighed. Not from impatience or frustration. He seemed tired. "My young friends, what is Satan the "father" of?"

"Lies." Most of us knew that one.

"Who is he the ruler of?"

Less voices on this one. "This world."

"So we're on his turf, and he's the master of deception. Guess what? That is how he operates. Not with dramatic flourish, Hollywood-style—though something tells me he appreciates all the free advertisement he gets there. But be warned: Satan prefers to stay hidden as long as possible. The Bible says he prowls around like a hungry lion, looking for someone to devour. A lion doesn't run snarling and growling for a half mile up to a herd of zebras. He lies in wait; he camouflages. The stuff of this world—that's his cover.

"And know this: Satan does not have to be named to be worshipped." He let that sink in.

"Ask a Satanist, they'll tell you. They don't necessarily gather to worship Satan. They worship *themselves*…and, in the words of one Satanist, 'Satan shows up.'

"He's going to show up whenever we seek to fill a God-given desire with an ungodly substitute." He clicked his remote at the big screen.

PROSPERITY → greed

"Jesus wants us to have life and have it abundantly. Satan wants us never to be satisfied—to always want *more*."

INTIMACY → lust

"God created us to enjoy a beautiful, soul-deep union with one person for life. Satan sells us cheap, meaningless pleasure that destroys our bodies and starves our souls."

COMMUNION with GOD → to be god

"We are made in His image, with an eternal soul. We're spiritual beings who instinctively reach out for something bigger and deeper than the physical world around us.

"Your Enemy knows this, and he will twist it whenever he can. In the life of a follower of Christ, weakness is an opportunity for the Lord to move in and be strong on our behalf. For a nonbeliever, weakness is a thing to be feared or despised or corrected—and in seeking power for one's own self, a person can easily be led down the path of destruction.

"It might be the lure of 'ordinary' power: control over your circumstances, the ability to do what you want when you want. That doesn't sound like such a bad thing, until you consider that it was Adam and Eve's fatal error. They decided to do it their way, not God's way—and what was it the tree supposedly offered? That they could *be like God*.

"Not so different, then, are those who seek a supernatural sort of power. Who here hasn't fantasized about having that kind of power? Wave a wand, wiggle your nose, and presto! Your room is clean, your homework is done. Your brother is a frog.

"But it's not all harmless, storybook stuff. There is real power out there, working for us or against us. Two sources of supernatural power, folks. And it's not from inside you, or from the earth, or anything like that. It's either from God and His angels, or from Satan, the fallen angel, and his."

He powered off the screen, and for some reason the room seemed darker. "We can't talk about spiritual warfare without talking about the occult."

But we didn't talk about the occult. The talk got stuck on Worldly Things, and from there it somehow got swept up into *ePeople* and InterFace and other internet stuff. Two days ago I wouldn't have had a clue about it—well, I still didn't have much of a clue, but now I could honestly say I had an InterFace account, thanks to Bliss. And I was already getting friend requests, mostly from interesting (odd) people who knew Bliss.

Obviously a lot can happen in two days. Two hours, even—and I still had to get through these two. I wasn't about to make it easy on myself.

Martina wasn't, either. "Did everyone do their assigned reading?" She asked all the girls, but she looked straight at me. Assignment…right. I pulled the paper out of my Bible. Very handy, right where I'd left it last Saturday. My eyes flicked over the sheet.

"James, mm-hmm ," I said.

"Questions on the reading, Rory?"

"Um, no…"

"So you understand it. Great. How about summing it up in your own words."

Most unhelpfully, this put me in mind of my dad, who used to joke about putting things in his own words—at which point he'd actually make up his own words. I squeezed back the urge to say something like, 'James shmurfum gobbit plinky doo.' Instead I said the only slightly more intelligent, "Well, maybe I didn't exactly understand."

"Let's have a look, then."

Oh, yeah, I was good. Now I could re-read the verses (for the first time) and no one would be the wiser. To make it look even better, my Bible opened right up to the first chapter of James as if by magic.

Only it wasn't magic—it was a bookmark. I stared, because I hadn't left a bookmark there. I stared harder, because it wasn't a bookmark.

"Hey," I announced. "There's twenty dollars in my Bible."

Long, burgundy-nailed fingers swooped in and plucked it away. "Yes, I know," Martina said. "I put it there."

I stared dumbly. Dumbly, as in *not saying a word*. Also dumbly as in *I'm such an idiot*.

"I would've let you keep it, if you'd found it during the week."

The girls groaned on my behalf.

"Denied," Mary K hissed.

In one of those half-minutes that stretches on for forty years or so, I realized I'd been had. And there was no wiggling my way out. Sure, I could claim that I'd read every book of the Bible except James, but what if there were other twenty dollar bills tucked in there? I could be walking around with a Bible ATM for all I knew.

You might think that under the influence of intense humiliation I wasn't able to listen to the discussion. But maybe because of all the extra blood in my big hot red head, the words Martina read were tattooed on my memory.

"'If anyone among you thinks he is religious, and does not bridle his tongue but deceives his own heart, this one's religion is useless. Pure and undefiled religion before God and the Father is this: to visit orphans and widows in their trouble, and to keep oneself unspotted from the world.'"

I didn't really think hard on them until later—maybe too late—but they were stored in my permanent memory bank.

"You okay?" Shayne asked me after our group broke up.

"Wonderful."

Allie already had a basketball under her arm; her eyes were across the room when she asked, "So, you think the guys'll want to play HORSE today?"

We followed her gaze, saw Jake and Silas glance our way. Sam didn't. He looked as if he were hanging back. I turned my back to them. Stinkin' boys, who needed them?

"You mean you guys still aren't talking?" Shayne asked, hands on hips.

"This is getting serious," Allie said. So serious she looked like she was trying not to smile.

"How'd it all start, anyway? I can't even remember." Shayne chomped her bubble gum fiercely. "This is stupid. I'm getting him over here and we're going to fix this so we can get back to normal."

Yeah, that sounded like fun. Good, horribly awkward, publicly humiliating fun. Not that awkwardness and humiliation were anything new to me, and any given Saturday night might include a dose of both and still come out pretty successful. But Martina's twenty-dollar truth test had knocked my legs out from under me. Enough for one night.

"Look, you guys," I said loudly, over the echoing sounds of bouncing balls and voices. "Forget it. Sam's like the last person in the world I want to talk to right now. Totally not worth it."

They both just gave me a weird look. In a movie, this would've been one of those funny moments when the person asks, *He's right behind me, isn't he?* Too bad it was life and not a movie. No rewind. No off button. No funny.

I looked over my shoulder and saw Sam just as he turned to walk away.

twenty-one

Sometimes life gets really uncomfortable, and you just have to run the other way.

Yes, there are times when this is a bad idea, like when you're in the dentist's chair. Or when it's your true friends making you uncomfortable.

But I couldn't help it. Nothing felt right with Shayne, Allie, Jake and Sam. It wasn't anything they did. Something had broken, and it felt better just to avoid the painful spot altogether.

A logic I wished my dentist would follow. He seemed to be a big fan of the Relentlessly Probe the Painful Spot philosophy of life. It did turn my thoughts away from my friends for a while, but since the thoughts now turned to slugging a little old guy it probably wasn't a big improvement.

I was saved when my pocket started chirping. The dentist jerked back in his chair and rolled about two feet away.

"Sorry," I said, wiping drool from my lip. "Forgot to turn off my phone."

He flapped his smooth white rubber-gloved hand with a shake of his head to match. "I have to get more procaine. Go ahead and talk while you still can."

I wasn't sure I liked the sound of that. He left the room and I checked the phone. It chirped at me a lot—sometimes calls but mostly text messages, all for Bliss from people who didn't have her new number. I'd stopped reading them days ago since they were really none of my business...plus I didn't know any of the people and they were mostly sending strings of nonsense letters. I didn't speak Textmessagese.

This one looked like a legitimate phone call. From Bliss, actually. I found the right button. "Hello?"

"Where are you? I thought you were coming over."

"So did I. My mom forgot to mention I had a dentist's appointment."

"That bites." She laughed at her little joke, or maybe at me.

"And get this: the guy's name? Dr. Hertz. Born to be a dentist."

"I guess. How's the phone?"

"It's great. It's a great phone. But maybe you should take it back. You're getting all kinds of messages."

"Not from anyone I'm interested in. That's why I got rid of it—easiest way to get them off my back."

And onto mine, a little voice said in my head. I pushed it away. Having this phone hadn't exactly scored me any points at home, either. My mom seemed impressed that I had a friend who'd give me such a nice gift. Sheelan, on the other hand, nearly burst into flames when it rang one evening and she saw me slip it out of my pocket. She was convinced she was the only seventeen-year-old in the western hemisphere who didn't own a cell phone.

Okay, I enjoyed that moment a little bit, but not as much as I'd expected.

"Have you InterFaced today?" Bliss asked.

"No, my sister brought me straight here after school." Another happy-happy-joy-joy moment for Sheelan.

"You need a smart phone. I joined you up on all of my networks. You have about two hundred new best buds."

"You did?" Bliss knew my username and password because she'd helped set me up. I guess that meant she could sign on as me.

"I know how slow your connection is at home. By the way, I figured out how we could amp that up a little. Can you get your hands on your last phone bill?"

"Maybe..." My mom always paid the bills at the same desk, and there was usually a pile of them sitting out.

"I'll explain it later. I've got to go." And she did, just like that. Click.

"Mmhmn, okay, bye," I said to no one. Dr. Hertz had walked in, and it didn't feel right just hanging up without a goodbye.

"Ready?" he asked, not bothering to hide the needle in his hand.

"Can't wait," I sighed.

At home later I got on the internet to find some good stuff for my *Fact vs. Faith* report. I thought about the books Sam had lent me, too—thought about them for the first time in a while. I guiltily wondered where they'd ended up. Under my bed, probably.

The soft *plink* of a new email coming in distracted me. I checked it out. No, not one email...about two dozen. Notifications that my InterFace friend requests had been accepted. Of course, I had to check this out.

The next hour or so was a blur of bizarre profiles, reading posts I only half understood and viewing photos that I was a bit surprised to see posted as these people's profile pictures. Even the reasonably normal-looking kids had some very interesting things to share about themselves. And by interesting, I mean eyebrow-raising. I wondered why they even wanted to be friends with me. Some of them weren't even kids. One guy was twenty-seven.

Almost without me realizing it, I was sucked into a world that I'd known was out there but had only vaguely understood, kind of like the teachers' lounge. School suddenly changed. Once it had been Us or Them; then it became Bliss or un-Bliss. Now I started seeing people as InterFacers or non-InterFacers, text messagers or non-text messagers. Some were both, or one or the other. Jasmine, for instance, didn't have a cell phone (more than once I caught her eyeing mine as if it were the Special of the Day to beat all Specials of the Day), but she did have an InterFace account. Sometimes we would exchange messages or send each other personality quizzes, though we never talked about it at school. It was like a completely separate universe, virtual unreality.

There seemed to be less and less time for actual school at school. At home, too, come to think of it. I managed to squeak out the homework assignments when necessary, but the evolution paper pretty much fell off the radar. I decided the long Thanksgiving weekend would be perfect for knocking that thing out once and for all.

Sheelan got her way and spent Thanksgiving with her 'other invitation'—Jeph Svoboda and family. The night before I got an email from Shayne:

Hey, RJ! Your sis is coming here tomorrow for my dad's Turkey Jerky. Weird, huh??? You wanna come, too? When their lovie-dovieness makes us lose our appetites, we won't even be sorry because my dad's a pretty sad cook. Just don't tell him I said that!!

Lemme know if you want to share some leather turkey, lumpy potatoes, stuffing from a box and cranberry sauce from a can, baby. WHO COULD RESIST??

Luv 'n' stuffing—SS

P.S. If any of the rest of you have a change in plans, you're invited, too. Please save me from loads and loads of leftovers.

She'd sent the email to Jake, Allie and Sam, too. I suspected a trap. Get us all there, force Sam and me to speak to each other again. A tiny part of me (a part around my heart somewhere) was tempted. After all, I wasn't really mad at Sam. I couldn't remember him actually saying anything that bad... Why had I blown up at him?

Hadn't I been the one to say the mean things? Maybe... No, wait, this was about him sharing my personal business with Jake, who then blabbed to Bliss, who made it all part of her 'séance'. And then he had the nerve to scold me for being involved in a séance that probably wouldn't have happened if he hadn't blabbed in the first place.

And even if I'd said some hasty things to Sam, he sure wasn't giving me any sort of a chance to make it up to him. He was keeping a quarantine-level distance. So much for forgiveness. Just like Bliss was always saying: a lot of the kids who called themselves Christian were quick to criticize the faults in other kids, but they didn't seem to notice it in themselves.

I replied, just to Shayne:

Thanks, Shayne, but my Gran's expecting me and I don't want her to spend Thanksgiving alone.

There. What a good Christian kid I was.

Good luck with the leftovers! -RJ

I was wrong about one thing. Well, I was wrong about more than one thing, but the first thing I realized I was wrong about was the chance of Gran Judy spending Thanksgiving alone.

When my mom dropped me off, there were two cars in the driveway already.

"Who's that?" I asked.

Mom shrugged, applying some quick mascara in the rearview mirror. "She said something about inviting some widows from her church. People who would otherwise be alone today."

"Oh." I pictured little old ladies bearing scrumptious homemade pies and cobblers. That might be okay.

"Help Grandma today, alright?"

"Yeah."

She looked at the car clock. She was worried about being late. I wasn't moving fast enough. Still, she felt she had to say something. "Next year we'll do our own meal, right? We'll do it up big."

"Yeah. Sure."

Still not enough. "You're probably going to have the best Thanksgiving dinner in town today, though."

"It'll be great, Mom. You'd better go."

"I suppose I'd better." She sighed. "Grandma said she'll drive you home."

"'Kay." I started to climb out. For a second I paused, like I'd forgotten something. I had memories of giving my mom a kiss before hopping out of the car, but I hadn't done that for a while. I couldn't remember exactly when I'd stopped.

"Bye, hon."

"Bye." I was out, and she was off.

What came next was a barely normal, highly memorable Thanksgiving. There were no little old ladies with pie. Gran Judy was the oldest, and she did have a pumpkin pie (the one pie I don't like). The other guests included a short, roundish woman with a tight sparkly shirt and plenty to fill it, who talked nonstop but not in English. I don't know if anyone understood her, but it didn't seem to matter. Her hands never stopped working, chopping some strange vegetables that had no place on a traditional Thanksgiving menu.

Next to Chatty Foreign Woman was a skinny balding guy with a nose like a red Christmas bulb. I'm not sure I heard him speak at all. I was alright with Silent Bald Guy, no problem. It was Huggy Bad Breath Lady who made it an especially long day. She sat next to me, and these folks were hand-holders when it came to prayer time, so I got my hand squeezed until it turned purple while she prayed over the food. If I leaned a little to my left, the smell of the corn pone was just strong enough to cover the smell of halitosis. (In case you don't watch enough TV commercials, that's medicalese for bad breath.)

But the breathing didn't stop with the *amen*. Huggy Bad Breath Lady was endlessly fascinated by me and had to talk to me for the entire meal. Mostly she asked questions.

"So, do you like to cook, Rory?"

Do microwave burritos count?

"Do you play sports?"

Sure, don't you know every tall girl is a basketball prodigy?

"Are you saved?"

I'm waiting for someone to save me right now.

"What's the square root of π?"

I can't stand pumpkin π, but I'll cram some in my mouth if it will end this conversation.

Maybe this wasn't exactly how it went, but it felt like it. Everyone else had a grand old time. When grand old Grandma Judy drove me home later with a shopping bag full of Tupperware-encased leftovers, she asked, "You sure you don't want to grab some overnight things and come stay for a day or two? We could finish that pie off tomorrow morning for breakfast."

"I've got a big paper to work on this weekend, Gran. And you don't have a computer."

She shooed the very thought of computers away with a swipe of her hand. "Never had time to learn how to use one. Never needed to." She was quiet for a minute or two. "This is the weekend I usually start pulling out the Christmas decorations. That might be fun."

She was dipping her toe in the water, testing out the beaches of Rory's First Christmas Without Her Dad.

"I've got to concentrate on the paper," I said.

As far as I was concerned, that beach was closed.

Unlike the White Witch in Narnia, I couldn't make it winter but never Christmas. All I could do was act witchy about it.

It started snowing during the night, and I could tell by the brightness of my room when I woke up the next morning that everything outside was white. I ignored it. Everyone else seemed positively tickled.

You've GOT to come.

So said Shayne at the top of this forwarded email:

That huge mound of dirt the construction crew piled down the street is loaded with snow and begging for sleds. Anyone who's got one, come over this afternoon. Let me know if you can. —Sam

Sledding. One of the few things that made Midwestern winters bearable. It must've been two years since I'd been sledding. That had been with the most horribly great person in the world to hit the slopes with.

Sledding with my dad was hazardous. He managed to find the hills that were a little too steep, the ones with the unexpected humps that projected you into midair, the ones that had a half-frozen creek at the end of the run if you skidded a bit too far. Dad always took your *No way, I'm not trying that* very seriously while he very treacherously maneuvered you into position and shoved you off, delighting in your screams. The screams almost always turned into laughter. The frozen fingers were always rewarded afterwards with a steaming cup from Edith's, the little gourmet place that mom said charged way too much for a cup of cocoa, where they put a huge dollop of real whipped cream and chocolate shavings on top. The feel and the taste of winter.

I'm not sure how long I was staring out the window, but when I turned back to the computer screen, I had big fuzzy pink and green squares dancing across my eyes. I was snow-dazzled.

Sorry, Shayne, I've got this dumb paper to write. -RJ

It wasn't an excuse. It was a legitimate reason. So why did it feel like an excuse?

That afternoon I finally located Ericson's books—not under my bed, just under a pile of papers and books next to my bed—and took them downstairs when I heard a faint chirping. Sheelan looked up from her flavored coffee, narrow-eyed. My mom came into the kitchen.

"Something's beeping in the front hall," she said.

I dug in my coat pocket for Bliss's phone. "Hello?" No answer, because it was a text message. Sheelan snorted at my mobile incompetence.

Look in your driveway.

I went to the living room window. Nothing in the driveway. Then a black car with tinted windows peeled up and nearly took out the lamppost. Three long honks.

I fumbled with the phone's tiny buttons. *WU?*

Picking you up. She typed so fast, she didn't even need shorthand. And she probably knew I couldn't read it anyway.

I couldn't decide how to respond. Where are you going? Maybe. The phone rang because I took too long.

"Hey," I said.

"Come on."

"Where?"

"For a drive."

With angry Cody in the postage-stamp sized backseat? Not so tempting. "Um, I'll have to ask my mom." I heard them both laughing. Was I on speakerphone? "Hang on."

Mom was watching me expectantly in the kitchen. "Well?"

"Bliss wants me to go with her."

"Where?"

"Just driving, I guess."

"Who's driving?"

"A neighbor kid, Cody. He's a senior." Here it was, my handy excuse. Take it away, Mom.

"Do I know him? Do you know him, Sheelan?"

"Cody? A senior? Must be Cody Desplat." She gave a one-shoulder, I-could-take-him-or-leave-him shrug.

This was where my mom was supposed to hand me the one-way ticket to No-town. Instead, she said, "I suppose you'll be bored if you're just hanging around the house all day."

"Well, I have a big paper to write." There, Mom, I gave it to you on a silver platter. Just say no to cruising with Cody.

"So don't be gone all day," she said.

"It's about time," I heard a tinny little voice say. I put the phone back to my ear. "So get out here," Bliss was saying. She'd heard the whole thing.

As we tore out of the driveway, my knees crammed up almost to my ears, I figured it all out. This was the day we always dragged the tree and the boxes of decorations out of the attic. Mom wasn't just avoiding Thanksgiving this year. It was beginning to look like she might just try to avoid Christmas, too.

twenty-two

Life had just gotten significantly more uncomfortable. Cody lacked a basic understanding of physics and would actually speed up before taking corners. I suppose he liked the way his tires squealed. Or maybe he wanted us to squeal, but Bliss only sneered at him, while I clung silently to the back of the passenger seat for dear life.

It became obvious that Bliss did have a destination. We bulleted down Highway 2—Sam's house whizzed by, even the big snowy mound that had beckoned to him that morning, empty now—and sped towards Westhaven.

Unlike Whitestone, Westhaven had a bit of history. There was an old downtown district (about four blocks of old-fashioned storefronts along Main Street), which was already festooned with red ribbons and twinkly lights in the trees. The place was packed with shoppers.

Cody double-parked in front of one of the few shops that didn't have a Santa or a tree or a nativity scene in its window display. There was simply a curtain of midnight blue velvet that puddled on the floor, a silver tray with three bottles of different shapes and sizes but all a swirly white glass, and a sparkling crystal the size of a plum hanging from an invisible string.

I looked at the used book store to the right and the barbershop to the left. "I think this used to be a gourmet candy shop," I said. I didn't think—I knew. It had been Edith's. Who would want to change a candy shop into a…a what, exactly? I stepped back and looked at the wooden plaque that swung over the door. *The Gloaming*, it said, then in smaller letters beneath, *Cures and Curios.*

Cures? Obviously these people had never had one of Edith's hot cocoas after sledding. Nothing could cure better than that mountain of chocolate-sprinkled whipped cream.

Bliss pulled the door open with a tinkling of bells. "Well, it's Tam's shop now. Come on in."

If she hadn't told me it was Tam's place I would've known anyway, because it smelled like Tam. It smelled like about a hundred Tams. The wave of earthy, sweet perfume engulfed me, poured into my lungs and maybe altered my DNA.

Gone were the round, red-vinyl cushioned stools and the little round tables. Gone the glass cases with the glass plates perfectly stacked with handmade chocolates and fudges. Ice cream, gone. Soda, cocoa. Gone.

There were plenty of people, though. I eyed them accusingly. What ever happened to loyalty? Edith was booted out (or whoever ran the place in Edith's name), and everyone was perfectly happy to come and buy…

I picked up a bottle off a glass shelf. Evening primrose oil. Oh, yeah, who needs fudge when you can have evening primrose oil?

"That's wonderful stuff," a voice said in my ear, "for eczema, arthritis, PMS—"

I quickly set it down. Tam gave my shoulder a squeeze. "How nice to see you here, Rory. And Bliss, thank you." She took the folder Bliss was holding out to her. "I can't believe I forgot this, today of all days. You're an angel to bring it. See how busy we are? Isn't it wonderful?"

"Just great," Bliss said with about the same level of excitement I'd showed when my mom told me I was going to the dentist. "It's crowded, so we'll get out of the way."

"Don't go yet. Show Rory around first. I have to go help this customer, excuse me, ladies."

Bliss showed me around with a wave of her hand that said *Here it all is, look if you care*. I spied a handpainted sign above the door: FOLLOW YOUR BLISS, it said. She saw me noticing it and shrugged. "She's had that thing forever, hangs it wherever she goes. It's her life philosophy."

"So, what came first, you or the sign?"

"It inspired my name." She rolled her eyes. "I hate that thing."

Tam was ringing up a sale at the register but looking at us. I glanced at a few things to be polite, reading bottles until I came across some embarrassing 'cures'; examining objects whose purpose remained a mystery—except for the candles. Candles everywhere, some of them already burning, with heavy fragrances that made me fuzzy in the head. And the books. Astrology, deep ecology, astral projection, whatever that was. Ecoactivism. Some of the titles suggested topics that I could only begin to understand and uses I could barely suspect—but just enough of a suspicion to make me embarrassed all over again.

One title caught my eye. *Communicating With Your Angels*. I pulled it from the shelf, and at the same time I became aware of the music droning softly in the store. The sounds, the thick sweet smells, brought me back to the Halloween party, the white living room… I could almost taste guacamole and sickness in my mouth.

"You can borrow that if you want." A woman I assumed worked there came up alongside me. "Friends are allowed to use this like a library."

"No, it's okay." I almost threw the book down. I just wanted to leave. "I feel funny."

"Really." She inspected me. "Maybe someone or something," and she nodded meaningfully, "wants you to read that book."

"I think I just need oxygen," I said. But everywhere I tried to move, a customer stepped in my way. I dodged and skirted and changed course; it felt like I was moving farther away from the door. "Excuse me," I finally said, just pushing my way through. With a tinkle of bells, I was out on the sidewalk.

In what felt like half an hour but was less than half a minute, several things hit me. First the cold air, smelling like dusty snow and car fumes, but a relief all the same. Then the tinkling of the door behind me as Bliss followed me out; both of us looked up as Cody laid on the horn. Still double-parked and causing a car clog, he had also turned his stereo up and the bass vibrated the air.

My eyes lifted to look beyond him at the opposite side of the street. The one other shop without Christmas decorations was a little bakery. Its door swung open and out stepped Allie. Followed by Jake and Shayne. Then came Sam, holding a brown paper bag.

I lunged for Cody's car. The door was locked. He flicked the locks, then pressed them again before I could open the door. I could see him laughing. He did it again.

I looked up; Sam was looking back at me. I pretended I was looking at something else, that I hadn't seen him. Now Shayne was waving, but still I made like I didn't notice. By the time they called my name, I was already climbing into the car and could therefore say I didn't hear them.

Didn't change the fact that they'd seen me coming out of a Wiccan wonderland with Bliss Hathaway on the day I was too busy 'writing my paper' to go sledding with them.

I skipped the Scene the next day. It was easy, because Jeph wasn't driving. Sheelan had talked him into going to the Super Everything Youth Experience instead. I heard her convincing him on the phone, sweetly pointing out the fairness of it all. (Nevermind that Jeph hadn't missed a Scene in like three years.) All I had to do was have her tell Jeph that I wasn't feeling well, so I wouldn't need a ride—from whoever ended up driving. Piece of cake.

The cake tasted like cardboard.

Maybe you've noticed: when there's something you really should be thinking about that you don't want to think about, there are a million distractions in life to help you bury it. Kind of like slathering that cardboard cake with double-fudge frosting and ice cream—you know underneath it's the most unsatisfying treat in the world, but you keep on chewing and smiling.

I spent Saturday evening alone at home. Ever since my experiences home alone earlier that year, I didn't do it much. But now my mom was taking more and more late waitressing shifts, and she could barely keep Sheelan home on weeknights, let alone weekends. Even so, I'd sometimes be babysitting for the Fishers or hanging out at Grandma Judy's, so home alone didn't happen a lot.

I didn't mind so much this time. I parked myself in front of the computer with a bowl of cereal—okay, two bowls—and wrote my paper. Okay, not my paper. I went on InterFace for three straight hours. I had messages from people I didn't know but who seemed determined to change that; photos of other people in their fairy costumes (apparently there's a whole sub-culture of overgrown fairies out there, and they mistook me for one of their own); games to play against some people I did know (Jasmine and Tiffany, who I guess had forgiven me for not voting for her, even though I had) and some people I didn't. I even got invited by instant message to chat with a girl named Angelica Lyte. I saw she was in Bliss's friend network. Which was now my friend network.

There's something electric about encountering another real, live person when you're clicking around in internet outer space, like when you stick your hand in the pocket of a coat you haven't worn for months and find some money, or a candy bar that got pushed to the back of your sock drawer. It's a bonus—you can't help but grab it. Especially when you're home alone.

I exchanged hellos with her.

Fairy316: *So you're Bliss's friend?*
Angelyte: *I know her. You go to her school, right? West something?*
Fairy316: *Whitestone Elementary*
Angelyte: *Right. Named after the town.*
Fairy316: *Yep. Original, I know. Where are you?*
Angelyte: *Not far from you.*
Fairy316: *I'm clicking on your profile now...hey, no fair.*
Angelyte: *??*
Fairy316: *no photos!*
Angelyte: *That's because my people believe when a camera takes your picture, it captures your soul.*
Fairy316: *oh*
Angelyte: *Just kidding. My dad won't let me post a photo yet. He's not sure about this InterFace stuff. All the perverts and weirdoes, you know.*
Fairy316: *LOL*
Angelyte: *gotcha*

We must've chatted for a good half hour, maybe more. She was easy to talk to, almost like it was just another me talking back to myself. I even told her about my awkward moment outside The Gloaming the day before.

Angelyte: *I think I know that shop.*
Fairy316: *Lots of potions, used to be a chocolate shop? In Westhaven.*

Angelyte: *That's the one.*

Fairy316: *Well, I was walking out, and there they all were, across the street.*

Angelyte: *The friends you stood up?*

Fairy316: *Ouch. I guess you could call it that.*

Angelyte: *Oops.*

Fairy316: *Now I suppose I'll just have to hide from them until I die of old age.*

Angelyte: *Why, because you decided to hang out with someone else, or because they saw you coming out of a New Age shop?*

Fairy316: *I don't know. Both, maybe.*

Angelyte: *I'm guessing they're Christians.*

Fairy316: *Yeah.*

Now I'm forced to admit that my pinky finger hopped over and hit the 'return' key. Wicked pinky, weakest of all digits. But in my shame, before she could think otherwise, I quickly added:

Fairy316: *so am I.*

Angelyte: *That's cool. So what's their problem? They afraid you'll convert to the other side?*

Fairy316: *Well, we've been talking about avoiding this kind of stuff in our youth group.*

Angelyte: *So you're only supposed to hang out with other Christians?*

Fairy316: *I don't think so...*

Angelyte: *I'm no expert in religious stuff, but aren't you guys supposed to be Sugar and Spice to the world, something like that?*

Fairy316: *salt and light*

Angelyte: *Whatever. How can you be that for the world if you're not allowed to get out into the world?*

Fairy316: *Yeah, well, we've been talking about that, too.*

Problem was, I hadn't been listening very well.

> **Angelyte:** *Just be careful.*
> **Fairy316:** *of what?*
> **Angelyte:** *Of friends who start telling you who you can and can't be friends with. Especially when it's based on religion.*
> **Fairy316:** *Has it happened to you?*

I had to wait a while for her answer. Maybe she was deciding what was safe to tell me. Maybe she was just a slow typist like me.

> **Angelyte:** *When my best friend became a Christian. She tried to be all nice about it, but it was obviously eating her up inside that I wasn't exactly like her. I mean, I think the Bible's got lots of good stuff in it, but she just couldn't accept the fact that I had some different beliefs.*
> **Fairy316:** *Like what?*
> **Angelyte:** *Oh, I could go on and on. The point is, there's a lot we had in common. I'm all about angels, and Jesus was an awesome teacher. But come on, you've got to admit: the idea that, in this whole wide world, with all the different cultures and religions, saying that a Jewish carpenter born 2000 years ago in the middle of nowhere is the one and only way to God and heaven and all that? It doesn't make a lot of sense.*

It was strange. Bliss had said almost the same thing on the way home from Westhaven yesterday.

> **Angelyte:** *Don't get me wrong, I totally respect your beliefs. I know that's your truth. But God is big, right? He can reach out to people in a lot of ways, with a lot of different names. If more people believed that, I think this world would be a peaceful place.*

It sounded so good. In my memory I saw the graceful script painted across the upper wall in Tam's shop: *Diversity, Harmony, Peace.* Who could argue with that? No little alarms buzzed in my head at any of these warm and fuzzy thoughts. Why should they?

Surely a Christian could navigate through the world without making waves, splashing everyone else in the face, giving Christianity a bad name. I wasn't an in-your-face kind of person; getting along was more my style.

I sat back in the chair, feeling more comfortable than I had in a while. All I had to do was be myself, just the way God made me, and everything would be alright. Keeping it real, humble old me.

I heard a gentle *ding*, different from Angelyte's *bleep*. The little window for my old instant message application popped up into the corner of the screen.

>**samIam:** *You there?*

I froze while it slowly registered in my brain. Then, the *bleep*.

>**Angelyte:** *You still there?*

My fingers hung over the keyboard.

>**Fairy316:** *Yeah. I just got another IM.*
>**Angelyte:** *Let me guess. One of those friends.*

Ding.

>**samIam:** *Where were you tonight?*

Bleep.

>**Angelyte:** *What do they want?*

> **Fairy316:** *to know why I missed youth group tonight*
> **Angelyte:** *Uh oh, here you go. The God Police!!*

Ding.

> **samIam:** *If you're there, can we talk?*

Bleep.

> **Angelyte:** *If you need to go, just go. I get it.*

My hand settled on the mouse. I couldn't manage instant message ping pong. One of them had to go. My eyes kept moving back to Sam's last words. Why, when any other day of my life I would've leaped all over that invitation, why now did it have all the appeal of a cardboard cupcake? But still...

I clicked on a little red button to make one of the windows disappear. Part of me shriveled up inside, but I did it anyway.

Bleep.

> **Angelyte:** *Still with me?*
> **Fairy316:** *Yeah. I was talking to you first.*
> **Angelyte:** *And if you want to hear a sermon, you'll go to church tomorrow, right?*
> **Fairy316:** *right*
> **Angelyte:** *Now, tell me more about you, Rory. I feel like I'm just getting to know you.*

Funny, I kind of felt that way myself.

twenty-three

My brain was everywhere except where it should've been.

Mentally I had taken up residence in the world of InterFace. I couldn't believe what some of these other kids—some older, but a lot of them my age—were doing and writing about. I began to look at my own life as Bliss must see it. If this was the sort of world she'd come from, Whitestone had to seem like the Land that Time Forgot, or just a bad dream.

Dreams. I'd got to thinking about them, too. The lack of them, really. When I tried, I couldn't remember a single dream from the last two weeks at least. I know dreams are mostly forgotten, but usually there's this sense of them that lingers for a while: fuzzy pictures, emotions, some kind of meaning that keeps just outside your grasp. I searched for this, but even right after I woke up, I had nothing. Not the nothing of a deep night's sleep, either. More than just blankness. Darkness, almost thick enough to touch.

And because these distractions weren't enough, I also kept seeing the words *If you're there, can we talk?* In my imagination, I had answered him a hundred times, had a hundred different conversations. Most of them went something like this:

> **samIam:** *If you're there, can we talk?*
> **REJoyce316:** *I'm here.*
> **samIam:** *Why'd you miss the Scene? You're not really sick.*
> **REJoyce316:** *Am so. Sick of feeling out of place, out of sync, out of my mind.*
> **samIam:** *You wouldn't be if you just did the right things.*
> **REJoyce316:** *Such as?*
> **samIam:** *Be a better Christian, a better friend.*
> **REJoyce316:** *If I am, will things be like they were at first, when you and Jake and Shayne and Allie and I were friends?*
> **samIam:** *Don't worry. Just do as we say and we'll forgive you.*
> **REJoyce316:** *Great! I don't know what I was thinking, having other friends, thinking original thoughts, all that. Thanks for setting me straight.*
> **samIam:** *No problem. Anytime you want to feel judged or not good enough, you can count on your Christian friends.*

Yes, it sounds stupid to me now, too. But daydreams can be a lot like night dreams—at the time, they seem very plausible. Only later when you talk about them do they sound ridiculous. I didn't talk about these particular daydreams with anyone, so my imagined conversations with Sam grew into imagined confrontations, then nasty little imagined spats that made me avoid my email and the phone and the front steps on Tuesday and Thursday afternoons.

Daydreams pose an additional challenge—they can strike at the worst possible times. Like when you're standing at the board in your classroom, dry erase marker in hand, with your back to a class that's starting to laugh and make comments.

How long have I been standing here staring at you? I silently asked the algebra problem. It gazed back at me with its ornery X and wistful Y. Never get in a staring contest with an algebra equation.

"Solve for Y, Rory," Mrs. Palmer said, I'm guessing not for the first time.

If I could solve for Y, life would be so tidy. For instance:

Y did Mrs. Palmer always seem to get one of her headaches after she called on me?

Y did my armpits have to get so soggy at times like these?

Y did Jasmine look slightly disgusted whenever she looked at me lately? (And did it have something to do with my soggy armpits?)

Y did my mom think working all the time would help her escape the holidays?

Y did we say 'happy holidays' and 'winter break' when it used to be Merry Christmas and Christmas break?

…Y did my dad have to die over Christmas break?

Y didn't I have night dreams anymore?

"Rory?" Mrs. Palmer was rubbing her temple.

"Sorry," I said, managing a helpless half-smile. "I kind of draw a blank when I get up here."

"Someone else want to give it a try? Ronnie, come on up. Rory, sit."

That wasn't so terrible. No one seemed to care if my brain imploded when I stood in front of the class. Or so I thought. After school, Mrs. Palmer asked me to stay for a minute.

"What happened during math today?" she asked.

"Oh, that? I lost a staring contest with X and Y." I sighed. "It's bizarre. My mind totally blanks when I get up there."

"I know you can do that problem. It's just like the ones you've been doing in your homework." She shuffled through a stack of graded papers and pulled one out. I recognized my handwriting. I also recognized the assignment I'd copied off Bliss in my big hurry. With several red marks on it. "Though I think maybe your mind 'blanked' a little on this one," she added, watching me over her glasses.

I fought the redness I felt creeping into my face. "Math isn't my strong subject."

"Actually, you're doing quite well, your little drama up at the board notwithstanding."

Drama? I straightened up a bit. "It wasn't an act. I'm just not a math genius, I'm sorry."

"No, you're not a genius. So what? Join the club: it's called the rest of the class. Why not just give it a shot? What I see isn't a girl who can't do it—I see a girl who doesn't want to try and fail in front of everyone. Could this thing you're trying to pass off as humility really be pride in disguise?"

Pride? I gave her the mouth-slightly-open look. I'd say I was the poster child for low self-esteem, but I was more like the mascot of low self-esteem, the kind of mascot trapped in the big clumsy costume that little kids like to kick in the shins. "Wow," I finally said. "That would be great, because it would mean I had something to be proud of."

She shook her head. "I'm talking about a different kind of pride. Be careful, Miss Joyce. It's the sort of thing that's hard to spot in yourself. It covers its tracks—camouflages by its very nature."

It would be neat to occasionally understand the stuff adults say.

So why did I keep ending up over at Bliss's house? Now there were two women who'd mastered the mysterious sounds-like-English-but-does-not-compute language of adults. But Sylvie and Tam talked to me as if I was perfectly capable of understanding, and that made me want to.

Bliss just wanted me to help plan a holiday assembly. After school she would pass my locker and say, "Coming?" On those days I ended up at her house.

We didn't do much holiday planning. "Forget it," she finally decided. "There's no point in doing a Winter Holiday thing. Thanks to school policy, all we're allowed is candy canes and 'Jingle Bells'. But it's all good—I've got way bigger plans for an Earth Day celebration."

"You mean that day in April? I think we had an assembly last year—some people came and talked about being 'green'—but I wouldn't call it a celebration."

"That's because I wasn't in charge of it. I might as well put this student council position to some use."

Since April wasn't exactly ready to burst out in bloom, we mostly just sat around the kitchen island and talked. Well, Bliss flipped open her laptop and got on InterFace while Tam and Sylvie talked to me. Lots of questions. This was embarrassing for all of three minutes; then, I admit, the 'all about me' part of me began to enjoy it. When adults show that kind of interest in you, it's hard to resist.

Some of their questions were a little out there, but Tam really flew in from left field when she asked, "Has there been anything unusual about your dreams lately?"

My face gave it away before I even had a chance to think about how to answer that. Tam nodded. "I thought so," she said. "Vivid dreams? You wake up feeling like there's something urgent to do?"

"Well, not..." I searched for the thing to say. I don't know what I was concerned about most, making myself look good or not making her look bad because she was wrong. I can say this: the truth is always simplest. I ended up telling the truth, but only because I didn't come up with a more attractive alternative. "I've had those kinds of dreams, but lately I haven't had any."

"Any vivid ones?"

"Any dreams at all. It's been weird. You know how usually you wake up with that feeling that you've been doing something or seeing and hearing something, even if you can't remember what it was? I don't even have that."

Tam and Sylvie exchanged a look. Tam reached across the shiny black countertop and laid a hand on my arm. "Are you sleeping soundly? Waking up and finding it's morning already, when it feels like you just closed your eyes?"

"No, I wake up and go back to sleep a lot. The nights seem long."

She said nothing, but her forehead scrunched up.

"Why?" I asked. "Is that bad?"

Now she squeezed my arm and smiled, the kind adults use to reassure you without knowing how unreassuring they look. "Life is rarely as simple as good and bad, black and white. And I can't say for certain without exploring further with you, but I suspect it's not that you aren't dreaming. It's just that something is blocking your dreams."

I tried to swallow, but I didn't seem to have any saliva. "Something…like something I ate?" Grandma Judy hadn't been by recently, so most of my dinners had come from the microwave, a can, or a cereal box.

"Dreams certainly can be affected by natural causes, but in cases like yours, I would suspect the supernatural."

"You mean…"

"We've all sensed a strong spiritual aura around you, Rory. I believe your lack of dreams has a spiritual cause. I don't know the reasons, but something or someone may be trying to communicate with you, and perhaps you are most open to it in a sleeping state."

A chill raced up my right arm and down my right leg. A thrill or a warning, I was too muddled to tell. "Has it ever happened to you?" I asked.

"From time to time. I usually interpret it as someone trying to get my attention, so I help them by seeking them out in return."

"And by 'someone', you're talking about…"

"Someone who has thrown off the mortal coil, gone on to the next great adventure—or perhaps gotten lost along the way. Death isn't an evil to be feared. It is simply the natural ending of one state of being and the beginning of the next. It is a metamorph—"

"You think some dead person is trying to talk to me?" I pulled my arm away. My voice quivered a little. "Is that what you're saying?"

"Don't be upset, dear. I only mention it because I believed you would be more open to the idea than most—

"Because of my dad—you figured I'd want—" I didn't even know how to finish that one.

She shook her head with a look of pity. "Because your faith includes belief in an eternal soul. The everlasting spirit. Not everyone believes even that much."

"Not sure I do," Bliss contributed, her eyes glued to her laptop, fingers tick-tacking the keys.

Tam smiled indulgently at Bliss, like a mother cat who knows her kitten is testing its claws on a bigger doggie than it can handle, but that it will come scrambling home smarter for it.

Sylvie came up beside me and offered to refill my glass of unsweetened green tea. "Thanks, I'm good," I said.

"You are, aren't you?" She was dressed more casually today, but still a crisp, expensive-store-mannequin kind of casual. She smiled, all glistening teeth and blond hair. "You have a good heart, Rory. Trust it. It will lead you to what's true. Ultimately we find truth through our experience, our conscience, and our reason."

"She's right," Tam said. "So I can't help but think, Rory, that you don't mention your father by accident. I would never wish to put you in an uncomfortable situation, but if he or anyone else is reaching out to you, I might be able to help you."

Uncomfortable? I wasn't sure the word adequately described how I felt every time I passed the white-carpeted living room. Could she have already forgotten the blood-red candle wax and the guacamole-green…recycled guacamole? But the carpet was pristine white again, as if all of that had never happened.

They were all watching me, even Bliss, though her fingers were still tapping. "I don't know," I murmured. "No. Not my dad. That's not… No."

She squeezed my arm again. "Perhaps someone—something—else?"

They were so focused on me, so interested. It was like the nitrous oxide at the dentist; it make me feel weird and giddy. "In my dreams I used to… It was almost like I'd get messages, or visits…"

"From your spirit guide?" Tam pounced on it.

Was I really about to talk about this? "From angels."

They all looked at each other. There was no skepticism there, not even in Bliss's face. Tam's voice sounded especially smooth, as if she were making an effort to keep it that way. "But they haven't been communicating to you lately?"

I shook my head.

"Maybe it is time you reached out to them." She nailed me in place with those searching eyes, the same iron gray as her hair. "You think about it, do what you feel is right. I'll make the preparations, and if you like you can even come back tomorrow."

"But for now, how about joining us for some sushi? Then Tam can drive you home."

Food. Home. Ordinary things I understood. "Thanks, that'd be great."

Later I sat at home, discovering that I couldn't simultaneously digest sushi and write an essay on American poet, Walt Whitman.

So I flicked on the tube, decided against one of my least favorite sitcom re-runs, and flipped to the Amazing Nature Channel. My ears perked up at the words *survival of the fittest*. That was the whole gist of that natural selection stuff we'd talked about for evolution; maybe I'd get some ideas for my paper.

I watched as the lions crept belly-low through the yellow savannah grass, inching their way towards the herd of grazing antelopes or gazelles or whatever they were called. The lions wanted to call them dinner. But something warned one of the gazelles; the whole herd sprang into motion. The lions could barely keep pace as their dinner darted, swerved and turned like one massive creature with a thousand horns and hooves.

Then it happened: one swerved left when the others went right, and suddenly it was singled out.

"No, dummy," I cried to the TV gazelle, "stay with the others! Don't you ever watch these programs? Nope...you're done for."

And down she went under a mountain of fangs, fur, and muscle. For the first time, I realized how little enjoyment I got from these nature programs. Either you followed the lion families around and worried about them starving, or you followed the gazelles around and worried about them being eaten. They called it the 'circle of life' or the 'lethal beauty of nature', but it always seemed to end in death.

If that was natural — how the world was supposed to be — why did it feel so wrong?

If I'd followed that thought to its logical conclusion, I would've ended up in a much better place. Instead, another thought jumped in and short-circuited my logic boards.

What if I could still somehow communicate with my dad? Even just a few words...

Was it wrong?

I shoved the thought away. Even if it were possible, it had to be wrong.

But what about my angels? Hadn't God first sent them to communicate with me? Why not reach out to them? How could it even happen, unless God allowed it to? If it were wrong, He wouldn't let it happen. So if it worked, it must be okay.

This was too much to grapple with by myself. But I knew someone I could talk to about this sort of thing. I looked at the computer; the screen saver comet streaked in beckoning rainbow trails. I sat, took a deep breath, typed, *If you're there, can we talk?*

I clicked the send button and waited. Behind me, hyenas came and stole the gazelle carcass from the lions. The narrator spoke of lion cubs and starvation.

The computer did nothing. The hyenas hooted and laughed so loudly I had to turn and look. Now they snapped at each other, fighting over the scraps. Creepy, obnoxious things.

Bloop.

I smiled and turned back to the computer.

Angelyte: *Yeah, I'm here, and I'm all ears.*

twenty-four

"Coming?"

I pressed my locker quietly shut, twisted the combination lock, felt the click-click-click of the mechanism beneath my fingertips. Each second swung in the air, slow and sticky like the flypaper in Grandma Judy's potting shed. All my reasons for saying no, and all my reasons for saying yes, got stuck hanging in the air, and I was left with only the usual response when Bliss asked for something.

"Yeah, sure."

I followed her out the school's side doors. Various cars waited along the snowy curb, but she passed them by. Apparently we'd be walking. It was a good day for it. Fresh snow had covered the dirty stuff, and even though you knew the polluted snow was right under the surface, it looked clean and bright. We crunched along, silent under a soft sky almost as white as the ground. Bliss didn't even play with her phone.

Eventually she looked at me. "I just want to say, I think it's pretty brave, what you're doing."

Brave? I didn't want to be brave. Brave suggested that I was about to do something scary. "Oh."

"I mean, you're seeking your truth, no matter what your family and friends might think."

Think? No, just move forward, don't think. No reason to mention that I hadn't exactly told my family and friends what I was about to do. Or that I wasn't sure they'd care anyway.

There was one person I'd told: Angelica Lyte. I'd been chatting with her a lot lately. We could talk about practically anything. She always made so much sense—and said things exactly the way I would've said them if I'd been able to say them that way. So when I told Angelica about Tam's offer, I was prepared to let her answer guide me.

Sounds like Tam's the only person interested in helping you right now. To really DO something, I mean. Besides, you've got to find a way to start dreaming again. I've heard that if you don't dream, after a while you go nuts... Hey, you don't have a history of mental illness you're keeping from me, do you?? LOL

Okay, there were a few things we hadn't talked about yet.

Soon we were clomping our boots on the *LeVey* doormat, shedding our coats inside the door. Journey walked out of the kitchen, already out of her school uniform and back into her black garb. She sipped a mug of something steamy as she passed us, saying nothing. Her eyes locked onto mine, then I thought she might've shook her head. She looked away.

There was an odd smell in the house, as if something had been burning, and then someone lit a candle or incense to cover the smell.

"Tam's getting ready in the back room," Bliss said, leading me to the suede sofa.

Instantly my palms began to sweat. This was probably a great big nothing, so why was I nervous? Whether it worked or not, it was a one-time thing. And I doubted it would work. But I couldn't stand much more of the dream blindness. Or the darkness. It's wasn't just at night anymore. I swear I could see it in the corner of my eye when I was awake, creeping around my edges. I had to do something.

"She recommends that we pray silently while she cleanses the room. I prefer meditation—you can do whatever you want." She crossed her legs on the sofa.

I sat on the edge, elbows on my knees. Pray. So... Hmm. I still wasn't very good at the prayer thing. *God*, I tried, *I'm not sure how... I don't know if...*

I just need help.

Nothing happened. Bliss closed her eyes and let out a slow breath. I watched, but it didn't look like she took a breath back in. Maybe I wasn't breathing, watching her, because I started to feel like I was suffocating. The weird smell in the house suddenly seemed like a hot, scorched smell, oil and rubber and a sick smell like burnt hair, and for a split second I imagined I was crushed, my chest gripped in a huge metal vice, and I wanted to cry out but couldn't. I was my dad, in his last moments of life. I was sure of it.

A gentle chime sounded in the front hall, and just like that, the feeling was gone. I sucked in a raggedy breath.

Bliss didn't move, but I heard footsteps on the stairs. A second later, Journey appeared.

"Someone's at the door for you," she said.

Bliss said nothing, eyes closed. I looked from her to Journey. "Should I...?" I made like I was going to shake Bliss out of her trance.

"No, not for her. You."

I blinked, then went up to see who knew I was here, when I hadn't told anybody I was here. My knees shook a little. I pulled the big wooden door inwards to a gust of delicious, clean cold air. For some reason, the house had no storm door. I shivered as I looked out on four faces I knew very well.

"Hi," Shayne said.

"We were at Jake's," Allie said, beside her. "We saw you go in."

Jake elbowed his way between them. "We were spying on you." He looked past me. "Hey, Bliss, how's it going?"

Now I could feel her right behind me, though I hadn't heard her come. So much for her deep meditative state. My eyes dragged themselves to the fourth person, whose army green coat and rusty orange cap I'd recognized without looking. His face looked pale, which made his eyes look big and black under the dark eyebrows. He gave me a nod, like he was answering a question I hadn't known I'd asked.

Bliss nudged in next to me. "Um, these are my friends," I told her. "Allie, Shayne, Sam. Guys, this is Bliss."

"Actually, they're my friends," Jake said. They ignored him, saying hello. She nodded at them, really more of a chin lift. Then she looked at me, and for some reason from me to Sam, and he looked back at her. It was an agonizing hour, or maybe just a few seconds, while they were locked in that stare like it was one of those killer handshake duels. Then Shayne dug an elbow into Allie.

"Hey," Allie said, "we know it's last minute, and we don't mean to barge in or anything, but we all managed to get together and we have sort of a surprise for you, Rory. Think you could come for a little while?"

"It's kind of a bad time," Bliss answered for me.

"That's just the thing," Shayne said quickly. "This was the only time we could get it together. You understand."

"Not really," said Bliss.

"Okay, true. But it's a surprise, so we can't really…" She petered out when Tam appeared behind us.

"Greetings, all," Tam said in a sing-song voice. "You're going to have to excuse us, I'm afraid." She turned to me, took my arm in hers and led me a few steps away, but not before giving Bliss a meaningful look.

"All is in readiness, Rory," she said softly. "It will not do to become distracted now. The moment you first entered the house, I sensed the presence around you, the one who influences your dreams. Now is the time for discovery."

"Maybe. I'm just not…"

"There is nothing to fear. The spirit world is just one more link in the circle of birth, life, death, and rebirth, as natural as wildflowers sprouting, blooming, and fading to rejoin the earth and grow again in season. It's a beautiful thing."

I could hear Bliss exchanging words with my friends, but Tam's murmur in my ear made it impossible to tell what they were saying. Then Bliss shut the door, but not all the way, and came over to us. "They need to hear it from you," she told me.

Tam squeezed my arm. "You can always join them when we're finished. It may be over quickly. Certainly an hour will be plenty. Tell them that, then you may join us below. Come, Bliss."

Bliss held my eyes for a long moment. I didn't have the feeling that she was bossing me into anything. This was important to her, for reasons I couldn't understand. "Moment of truth, Rory," she said quietly before following Tam downstairs.

Only then did I look around and realize I was standing pretty much in the very spot I'd had my guacamole incident. The carpet was spotless.

The house was suddenly freezing. The door hadn't been open that long, had it? It felt like a meat locker. I grabbed my coat from the coat rack and pushed my goosebumpy arms into the sleeves before opening the door again.

They all turned to me, and Shayne's face lit up when she saw my coat. I should've thought of that. "Hey, you ready?" she asked.

"Um, actually I was just cold."

"You're not coming?" Allie asked.

"Told you she wouldn't." Jake said it like he'd won a bet.

"Sorry," I said, "it's just—" Sheesh, was Sam trying to drill holes into me with those eyes? "I promised to do something here first, but it probably won't take that long. I could come over when we're done."

Shayne stamped her boots. "Aw, man. We're not going to be here. We're going—hang on, is it still a surprise, you guys?"

"You sure?" Allie asked me.

'Sure' wasn't a word I'd use to describe how I felt about anything lately. What I was pretty sure of, though, was that if I let these guys down, they'd still be my friends. If I let Bliss and Tam down, I wasn't sure what they'd be. Ticked off, maybe. This should've told me then and there who were the right ones to be with, but my logic was as twisted as a car wreck.

I sighed. "Sorry."

Both Shayne and Allie seemed to cast quick glances over at Sam, but he only chewed his bottom lip. So Allie just said, "Okay. Well, maybe we'll see you next time."

"Bye." Then I did it. I closed the door on them.

I blinked hard, blinked hard again, but when I opened my eyes, I could still see the blackness at the edges. But the emptiness wasn't at the edges—it was in my very center.

What difference does it make? The voice in my head sounded a lot like Angelica Lyte's. Or that's what I thought for a split second before I remembered that I'd never heard her voice.

I moved towards the kitchen. Upstairs, I saw Journey sitting in the hall, watching me. She and Sam must've taken the same stare-straight-into-their-soul-with-your-great-big-eyes lessons. I passed by and started down the steps to the family room.

Ding-ding-dong-ding.

The doorbell again. I turned back, then remembered it wasn't my house. Journey stood but then just disappeared into her bedroom. I waited, then it rang again. No one else appeared. I walked across the shining hardwood floor and opened the door.

It was Sam. Just him. He reached in, took me by the wrist, and pulled me out of the house.

twenty-five

Glad I have my coat on.

That was the best my brain had to offer at the moment. Sam led me towards Jake's house without looking at me. I somehow knew this without looking at him. His hand felt hot on my cold wrist.

My feet flopped around in my unfastened boots (I'd barely had time to step into them). My heart bounced around in my chest like a rubber ball in a coffee can. This, I told myself, was because I was gearing up for the Big Confrontation, the long-dreaded, oft-imagined showdown with Sam.

The others stood on Jake's driveway. They stared. Sam pulled me right past them while they stared. I sensed that Sam had implemented Plan B and that they had never discussed anything beyond Plan A.

We'd traveled halfway along the footpath that led to Jake's backyard before I finally wriggled my captive arm. "Alright, already. Am I a fugitive or something?"

He let go. "Practically. You don't answer Shayne and Allie's emails, you don't IM or answer your phone."

That last one wasn't my fault. Ever since Sheelan spied my cell phone, her policy was to ignore any call-waiting signals on the home phone that might be for me. But I hadn't given the cell number to my Scene friends.

"Well, if they need to tell me something—"

He stopped me from turning back, again the hand on the wrist. This time he dropped it right away. "Wait. First I have to talk to you."

"Can't we do it up there?" I gestured towards the driveway, now out of sight. What were the others thinking?

"No. They won't—" He pulled off his cap and raked his hand through his sloppy curls. "It's kind of hard to…"

Here it comes, I thought. This was where he'd finally give me a piece of his mind. And not just about the things I'd said weeks ago, but the things I'd been doing since. Angelica had warned me this was coming. Bliss had warned me this was coming. No problem, I was ready. I watched the words come to his lips and braced myself.

"I'm sorry," he said.

Hunh? I already had sass on the tip of my tongue. Now what was I supposed to do with it? "You are?"

He nodded. No hot face—he still looked pale.

"But I'm the one who said the stupid things," I said. Why did I say that? Not what you'd call an argument-winning strategy.

"Yeah, but—" He stopped himself. "What I mean is, it shouldn't matter what you said. But I let it stop me from telling you something I should've told you weeks ago."

I zipped up my coat, hugging myself against the cold. "Tell me what?"

Round and round went his hat in his hands. "It's hard to explain."

Harder than apologizing to a person who'd been a jerk to you?

"It's pretty strange," he added.

So strange things were happening to people besides myself. It was such a refreshing thought, I couldn't resist stretching out my hand. "Hi," I said. "I don't believe we've met. I'm the mayor of Strangeville. Welcome."

He shook my hand with a straight face. "Thanks. I might be relocating here."

"Always room for one more."

"Good. Because I've been having these dreams."

I dropped his hand like a hot potato. "Really."

"For the last couple of weeks, at least. Just a few at first, but more and more, now every night. And since I can't come up with of a way to say this without sounding *loco*, I'll just tell you: I think I'm supposed to tell you something."

"Really." I was stalling. Part of me—a small, shriveled part, a moldy old prune part—didn't trust Sam. Or it didn't want to trust him. It already whispered to me that Bliss must've told Jake about my undreaming problem, and Jake had told Sam, and now Sam was going to try to use it to... To do what, exactly? Lure me away from Bliss and Tam and Sylvie and the answers they always seemed to dangle just outside my reach.

Sam was no dummy. "You don't believe me."

"How can I believe or not believe what you haven't told me yet? What's the message?" Now I might be able to tell if he or Jake dreamed this up. Or why not all four of them? This could all be an elaborate joke, or a ploy to get me out of Bliss's house. Rory's hanging out too much with that obnostic girl and her freaky family. How can we rescue her? Oh yeah, tell her we had dream messages about her—she loves all that kind of stuff, angels and whatnot.

"Okay," he said with a sigh. "Hopefully it makes sense to you. I think I'm supposed to tell you that there's Kingdom work to be done, but your sword is rusting." He met my eyes, searching for some sign, some light to come on.

No light bulb dinged over my head. "That's it?"

"Yes."

"It took three weeks of dreaming to get 'Rory's sword is rusty'?"

"No. There was more than that, but… You know how dreams are. That's the part I can put into words."

"You realize I don't own a sword."

I was letting him down, I knew it. He put himself out there, and I let him flounder around like a fish in a bucket.

"You realize," he said, "that it could mean more than a sword. I know Kellie died before we got to the lesson about the sword of the Spirit—"

"I remember, Sam. I get it. The sword of the Spirit is the Word of God. You're telling me that I haven't been reading my Bible enough. Thanks. Can we go now?"

Funny thing about Sam. When you hurt him, it showed, but right underneath it was something rock solid. "No, Rory, not me. It was her. She wanted to tell you. I don't know why she didn't just visit your dreams."

"She?"

His eyes snapped up to mine. "Yes. I didn't remember until I just said it now. But there was a girl."

"A little girl."

"An older girl. Really old, I think…" His eyes got kind of fuzzy, then he came back. "But no, she looked young. A little bit scary, though—no, intimidating? But then she just looked like a regular sort of girl."

"Like what?"

"I don't know, just a girl. Have you ever met Silas's sister?"

"No."

"She looked a little like her, the hair. Not an afro, but super curly. Light brown skin. And the eyes." He went all far-away again.

"Greenish," I guessed. "Kind of lit up."

He just looked at me. Then another memory resurfaced. "Flip-flops…?" he said.

"Big book," I added. "Reads with her finger."

"How…?"

Something touched my face. I looked up into the white sky and blinked as snowflakes melted against my eyelashes. I closed my eyes and kept my face tilted back. "You know how I told you about Rafie and Micah and Gabby…and Uri."

He seemed like he would say something, but he just nodded.

"Sounds like you met Gabby."

His dark brows scrunched together, and he leaned against the brick house. "But how can—"

"Something go from my head into yours?"

"No. I never thought it was all in your head. You know that. But there's something else that's been bothering me, and what you just said—it made me remember."

"About Gabby?"

"No. Uri."

My mouth clenched up. My whole body did, really.

He pushed on. "The last time we talked—"

"Fought."

"Okay, yeah. You said something then about Uri—"

"Listen, if we're going to talk about him, could we at least not keep saying his name?"

"You're right. I'm sorry." He shoved his hands deep into his coat pockets. "But you accused me of telling Jake about…him. About all of them."

So finally we'd come to it. Only now I couldn't just be mad at Sam, plain and simple. He'd dreamed of Gabby, so now he and I were all sort of tangled up together. But that didn't make it all go away, either. "Yeah," I said, "and Jake would naturally tell Bliss, so she got to stage the whole Halloween gag with the ouija board."

He was already shaking his head, just barely. "But you never gave me a chance to tell you. I never talked to Jake about any of that."

"Well, he knew about the angels. Not their names—not from me—but he had to find out somehow. Maybe you don't even remember telling—"

"No, Rory, you don't understand. *You* never even mentioned Ur—*his*—name. Not to me. Gabby and the others' names, yes. But not his."

I could feel what he was implying hanging over me, but I refused to look it in the face. "But how could Bliss have known?" I asked stubbornly.

"If you didn't tell her, she couldn't have." His voice was quiet.

And all the dark that had stained the edges of my life these past weeks rose up like a wave that would just wash over me. Only it didn't. I stood there, shivering all the way down into the pit my chest, and I thought of where I'd meant to be right now and what we'd meant to do. I'd figured that reaching out to 'the spirit world' would be, at worst, be nothing more than a ouija board gag.

But the gag hadn't been one. And it make me want to gag all over again.

"How'd you know what we were going to do today?" I asked. My voice shook a little.

"Jake told us."

"I'm surprised Bliss told him."

"I don't think she did. He said it was her sister."

Journey? I chewed on that. Unexpected, but it made sense. She'd probably done it to get back at Bliss for something. "So," I said slowly, tilting my head towards the driveway, "they all know that I was trying to...contact my angels?"

His eyes seemed to get even bigger and darker. He shook his head. "They just know that Bliss wanted to get you involved in a séance or some kind of spiritist thing." Obviously it was the first he'd heard about the specifics.

But that wasn't all he knew. He'd known the ouija board incident must've been real. And if they hadn't come today, if he hadn't rung that doorbell a second time...? I had no doubt which 'angel' we would've contacted.

We stood there, snow collecting in our hair. I opened my mouth, wanting to say something, but it was Shayne who spoke.

"How's it going back there?" she called, peeking around the corner of the house. "Hey, you guys okay? You both look as white as ghosts."

Faintly we heard Allie comment on Shayne's interesting choice of words. Then Jake came alongside Shayne.

"Would you two just kiss and make up so we can go? Our ride's waiting."

Ride? I looked questioningly at Sam, but it was Shayne who grabbed my wrist this time and dragged me forward. "It's the surprise. You can come, can't you?"

"Come where?" But now I could see the dark blue van in the driveway, vaguely familiar. The window rolled down, and Ericson Greene leaned out with a short wave.

"Ericson's house," Shayne said, then she grinned. "It's the first official meeting of the Jesus Machine."

twenty-six

"Coming?"

That again. But this time it was Sam asking. The others climbed into the van like it was a done deal.

"I'd better tell Bliss," I said.

"Have fun," Jake called from the shotgun position. *She's gonna eat you alive,* his jolly smile said.

I shuffled through the snow to the big oak door, standing on the *LeVey* mat for a second before I raised my finger to the doorbell. The door opened before I rang.

It was Journey, but Bliss shouldered her aside. "So?" she asked.

"Well..." I searched for words, but they were like those tiny marshmallows in hot cocoa, melting away before I could scoop them up.

"Say no more." Her mouth twisted into a mocking little half-smile. "I see where this is going."

"It's just—I guess they've been planning this for a while, and they wanted to surprise me." I gestured towards Jake's house.

Sam was taking his time getting into Ericson's van. He still stood out there with a casual pose, but his eyes were on us. I turned back to Bliss and saw that her eyes were on him.

"Enjoy yourself," she said. Before she could close the door, Journey caught it and handed me my backpack.

"Don't forget this," she said. Maybe my eyes were snow-dazzled, but it looked like she was smiling.

I was hardly back at the van when a black car careened into Bliss's driveway. Bliss came out in her coat and hat and climbed into Cody's car. It had taken her all of thirty seconds to find an alternate activity.

Her window rolled down as they backed away. "Forget Tam and all that," she called. "Come with us. Last chance — you don't have to follow the herd."

Interesting choice of words. The image of a lone gazelle torn by starving lions popped into my head. "I think I do," I answered her.

She shrugged and the window went up, but not fast enough to contain Cody's bleating impression of a sheep. I climbed into the middle seat beside Allie. Sam and Shayne were in the back.

"Hey, Rory," Ericson said. "Nice to see you again."

"Yeah, you too."

"Is your mom home?"

"I think so. I'd better call her and let her know where I'm going."

But Ericson wouldn't accept anything less than driving to my house and getting permission from my mom in person. She remembered him from Kellie's funeral, recognized my friends (or at least their faces) and thankfully gave the go-ahead without anything embarrassing like a prolonged conversation.

"Just so you finish your homework and get to bed on time," she said.

"Sure, Mom."

Ericson explained as we drove away, "It was different when Kellie and I had kids over at the house together. A man alone has to be a little more... I don't know if 'careful' is the word I'm looking for."

"I understand," I said. "Thanks for doing this. It came at a pretty good time." What I meant was, *you* came at a *really* good time, and I meant it for Sam, but bursting with courage to speak from my heart I was not.

"If you feel like it, we can talk about it at the house," he said. "But there's something we need to do first."

And that something hit us the second we walked through the door, hit hard enough to make our eyes water...and our mouths. The house was saturated with the smell of meatballs.

"Have you guys ever used one of these?" Ericson cranked the handle of a metal contraption on the table.

"Looks like some kind of extruder," Sam said.

"Oh!" Shayne laughed. "It's a noodle extruder."

"A nextroodler," Jake corrected.

I confess that I'd never given a second thought to where pasta came from, other than a box. Maybe I would've guessed that it grew on bushes, I don't know. But Ericson showed us how to make fresh, homemade pasta with just flour, salt and eggs.

Sam actually seemed to know what to do already—he mounded the flour and made a well in the middle where we cracked a few eggs. Allie stirred them up carefully, blending the flour in a bit at a time. Jake tried to re-enact the eruption of Mount Vesuvius. Somehow we ended up with a ball of dough that we had to put in the fridge to cool. Ericson got a big pot of water boiling on the stove, and pretty soon we were smushing globs of dough and cranking them through the flattener part of the pasta machine, and then the 'noodler' to get long strips.

"What's this size called?" Allie asked. "Fettuccine? Tagliatelle?"

"Tapewormini," Jake said, flinging one into her hair.

Shayne refused to eat the 'worms'—until they were cooked, smothered in sauce, crowned with an enormous meatball and cozied up next to a hot hunk of garlic bread. Then she touched a whole plateful, as did I. The boys touched two platefuls and Jake inquired about possibly touching a third. We watched and groaned in horror, clutching our guts.

"How about we move to the music room?" Ericson asked after we piled our plates into a sink already almost full of dirty dishes. One of a hundred little ways you could tell that Kellie was missing.

We trooped down to the basement, which was half linoleum laundry room and half carpeted 'music room'—basically a collection of various instruments, mismatched chairs, stools and music stands, boxes of sheet music and books, and some amplifiers and other electronic equipment I didn't recognize.

"Try anything you want," he said.

Jake dove on the electric guitar, which thankfully was not connected to the amps. Allie and Shayne experimented with the electric drum pad, but Sam just sank into an olive green chair that had obviously seen a garage sale or two. I settled on the bench of the instrument most familiar to me, the piano, and plinked out a few notes from one of the two songs I vaguely remembered.

"Do you play?" Ericson asked.

"I used to. Well, I took lessons when I was like nine. Can't say I ever really played."

"Hated it?" He smiled.

"Pretty much. I wanted to play piano, but I didn't want to learn how to play. If that makes any sense."

"Perfect sense. Practice and discipline rarely appeal to a nine-year-old."

"I kind of wish I hadn't quit." It would've been pretty cool to be able to sit here right now and actually play. With five years' experience I probably would've been fairly decent.

"Life lesson," Ericson said. "But you're not a fifty-year-old, looking back and wishing. You're at a great age to take it up again."

"You think?"

"I know. The theory—the nuts and bolts of it—will make more sense now. And the discipline will come easier if you're doing it by your own choice, not just your parents'. Longer fingers don't hurt, either."

"Yeah, I guess so." I plucked up my courage. "Do you teach piano?"

"Not currently. But I used to, when I was still at the conservatory."

Jake stopped his rock star impersonation in mid-thrash. "Conservatory? Isn't that where rare little birdies live? Did you play piano for little birdies?"

"That's a sanctuary, you cornball," Shayne said. "A conservatory is like a greenhouse, right Ericson?"

"Well," he said with a laugh, "it can mean that. But it also means a school of music."

Sam scratched his head. "The real question here is, what exactly is a 'cornball'?"

"You know." Shayne rolled her eyes as if it were obvious. "Cornball. Like a…corny goofball. What?"

We giggled.

"Everyone's entitled to invent their own word now and then," Ericson said.

"Grammy does all the time," Allie said. "She loves to pinch the squidge on a baby's tookus."

"And Sammy-boy's cheekus," Jake said.

The others weren't, but I happened to be looking at Ericson when Allie spoke, and I saw a shadow cross his face. Then I remembered. By now there was supposed to be a new baby in this house. My eyes flicked over to the only other person in the room who knew, and he was already looking at me. We shared the thought of a little white rosebud tucked alongside seven red roses.

"How is your grandmother, Allie?" Ericson asked.

"She's doing better now. Thanks for the prayers."

Everyone else seemed to know what she was talking about. Why didn't I?—oh, right. Because I'd been too busy being a jerk. How sick had Grammy been?

"But it's got her thinking about all kinds of stuff. Her will and estate, all that. She'll be seventy-five next year."

"Man, that's old," Jake so helpfully contributed.

Allie didn't even react to Jake; her eyes were on the floor, where her deep thoughts gathered. "She wants to adopt me. Well, something like that. She's my grandmother and my legal guardian, but she wants to make some things a little more legal, if that makes any sense."

"Not really," Jake said, sitting on the arm of Sam's chair.

Allie straightened up and met our gazes. Her fingers were playing with her white stone amulet, turning it over and back, over and back. She looked about twenty-two all of a sudden. "If anything happens to her, she doesn't want my mother to get custody of me."

Shayne dropped a drumstick. "Your mom's alive?" she asked softly.

Allie nodded. "She's living on the west coast somewhere, I think. I never knew her. She's got problems."

"What sort of problems?" Jake asked. Sam punched him.

"No, it's okay. Mental problems. And drugs."

No one said anything. What could we say?

"At least, that's all Grammy told me at first, after I pestered her about it for like five years. But then I heard some other things, and saw some old papers, and I started to put things together last year. When I asked her about it, Grammy couldn't really hide it anymore.

"My mother overdosed when she was pregnant with me. She couldn't handle it." She shrugged and let out a slow breath. "When they found her, she was barely alive. Me, too. Two months premature, but I survived."

Her hand had closed over the white stone and rested, very still, against her chest. I knew the name on that stone: *chosen*. I knew the verse, too, because I had memorized all five of our stone verses. Ephesians 1: 4-5. *Long ago, even before he made the world, God loved us and chose us in Christ to be holy and without fault in his eyes. His unchanging plan has always been to adopt us into his own family by bringing us to himself through Jesus Christ. And this gave him great pleasure.*

The first time we had read that verse together, right after Ericson gave us Kellie's gift, Allie had cried. Now I began to understand why. If you think you're unwanted, only here by accident, how sweet is it to hear that you've been planned all along?

Allie sat up straight and smacked the drumstick against her open palm. "But none of that is the problem now," she said crisply.

"So what is the problem?" Sam asked.

"Grammy wants me to take her last name."

Shayne scrunched up her forehead. "I thought she was a Rousseau, too."

"Nope. That was my mom's name."

"I still don't see the problem," Sam said.

"Her last name is Ughi."

We all sampled the name in our heads.

"Ah," Sam said.

"Exactly." Allie sighed.

Jake made a show of holding back laughter. "Oogie?" He sniggered.

"Don't even say it, Jake," I warned.

"Say what?"

"Oh, let me see," I said. "That it's like *alley-oop* and *ugly* and *boogie* all wrapped up in one, maybe?"

He rolled off the arm of the chair. I closed my eyes, but there was no escaping this big yap moment. Sam, Shayne, and even Ericson had their lips pressed tightly shut—until Allie gave a little snort, then a giggle, and everyone else joined her and Jake in a good laugh.

"Sorry," I said. "It's just my day for doing stupid things, I guess."

We all jumped at a sudden clang from the corner of the room. Shayne stood there with a little mallet and the metal object she had just beaten with it. "Order in the courtroom," she said, holding up the mallet threateningly. She took a closer look at the metal thingy. "This reminds me of one of those bells you see cows wearing around their necks in pictures. What's it called, Ericson?"

"A cowbell."

She clanged it again. "Good name. Oh, and Rory, speaking of what you've been doing today, what was up at Bliss Halfway's house, anyway?"

That took care of our last lingering giggles. This is usually where I would launch into a long, twisted explanation of why it was perfectly sensible, or practically unavoidable, for me to be with Bliss. But something about Allie's story made all of that seem like a load of bull pucky. So I went with the short version.

"They wanted to help me talk to my dad. But I was just going to try to talk to some angels."

twenty-seven

Eyes widened.

But not Jake's. "Yeah, that's what Bliss's sister told me," he said, yawning. "Journey—she's warped. Pathetically jealous of Bliss. Anyhoo, I figured she just meant you were going to play your little ouija board game again."

"You were concerned enough to tell Sam about it," Allie pointed out.

"Only because he kept asking me about Rory."

Sam was already out of his chair, grabbing an acoustic guitar, his back to us. Since we couldn't see his face, my cheeks took up the job and went pink on his behalf.

"Well, I'm glad Sam asked," Shayne said. "We all should've been asking more, after you missed a couple of Scenes, Rory. Sorry about that."

"You know," Allie said, "the five of us really have been going in different directions."

"Yeah," Shayne said. "What almost happened to Rory today... We really haven't been..." She laced her fingers together.

"Knit together in love?" Ericson said. He lifted a Bible off a stack of books beside him. "Can I share a passage with you guys that I read this morning? I think it fits."

They nodded and found cozy spots, mostly on the floor since music stools aren't what you'd call comfortable. I stayed on the piano bench. Comfort wasn't really an option for me at the moment. Shayne had been kind to say *what almost happened to Rory*, but *the stupid thing Rory almost did* would've been more accurate and we all knew it. It wasn't like I'd hoped the evening could go by without the subject coming up, but... Well, yeah, that's pretty much what I'd hoped.

I figured Ericson was going to read about how desperately wicked it was to meddle with the spirit world.

He read: "'I want you to know how much I have agonized for you and for the church at Laodicea, and for many other friends who have never known me personally. My goal is that they will be encouraged and knit together by strong ties of love. I want them to have full confidence because they have complete understanding of God's secret plan, which is Christ himself. In him lie hidden all the treasures of wisdom and knowledge.'"

Ericson looked up. "That was Paul talking to the Colossians, but it's a good goal for us, too." He gestured around the room, so the 'us' meant *us*. My heart leapt and clicked its heels together, leprechaun-style, and I remembered what I'd once wished for but sort of lost along the way: this little crew, knit together strong. Encouragement, confidence, understanding. Imagine that.

Ericson went on, and certain passages leapt out at me.

"'I am telling you this so that no one will be able to deceive you with persuasive arguments.'"

I'd been hanging around or chatting with some pretty persuasive people lately. But deceived? Surely not me.

"'...And now, just as you accepted Christ Jesus as your Lord, you must continue to live in obedience to him. Let your roots grow down into him and draw up nourishment from him, so you will grow in faith, strong and vigorous in the truth you were taught. Let your lives overflow with thanksgiving for all he has done.'"

The words made me thirsty, more in the area of my heart than my mouth. I had accepted Jesus as Savior, but right then I knew: I had no roots. Nothing growing down into Him, soaking up strength and truth. I was about as overflowing as a forgotten cup on the back shelf, nothing but a few dry bugs at the bottom. As for thanksgiving...Thanksgiving to me had just been a day to be annoyed at my mom and my grandma's friends.

So how to get my roots to grow? *...you must continue to live in obedience to him.* Obedience. Not a word to send shivers of excitement through my soul. But did I want to be a tree without roots? Like a too-tall woodland fairy, ready to topple over at the slightest push? The clumsy, jolly green giant of faith?

"'Don't let anyone lead you astray with empty philosophy and high-sounding nonsense that come from human thinking and from the evil powers of this world, and not from Christ. For in Christ the fullness of God lives in a human body, and you are complete through your union with Christ. He is the Lord over every ruler and authority in the universe.'"

Ericson paused again. "I don't want you to miss the meaning of 'rulers and authorities'—he uses these again in verse fifteen when he says 'God disarmed the evil rulers and authorities. He shamed them publicly by his victory over them on the cross of Christ.' Some translations use the phrase 'principalities and powers'."

My ears snapped to attention. I'd heard those words before. In the Armor of God passage in Ephesians.

"Satan and his demons," I heard myself say. "So you're saying that God has taken care of the evil spirits for us."

"Paul is saying that on the cross, Christ achieved victory over the spiritual forces of evil. And that in Christ that victory becomes ours, and we are free from any power they might have over us."

"So evil spirits are powerless against us," Jake said in his Deep Drama voice.

"Incorrect," Ericson said. "They are powerless against Christ. Remember, the choices we make, the way we live our lives—though none of that earns us or costs us our salvation, ungodly choices leave us vulnerable. And Satan wants nothing more than to lay waste to the followers of Christ wherever he can."

He picked up a guitar and absently began removing a broken string. He said, "When we engage in activities that God condemns—" The string jangled. "—we leave ourselves wide open to attack."

Everybody made it a point not to look at me, which felt almost exactly as if they'd all stared at me.

"But when we talk about obedience to Christ, it isn't just a simple matter of following some rules. A lot of people get this confused. Rory, can you read the rest of Colossians 2 for me while I fix this? Here, pick it up with the twentieth verse."

I cleared my throat. My voice shook anyway, but only a little, only at first. "'You have died with Christ, and he has set you free from the evil powers of this world. So why do you keep on following rules of the world, such as, "Don't handle, don't eat, don't touch"? Such rules are mere human teaching about things that are gone as soon as we use them. These rules may seem wise because they require strong devotion, humility, and severe bodily discipline. But they have no effect when it comes to conquering a person's evil thoughts and desires.'"

Jake rubbed his hands together. "So we toss the rules out the window. Coolness."

"Just the man-made ones, Cornball," Allie said.

"That's legalism, and it's just another way we try to save ourselves," Ericson said. "But when *God* says 'don't touch', I advise that you listen. And when it comes to the spirit world, He definitely says 'don't touch'."

Shayne's hand shot up.

"I don't think you need to raise your hand, Shayne," Sam said. His head practically rested on the curve of the guitar in his lap, and the fingers of his left hand were finding chords though his right hand wasn't strumming.

"I just have a question. I know that it's wrong to use astrology and to try to communicate with the spirits and know the future and all that, but I've got to admit, I don't know why exactly."

"Because it says not to in the Bible," Allie said. "What more do you need?"

"But Shayne asks the question we all should ask," Ericson said. "God's rules aren't just arbitrary. He ultimately seeks our good and His glory. But what are we doing when we try to see the future, or gain knowledge, through some supernatural means?"

"Playing God," I guessed.

"You could say that, yes. Ultimately, we're seeking hidden knowledge that God has not revealed. Or hidden power, so we can control our own destinies. We're not trusting Him."

Jake stole a drumstick from Allie and tapped it on a music stand. "You know," he said, "I can understand about not conjuring up demons or putting spells on people, but come on. At the Scene they were talking about the hideous evils of horoscopes and stuff. It's just fake and stupid, for fun. Do you know anyone who was damaged because they 'tried something different on Thursday' or 'watched out for a new love interest at work'? Or ouija boards. Other than making Rory puke green, what's the big scary?"

"One person's 'board game' is another person's enticement to investigate further, take it to the next level." Ericson snapped off the extra bit of guitar string with wire cutters, then started twisting the little knobs to tune the guitar. "Fantasy can be the bridge to reality. It wasn't so long ago that kids were just reading books about witches and wizards and watching witchy-teen sitcoms. Now there are loads of kids who consider themselves witches, with their own altars and magic spells. Fantasy triggers a need—in this case for something spiritual, something empowering—and something real will show up to fill it." He strummed a chord in a minor key.

Sam echoed it with his guitar. "But when Rory took part in the séance—"

"Jake was there, too." I couldn't help it.

"When Rory and Jake were involved in that, they were still safe, right? I mean, don't we have a special protection in Christ, like it just said in Colossians?"

Ericson's fingers moved over the strings, and for a moment we forgot about the question and just marveled at the music. Moments like that are never long enough. "Yes," he finally answered, slowly. "*In* Christ. The protection comes from walking in His path. You are also indwelt by the Holy Spirit, which most Bible scholars agree means you can't be possessed by an evil spirit. That doesn't mean you can't be oppressed by one, if you allow a foothold."

Shayne clanged the cowbell, and we all jumped. "Come on, guys," she said. "This is kind of freaking me out."

At the same time, Jake turned to me and said, "Well, Rory, I guess with you it was just a guacamole rerun and not demon puke, after all."

I gaped at him.

"Not at all funny, Jake," Allie said.

"What? Come on. That was all just a staged show for a Halloween party. You guys are like a bunch of little kids telling spooky stories at summer camp."

"Haven't you heard a thing we've talked about?"

"Haven't you considered that it could be a case of overactive imaginations—"

"Guys." I heard the quiet warning in Ericson's voice, but my eyes and most of my mind had drifted. I had partly turned away, leaning against the piano.

Was it all starting again? Somehow I'd thought Micah had taken care of Uri, but I guess that wasn't how it worked. You couldn't kill a spirit being, could you? But hadn't Micah chased him off for good?

Unless I was the one inviting him back.

I didn't want to go through that all over again. I couldn't.

I didn't notice how quiet the room had become until some guitar chords broke the silence. It wasn't Ericson's crisp, confident playing. I glanced over my shoulder and saw Sam bent over his guitar, carefully moving his fingers over the frets, strumming experimentally.

Ericson nodded. "Good choice." He added his own fingerpicking. "Martin Luther knew something about struggling with the Enemy. Do you have the words, Sam?"

Sam pulled a folded piece of notebook paper from his back pocket and for some reason handed it to me.

"I'll sing the first verse for those of you who don't know the tune," Ericson said. "Then you'd all better join in. It's in the red hymnal behind you, Allie." He strummed in a formal sort of way, and it reminded me of a medieval bard singing an ancient tale to his royal audience. He had a pleasant voice.

> A mighty fortress is our God,
> A bulwark never failing;
> Our helper He amid the flood
> Of mortal ills prevailing.
> For still our ancient foe

> Doth seek to work us woe–
> His craft and pow'r are great,
> And, armed with cruel hate,
> On earth is not His equal.

He started chugging out the chords then, and Sam joined him. My pulse surged with the tempo. Allie had found the song in the hymnal, and she and Shayne joined in.

> Did we in our own strength confide,
> Our striving would be losing,
> Were not the right man on our side,
> The man of God's own choosing.
> Dost ask who that may be?
> Christ Jesus, it is He–
> Lord Sabaoth His name,
> From age to age the same,
> And He must win the battle.

It sounded good, their sopranos with his baritone. I always wished I could sing high and clear like that, but in music class I'd been a lowly alto.

Ericson nodded a signal to Sam, and they changed key, an upward shift that made it sound more urgent. Eyes on his guitar, Sam added his voice to the others. He didn't have to look at me; I knew he wanted me to listen.

> And though this world, with devils filled,
> Should threaten to undo us,
> We will not fear, for God hath willed
> His truth to triumph through us.
> The prince of darkness grim,
> We tremble not for him–

> His rage we can endure,
> For lo! his doom is sure:
> One little word shall fell him.

I couldn't help myself. I joined in the last verse.

> That word above all earthly pow'rs,
> No thanks to them, abideth;
> The Spirit and the gifts are ours
> Through Him who with us sideth.
> Let goods and kindred go,
> This mortal life also–
> The body they may kill;
> God's truth abideth still:
> His kingdom is forever.

I guess I got a little too into it, because at the end my voice rang out louder than anyone else's. I tried to bite it back, but it hung there in the air with the thrumming of the last chord.

"Rory's got some pipes," Shayne said.

"Sorry," I said.

"What do you mean?" Allie asked. "You sounded great."

"Yeah," Jake said. "If loudness is good, then you were definitely great."

"I didn't hear you join in, Jake," Sam said.

"Of course you couldn't hear me, what with Rory's shout-singing and all."

Ericson silenced everyone with a gesture of his hand. "Rory," he said, "you've revealed a hidden talent. Not just anyone can sing harmony."

I glowed a little, but it was mostly embarrassment. "Only because I can't sing soprano. I have to listen for the lower part."

"That's the thing most people can't do."

I shrugged. "Well, it's not the same as playing an actual instrument."

"The voice is an actual instrument. All the others were fashioned by the hands of men. The voice is fashioned by God."

Jake seemed about to offer an opinion about whether that really applied to me. A well-aimed pillow from Sam's direction put a quick stop to it.

"The clock tells me that's our closing song," Ericson said. "Time to get you guys home to hit the books." This was met with moans. "But I'm glad you could come. Kellie would be glad."

We were quiet for a few seconds. "Think we might do it again sometime?" Allie asked delicately.

"Oh, I think so. Probably after the holidays. I'm playing at a bunch of services. Plus I have a lot of invitations."

Sam snapped his guitar into its case. "I have an idea," he said, but that's all he would say about it.

Ericson wanted to pray before we left. He kept it short and simple. "Lord, help us to remain in You. Feed and strengthen us with Your Word. Remove the forces that block your truth from reaching our hearts. Deliver us from the Enemy's snares. And make us warriors for Your kingdom. Amen."

He drove us home, and Sam's house was the first stop. Through the gauzy curtains we could see twinkling white lights in the house. I had to climb out of the van with Sam so he could get his guitar out without bonking me on the head.

Mrs. Newman stepped out on the front porch with just a sweater pulled around her. She waved without unwrapping her arms.

"Hi," I said with a quick wave and eyes mostly on my snowy shoes.

"Hello, Rory."

I blushed that she remembered my name, though it didn't quite roll off her tongue. More of a *roe-ree* than a *roary*.

"See you Saturday, guys," Sam said. He fumbled around with his backpack and guitar to get them out of my way, but I wasn't exactly rushing to hop back into the van. There was unspoken stuff hanging out there—the dream, his wrist-grabbing rescue at Bliss's…big things we'd had no chance to talk about. Or maybe we just hadn't had the courage.

He looked at me, his dark eyes shadowed by his darker brows, all scrunched together in consternation.

"It's not getting any warmer in here," Jake called.

I rolled my eyes and climbed in. Before I could close the door, Sam asked a quiet, two-letter question.

"IM?"

It only made sense to give a two-letter answer.

"OK."

twenty-eight

Sam didn't IM me that night. But Angelica Lyte did.

    Angelyte: *So what happened?*
    Fairy316: *nothing, everything. craziness.*
    Angelyte: *I knew it. You didn't try to contact your angels.*

I could've taken that as a compliment. I don't think she meant it as one.

    Fairy316: *it was a mistake*
    Angelyte: *It was an amazing opportunity. But they got to you.*
    Fairy316: *they?*
    Angelyte: *You know. Your God Squad thought police.*
    Fairy316: *They're my friends. They saved me from*

I tried to find the right words.

    Angelyte: *From thinking an original thought?*

Fairy316: *It's not like that. They were worried about me.*
Angelyte: *Listen, I'm not here to slam your friends. But what if they're just trying to keep you from doing something because they've never had the guts to do it? Or the ability. People get nervous when one of their comfy clique members branches out on her own.*
Fairy316: *well, there's branching out and then there's spinning out of control*
Angelyte: *That's not you.*
Fairy316: *It wasn't about me going against my friends' rules. I was going against God's.*

I waited a while for a reply, and as I sat there in the quiet living room, I felt a weary weight pressing me down, like years and years of mistakes and shame and guilt. Too many ways to screw up in life. Who could hope to do even a half-decent job of it? I pulled an afghan around my shoulders, but I still felt cold.

Angelyte: *Some people seem to need a god of rules. Others find themselves a god of freedom.*

She had me. I didn't want to be a rigid, rule-locked person, shuffling along the narrow road with my narrow mind, destined to fall off eventually, a failure. Why not just relax, do whatever felt right at the time, do good but maybe enjoy myself a little along the way? Find a god of freedom...

I let my head roll back and my eyes close. "God," I whispered. "I don't even know what to pray." Would God even help me to pray? Seemed like a silly idea. I mean, wasn't there *anything* I could do right? Did God have to do everything for me?

Yeah, probably. I sighed. Yeah, definitely.

Then the words came. "God, I know you're not about rules. That's us. You're about righteousness. You're about setting people free."

And a memory washed over me, cool and sweet as a drink of water on a dusty road. It was Gabby's face, softly smiling as if with a sweet memory of her own. *Read the gospel written by John.* That had been her advice once, when I was struggling to understand. And I had read John's gospel, more than once. Some of the verses had nestled into my brain like baby birds.

I sat up and pushed aside a stack of mail and books, uncovering my Bible. It took a few minutes. Then one of those baby birds jumped out of the nest and flew.

Fairy316: *"Therefore if the Son makes you free, you shall be free indeed."*

Long pause.

Angelyte: *#!$%@?*

I'd gotten somewhat accustomed to bad language hanging around Bliss's world, though she liked to laugh when she caught me flinching at a particularly shocking word. She'd be laughing now. I pressed forward.

Fairy316: *John 8:36*
Angelyte: *You're going to quote the Bible at me now?*
Fairy316: *I just wanted to show you*
Angelyte: *How much brainwashing you enjoyed tonight?*
Fairy316: *how free I feel when I remember who I am*
Angelyte: *I see it as losing who you are, like what happens when you join a cult.*
Fairy316: *I know it looks that way sometimes*
Angelyte: *Because it is that way.*
Fairy316: *No. It's hard to explain, but I feel like I never really knew myself until I starting finding out who I am in Christ.*

And just like that, her IM status switched from the little green 'available' light to the forbidding red 'unavailable'. Sheesh.

I logged off InterFace and checked my other IM window. No sign of Sam. I imagined him doing his homework, then remembered that he might not technically get homework. But he did have parents and restricted use of a computer. I didn't have the feeling that he'd forgotten. Just that I had to be patient.

Patience is highly overrated. I mean, have you ever noticed that the people who dispense such nice advice about patience aren't the ones anxiously waiting for something?

Patience can backfire, too. December wasn't getting any younger, and still my mom hadn't even mentioned putting up the Christmas decorations. I can't say my heart brimmed with holiday cheer, either. The memory of taking those decorations down with my dad just days before he died hadn't been knocked out of my brain by the car accident. But even though opening the cardboard boxes of glass balls, tangled lights and shedding garland would be slightly horrible, it felt like a necessary sort of horrible. Someone needed to just say *ho ho ho, let's get through this, even if it's mostly fakey-fake*.

So, I tried to be patient, waiting for Mom to take the first step. Mostly she just stepped off to overtime at the office or extra waitressing shifts. Sheelan didn't seem bothered, and I figured out why when I got an email from Shayne the next night. That was after I'd endured an endless Friday at school , though at least I hadn't been forced to face up to Bliss. She'd been absent from school again (cutting class had come to be known as 'taking a Bliss Day' at Whitestone Elementary).

School was, by law, Christmas-less, and our house was un-Christmasized. But there was still a hint of hope in the air, and it smelled like gingerbread. The fragrance wafting from the Fisher's house that afternoon nearly brought eggnog tears to my eyes. Mrs. Fisher waved me inside with her oven mitts, and I ate marshmallow fudge while the twins decorated gingerbread men to look like themselves, which worked out nicely since the cookies happened to exactly match the color of their skin.

Sam was lucky I'd been tranquilized with plenty of chocolate, because there was still no sign of any IM activity from him when I got home and logged on. So I checked my email to see if Angelica was still speaking to me, or any of the other oddballs I occasionally InterFaced with.

First I saw Shayne's email.

Hey, R₂O! (Rory Rejoiced Over)

Groovy hanging with you yesterday. You should've come here with your sister tonight. She's pretty good at decking the halls. Good thing, since Jeph is basically just staring at her with his moony lovesick eyes and is otherwise useless. BLECH!

Sheelan's pretty cool, though. It's kind of nice having another female around to do this Christmas thing. Next time you come, too, K??

Your future sister-in-law, S-FOG (Shayne Friend of God)

Sheelan hadn't informed me that she was going out—unless you count the sound of the front door opening and closing as informing—let alone where she was going. Apparently she was getting her fill of holly jollies elsewhere.

I closed the email and finally noticed the long column of new emails popping up after it. They were all from InterFace, all notifications that I had messages waiting, or posts on my FaceBoard. Something must've gone haywire. No way would I get so many messages all at once. I didn't even recognize half of the names.

I logged on to my account. There they were, one after another. Messages, with pictures of the senders attached. Most of them I knew from Bliss's network—the one she had gone ahead and made my network, too—some looked only vaguely familiar. And most of the messages were capital letters.

But not LOL, CUL8R. I didn't understand most of them. And the few I did know...

My stomach clenched around the fudge. I couldn't be positive... But it seemed like I was getting hate mail. Or if not hate, then at least obnoxiousness. From people I hardly knew.

I ran away—which is to say I quickly clicked on something else to escape. And so I arrived at my FaceBoard, which now sported a collection of new photographs, compliments of the many so-called friends I hardly knew. I'm sorry to say, not many of the photos on my FaceBoard were of people's faces.

I fumbled around, clicking haphazardly until I finally quit the application. When had I changed from just another hen in the cozy virtual roost to the one weak chick that all the others turn on and peck to a pulp?

It had to be Bliss. Seemed like she'd been busy in her time off. I'd ticked her off, and this was payback, getting all my InterFace 'friends' to harass me. Her InterFace friends, that is.

But hang on—I'd ticked Angelica off, too. Could she have something to do with it? Suddenly I understood the joke, 'With friends like this, who needs enemies?' Not a very good joke.

Ding.

samIam: *there you are*

I was so relieved, I attacked.

REJoyce316: *Me? Where were you?*

> **samIam:** *Sorry, my dad said no computer last night.*

I couldn't exactly sympathize, since I never had to get permission to go online. My mom wasn't usually around to ask.

> **REJoyce316:** *uncool*

Crud. Maybe that sounded like I was calling his dad uncool.

> **samIam:** *he didn't really say no, he said later.*
> **REJoyce316:** *and later wasn't till now?*
> **samIam:** *yeah, because I kind of said "later" when he reminded me to put the garbage out yesterday morning*
> **REJoyce316:** *let me guess, you forgot*
> **samIam:** *afraid so*
> **REJoyce316:** *so he gave you the later treatment*
> **samIam:** *sad but true*
> **REJoyce316:** *fair but true*
> **samIam:** *hey*
> **REJoyce316:** *you know I'm right*
> **samIam:** *yeah… but hey anyway*

I laughed, and I could imagine him laughing, too, or at least grinning that sparkly Sam grin. Then, just like in a real conversation, there was a pause. We were both thinking about the reason we needed to talk. Only what could we say about it?

> **REJoyce316:** *so*
> **samIam:** *so*

So… Pull any other girls from pagan houses lately? No, no good. How about, have any more dreams about my angels lately? Oh— duh. That reminded me:

> **REJoyce316:** *I finally dreamed again last night!*
> **samIam:** *really? 'cause I finally didn't dream. About your Gabby, I mean. Just about an enormous pile of garbage swallowing my house, and riding a paper airplane, and falling into a giant banana cream pie, and Ben. The usual stuff.*

Ben. His twin who had died when they were little.

> **REJoyce316:** *do you dream about him a lot?*
> **samIam:** *yeah. But let's talk about yours*
> **REJoyce316:** *mine were just sock drawer dreams, you know*
> **samIam:** *??*
> **REJoyce316:** *just ordinary, everyday stuff*
> **samIam:** *I've never dreamed about my sock drawer. My jammie drawer, maybe, but socks? Come on.*
> **REJoyce316:** *ROFL*
> **samIam:** *????*
> **REJoyce316:** *GMBO*
> **samIam:** *either you just ralphed after you ate some bad gumbo, or you're acronyming at me*

You couldn't IM on InterFace without picking up a few shortcuts. I almost did it without thinking. Okay, I was showing off a little.

> **REJoyce316:** *it's my new bad habit*
> **samIam:** *you mean your NBH*
> **REJoyce316:** *exactly*
> **samIam:** *I'm not supposed to use them*
> **REJoyce316:** *why not?*
> **samIam:** *my dad says I need to learn to type, so no cheating*
> **REJoyce316:** *no problem. You write the long way, I'll write the short way*

samIam: *and I'll be in Scotland before ye*
REJoyce316: *???*
samIam: *you know, the song, You take the high road and I'll take the low road...*
REJoyce316: *???*
samIam: *nevermind :-}*
REJoyce316: *LOL*
samIam: *seriously, though, I'm not supposed to have 'strings of letters' in my IMs*
REJoyce316: *why not?*
samIam: *just a safety measure*
REJoyce316: *I don't get it*
samIam: *I guess some kids get into pretty messed up stuff online, and it's right under their parents' noses, but they don't understand the code*

So much for showing off. Now I looked like one of 'them'. But weren't Sam's parents being just a little overprotective? It's not like Sam was the kind of kid to get into trouble.

REJoyce316: *I actually don't understand most of it*
samIam: *I'm trying to memorize the periodic table of the elements for science, so I have enough letters swimming around in my head. PA— protactinium or...*
REJoyce316: *Parent Alert*
samIam: *Is that really what PA is?*
REJoyce316: *There's a lot of them for "my parents are coming"*
samIam: *proving my parents right, I guess*
REJoyce316: *I'm glad I don't know what most of them mean. I just got a bunch of messages in my InterFace mailbox, and I think some of them are messed up*
samIam: *you do InterFace?*
REJoyce316: *yeah, do you?*

I knew he didn't. I'd checked.

> **samIam:** *no. who's sending you messed up messages?*
> **REJoyce316:** *a bunch of people I hardly know*
> **samIam:** *why?*
> **REJoyce316:** *I think I ticked someone off. It might be revenge, or a weird joke.*
> **samIam:** *is it normal to get messages from people you hardly know?*
> **REJoyce316:** *I guess so. That's why people InterFace, to meet people they wouldn't ordinarily meet*
> **samIam:** *is it safe?*

First I felt a warmth swirl around in my chest, like the commercial for chocolate bars that showed a big vat of melted perfection stirred in satiny brown circles. Sam was being protective of me.

Then, maybe because it was easier to believe the less chocolaty possibility, it crossed my mind that maybe Sam's overprotective parents were rubbing off on him.

> **REJoyce316:** *as long as no one can reach through the computer and grab me, I guess it is*
> **samIam:** *but you never use your real name in chat rooms or anything like that*
> **REJoyce316:** *nah, even I know that*
> **samIam:** *interesting photo*
> **REJoyce316:** *whose?*
> **samIam:** *yours. Your InterFace photo.*
> **REJoyce316:** *you can see my profile?*
> **samIam:** *not the whole profile. I don't have "Friend Access". But I looked up your name and found your photo.*
> **REJoyce316:** *I need to change that*

> **samIam:** *maybe. You kind of stand out from the other Rory Joyces.*

> **REJoyce316:** *there's others?*
> **samIam:** *four others. All guys.*
> **REJoyce316:** *figures*
> **samIam:** *but only two of them are wearing fairy costumes*
> **REJoyce316:** *please tell me you're joking*
> **samIam:** *I'm joking*
> **REJoyce316:** *I really need to figure out how to change my photo*
> **samIam:** *I bet Kingston can show you*
> **REJoyce316:** *yeah*
> **samIam:** *or if it can wait til Tuesday, I'll help you after school*

I forgot how to type for a half a minute.

> **REJoyce316:** *Tuesday's good*

After another half a minute:

> **samIam:** *OK*

Fifteen seconds:

> **REJoyce316:** *hey, no acronyms*
> **samIam:** *oops*
> **samIam:** *well, maybe I'll see you at the Scene tomorrow*
> **REJoyce316:** *I think so, yeah*
> **samIam:** *oh, one other thing before I go*
> **REJoyce316:** *go ahead*
> **samIam:** *what are you doing on the first night of Chanukah?*
> **REJoyce316:** *that depends. when is the first night of Chanukah?*
> **samIam:** *a week from Monday*

Mind racing. Not getting anywhere, but racing.

> **REJoyce316:** *no school. That's the first week of winter break.*
> **samIam:** *my parents are having a "get-together"-- small group of people, large amount of food.*
> **REJoyce316:** *any chance of your mom's rugilock (did I spell that right)?*
> **samIam:** *rugelach. You had some at the Fisher's?*
> **REJoyce316:** *oh yeah*
> **samIam:** *liked it?*
> **REJoyce316:** *mmmm*
> **samIam:** *there might not be rugelach*
> **REJoyce316:** *darn*
> **samIam:** *but there will definitely be sufganiyot*
> **REJoyce316:** *oh, my favorite*
> **samIam:** *you've had it?*
> **REJoyce316:** *never heard of it. I think you made the word up.*
> **samIam:** *just for that, I'm not telling what it is. You'll have to come to find out.*
> **REJoyce316:** *no fair*
> **samIam:** *I know it's close to Christmas, so don't feel bad if you can't come*

I almost told him how I wasn't sure there'd be much of a Christmas at my house, but it burrowed deep inside me the way an exposed earthworm tries to escape back into the dark dirt. I was tired of looking pitiful. Maybe if everyone believed we were having a Merry Christmas in the Joyce house, it would be the next best thing to actually having one.

Maybe I'd just celebrate Chanukah instead.

> **REJoyce316:** *count me in, already*
> **samIam:** *roger, copy that*

REJoyce316: *Roger? I thought I was Shirley*
samIam: *Wasn't I Shirley?*
REJoyce316: *life is confusing*
samIam: *you can say that again*
REJoyce316: *life is*
samIam: *don't*
REJoyce316: *: P*
REJoyce316: *oh, are you allowed to do emoticons?*
samIam: *let me check the rule book…hmm. Yep. Emoticons are OK.*
REJoyce316: *you mean "Okay"*
samIam: *right, right. :0 Life is confusing.*
REJoyce316: *you can say that again*
samIam: *but I won't*
samIam: *uh oh*
REJoyce316: *what?*
samIam: *PA*
REJoyce316: *rulebreaker!*
samIam: *my dad's looking for his laptop*
REJoyce316: *so I guess it's time to say shalom*
samIam: *shalom aleichem*

His little symbol switched from 'online' to 'away'. I sat there, reading our conversation over again (okay, three times). Funny, we hadn't actually talked about his dreams of Gabby, or my narrow escape from Bliss Hathaway's house. It was enough that we'd talked.

And it was enough to remind me of something that shouldn't have required reminding. I grabbed my rusting Sword, and it opened to where I had stuck a sheet of paper one week at the Scene, a while back. It was in the thirteenth chapter of Matthew. I read about the kingdom of heaven.

That night I dreamed I was digging in an open field, struggling to chip away at the frozen ground. My shovel struck something; it dazzled my eyes with its beauty. Everything in me wanted to dig it out, to claim this precious thing for my own, but I could only have it if I bought the entire field. I would have to leave it, go back, sell every single thing of value that I owned if I hoped to possess this field and this treasure. I agonized over it. I couldn't bear to leave it. Dropping to my knees, I tried to pry it from the ground with my aching cold fingers. It wouldn't budge.

twenty-nine

Two things stand out in my memory of the Scene that Saturday. First, walking in with a fluttery kind of feeling, like the way you feel before you open a present. You're not sure what you're gonna get, if you'll even like it or if you'll just have to pretend, but hey, it's a present.

I was calculating how I might mention to Allie and Shayne that Sam had invited me to his family Chanukah party. I could just mention it in passing, work it into a conversation. Or maybe say nothing at all, and keep it just between him and me? No, I had to tell somebody, even if I had to act all casual about it.

Shayne helped me out on this one. "Hey," she asked casually, in passing, "you going to the Newman's Chanukah party?"

I'm not sure why it hadn't occurred to me that we were all invited. It just hadn't.

"Yeah, probably," I managed to say.

"Well, we need to work out a ride. Jeph already informed me that he can't be our chauffeur. Plans with Sheelie-pooh, I guess."

The second thing I remember is a little more encouraging. Proving that if I actually paid attention, I might not miss the blessings God sent my way.

"Get a load of this," Pastor said, and he zapped his little remote at the screen. A video clip began to play—a famous actor in a well-known flick about a shaggy Scotsman who leads a raggedy army to victory against all odds. We watched him give a rousing pep talk about freedom.

It took a minute after it finished for the room to quiet down, since half the kids had to try their own Scottish accent. Mostly the boy half, big surprise.

"What would ye do without freedom?" Jake demanded to know, standing with a fist raised.

"You'll find out if we have to lock ye in the broom closet, Mr. Dean," Pastor Dan told him. Sam dragged Jake down by the back of his shirt. Pastor shook his head while he opened his Bible. "Done with a real thespian flourish, I have to say, Jake. You could have a future in film."

"All he needs now is looks and talent," Allie whispered, just loud enough for Jake to hear. He had no chance to retaliate.

"So, Jake," Pastor said, "why don't you give us your thoughts on freedom. What is it, exactly?"

"Easy. Doing what I want, when I want."

"You're confusing freedom with complete self-absorption," Allie said.

"I think a lot of people would agree with Jake." Pastor passed a hand over his head, like he was checking if his bald spot was still there. It was. "But we've spent these last several weeks talking about what it means to be a follower of Christ in a fallen world, and what that looks like. We know from the Bible that God doesn't want us just going around doing whatever the culture says is good at the time. God sets standards. He's got rules, and some of them are hard to follow. Really hard. What's with that? Doesn't He just want us to be happy, and free?"

Shayne raised her hand. "Not if what makes me happy hurts other people."

"Or what about hurting yourself? And damaging your relationship with God?" Pastor asked. "I've said it before, and I'll say it again: When God says 'Thou shalt not,' just go ahead and attach the words 'because you'll get hurt'. Maybe now, maybe later—but there's always a price attached to sin."

A boy's voice spoke. "So God's rules really give us freedom from sin."

"I'm glad you said that, Silas." Pastor said. His pacing warned us that the matter wasn't settled. "Would you then say that God's law brings freedom?"

"I guess so, yeah," Silas answered, but I saw Sam's head shake slightly. Not that I was watching him.

"Let's go to the book of Galatians and see what Paul has to say about it." He pressed the remote.

So Christ has really set us free. Now make sure that you stay free, and don't get tied up again in slavery to the law. ...For if you are trying to make yourselves right with God by keeping the law, you have been cut off from Christ! You have fallen away from God's grace. Galatians 5:1,4

"Slavery to the law?" Pastor asked. "What happened to freedom? Sam, you've got the answer written all over your face."

Sam scruffed a hand through his hair. I knew that meant he felt self-conscious. "The law shows us our sin, and how we can never be good enough," he said. He'd told me that same thing once when I'd been struggling to understand the Bible and the gospel.

Pastor Dan nodded. "But wait. What about the Apostle Paul? He was an expert on the law. He'd been a Pharisee, the spiritual elite. Now he's an apostle for Jesus. This guy's got credentials. Surely he didn't struggle with sin the way we do every day, right?" He flipped to the next screen, jam-packed with text.

"The seventh chapter of Romans. I know it's not the usual bite-sized passage, but you've just got to check this out. I want to read it aloud, all of us. Let's start over here and work our way across the room. Read a verse and then tap your neighbor to read the next one."

What happened next is what sticks most in my memory. They were Paul's words, but somehow as we read, the two thousand years between him and us evaporated, and I almost felt like I met Paul the man, the person, the human, not just Paul the apostle.

The kids on the other side of the group started reading about how as believers we somehow died with Christ on the cross, and so died to the power of the law. That made us free to really serve God in a new way, by the Spirit—not by just obeying a set of rules.

The verse relay wound its way towards us: The law showed us our sin, but then something happened. Our sin saw the law and stirred up all kinds of guilt and wrong desires in us. What should have shown us the way of life ended up handing us the death penalty.

Silas read a verse, the fourteenth. "'The law is good, then. The trouble is not with the law but with me, because I am sold into slavery, with sin as my master.'" He tagged Sam.

"'I don't understand myself at all, for I really want to do what is right, but I don't do it. Instead, I do the very thing I hate.'" Sam nudged Allie.

"'I know perfectly well that what I am doing is wrong, and my bad conscience shows that I agree that the law is good.'" Allie elbowed Jake.

"'But I can't help myself, because it is sin inside me that makes me do these evil things.'" Jake shot Allie the evil eye but gave me the poke in the ribs.

I started reading. "'I know I am rotten through and through so far as my old sinful nature is concerned. No matter which way I turn, I can't make myself do right. I want to, but I can't.'"

Somewhere around the word 'rotten', the words grabbed hold of me. Paul took a big step backwards and I jumped into his place. Maybe that's why I kept on reading.

"'When I want to do good, I don't. And when I try not to do wrong, I do it anyway. But if I am doing what I don't want to do, I am not really the one doing it; the sin within me is doing it. It seems to be a fact of life that when I want to do what is right, I inevitably do what is wrong. I love God's law with all my heart. But there is another law at work within me that is at war with my mind. This law wins the fight and makes me a slave to the sin that is still within me. Oh, what a miserable person I am! Who will free me from this life that is dominated by sin?'"

I stopped, but not because I finally remembered to tap someone else. I just sat there with the words passing into me, like arrows that puncture but then become part of a person, hard and strong and straight like bones. I suppose everyone was looking at me. I didn't notice.

Shayne came to my rescue, patting my knee as if we actually had to touch before I could pass the turn along to her. She read, "Thank God! The answer is in Jesus Christ our Lord. So you see how it is: In my mind I really want to obey God's law, but because of my sinful nature I am a slave to sin."

Everyone kept quiet when she finished. Pastor Dan's voice was softer than usual when he said, "Thank God! The freedom is in Christ. He breaks the bonds of our sin nature. He sets the captives free."

I bounced into school Monday morning (I know—bouncing on Monday, seriously?), ready to forgive just about everything: the school for being school, the teachers for teaching, Christmas for not being Christmassy. Who cared? For the first time in a long time, I felt free. All my sins and stupidities and failure to follow God's ways—forgiven. And the voice in my head that said *you're going to mess up again and you know it* was easily answered.

Yeah, probably. Being a Jesus follower doesn't mean I'm automatically good. It just means I'm so thankful that I want to try.

As if all this soul-deep giddiness wasn't enough, the countdown was on. At this time next Monday, I'd be rolling over in bed, punching my pillow into a comfy lump for another hour or two of sleep. Possibly dreaming of the Chanukah party that night. Seven more days until the party, and only five more until winter break. Winter break: the lushest oasis in the desert of the school year.

"I'm looking forward to reading your paper over winter break," Mr. Hayes told me after science class.

And the Monday-morning bounce screeched to a halt.

I smiled a *right you are!* sort of smile at him while panic scrambled around inside me like a rat in a burlap sack. The smile must've still been stretching my face out of shape when I sat opposite Jasmine at lunch.

"You tried the Chunky Meat Stew, didn't you?" she accused.

There sat the Chunky Meat Stew, steaming conspicuously on my tray. "Not yet," I said.

"Because you look like you just ate something bad."

"No." I sighed. "I just realized my evolution paper is due by Friday."

Her black eyes snapped wide for a second until she remembered it was my paper, not hers. "Oh, that. So?"

"So that gives me four nights."

"Let me guess: you haven't started writing it yet."

I poked at what might have been a potato. "Not exactly."

"Don't worry," she said. I looked up at her, startled by this thing that sounded like encouragement. She stabbed a forkful of salad. "If you've got all your notes organized, four nights is enough time." She munched that green leafy mouthful and was about to add a mandarin orange slice when she noticed my look. "You have the research done, I assume."

Assume. My dad used to have a saying about that word, and what it made out of 'u' and 'me'. This time it only seemed to apply to 'me'. "Well…"

She let out a hot puff of breath and smacked her fork down. "You know, Rory, that's dumber than eating stew with unidentified meat. Why bother and take a stand for your beliefs if you're just going to sit down on the job?"

She had a point, and she pressed it in like the lost thumbtack you find when you're walking barefoot. I was saved from having to answer by the swooshing arrival of Bliss Hathaway at our table, decked out in a flowing green dress, her hair swept back with a knotted scarf.

Since I wasn't exactly putting up a fight, Jasmine turned on Bliss for satisfaction. "So why do you get to scrap the uniform today? You guys studying hippies in history?"

"You like it?" Bliss asked, though Jasmine hadn't exactly been expressing admiration. She smoothed her hands over the crinkly fabric. It's 100% green."

"Yes, we're not blind."

"I don't mean the color. I mean it's eco-friendly, socially responsible, ethical, organic and sustainable. I'm allowed to wear it because I'm celebrating a day of spiritual significance." She waited for us to ask what it was.

Instead Jasmine asked, "Why do you get to? I don't see other kids wearing holiday clothes on other religious holidays. Rory doesn't get to wear black on Good Friday."

I'm not sure if I would, but she had a point.

Bliss smiled. "Well, the alternative was that my mom would allow me to stay home from school, so I guess they decided this was better than me missing a day."

"So what's the big occasion?" I asked.

She got a dreamy look on her face, but her hand remained very practical and casually stole the bread roll from my tray. "As you know, I've been a spiritual seeker for a while now. I'd gotten to the point where I was ready to forget the whole business—I mean, be a real materialist, just believe in what I could see and touch, you understand."

I did a sideways nod, since I didn't, really.

"That's all changed. I've become convinced that there's more to life than just what we experience on this plane. And since I'm a person who has to be passionate about something, and lately that something has been the environment, it seems perfectly natural for me to embrace Wicca."

"So you're a Wiccan now," Jasmine summed up.

Bliss tore my bread roll with a smile, nodded, took a bite.

"You cast spells and all that?"

Bliss shrugged and answered with eyes on me, as if I'd asked the question. "There can be that element to it, but I haven't really explored it much yet. That's one of the beauties of Wicca. It's different for each practitioner. It's very anti-rules, anti-establishment—it's about freedom. What really speaks to me is its reverence for nature and the empowerment of women."

Jasmine munched salad thoughtfully. Bliss scattered sunbeams over me, smiling as she 'borrowed' my bottle of lemonade. "I partly have you to thank for my decision," she told me. "Seriously, my experiences with you re-opened my eyes to the possibilities."

I felt full of…unidentified meat. "Tam must be happy," I said weakly.

"Major understatement." She laughed. "She's whipped up into a Yuletide frenzy, now that she knows I'll be celebrating with her. Speaking of which, she's having her little sisterhood over to the house on Saturday, kind of a Yule Eve celebration. Feasting, wassail, music, madness, frith. Gifting the living, honoring the dead—all are welcome!" She sipped my lemonade. "We don't discriminate against the flesh-and-blood-challenged."

"Sounds neato."

"So you'll come, then. You'll be most welcome." She leaned in, lowered her voice. "Tam even thinks it might be a good night to seek my companion spirit." She saw my wrinkled brow. "You know, like yours."

"Mine?"

She mouthed the letters *U-R-I*.

I gagged on stew. "No! That's—"

"Shh, I know, it's okay. I understand now. It's a private thing."

"But you don't understand. He's not a..." My jaw muscles grew tight, as if my body refused to talk about him.

"'He', you say? Interesting."

Jasmine cut in. "Are you talking about spirit guides? Like in animal form?"

"You're interested in that kind of thing?" Bliss turned to her, as if seeing her for the first time. "You should come and talk to some of these women. It's much more than just a party—very meaningful, with the solstice and all it represents. People were celebrating the birth of the sun long before the birth of the 'son' of god. No offense, Rory."

I struggled to snap back into the conversation, but the U-R-I had derailed me.

"Honestly," Jasmine said, "all the holiday insanity turns my stomach."

"Perfect. Forget the fat man in red and people beating each other up at toy stores. Come on Saturday and check out something deeper."

I watched to see how Jasmine would shred the idea into tatters. But she just shredded a piece of lettuce with her small fingers. No way could Jasmine be wavering.

"Hang on," I heard myself say. "My youth group is having a Christmas party on Saturday, too. You should come. You've never been to one."

Jasmine looked at me. Not with the cold eyes, either, just sort of flat. "Because you've never asked me."

Oh.

She turned to Bliss. "What time should I be there?"

thirty

If ever there was a week to fast-forward through, this was it. Sadly, the remote control for my life was lost in the sofa cushions of harsh reality.

Maybe I watched too much TV.

Rather than dwell on a school week that already slurped up way too much of my time, I'll try to boil it down to five Quotes of the Day. Monday definitely belonged to Jasmine and her "What time should I be there?" to Bliss. Which, filtered through my internal translator, came out something like, "Rory, as a witness for Jesus, you positively stink." Not only was I not drawing people towards Him, but I was actually pushing them towards alternative religions.

Tuesday held the potential to totally reverse my luck, with Sam's promise to fix my InterFace photo. But then came Tuesday's quote, compliments of Kingston Fisher: "Sam couldn't come for school today. He's got the flu."

By Wednesday I was punchy from lack of sleep. I'd spent two nights up late, scrambling to throw something together for *Fact vs. Faith*. I skated on the fragile icy patch between plagiarism and incoherence. Mr. Hayes' helpful reminder capped the day off nicely: "Don't forget to include your bibliography and footnotes."

By Thursday I understood what 'bibliography and footnotes' meant: that I should've been reading those books I'd borrowed from Ericson; that I couldn't just cut and paste stuff off the internet; that I was in deep doo-doo. Stinkin' Thursday.

Mr. Hayes must've sensed my dilemma, or smelled it, because he stopped me at the door as I left science class. "Regret not re-taking that test now, perhaps?" His smile was handsomely sympathetic. "What if I offered you another chance?"

I froze.

"Recant, or write-write-write," he said with a laugh.

Mrs. Palmer appeared in her classroom door across the hall. "Rory, do you have a minute before class starts?"

I looked from one teacher to the other. Hayes was looking at Palmer. Palmer was looking at me. I shuffled over. She led me to her desk and pushed a dictionary towards me. Strangely, I knew what she wanted.

I looked up *recant*. It means to change your beliefs. Mr. Hayes was giving me one more chance to cave in.

I looked up at Mrs. Palmer as the rest of my homeroom class began wandering in. She swiped at the white board with an eraser and didn't look at me. But she said, kind of from the corner of her mouth, "You know, technically you have until the final grading in May to eliminate that incomplete mark from first quarter."

Thursday's quote of the day. Sweet Thursday.

I couldn't get her to repeat it, or even acknowledge that she'd said it, but on Friday Mr. Hayes couldn't deny it. He had to give me until May to turn in the paper. My heart soared on wings of hope and relief. Then Mr. Hayes rounded off the school week with what I can only call a humdinger (nevermind the fact that the term 'humdinger' dates back to when the supposed feathered dinosaurs were evolving into the supposed dinobirds):

"If you choose to wait until May to submit your paper, I'll have to accept it then. But I'll be accepting fifteen pages instead of ten."

I shared my tale of woe with my friends on the way to the Newman's house the next Monday—though it was suddenly a lot less woeful, now months away from its deadline, and me on the way to a party. Mr. Fisher was driving because, come to find out, Kingston was invited, too.

"So now I've got to write fifteen pages," I said, waiting for the sympathetic groans.

Allie chuckled. "Serves you right for procrastinating."

"Hey, whose side are you on?" Shayne asked her.

"I'm on the side of knowledge and improving our minds. This paper isn't just something to crank out—it's a chance to learn about an important issue."

"Well said," Mr. Fisher's deep voice said from the front seat.

"Thanks. I'm in the Debate Club."

"A club especially for people who like to nag and argue," Jake observed. "How perfect for you."

I was only half-listening, because we had just pulled into the long gravel driveway of Sam's house. Except for the dim orange glare from the streetlights in the half-developed subdivision on the other side of a snowy field, the outside of the house was dark. But the windows were filled with light, and the light poured out with music and the smells of food and a dog's bark when the front door swung inwards. Sam beckoned us inside, wiping his hands on what appeared to be a white apron.

"Nice skirt," Jake said, stepping in first. "Though I prefer your pink lacy one." Allie and Shayne followed him.

Kingston waved hello to Sam, then looked past him. "Hey, Rory," he said. "Looks like you'll get to meet Tali tonight."

She came up alongside Sam, brushing elbows with him. But only for a second or two; then a yellow shape pushed between them and burst out the door. A second later my backside met the cold porch and a warm pink tongue met my cheeks.

"Roddy, stop it," Sam said sharply, but he couldn't help smiling. "He just really likes you."

"I guess I'm flattered," I said as he pulled Roddy off me and Kingston helped me up. "Or maybe I'm just flattened."

Behind Sam I saw Tali taking coats from the others, but her laughing cinnamon eyes were on me.

"Samuel, why is that dog not in the basement?" Mrs. Newman's voice emerged a moment before she did. She wore a deep blue dress that flared out and swung gracefully around her calves. "Come in, children, come in. And leave the cold outside." Roddy continued to jump joyfully in our midst as we removed our coats in the hall. "Samuel," she said in warning tones.

"I'm trying, Ma. Heel, Roddy. Come."

Jake reappeared, already sipping a soda. "Call him by his full name, Sammy. He always answers to that." He smiled wickedly.

"Don't go there, Jake."

"Come on. It's such a distinguished name, and you came up with it all by yourself."

"Now you've got to tell us, Sam," Kings said, scratching Roddy's velvety gold ears.

Sam shot Jake a withering glance.

"Oh, you want me to tell them." Jake said. "Sure. Let's see if I can get it right, now. Wasn't it Lord Roddenham of Shaggyshire? No, wait. Sir Roddiwick Scruffeldon."

Sam finally got Roddy to the basement door, just off the kitchen, and closed it behind him. "It's Sir Roderick Scruffs." His nostrils flared as Jake burst out laughing and even Kings chuckled. I pressed my lips together, hard. "Hey, I was five years old. I liked knights and tales of derring-do."

Jake bent over, hooting. "Tales of derring-do? Who talks like that?"

Dr. Newman ducked through the living room doorway. "Good evening, gentlemen, ladies," he said in his mellow voice. "We're ready for the kindling, if you'd care to join us. But first, Samuel. you should introduce the young lady to Sabra and Tali."

They were by the fireplace, Tali and a woman I assumed was Sam's so-called Aunt Sabra. They watched us approach, and the book-lined room felt about a mile long. Long enough to see the way the firelight made Tali's skin glow and the ripples of her wavy brown hair shine. Her simple white blouse was delicate, suggesting some faraway exotic place, timeless and yet youthfully fashionable. Her eyes were like warm embers. She smiled, and there were those perfect teeth. I felt like a clompy old goat scuttling over to meet a doe freshly stepped from the woods.

I wouldn't like her. I knew it already.

"Aunt Sabra," Sam was saying beside me, "you've met all my friends except Rory. Rory, this is Aunt Sabra." I shook her hand and returned her smile and polite words. She was small, pretty, plump. Her face was young, but her hair was almost all silvery white.

"And this is Tali," Sam went on. I turned to her, aware that Sam's hands were moving in a strange way, just at the corner of my eye, like he was making a gesture he didn't want me to see. And she was looking at him, not me.

"Nice to meet you," I said with a voice that sounded fake in my own ears.

"Nice to meet you," she said back, in a voice that made my wandering eyes snap back to her. She made some quick gestures, a few flicks of her fingers, and Sam said, "I think she likes your red hair."

Aunt Sabra laughed, made gestures at Tali, and Tali laughed, too. "No, Sam," his aunt said. "She said she loves Rory's red sweater."

Sam's face threatened to match my sweater—which was an amazing deep cranberry and did make my hair look especially red. "Sorry. This signing is harder than it looks."

Okay, so Tali was deaf. So I'd already decided to dislike a deaf girl. So I was a jerk. But you know, somebody might've mentioned it to me in advance, so I wouldn't have to stand here like a dumb cow. What had Kings said? *It was a little hard to understand her at first.* Had he mentioned why? Of course not. Because then I might've missed a chance to look like a jerk.

Tali made some signs while looking at me. Her mom said for her, "I do like your red hair, too. I always wanted red hair."

Okay, Tali was really nice, too. Perfect.

She would speak occasionally—mostly to say *excuse me* or *thank you,* or *hey* to get Sam's attention—but usually she would sign. Sam seemed to understand a lot of what she was 'saying', but his signing was clumsy, to her amusement.

"You've forgotten half of what I taught you last time we visited," she said through her mom.

"That was almost two years ago," he said. "A lot can happen in two years."

"That's for certain," Aunt Sabra said in her own voice (different than her Tali-translating voice, which sounded less Israeli and more American). She winked at Mrs. Newman. "Always, Elena, we've teased these two that we would see them married someday, and always they've protested. But I have not heard so much protesting from Tali on this visit. A lot can happen in two years, like our Samuel growing into a fine young man."

"Oh, Mama," Tali said, rolling her eyes but not looking as if she wanted the earth to open and swallow her. Tali, I saw, was not a blusher. I bet when she cried, she didn't get all puffy and splotchy, either.

"I interrupt this matchmaking to get on with the candle kindling," Dr. Newman said, standing behind poor speechless Sam with his hands on his shoulders. "Before we do, perhaps Samuel will remind us what we celebrate during Chanukah."

"Or tell us what we never knew in the first place," Jake said. This earned him some elbowed ribs. "What, like you guys know?"

Sam ignored this. "I'll do the short version." He cleared his throat. "So, it's 165 B.C., and the Syrians are ruling Judah and Israel with an iron hand. They're determined to wipe out Jewish culture, laws, and religion. They've even desecrated the Temple, turning it into a filthy pagan shrine. But a certain priest starts a revolt, which is led by his son, Judah, who's called the Maccabee or 'The Hammer'—that's *makabah* in Hebrew. Pretty good nickname, I think." He grinned. "Anyway, the revolt works, and before long the Maccabees, as they were called, win back all the lands of Judah and Israel.

"Chanukah is a celebration of their victory, and the cleansing and rededication of the Temple after the revolt. The Talmud—that's a Jewish book of laws and legends—tells of a miracle that happened with the rededication. They could only find one jar of lamp oil to light the Temple menorah, which was only enough to burn for one day and night. But it burned for eight whole days, and this was taken as a sign of God's acceptance of the Temple's rededication."

Shayne raised her hand. "Oh, oh—is that why the menorah has eight candles?"

"Ding-ding-ding! We have a winner," Jake announced in his Game Show Host voice.

"So that's why it's called the 'Festival of Lights'," Allie said.

"Yep." Sam led us over to the front window, where the menorah stood on a gleaming antique wooden table. "And we're supposed to put the lights in a place where everyone can see them, to publicize the miracle."

"You have the most beautiful *hanukiyah*, Aunt Elena," Tali signed.

I guess she meant the menorah, which was beautiful. It was silver and wrought like a tree with eight branches that ended in the candleholders. As we watched, Sam placed a slender blue candle in the holder farthest to the right. He also put a smaller white candle in a holder lower down, in the center.

"This is the *shamash*. It's the candle we use to light the other candles, because the Chanukah lights can't be used for anything else—you can't even use one of them to light the others."

Dr. Newman struck a match and lit the *shamash*. "Samuel will say the blessings."

Tali gave him an impressed look. He shrugged modestly. Then he lifted the *shamash* candle and said, "Blessed are You, Lord our God, King of the universe, who has sanctified us with His commandments, and has commanded us to kindle the lights of Chanukah.

"Blessed are You, Lord our God, king of the universe, who has performed miracles for our ancestors in olden times and in our times.

"Blessed are You, Lord our God, king of the universe, who has given us life and sustained us and brought us to this happy season."

He lit the candle. As he did, Aunt Sabra began to sing in Hebrew. Mrs. Newman joined her, harmonizing. It was pretty, and we listened politely, but I wasn't sure where to look. Stare at the singers? Look at Shayne and Allie and risk getting the giggles? Definitely didn't care to look at Jake. So I just gazed at the one blue candle. Thankfully it wasn't a long song, or I'd be seeing a ghost spot of a candle flame burnt onto my retina for a half hour.

"That was beautiful," Shayne said. "I wish I spoke Hebrew."

"Thank you, Shayne," Mrs. Newman said. "It is a traditional song, about why we kindle the lights, and how we kindle them only to look at them and praise God and remember what He has done for us."

"But only one candle?" Jake asked.

"On the first night, yes."

"No offense, but it's a bit anti-climactic."

Tali made all sorts of signs. Her mother just shook her head.

Sam laughed. "I understood that."

"What did she say?" Jake asked.

Aunt Sabra warned him with a lifted finger, but he gave her the sparkle-eyed Sam Special. "She said you Christians aren't happy until you've covered everything with lights."

Tali snickered and signed some more.

"Go down to the den and rock around the Christmas tree."

Everyone laughed. I joined them, a few seconds late. I'd gotten hung up on Sam's words: *you Christians*. He'd probably just translated it like she said it. Or was there an us-and-them thing happening here?

If so, maybe I'd just score a point for the Them team (which was Us). "Can we go down and see the tree?" I asked. Maybe Tali read my lips, because she laughed.

"The Newmans don't do a tree," Kings told me.

"Oh," I said. I had achieved Idiot Equilibrium: when you look as foolish as you feel.

"We still have to sing the *Maoz Tzur*," Sam said.

Aunt Sabra waved her hand. "Oh, let them go," she said with a smile. "They don't wish to hear a pair of old ladies sing another Hebrew hymn."

"Yeah, let's go peek at all of Sammy's presents," Jake said.

Off they trooped, expecting me to follow. Yeah, but...I actually wanted to hear the hymn. Plus it felt a bit impolite to walk off in the middle of an ancient ritual. Sort of Gentile-ish.

Tali was watching me. Then I copped on—I was sort of Gentile-ish. 100% Gentile-ish. Maybe they wanted to share this Jewish thing just among themselves. I followed the others. Sam's eyes followed me for a second. Maybe he'd been watching to see if I'd stay. But I had to keep walking. If I turned back now, I'd look like an idiot.

Maybe sometimes it's okay to look like an idiot?

By now I was in the kitchen, the shortest way to the den. There was something in the oven, covered with foil but smelling insanely good. And on the countertop, a mound of dough on a floured board, and a tray holding rows of doughy circles with pinched edges. This looked promising.

From the living room drifted the hymn, a jumble of meaningless syllables to me, except that right at the beginning I almost thought I heard 'Yeshua'. I'd assumed that Tali and Sabra would be Messianic Jews—Jewish but Christian, like the Newmans—but after Tali's comment I was pretty sure they weren't. Now I was confused. In other words, things were pretty much the same as usual.

A guitar joined the voices, and the melody stayed the same but the lyrics were in English.

> *Rock of ages, let our song*
> *Praise Your saving power;*
> *You, amid the raging foes,*
> *Were our sheltering tower.*
> *Furious they assailed us,*
> *But Your arm availed us,*
> *And Your word,*
> *Broke their sword,*
> *When our own strength failed us.*

If that was a Chanukah hymn, it obviously wouldn't be about

Jesus. Strange, because it easily could've been. Except it would be in the present tense. You *are* our sheltering tower…

"Rory?" I heard Allie call from the den.

"Coming," I called back. But there was one thing I had to know before I went. These doughy things were filled with something. One of them wasn't pinched all the way shut. If I just pulled the two sides apart a tiny bit…

"Hands off the *sufganiyot*, Shirley."

thirty-one

I spun around to find Sam tying his apron back on.

"I wasn't—"

"Sure you weren't. Hold out your hands."

I did. He inspected. "Mm-hmm. Flour. Just as I thought. Lucky for you, no signs of filling. No, don't bother peeking, you won't find any clues. I covered my tracks. It's a surprise."

I leaned against the counter, watching him pinch the doughy edges of the last pastry together. "So how long do they need to bake?"

He shook his head, sighed. "So much to learn. A *sufganiyah* is a doughnut."

"So?"

"So doughnuts are fried. Tell me you knew that doughnuts are fried."

"Hey, I just get them in the big orange box from Doughy Holes. I never thought much about how they got there."

He groaned and pulled the lid off a huge skillet. "Those are not doughnuts. Those are..." He gestured but didn't have a word for what Doughy Holes were. "But here, this oil looks ready. You'll be tasting a real doughnut pretty soon. Stand back. It may spit." He began dropping the crimped balls of dough into the hot oil. It was at least four inches deep.

I said, "I'm beginning to understand why they say doughnuts aren't good for you."

"Yeah, well, on Chanukah we stuff ourselves with them."

"Have you ever tried baking them?"

He brandished his spatula furiously at me, but the fury didn't reach his eyes. "It's a doughnut. Do I have to go over this again? Besides, the oil reminds us of the miracle of the oil lasting eight days. We eat lots of fried stuff this week."

"Samuel Solomon, what have I told you about waving utensils in young ladies' faces?" Mrs. Newman demanded, nudging past him to peek in the oven.

Sam had a searching look. "I'm coming up blank, Ma. What have you told me about utensil waving?"

"Not to do it. Especially in young ladies' faces." She gave him a swat.

Aunt Sabra entered and began pulling food from fridge, cupboards, and crock pots. Tali was close beside her, sampling whatever she could get her hands on.

"Tali Shoshanna," her mother scolded. Tali pretended not to hear. See. (Sigh.) Tali smiled and kept nibbling.

"So moms in Israel use their kids' middle names when they're in trouble, too," I observed.

"I think it's universal," Sam said.

"At least yours is pretty," I said to Tali, moving my lips probably more exaggeratedly than I needed to. I was a total novice when it came to deafness. I knew it showed.

"Tali Shoshanna, 'dew of the rose'," Mrs. Newman said, slipping on oven mitts. Tali was watching our mouths intently, following along. "I don't believe many people think about the meaning of a name anymore, when they choose it for their child. Your mother chose beautifully for you, Tali."

Tali signed at Sam.

"My name?" he asked. "Um, it means something about God."

Mrs. Newman pulled the foil-covered pan from the oven. "It does not mean 'something about God'. Samuel means 'my name is God' and Solomon is 'peace'. You were named for the God of peace."

"Could I change it to Maccabee?" Sam tried. "You can call me The Hammer."

Tali signed again, this time looking at me. Her mom asked, "What about your name, Rory? Somewhat unusual, no?"

"Oh. Well." I scrambled to reinterpret my name as anything that sounded remotely as lovely as 'dew of the rose'. "They called me Rory Erin, because my grandmother was from Ireland. My dad's mom. I never knew her."

"So what does it mean?"

"Rory means 'red chieftain', and Erin is another name for Ireland." I shrugged. "I guess my parents were the kind who didn't think much about the name they picked."

Tali looked from my lips to my eyes and shook her head sharply, once. "No, it's good," she actually said, in her soft, throaty voice. Then she signed, and it was Sam who spoke for her.

"Red queen of Ireland," he interpreted, with a small quirk at the corner of his mouth. Tali gestured from head down to my dark red sweater, looking satisfied. My hair was twisted and caught in a clip at the crown of my head, not exactly regal but more dignified than my usual wavy mess. For a second, she'd made me feel just a bit queenly.

"Oh," Sam said sharply. "They'll call me the Sufganiyot Scorcher of Whitestone if I don't get these out of the oil. Stand back, everyone."

Then everything happened at once. Loud music began playing in the den, someone opened the basement door and let Roddy escape, the doorbell rang, and chaos ruled. I caught a glimpse of Ericson Greene before Roddy leapt up and licked my nose while Sam simultaneously yelled, "Rory, the platter!"

I grabbed a paper towel-lined glass plate just in time to catch the first hot doughnut. Nine others followed, all golden brown and lightly sizzling.

"The next ten are going in," he said, easing some uncooked ones into the hot oil.

"Where did you learn to make these?" I asked.

"My grandpa. Old family recipe."

I leaned over the plate and breathed in the perfume of fried dough. Sam wagged his eyebrows in shared appreciation. Roddy wagged his tail, stood on his hind legs and snagged a doughnut.

"Roddy!" Sam lunged after him.

"Sir Roderick Scruffs!" I scolded, giggling like a first grader.

"Samuel Solomon," Mrs. Newman put in. Then, "Ro-ree Er-ee—Rory Air—" She gave up trying to say my names. "*Yaroni*, put that plate up on the counter and flip those *sufganiyot* for Sam. Samuel, leave that clown of a dog alone. Do you really want the doughnut back now?" She continued to mutter in Hebrew, cheerfully.

Ericson entered the kitchen. "Can I help?"

"Not this time. You need a night out of the kitchen."

"I'm sorry I missed the lighting of the menorah, Elena."

"No, no. You are wanted many places, you can only be at one at a time. Did you see anyone else arriving?" The doorbell rang. "That must be her now. Just in time—all is ready."

Sam reappeared and pulled the spatula scoop from my hand. "I've got it."

"I know: hands off the *sufganiyot*," I said.

"The platter?"

I held it out while he deposited the hot batch next to the cooling one. "You know," I said, "you're very bossy when you're in the kitchen."

"Businesslike," he corrected.

"Whatever you say, boss."

"Gather in the dining room, if you please," Dr. Newman called.

Sam frowned. "I need to make more of these."

"We have twenty—"

"Nineteen."

"Right. Well, there's only, what, twelve people here?"

"Exactly. There should be at least three for everyone." He looked at me. "What? I usually eat five or six."

"Unreal."

Shayne's head poked in from the dining room. "Hey, guys. Mrs. Newman says the latkes are getting cold."

Sam abandoned his spatula. "Hurry."

We were intercepted by Mr. Newman. "May I suggest you escort the dog outside, Samuel?"

"He has to make his derring-doo-doo," Jake called from the table. Shayne smacked him.

I guarded the plate of doughnuts while Sam shoved Roddy out the kitchen door. We narrowly escaped the wrath of Cold Latke Mama, grabbing the last two places at the table. Sam sat between Ericson and Tali. I found myself beside Kingston and, requiring a double-take, Martina Thistlethwaite.

"I didn't know you were here," I said, not meaning it to sound unfriendly, which unfortunately it kind of did.

"I just got here," she whispered. She smoothed the sides of her tight boy-cut black hair with glistening silver fingernails. They coordinated with the table, all decked out in white and silver and glass and touches of blue. "I feel bad—I'm just in time for the food."

"It would be worse if you weren't in time for it," I said, speaking for her and not necessarily myself. Having her there was kind of like having a scorekeeper, watching and evaluating my performance. How Christian would Rory's behavior rate tonight? Any twenty-dollar-bill-in-the-Bible tricks to play on her?

"Thanks, Rory. That's sweet."

I was saved from guilty self-evaluation by the arrival of the food. Beef brisket in gravy that fell apart under the fork, crisp potato latkes, salads, homemade applesauce—the dishes kept circling the table. Everyone seemed to be talking at once, even Tali. She signed, and Sam nearly choked on a latke.

"She says she's lucky," he explained. "She gets to talk with her mouth full." He smiled, watched her gesture some more, and began to translate. "This is the first Chanukah she's ever celebrated with a bunch—" he broke off, smile fading.

"Tali," her mother shook her head.

Tali's motions clearly meant to make light of what she'd said. Aunt Sabra felt the need to explain. "This is unusual for Tali and I. Ordinarily we are home in Tel Aviv at this time, where everyone celebrates Chanukah and—no offense—there is no sign of Christmas. It is a unique experience to celebrate Chanukah with Christians."

"It's unique for most of us here to celebrate it," Ericson said. "We're honored to share it with you."

Aunt Sabra's smile relaxed, and the chatting resumed. Tali seemed to be trying to draw Sam into conversation, but he kept his replies rather short. Closer to my end of the table, Allie and Shayne were happily arguing about whether latkes and plotskis were the same or different, and Kingston was happily devouring latkes while taking Shayne's side.

Martina leaned over and spoke low. "Don't you find it odd that we didn't say grace before the meal? I mean, with all the observance of ritual, you'd think that would be included."

I wasn't the only one being evaluated, I thought. I felt I should defend the Newmans. "There were blessings when we lit the menorah, but you weren't here for that." Reminding her of her late arrival seemed to work. She concentrated on her salad greens.

"I missed it, too," Ericson said, turning to Martina. "And I'm sorry I did. Knowing the Newmans has taught me a new appreciation for the Jewish tradition, which in a sense is part of our heritage, too."

"Romans eleven," she guessed. "We're like a wild branch that is grafted in, fed by the sap of the root."

I saw Aunt Sabra signing to Tali, translating what Ericson and Martina said, though by her face I don't think she understood it herself.

As for us, what we had failed to understand was that mealtime prayers had not been forgotten—they came after the meal. And they were long. But Dr. Newman said them, and he did it in English. He was barely finished when Sam pulled a wooden object from his pocket, like a small spinning top, and announced, "Dreidel challenge in the den."

He and Jake were already halfway to the door when Dr. Newman called, "Plates—"

"No," Mrs. Newman cut in. "They'll only toss my china in the sink. Let the children go and play. I'll clear the table."

"Let me help," Martina said. "To say thanks for an amazing meal."

In the den, Sam showed us the dreidel, which had four sides, each with a different symbol. "Okay, it's easy. This one is *nun*, for 'nothing'. This is *gimel*, for 'all'. This is *hei*, 'half', and this is *shin*, 'put in'—in other words, put two tokens into the pot. Everyone gets to spin, and whatever you spin, that's what you do."

"But what do you use as tokens?" Allie asked.

"Pennies, usually."

Jake gasped. "Ooh, too rich for my blood."

Tali signed.

"Something better?" Sam asked.

She smiled, skipped from the room, and sauntered back in with a mesh bag full of gold coins.

"Now you're talking," Jake said.

Tali made a C-shape with one hand and circled it around on the back of her other hand.

"Chocolate!" Shayne guessed.

Tali pointed at her and winked.

"Chocolate *gelt*," Sam said, grinning. "Perfect." Tali dumped the coins into a pile on the floor, and we all circled around it like pagan chocolate worshippers. "Usually everyone takes at least ten tokens, but there's a lot of us, so we'll have to start with less."

I reached for the pile, and Jake slapped my hand, girlishly.

"Hang on," I said, and fished another dreidel out of the pile.

"Oh," Tali exclaimed, pointing to herself and taking it from my hand.

"She says it's hers," Shayne translated.

"Wow, Shayne. How would we possibly understand without you?" Jake asked.

"Hey, should we play two separate games, since we have two dreidels?" Allie asked, motioning like she was dividing the group in half. We were all talking with our hands more than usual, as if that was somehow the same as sign language. Tali shook her head, so Allie tried to explain a different way. But Tali kept shaking her head, pointing at one side of her dreidel.

"Hey, look." Kingston took Sam's dreidel and held it up to Tali's. "All the letters are the same except for this one."

"What do you mean, letters? They're just squiggles," Jake said.

Sam frisbeed a chocolate coin at Jake's head. "You know they're Hebrew letters. But he's right. I'm impressed that you noticed, Kings."

"So why is hers different?" Shayne asked.

"Each of the letters stands for a word. On mine, they're short for 'A great miracle happened there'—meaning the miracle in the Temple. But Tali's is from Israel, so her letters stand for 'A great miracle happened *here*'."

"Well, we can still play by the same rules, right?" Allie asked. "The game's no different."

Tali signed and slipped her dreidel into her pocket.

Sam shook his head. "It's not meant to be used here. Only in Israel." He took his own dreidel back from Kingston. I saw him look at it as if it weren't as good.

"Too much talking, not enough chocolate winning," Jake announced. "Let's rumble."

So we played, spinning the dreidel, taking coins from the pot or putting coins in—except for me. I managed to spin *nun* every time, which meant that I did nothing. By the third *nun* I was annoyed; by the sixth, we were laughing so hard our faces hurt. In the end, Tali won the entire pot, which she then graciously divided amongst all seven of us.

Dr. Newman and Ericson had come in during the game. "The women kicked us out of the kitchen," Ericson said. "Believe it or not, they're discussing dessert. When we left, they were stacking about a hundred doughnuts on a platter the size of a manhole cover."

I looked at Sam, puzzled. "But you only made twenty."

"And about two dozen this morning. Plus the ones we brought home from the bakery after Temple."

"And you thought there weren't enough?"

"I'd say there's definitely enough for Jake, Kingston and myself."

"You guys make me ill," Allie said.

"Please don't talk about dessert yet," Shayne agreed. "How about another round of dreidel? This time winner takes all."

I shook my head, clutching my chocolate gold. "I'm not testing my luck again. Count me out."

Kings tossed his down by Shayne's feet with a shy grin. "I'm in."

Tali and Allie joined them, but Sam had something to show Jake on his dad's laptop, a war game by the look of it.

"What's that?" I asked, interested not as a gamer but as a nosy passerby.

"It's a magic book," Jake said, explaining as if to a Stone Age person. "Filled with magic voodoo spirits."

"And World War II battle games," Sam added.

"Let me play." Jake tried to shoulder him aside.

"Not now. I'll let you borrow it. Hey, Rory, did Kingston ever fix that photo you wanted changed?"

"No. It slipped my mind. I was working on my dumb paper all last week—I didn't even have time to go on InterFace." I was immediately sorry I'd said that.

"Oh, your InterFace picture." Jake nodded knowingly. "I've seen it. The Jolly Green Giant Girl captured on film. Not unlike a Bigfoot sighting. I can see why you'd want to change it. Though it's pretty tame compared to some of the photos of all your 'friends'."

"You've been on my page?"

"Sure. I sent you a Friend Request, though it took you about a month to accept it. I was crushed, of course."

"You mean I have to accept a friend request?"

"Duh. How do you think you got all those friendly, twisted deviants' pictures in your Friend File? You had to accept them first."

"I don't remember doing that. Bliss must've done it for me."

"What do you mean?" Sam asked.

"Bliss is the one who helped me set up the account."

"You mean she knows your password?"

I nodded. It sounded bad when he said it. Sam and Jake exchanged a look.

"Bad plan, Jolly Green," Jake said.

"You might want to change your password while you're changing your picture."

"Okay." I nodded like I knew how to do that.

"Do you know how to do that?"

I shook my head.

Jake let out an exasperated sigh. "Here." He slipped a cell phone from his pocket, flipped it open, and snapped my picture. Sam found him a little cord and he plugged his phone into the laptop. With a few taps, he had my new picture up on the screen.

"Not my best work," he said, shaking his head.

I shrugged. "It's better than the other one." Secretly, I was delighted. My skin looked a bit pale, but all the other colors were vivid: my cranberry sweater looked almost blood red, and my hair looked auburn, my eyes almost green. And over my shoulder, was half a head of loose dark curly hair and an intensely black eye over half a nose and a half-smiling mouth.

"I can crop him out," Jake said.

"Don't worry about it. Just get it on there."

"It's a great shot of my left nostril," Sam said.

"Yeah, I thought so, too," I said with a straight face.

Jake tapped at the keyboard. "Okay, what's your password?"

I started to say it. Sam glared at me. "How many times do we have to tell you?"

"Just testing you, Jolly Green." Jake turned the keyboard towards me. "Enter it yourself. And remember—" switch to Kindergarten Teacher voice, "—passwords are for keeping secrets, so keep 'em secret."

I typed it in, and up came my home page and the awful awful woodland fairy picture. I hadn't realized how awful until that moment. Did I mention it was awful?

Jake slapped his leg with a grin. "Always good for a giggle. Are you sure you want to change it?"

"I never wanted it up there to begin with. Bliss picked it."

"You are the pushover of the century. Okay, look. Just go up here, click there, and there, and select that. There you go."

Jolly Green Me disappeared, replaced by Red Queen Me. Immediately I felt better. It lasted for a glorious ten seconds.

"What's that?" Sam asked, pointing at a small picture of one of my supposed InterFace friends.

"I'm not sure. Someone got a new tongue piercing, I guess."

"Click on it," Jake said.

"No, don't." I quickly scrolled away from all the strange little faces (just their faces if I was lucky). "I don't really know any of these people."

"Well, they seem to know you pretty well." Jake pointed to my Bulletin Board, where my 'friends' had posted lots of new comments. Several crude words leapt off the screen at me. I fumbled with the touchpad, trying to click on something, anything else, but in the eternal moment it took to load up another screen, the obscene suggestions written by my dear InterFace pals had seared themselves into my eyeballs. Sam looked away, but I knew he had seen. Jake clicked his tongue and said nothing. My face was blazing.

I had clicked on my Inbox, where a message from Angelica Lyte waited for me. The subject read: *finally my parents let me post a photo!*

For some reason this came as a great relief to me. The picture was just a thumbnail, but I could see it was a girl's face—just a face, no inappropriate body parts—and I realized that although I'd never really believed it possible, a small suspicious part of me had always been troubled by the possibility that Angelica was the archetypical 40-year-old internet predator masquerading as a 14-year-old girl.

"Who's this?" Jake asked.

"A girl I chat with sometimes. She's alright, though the last time we talked, I think I made her mad." I was about to add that I'd made her mad by quoting a Bible verse. Then I rethought it. The I-talk-Bible-to-my-online-friends point I scored might be cancelled out by the my-online-friends-are-the-kind-who-get-mad-when-I-talk-Bible penalty.

"Is she a hottie?" Jake asked.

There were so many things wrong with that, I didn't touch it. "I wouldn't know."

"Click on her thumbnail."

I did, and it opened her InterFace main page.

"Not bad," Jake said.

Blue eyes, freckles, light brown or dark blond hair, smiling without showing teeth. One shoulder was forward, and part of her upper arm was visible—she had taken the picture herself. She looked safely, blessedly normal.

I didn't notice it at first, but in the mostly dark background there was a lighter patch, the shape of another face. The flash had cast Angelica's shadow behind her and almost hidden it. But as I looked, the color pixels resolved themselves into features. Definitely male. Her father? No, younger. A brother, maybe—she talked about her lack of a boyfriend. Not bad looking, whoever he was. Gorgeous, really. Drop-dead gorgeous.

I jerked away from the laptop, or maybe pushed it away from me. It slid off the coffee table and smacked onto the hardwood floor. I ran out of the room.

thirty-two

I stared out from the backseat of the Newman's car, letting my eyes go unfocused so all the Christmas lights fuzzed by in a blur. Even then I could tell which houses had the tackiest decorations. The grand prize winner had to be the one with Santa and Rudolph standing amidst the shepherds and wise men around a manger. Overlooking all was an enormous inflated Frosty the Snowman. As an added touch, the house was blanketed in lights from the satellite dish on top to the garden gnomes down below. Even the mailbox had lights on it. And they were blinkers. I could almost hear Tali laugh.

The duplexes weren't as festive, maybe because it was a little trickier to do a half-and-half job—or sometimes just a half-job—that looked halfway decent. But the Fishers had wound pine garland and red ribbon around the stair rail and their front door, and their front windows were outlined in strands of gently twinkling white lights. Candles illuminated the nativity set in the front window.

The Joyce half of the duplex was dark.

We pulled slowly into the driveway. Mrs. Newman turned around to look at me. "Is anyone home at your house?" she asked.

Kings must've known. It's probably why he drove home with me when he could've stayed at the party, though he claimed it was to save Shayne's dad the trouble later. He asked, "Why don'tcha come over, Rory? We'll watch old black and white Christmas movies or something."

"It's okay, Kings. They'll be back any minute." Hour. Whatever. "There's something I need to do, anyway."

"Okay. Come on over if you change your mind. Thanks for the ride, Mrs. Newman. And all the great food. I had fun."

"Goodnight, Kingston."

He climbed out, and I opened my own door to slide out. I hesitated. "I'm really sorry about…the laptop," I said lamely. "I hope I didn't damage it."

She shook her head. "Samuel dropped it twice last week, and it was fine. His father was not so fine, but the computer and Samuel both survived. Sometimes I wish it were not so sturdy."

I closed the door. Her window rolled down. She was reaching for something on the floor.

"I'm sorry if I ruined—" I blurted, then tried again. "I'm sorry you had to leave in the middle of the party. It was really great. At least until…" Hmm, how to say that, exactly? *Until I saw a demon face on InterFace*?

She smiled gently. "I didn't have to leave. I wished to. Truly, it's not always easy for me to be among many people, though we keep the parties small. This cold air and these sharp stars revive me." She glanced up at the night sky, sparkling like a sheet of black ice. "You needn't worry, child. These days are blessed."

I didn't know which days she meant—the Christmas season, this millennium, or just these particular days of this particular month of this particular year.

"Thank you," I said, because it was enough. There was something about Mrs. Newman that kept the words from always tumbling out of my mouth. The silences weren't so awkward.

"I will wait to make sure you get in," she said. "Oh, and before I forget it—here." She pressed a paper bag into my hands. "Samuel sent this along for you."

"Oh, thanks. Goodnight, Mrs. Newman."

"Goodnight, *Yaroni*."

There was that word again. It had almost slipped past me the first time. Now I latched onto it: *yaroni*. Nevermind that I didn't know what it was. It almost made me smile.

I got inside and closed the door tightly behind me, flipping on any light switch I passed. A peek out the front window showed that Mrs. Newman was true to her word. She waited until I waved before she pulled away.

I found one of those old Christmas movies on TV and turned it on for cheerful background noise. Then I took a deep breath, marched across the room and turned on the computer.

"God," I said out loud, "I've been stupid. I know you're biggest and strongest, but I'm scared that I'm going to be scared again, even though I don't have to be. Holy Spirit, I know you're inside me. I've squashed you down and ignored you a lot lately—please forgive me. I need to know I'm not alone."

Behind me, the movie gave way to a super-charged infomercial featuring something so amazing the guy selling it was practically weeping with joy. In front of me, the email window opened. Mostly InterFace notices informing me that I had messages waiting. I'd been ignoring those. But buried in there I spotted one from ThistleSis3, which was Martina. It was from last Saturday night.

Hi, girls. I just realized that I forgot to assign your reading for the week, Isaiah 43. Enjoy.

Since I might not get to see or talk to some of you before Christmas, I wish you a blessed one. No Teen Scene next Saturday (the 26th), so we'll see you NEXT YEAR! -MT-

I caught myself thinking, *She just couldn't resist giving us homework over Christmas,* and had to pinch the thought off like a rotten tomato off a vine. What if, maybe, just maybe...

I grabbed Dad's Bible and opened it to Isaiah 43. *The Redeemer of Israel,* the title read. I began to read, and the first line or two slipped past. Reading the Bible could be like holding water in my hands. Sometimes most of it just trickled through, and only the wetness remained. But even when I couldn't hold onto it all, it still changed me. "I need to know," I whispered.

The words started leaping off the page at me:

> *Fear not, for I have redeemed you;*
> *I have called you by your name;*
> *You are mine....*
> *I will be with you...*
>
> *Bring My sons from afar,*
> *And my daughters from the ends of the earth —*
> *Everyone who is called by My name,*
> *Whom I have created for glory...*
>
> *Do not remember the former things,*
> *Nor consider the things of old.*
> *Behold, I will do a new thing,*
> *Now it shall spring forth;*
> *Shall you not know it?*
>
> *But you have not called upon me...*
> *...you have burdened me with your sins,*

> *You have wearied me with your iniquities.*
>
> *I, even I, am He who blots out your transgressions*
> *for My own sake;*
> *And I will not remember your sins.*

I sat back in my chair. Took another deep breath. Logged onto InterFace.

It takes about three minutes to cancel an InterFace account. But there was something I had to do first—send a message to Angelica. I couldn't just cut and run. (But I didn't have to look at her profile picture, either. I went right to my mailbox and typed her name, avoiding her homepage. And that photo.)

Angelica,

I saw your picture. We need to talk, but I can't do InterFace anymore. Here's my email address. Can we talk that way instead? Please write.

I signed with my name and email address. Then I erased myself from InterFace.

I spent the next five or ten minutes enthralled by an astounding slicing-dicing-shrink-wrapping kitchen gadget and its worshipful TV spokesperson. Beside me was the largest glass our kitchen had to offer, brimming with milk, and in my lap a paper bag with a crumpled top. Its smell had given it away. I delicately pried the bag open and breathed in the fragrance of fried dough.

One of the *sufganiyot* had suffered for its journey: I saw a blob of deep red seedy stickiness oozing out a crack. It looked scrumptious. *But wait, there's more,* the TV voice urged, and my gaze fell upon the mystery doughnut. It felt promisingly heavy as I pulled its sugar-dusted self from the bag.

And that's not all! Before I took the first bite, I zapped the infomercial with the remote and found yet another old Christmas movie.

Then I sank my teeth in. A dark and sweet, fruit-and-nutty gorgeousness melted into my mouth. I knew the taste. I smiled and melted into the chair. Sam's secret filling tasted remarkably like rugelach. A Wonderful Life, indeed.

I woke in my bed the next morning with a very sketchy memory of how I'd gotten there. There was a thumping and rustling outside my bedroom door.

I don't know what I was expecting to find, but it wasn't the lower half of Grandma Judy's body sticking out of the hallway ceiling. She was on a stepladder, rummaging in the attic.

"Oh, good, you're up." Her muffled voice descended from on high. Apparently she had eyes in her jean pockets. "Here, let me hand stuff down to you."

A shoebox came down at my head, followed by various other cardboard boxes and plastic bins, so I didn't have much choice in the matter. "What are you doing?" I asked. I didn't have to ask. I knew these boxes.

She climbed down, gave me a hug. She smelled like perfume and attic. "Good morning, hon. Why don't you change clothes and I'll make you some breakfast."

She said 'change clothes' instead of 'get dressed' because I was still wearing yesterday's. I threw on some comfy (worn twice already) jeans and a sweatshirt, slipped into my fuzzy slippers and met her in the kitchen, where the eggs were already sizzling. But my eyes were on the family room.

Gran saw me looking. So she finally answered my question. "Your mom's been so busy, and I suppose I have, too—I never meant it to get this late into December before coming over to help put up the tree."

She had it set up in the downstairs corner. "Mom likes it up in the living room window," I said, "where everyone can see it from outside."

"I know." She chopped ham for the omelet.

"But Dad always wanted it down there," I went on. Because that's where we'd spent the most time.

"I know." She winked at me. "Well, as you can see, I've only put it up. You and Sheelan have to do the decorating."

I sipped my orange juice. "With your help?" I sampled images of me and Sheelan working on it together, just us. Not exactly warm and fuzzy.

"Sure, but I want to hang a few lights in the front window first—appease your mother. It would be nice if we could all decorate the tree together when she gets home. Honey, could you butter that toast?" On cue, the toast popped up.

For a few moments, the only sounds were eggs sizzling and the knife dragging across the crunchy surface of the bread. "I don't know, Gran," I said. "Mom might go straight to the restaurant from the office."

Then she was beside me, giving me a sidelong hug. Grandmas didn't care that teenagers supposedly didn't want hugs anymore and gave them anyway. These were much nicer hugs than the ones from parents, who *did* care that you supposedly didn't want the hug but gave you one anyway, uncomfortably.

"Your mom has been working a lot," she said.

"I understand why."

"You're a good kid, Rory Erin. Your mom is lucky to have a daughter as patient as you. But she can't run away from this holiday and leave you girls to handle it alone. She didn't let me do it when your grandfather died."

I bit the toast, sat down as she put a steaming plate-sized omelet on the table in front of me. "How old was she?" I asked.

"Older than you, but not by too much. It was different in some ways. He was sick for almost a year, so it wasn't so sudden. But it's always a shock. You live in a fog for a while. Busyness is a way of coping. It breaks my heart to see my daughter going through it now." She sighed. "But I won't forget our first Christmas without Roy. It was your mom who dragged out the tree and the lights. Even the yard decorations, which we hadn't used for years—since she'd gotten old enough to consider them babyish."

She laughed and cut off a piece of my omelet, sliding it onto her own plate. "You didn't think that whole thing was for you, did you? You couldn't eat that much."

I had, and I could. But I just chewed and smiled.

"Losing Grandpa was hard on your mom, very hard," she said quietly. "Now it's your dad. We just have to find ways to cope. Do the old things in a new way. For instance, if you'd like to invite some friends over to help decorate, that would be fun," Gran went on after sipping her coffee. "Goes a lot faster that way, too. I brought six tins of Christmas cookies and a jumbo can of cocoa mix, so we can make a party out of it."

A half an hour later I'd enlisted Shayne and Allie, and they promised to hunt down Sam and Jake. Then Sheelan showed up and caught wind of the plan.

"Give me the phone," she said.

It only took her two minutes to arrange for Jeph to chauffeur my friends over. She left voice mails summoning a couple of her friends, too, but indicated that only Jephy-poo was crucial to her happiness. I made gagging motions.

"They're coming at 2:00," she said. "Start cleaning."

Aside from the commands from Her Royal Highness, the next few hours weren't so bad. Gran played the Nutcracker Suite on the stereo, and we danced around, cleaning as we went. Well, I danced. When no one was watching.

I vacuumed, Sheelan dusted. I cleaned the downstairs bathroom, she took the upstairs one. Grandma cleaned the kitchen, washed, dried and ironed the Christmas tablecloths, washed the Christmas serving plates and arranged the cookies, made cocoa, mopped the kitchen floor and the front hallway, and cleaned the glass and mirrors. Somewhere in there she might've stitched a torn seam in the Christmas tree skirt, too.

"I get the shower first," Sheelan told me.

"Whatever."

"Oh, please tell me you are planning to shower? Your friends may not care how you smell, but you will not embarrass me in front of mine."

I was showered and dressed by 2:00. For the sake of peace, I even chose clean corduroys and a white sweater. When she wasn't looking, I put on my red and white striped socks with the green toes.

Jeph crunched into the driveway with four other people squished into his two-door hatchback. In the front was a school friend of Sheelan's I'd seen once or twice; out of the back crawled Allie, Shayne, and Jake.

Allie handed me what felt like a foil-wrapped brick. "Grammy sends love. And fruitcake."

Jake grabbed it. "You're kidding me. An actual fruitcake? I thought they were like an urban legend. I've never seen one."

"Grammy's fruitcake is really good," Allie defended.

"Well, if it's not, we can use it as a weapon."

Shayne saw me looking. "Sam wasn't home. His mom said he's doing school today. I don't get it. You can make your own schedule, and you choose to have school three days before Christmas?"

"You didn't tell me he was doing school," Jake complained.

"Only because you're always making fun of him for it."

"Um, hello, Shayne-Brain. Where does Sam do school when he's not at home?"

Her brown eyes lit up beneath the blue stocking cap. "You're right!" She shoved Jake aside happily; he nearly toppled over the stair railing. Shayne skipped up the Fisher's steps. "Think it's okay if I ring the bell?"

"You won't have to," I said. Sure enough, Tee-Tee and Cherry ran from the front window and opened the door.

"Hi," Shayne said. "Is Kingston here?"

Tee-Tee chewed on a beaded braid and eyed her carefully. "Are you his girlfriend?" she asked.

"I'm his friend. Are you his sister?"

But Tee-Tee had her back turned already. "Kingston, your girlfriend is here!"

Kings arrived quicker than usual, with a curious Sam behind him. Sam grinned at Shayne's *here I am* pose, but Kingston's color deepened.

"What're you guys all doing here?" he asked.

"Inviting you over to Rory's house for a Christmas decorating blitz. Can you come?"

"Well, we were working on a Fibonacci series for math," Kings began. Behind him, Sam had disappeared. He was back in a few seconds.

"Your mom said it's fine."

"Okay, I guess we're coming."

By this time my teeth were chattering. "Come on, then." Another car pulled up into the driveway, which I assumed belonged to some other friend of Sheelan. I assumed wrong.

"Oops, we forgot." Allie looked apologetic. "I hope it's okay. We saw Bliss's sister when we went to pick up Jake, and we told her to come if she wanted—we just didn't have room in Jeph's car."

"Oh." I watched as Journey climbed out of the unfamiliar car. Well, that wasn't so bad. It was actually pretty cool. I had way more friends here than Sheelan.

Then the car's front passenger door opened.

"Oh, yeah," Jake said casually. "And I invited Bliss."

Bliss stepped out onto my driveway.

thirty-three

If you'd told me Tuesday morning that by mid-afternoon I'd have a dozen people in my house all decorating like over-caffeinated elves, I would've... probably believed you, because it sounds just strange enough to be my life. But more than once I stopped to just watch it all, as if I'd walked into a story about someone else's life.

During one such moment of stopping and watching, Gran Judy found me. "Here, two cocoas for the pretty brunettes unwinding garland over there. Grab the handles, they're hot." Nevermind that she held the mugs by their piping hot middles. Gran had hands of steel.

I brought the cocoa to Shayne and Bliss, who chatted and laughed as they adorned themselves with the fluffy gold garland. Shayne always had an easy way with people; Bliss was 'doing my head in', as my dad used to put it. She showed no sign of annoyance with the people who had pulled me out of her house — gave no indication that she had ever compared us to sheep.

Ah, but surely she wouldn't be so easy with Sam, the one who'd actually done the pulling. I waited to see what sort of silent staring battles they might get into this time.

Sam was nearby, untangling strings of lights. "Ever seen a Maypole?" he asked me, or maybe just everyone in general.

I set the cocoas on the coffee table, sloshing a little. "You mean the pole with the ribbons? Kids hold the end of a ribbon and dance around it?"

"Yeah, they weave in and out, in and out." He held up a scrambled mess of lights. "Admit it. You guys did the same thing with these lights last Christmas."

I zipped back in memory to those first days of the year, when my dad made us take down the Christmas decorations. He always insisted they be down by January 6th, though he couldn't say why it had to be that date exactly. It was something his mother made him do, he'd say, and she came from Ireland, where they had reasons for everything they did. In his mind, that was explanation enough.

We'd taken the decorations down, though not very willingly or very well. A couple of days later, Dad was gone and I was in the hospital in a coma. Almost a year ago.

Sam realized what he had done, I saw it in his eyes. His eyebrows pulled together, saying sorry without speaking. Then Bliss slid up alongside him. She took a sip of cocoa and examined the tangled lights.

"Allow me." She reached for them, not requiring approval. "I'm very good with twisted things. Just hold onto that end, and watch me."

Sam did as he was told. I wondered, was it really necessary for him to watch her? Her cashmere sweater was advertising her unfair advantages. As she worked, her eyes were on him as much as the lights, making sure his eyes were on her. Okay, where was the hostility, the battle of the glares?

I turned to find something else to do. Jake was putting hooks on ornaments for Sheelan, who clearly thought it was great fun to have an eighth grader fawning over her in front of her boyfriend who was too nice to pound him for it. Allie came to help Shayne, and their conversation turned to school.

"You'll be in first period Algebra 2 with me next semester, right?" Allie asked.

"Yep."

"It's cool that they're moving you up."

"Yeah, and you know who else? Dylan Graham and Will Darby."

"Seriously?"

"Oh, yeah. I knew you'd be happy. But you're going to have to choose once and for all which one to be in love with."

"Give me a break. I just think they're cute."

"Especially Will, right?"

"He's okay, but have you seen his brother? He's a junior. Gorgeous."

Sheelan's guy-talk sonar picked up this signal. "You mean Jack Darby. Watch, next year he'll be senior class president, captain of the football team, homecoming king, the whole package." Jeph stood by and listened silently to her glowing endorsement of some other guy, though I saw a certain tightening of his face.

This talk of boys—and now the sounds of Bliss and Sam actually talking and laughing—caused a certain tightening of my brain, so I jogged up the steps to the kitchen. "Need any help, Gran?"

"No, just tossing a casserole together for dinner later. But there's someone working by herself in the living room."

I found Journey at the bay window, setting up our old nativity set of painted wooden figures. She didn't turn around, but kept rearranging the figures. "No, I'm not playing with them," she said, her back to me. "I'm just trying to see what looks right. Is there a right way and a wrong way?"

"Not really. Baby Jesus just usually goes in the middle, with Joseph and Mary beside him. Everyone else just gathers around."

"The shepherds get the same front-row seats as the kings?"

"Sure. I don't think rank matters much to Jesus."

She nodded, then sat back, satisfied with her presentation. "But what about this?" She held up a yellow-painted four-point star dangling on a long thread.

"We hang that over the stable. Look above the window, the little nail is probably still there."

"I see it." She reached up to wrap the thread around the nail, and her black sleeve pulled back from her wrist. I saw a pink line, then more than one, on her pale skin. They looked like small scars.

Journey lowered her arm and tweaked her sleeve back into place. She looked at me with those steady gray eyes and said, "I believe I just earned myself a cookie."

"Maybe even some cocoa." The floor creaked behind me, and we both turned to find Sam.

"Excuse me," Journey said. "I am owed cookies and I mean to collect." She stepped with silent stockinged feet into the kitchen, like a black cat with white paws.

Sam took off his glasses and polished them with the edge of his shirt, so I knew he came to say something. It was always a little startling to see him without his glasses. Not because he looked all that different without them—it was kind of like surprising someone in their pajamas. They're completely covered, but still somehow vulnerable.

He slipped them back on. "You okay today?" he asked hesitantly.

"Me? Oh, after last night?"

"Is everything..."

I shrugged, one shoulder. "I cancelled my InterFace account."

He sat on the edge of the armchair. "Yeah. Good move."

"I gave Angelica my email address, though. I hope she writes to me. I need to tell her what I saw."

He fidgeted. I thought maybe I knew why.

I asked him, "What did you see?"

He didn't answer for a moment. It was the question he'd wanted to ask me but couldn't. "Um, I saw her. Her name is Angelica?"

"Yes. But did you see anything else? Behind her?"

"For a second, I thought—" He cleared his throat. "The background was shadowy…" Then he shook his head. "Sorry. I looked at it after you left. I didn't see anything unusual."

I sat in the bay window beside the nativity scene and sighed. "It's okay. I guess I'm glad."

"You are?"

"Well, yeah. I don't think I imagined it, but I'm glad he's not really there in the picture, plain as day."

"He…You mean *him*?"

I pulled my white stone from under my sweater and rubbed it between my thumb and finger, almost without realizing it. It was becoming a habit. "Unfortunately, yes. I'm just not sure what it means."

"You saw him instead of Angelica?"

"No, I saw him behind Angelica."

He began pressing each of his fingers down with his thumbs, making the knuckles crack. "Rory, have you given this girl any information besides your email address?"

"You mean like my phone number and address? No, I know not to do that."

"What about the name of your school?"

"I think she already knew that. She was from Bliss's friend network, and that's how she got onto mine."

"So she knows you go to a school called Whitestone Elementary."

"Probably. Yeah. I don't think she cares."

"What about any other names? Have you mentioned any?"

I stood up again. "What, do you think she's going to come find me and beat me up or something?" He ignored that, waiting for an answer. "Well, I might've mentioned Front Street Temple and the Believers Church. We talked about religion sometimes. And I think I mentioned Bliss's mom's friend's shop in Westhaven. But she already knew about most of this stuff, from Bliss I guess."

He stood up, too. "Don't you get it? With the names Whitestone and Westhaven, plus your full name—how hard do you think it would be for her to find you?"

"So?" I began, then faltered. So a girl who I was practically positive I'd seen in a photo with Uri probably knew where I lived.

"How can you even be sure she's who she says she is? That it's even a girl at all?"

"The picture…"

"Could be of anyone."

I turned and stared out the window. The sky was the color of the white socks that accidentally got washed with a load of dark jeans. "You know," I said quietly, "I'm tired of hearing about what I should've or shouldn't've done after I've already screwed up. It'd sure be great if someone could tell me ahead of time for once."

"I don't mean to—"

"I know, I know. You're trying to help. Now I know I should steer clear of the mysterious Angelytes of this world. She was just out there when I needed someone to talk to, you know? I'll probably never hear from her again."

Sam sat on the edge of a lamp table, nearly knocking over a picture frame. He caught it, got a little red, then said. "Well, now

I'm going to tell you what you should do ahead of time. When you need someone to talk to, just come to—"

"Hey, there you are."

Bliss entered the room with all her swerves on. It wasn't clear which 'you' she meant.

"—us," Sam finished. He tapped his chest, where the white stone must've hung under his shirt.

I nodded. For a split second, I'd thought he was going to say *When you need someone to talk to, come to me.* But *us* was a good thing, too.

"Sorry to interrupt," Bliss said, "but Jake says you're needed downstairs, Sam."

"Thanks."

"My pleasure." She used a voice that might best be described as chocolaty, then laughed some sprinkles on top.

Sam stood quickly and set the picture frame back on the lamp table. He looked at it, then at me. "Your dad?"

I nodded.

"I remember seeing him—at school events, I guess. Did he have a loud laugh?"

"The good kind of loud," I said.

"Yeah." His eyes flicked over to Bliss, who hadn't moved. "I guess I'd better…"

"Yeah, go ahead," I said. "Thanks."

Bliss watched him leave, then her eyes slid over to me, all sly. "He's kind of cute, in an eastern Mediterranean kind of way."

"He's a good person," I said.

"No doubt." She smiled at me. "What? Why the suspicious eyes?"

"I'm just surprised, I guess. I thought you'd be ticked off at him."

"Why? Because he dragged you out of my house that day? No, I appreciate a guy with guts. They keep things interesting."

If I had actual guts, I might've told her to keep her interest to herself. Instead I said, "I'm going back downstairs."

"Let's go, then." She took my arm and led me.

We walked in just in time to hear Sheelan make a royal announcement. "Believers' Youth Experience is way superior to Teen Scene." Her position standing on a chair beside the Christmas tree gave her an air of authority. Her strawberry blond curls and aqua sweater that exactly matched her eyes gave her an air of adorableness. I couldn't decide which was more sickening. "No offense to your church, but I mean, all you do is sit around and study the Bible, then play basketball."

"Sometimes we play volleyball," Shayne said. Everyone looked at her. "Well, we did once."

Jeph handed garland up to Sheelan. "We want to keep the focus on what's most important, that's all."

"But Jeph," she said, wielding her insidious power over him just by saying his name—seriously, I could see him sweating—"Teen Scene is never going to draw a crowd. Even if people forgive the atrocious name and come in the first place, they're going to bail out once they realize that's all there is."

"She's right," Jake said.

Allie shot him a look of disgust. "How do you suggest we draw the crowds, then?" she asked.

Sheelan cocked her head to the side, curls bouncing. "Come to Believers and see for yourself. We go to concerts, get guest speakers—I mean, like professional athletes and state senators—and the food is amazing, all catered."

"We get pizza sometimes," Shayne said.

"I'm not sure you're helping," Sam told her.

Sheelan put a hand on Jeph's shoulder. "Jeph's been there. Tell them, Jeph."

"It's pretty good," he admitted.

Since by an evil twist of fate she was my sister, and since Jeph had misplaced his spine, I felt it was my duty to defend the unfortunately-named but rock-solid Teen Scene. Just as my mouth opened, the door to the garage opened, and my mom stepped in.

My mouth stayed open. My mom's mouth opened. She looked around at the sea of faces, the sea of lights, glass balls and garland. She looked slightly seasick.

This was the moment when, if we had an old record player, you would hear the needle drag across the record and the music stop. Our CD player just kept crooning *White Christmas* without a care in the world.

My friends were now looking at me. "We just—" I started, since Sheelan was also, ever-so-helpfully, just looking at me. "We thought..." Now Mom's eyes swung over to me. "We're decorating," I said lamely.

"Yes, Rory, I can see that."

Then, finally, Grandma Judy came down the stairs. "Hello, Maggie. This was my idea—forgive me for not giving you fair warning. It was a spur-of-the-moment sort of thing."

Mom let Grandma take her coat, hat and purse.

"Hi, Mrs. Joyce," Allie ventured. I guess her Grammy's lessons on good manners outweighed my mom's scariness.

"Hello..."

"You remember Allie," I jumped in. "And Shayne. Jake, Sam. Bliss. And this is Journey. Kingston's here, too." They all waved or said a quiet 'hi'.

"Hello. Hello, Jeph."

"Nice to see you, Mrs. Joyce."

"I suppose you'll all be wanting something to eat," Mom said.

Gran said quickly, "I do have a casserole that just needs to bake for an hour—"

"No." Mom cut her off. "No casseroles. With a crowd like this, we'd better order some pizzas."

thirty-four

Forty-five minutes later, I sat watching out the window as the pizza delivery guy pulled into our driveway and Mrs. Newman pulled out.

"Too bad Sammy has to miss the pizza," Jake sighed. Then he clapped his hands together. "Oh well. More for me."

"Jake," Shayne said.

"Come on, you've seen how much he can eat. He's like a cross between a scarecrow and a shark."

She smacked him. I honestly think Jake enjoyed being smacked.

Everyone crowded into the kitchen, but I hung back in the living room. Sam had explained that it was the second night of Chanukah, and it was traditional to kindle the lights as soon as it was dark—pretty early at this time of year.

"My mom would probably let me stay," he said, "but it's just the three of us tonight, and…"

"No, right. I mean, yeah, you should go," I said.

And he had, and now Sheelan was bringing her plate of pizza, her soda and her boyfriend to sit in the living room and eat. "We thought you and the other youngsters could eat downstairs," she hinted subtly.

"I'm going."

She watched me. "Poor Rory."

"What?"

"Don't 'what' me. I'm not blind." She smiled and looked out the window where the Newman's car had pulled away. I left before she could become any more irritating.

Gran Judy's gamble had paid off. Mom ate pizza like she was hungry, not just putting necessary fuel into a machine. She laughed with my friends and teased Jeph and Sheelan. She thanked everyone for their help as they left that evening.

It wasn't that Mom didn't want to do Christmas. She just didn't know how she could. She needed a little nudge—or a big one. A big old tinsel-smothered nudge.

The decorations made the countdown to Christmas feel more electrified, you might say, if you liked saying punny things like that. Even being home alone on Wednesday didn't feel alone-ly. Twinkling lights (and leftover pizza) refuse to let you get down in the dumps. I spent the day wrapping the gifts I had bought for Sheelan (some teen-angst novel all her friends had read) and Mom (a new purse to replace the one her bottle of liquid foundation had spilled inside of as she applied makeup in the car on the way to work). When I say 'I bought', I of course mean 'Grandma helped me buy'. And when I say 'wrapped' I mean 'plopped them into a gift bag'. Lastly, 'spent the day' means it took five minutes and the rest of the time I read a book, watched TV, snacked on cookies, listened to music.

Oh, and by 'listened to music' I mean 'danced and lip-synched in front of my mirror'.

There were a few other unmarked boxes under the tree by Thursday afternoon. Mom only had to work a half day, so we had plenty of time to get to the Christmas Eve service at the Believers' Church. I will admit, when everyone lit their candles for *Silent Night* and the darkened church auditorium blazed with light, it was pretty breathtaking. And the refreshments afterwards were top-notch. They didn't quite compare to homemade *rugelach* or *sufganiyot*, but they were good.

Without ever saying anything to each other, neither Sheelan nor I asked to open a present that night, like we always do on Christmas Eve. There weren't that many under the tree. I didn't want to ask to open one of my gifts and then find out there was only one.

As for Christmas Day…we survived it. By another unspoken agreement, we did it differently this year, I suppose so the gaping Dad-shaped hole in our lives wouldn't feel so huge. Gran Judy came early and helped Mom cook breakfast before we opened presents (Dad was a gifts-first kind of guy). Blueberry crepes (not sticky cinnamon buns, Dad's favorite). We got dressed (Dad practically insisted on jammies all day). We opened gifts one at a time (Dad preferred the free-for-all approach).

Sheelan was happy with her cell phone. She would've been thrilled to death with a cell phone that had unlimited minutes and a monthly bill paid by my mother, but a pay-as-you-go phone was better than no cell at all. I got a digital music player, which was cool. It was a clunky little off-brand guy, and for some reason that made me feel sorry for my mom, not myself. But I smiled and showed it to Gran and told her what it was and how nifty it was. Gran gave us new winter coats, hats and scarves.

Mom watched us fiddle with our new gadgets for a while. I eventually noticed that she was fiddling with a big white envelope. "What's that?" I asked.

She made one of those smile attempts that moves the mouth but doesn't make it to the eyes. "This is another gift. It came in the mail two weeks ago."

"Can I see?" Sheelan already had it in her hands. She flipped it over, and her face went flat. "It's addressed to Dad."

Mom nodded, cleared her throat. "Apparently this is something your dad set into motion a while ago. He had talked about it, but I didn't realize that he'd been— Well, see for yourself."

Sheelan opened the clasp and pulled out a thick brochure. I saw images of beaches and amusement parks and sunshine. "It's stuff about a resort in Orlando," Sheelan said.

"A time-share," Mom said. "You pay an annual fee, and you get to reserve vacation time in these condos."

"Ooh, look. Luxury accommodations. Whirlpool baths. Fully equipped kitchen. Indoor and outdoor pools. Dad bought this?"

"He bought into it, so we can use it. There's a week open in March. He also got these." She pulled out what looked like airline tickets. "They're vouchers. The flight is paid for."

I took them from her hand, but the printed words were incomprehensible to me, like everything else about this. I swallowed to make sure my voice was steady. "This is from Dad?"

Mom nodded but didn't try to talk. Gran did it for her. "He must've taken care of all this last year, and planned to have it all ready for this Christmas."

That's how we got a Christmas gift from my Dad.

Of course, he followed it with a New Year's kick in the gut.

I didn't really blame him for dying. Well, I had once, for a little while, but that was a long time ago. Blaming myself had taken up a lot more time, but even that I'd gotten past, with help. I still got angry at the truck driver who fell asleep and ran the red light. Only when I thought about it too much.

Hard not to think about it too much on the anniversary of IT. It was the time of year to be doing the whole mental 'year in review' thing anyway. And in some ways, even that wasn't as hard as staring down the long dark corridor of the year ahead. If you stared too hard, all the years to follow began stretching out in front of you, who knew how many years, all of them without your dad.

And so New Year's passed, but hard on its heels was the first anniversary of the accident, and we all had to cope with it somehow.

At first, our coping strategy seemed to involve a lot of sitting around and staring at nothing. Mom stayed home from the office that day, and honestly, I think she intended to sit with us, reminisce about Dad, and eat ice cream (I saw Rocky Road and Mint Cookie Crunch in the freezer). But when crunch time came, there was no mint or cookie. A rocky road, maybe. We just sat, and the house was quiet.

So the phone made us jump. Rocky's, short-staffed, pleading with Mom to come in. They didn't know what day it was.

"Ruthie, I don't think—" Mom stopped. "I understand, but... Both of them are sick?" She didn't look at us, but I had a feeling she was repeating everything for our benefit. "Two parties and another big reservation?" Her eyes slid over to us.

"You may as well go, Mom," Sheelan said. "It's fine. Right, Rory?"

I shrugged, which apparently means *yes* to someone who wants it to. I couldn't really blame her for going. I'd run away, too, if I had somewhere to go.

Sheelan found somewhere: up in her room with the phone. She took the Mint Cookie Crunch with her. I grabbed the Rocky Road, changed my mind and went for a bowl of cereal instead.

My email inbox had some messages. Nothing from Angelica; I'd been feeling anxious about it, impatient, but tonight I was glad. Some back-and-forths from Shayne and Allie. Jake and Sam had been involved at first, but then both of them had to go out of town, Jake to his mom's in California and Sam to his dad's family out east. So we girls went from comparing what we got for Christmas (Shayne scored in the Bestest Gift Ever category: a puppy) to who spent the lamest New Year's Eve (Allie's night of babysitting tied with my night of nothing, though I pointed out that at least she walked away with some cash). Now the contest was, who had the best New Year's resolution?

My fingers hung over the keyboard. I tried—tried to share in their carefree spirit, to look ahead and envision something better. I blanked.

Ding.

I scrambled for the mouse, clicked. Let it be...

    samIam: *that you, Shirley?*

I took a deep breath, let it out.

    REJoyce316: *Sir Roger Scruffs?*
    samIam: *hey*
    REJoyce316 >:)
    samIam: *sadly, I'm not a scruffster anymore*
    REJoyce316: ??
    samIam: *mom made me get a haircut before we went to my Aunt Bekah's*

I groaned for the loss of those fat sloppy curls.

REJoyce316: *short-short?*
samIam: *no, but I feel naked*

My brain didn't know what to do with that one. I lunged ahead.

REJoyce316: *Happy New Year*
samIam: *thanks, you too.*
REJoyce316: *good trip?*
samIam: *yes, except for the army cot I had to sleep on. I named him Lumpy.*
REJoyce316: *isn't that what Shayne named her new puppy?*
samIam: *no, I think he's Plumpy, like the Candyland character*
REJoyce316: *the board game?*
samIam: *well, yeah*
REJoyce316: *I'll have to take your word for it— the last time I played Candyland was like ten months ago. Or wait, no, it was ten YEARS.*
samIam: *your loss*
REJoyce316: *so what's up over there?*
samIam: *just crashing. You?*
REJoyce316: *crash and burn*
samIam: *?*
REJoyce316: *school starts up again tomorrow*
samIam: *I always dreaded that*
REJoyce316: *I'm ready to go back. This holiday stuff...*

There was nothing for a half minute.

samIam: *I guess for your family this was just one to get through*
REJoyce316: *pretty much*
samIam: *but you made it*
REJoyce316: *that remains to be seen*

I was all but asking for him to ask me. I wanted him to and yet didn't.

> **samIam:** *what is it?*
> **REJoyce316:** *today was*

I couldn't even type it. Didn't have to.

> **samIam:** *oh*
> **REJoyce316:** *:(*
> **samIam:** *sorry, Rory*

His words—and that stupid little frowny-face symbol I'd made—blurred. I choked back a hard knot in my throat, but a warm tear slid out of the corner of each eye and plopped down on the keyboard.

Neither of us typed for a little while. But I knew he was there.

> **REJoyce316:** *I didn't mean to turn this into a pity Rory session*
> **samIam:** *you haven't*
> **REJoyce316:** *I just can't figure out how to deal. It's been a year and I still haven't figured it out. I feel like there's two of me. The one who acts like life is normal and okay—hey, sometimes I even fool myself—but it's fake. Then there's the me who's stuck and barely functioning, basically useless.*
> **samIam:** *is that how you feel when you're with people?*
> **REJoyce316:** *most people*

But not him. That's what made Sam irresistible and dangerous. I felt more like the real me with him. I just wasn't sure that was always a good thing.

> **samIam:** *what about with God?*

REJoyce316: *not sure I'm tracking*
samIam: *which "you" is the one who comes to God?*
REJoyce316: *you mean prayer? I pray.*
samIam: *you can be real with Jesus.*
REJoyce316: *I know. And I know because of Jesus there's a happy ending to all this, eventually. But what about right now? Today. And tomorrow. There's so much horse pucky to deal with right here, right now, before the happily ever after.*
samIam: *plenty of pucky, yes*
REJoyce316: *pucky o'plenty*
samIam: *but*
REJoyce316: *uh oh*
samIam: *what?*
REJoyce316: *I said something wrong, didn't I?*
samIam: *no, I was just thinking*
REJoyce316: *and?*
samIam: *and you trust Jesus with your eternity, right?*
REJoyce316: *yes*
samIam: *so can't you trust him with your tomorrow?*

I sat back and thought about that. Could I? I wasn't sure what that looked like.

samIam: *God's grace isn't just something that kicks in when we die. Our eternal life begins the moment we're saved. That's when the Holy Spirit moved in and made you his permanent residence. Jesus called him the Helper, and the Comforter.*
REJoyce316: *so where is He, then?*
samIam: *He has to be where He promised to be—in you*

Then where was the help? Where was the comfort?

REJoyce316: *so what you're saying is, if I'm not feeling all that happy-clappy peace that passeth understanding down in my heart all the time, it's my own fault*

I sat there a few seconds, waiting for him to tell me I was wrong. I sat there a whole minute, waiting for him to tell me I was wrong.

Like a come-lately Christmas miracle, the phone rang. Sheelan's cell phone (which she was foolishly using at home even though it was costing her precious money-minutes) had set our house phone free from bondage.

Newman, Isaac

I swallowed hard. "Hello?"

"That's not what I'm saying, and you know it."

thirty-five

"Um," I said. "Uh…" Articulate, Rory.

"It's okay that I called?"

How to answer that?

"Um-hmm." That would have to do.

"Things get lost in translation when I chat online," Sam said. "Maybe because I type with two fingers and a thumb."

"Could be that."

"Yeah." He paused, and for a terrifying moment I thought I'd have to come up with some actual conversation, but then he continued. "Anyway, I didn't mean to say that Christians are supposed to feel happy-happy all the time—and that if you don't, you're not doing it right."

"Yeah, I know."

"I mean, today is… For you, today is not happy." He cleared his throat. "Sorry, that sounds stupid when I say it out loud."

Welcome to my world. "No. I know what you're trying to say. And I don't expect to be happy all the time. It's all that business about God's peace…it really does pass my understanding. I *think* it means that, even when life is sad and hard and it stinks, that there's this rock solid sureness inside you that it's all okay, that God's handling it, that you're ultimately safe."

"Sounds to me like you understand it okay."

"In my head. I just don't know how to get it into my heart."

He was quiet a moment. For some reason I pictured him without his glasses. "I think I know what you mean," he said. "Like when I read the Bible, or pray, and it's just words, and they don't feel like they're sinking in or going anywhere."

"You mean you feel that way, too?"

"Sure. I think everyone does sometimes."

"Oh."

"You sound disappointed," he said.

"I guess I was hoping I'd grow out of that. Just like I was hoping this walking with Jesus thing would get easier as I went along."

"Yeah, that'd be nice. But let's both check, and the first one who finds in the Bible where it says following Jesus will be easy, wins."

A seemingly random thought popped into my head. "Follow your bliss."

"What? Who?"

"I was just remembering the sign hanging in Tam's shop. *Follow your bliss.* Bliss says that's where her mom got the idea for her name. Anyway, I guess it's their philosophy of life. Go where your happiness leads you."

"*Follow your bliss* versus *Take up your cross and follow me,* huh?"

"That's what Jesus said?"

"Yep. And he wasn't talking about taking up a cross on your necklace. Or your bumper sticker."

I sighed. "Take Up Your Cross isn't going to tempt many people away from Follow Your Bliss."

"Only when we figure out that what we think we want is never what we really need." Sam's words were followed by silence, then a thud.

"You still there?" I asked.

He groaned faintly. "Yeah. Sorry. I always lose consciousness when I try to be philosophical but it comes out sounding like song lyrics."

"Ha ha."

"Hey, guess what?" he asked.

"Chicken butt."

Mystified silence. "What?"

"Chicken butt. Are you telling me you've never heard that one?"

"It doesn't make any sense."

"Exactly," I said. "But nevermind. Tell me—what."

"Chicken butt."

"Sam."

"Just trying it on for size."

Interesting choice of words. I let it go.

"So I was going to say that I want to have you guys over this week, or maybe next. A really cold night. I got a telescope for Christmas. We can take it up on the roof—"

"Wait a sec. You really get to do Chanukah and Christmas?"

"Oh yeah." He chuckled. "Well, no. We don't exactly 'do' Christmas. This year Christmas fell during Chanukah, so my Christmas gift was really one of my Chanukah gifts—the big one."

"A telescope, huh? But why a really cold night?"

"So we can suffer. But mostly because the sky's super clear."

"Oh, right." I'd never thought about it before. "Sounds cool. Cold, but cool."

"Yep," he said.

There was a pause.

"So…" I tried.

"So we'll figure out a night."

"Yep," I said.

"So..." he said.

"So I'd better go." I wanted to bite the words, suck them back in. Too late. I'd hit the panic button.

"Sure, okay. Maybe I'll see you at the Fisher's this week."

"Okay."

"Okay." Slight pause. "Bye, Rory."

"Bye."

I placed the receiver on the base. Then I picked it up again, pressed *calls received* and looked at *Newman, Isaac* again. I pressed *save*. Because you never know when you might grow a backbone and have the courage to make a phone call to a friend. Who happens to be a boy. One of the nicest people you've ever met. Who happens to be a —

Ding.

samIam: *that's not what I'm saying at all*

I gave the computer my *whatchu talkin' bout?* look.

REJoyce316: *???*
samIam: *I'm answering your last message*
REJoyce316: *um, I think you took care of that on the phone*
samIam: *on the phone?*
REJoyce316: *like a minute ago?*
samIam: *I haven't been on the phone*
REJoyce316: *?????*
samIam: *just kidding. I forgot to ask you something. A favor — can you help me out with an assignment?*
REJoyce316: *tell me what it is first*
samIam: *what, you've got your lawyer there with you? Okay, I'm supposed to find as many Biblical names for Jesus as I can.*

> **REJoyce316:** *I know two: Jesus and Christ.*
> **samIam:** *very good, ha ha. Seriously, though, if you come across any while you're reading, let me know.*

I was being serious. I didn't know Jesus had any other names. I always thought it was kind of like a first name, Jesus, and a last name, Christ. Did he have a middle name?

> **samIam:** *If I find the most, I win a prize. Oh, and I can't use the internet, so I guess you can't, either. Only the Bible.*
> **REJoyce316:** *Rules, now? Do I get a share of the prize?*
> **samIam:** *your lawyer again? Sure, but I don't know what it is yet.*
> **REJoyce316:** *I'll see what I can do.*
> **samIam:** *have your people call my people*
> **REJoyce316:** *Roger that.*
> **samIam:** *bye, Shirley. Hang in there.*
> **REJoyce316:** *hanging. Bye*

Naturally I grabbed my Bible. I took it upstairs and sprawled across my bed. Where to begin?

How about with prayer?

I'm pretty sure the thought was my own. Half sure. But seeing as it was such a good idea, maybe not.

"God," I said quietly, then tried, "Jesus? Help me to find you in this book. I'm a few days late for a new year's resolution, but I want to try to read it every day if I can. I'm definitely going to need your help on that. Maybe… maybe you could make me as hungry for the Word as I am for food." I thought about it. "Or maybe make me a little less hungry for food and a lot hungrier for your Word. Thank you. Amen." I swallowed hard. "Oh, and if it's possible… I mean, if things work that way up there, could you give my dad a hug from me? Amen."

My Bible opened to the Gospel of John, which is where I'd happened to shove Martina's bookmark when I found it under a pile of dirty laundry a week ago. But it was hard to call it mere coincidence when my eyes fell on Jesus' words in the sixth chapter: 'I am the bread of life. He who comes to Me shall never hunger, and he who believes in Me shall never thirst.'

"Wow," I said out loud. I leapt up, grabbed a pencil and paper. *Bread of Life*, I wrote. Names for Jesus. Now I got it.

Because she'd gone in early, Mom was home from work before I went to bed. She made sure I'd had some dinner. She made sure I had a clean uniform for school in the morning. She even sat on the edge of my bed when I was about to turn out the light. She wanted to say something about Dad, so the day wouldn't go by without saying something about Dad.

She looked around the room, as if she hadn't seen it in years. I saw her chin quiver.

"It's okay, Mom," I whispered.

She squeezed my hand, then went into her room and cried.

I cried, too, my tears running down into hair still wet from the shower. Washed with my dad's shampoo—after he died I had sneaked the bottle from his bathroom, a 2-in-1 with rosemary and eucalyptus, rationed all these months like liquid gold. I only used it when I missed him the worst. Today I had gotten the very last drips out. Now it was gone.

My tears seemed to make the fragrance stronger. It's a soggy way to fall asleep, but it works.

I sank through scattered, nonsensical images, voices that seemed to speak English but made no sense. I glimpsed a familiar face and tried to stop there, hang on to something comforting. *Rafie?* I called, sure it was him, though he looked remarkably changed. Not at all childlike—utterly ageless, scattering trails of light when he reached for my hand. But something tore me away.

I stumbled, head hanging down, a horrible weight pressing on my shoulders and outstretched arms. Breaking my back. *Take up your cross?* a voice mocked smoothly, like a serrated blade with a velvet handle. *Watch it take you down, and despair.* And it would, I knew. The burden would cut through flesh and bone and soul and crush me down to agony and darkness. I was lost. Dead. I gave up.

And the load lifted. An arm lay solidly along my own; a hand gripped me firmly below the elbow. I lifted my head, saw that the cross wasn't a cross at all, but a yoke. My legs straightened and my steps steadied. I took up the gentle pace of the One beside me. He carried the weight, and he kept us moving straight. He let me work alongside.

The mood of the dream stayed with me. I moved through the next day calm and alert, thoughtful. This is probably what saved Bliss from a strangling.

Our teachers had obviously made New Year's resolutions to squeeze twice as much work out of us, so classes had been all business. Bliss didn't have a chance to get chatty with me until lunchtime.

"Want to go out and get lunch?" she asked me.

I was already handing the lunch lady my money. "Isn't it like ten below zero outside?"

"Cody can pick us up."

Wouldn't Cody be at the high school, in class, right now? I didn't bother to ask. "Thanks, but I've got my lunch."

I headed for the usual table. She sat across from me. "I'm not really hungry, anyway," she said. "Hi, Jasmine."

"Hi." Jasmine—or the replica that the body snatchers had supplied in place of the real Jasmine—slipped a bookmark into her historical novel, set it aside, and smiled at Bliss. I nearly choked on my mixed veggies. She didn't notice, focused as she was on smiling at Bliss. Did I mention she was smiling? "I talked to my mom about Wicca," she said.

"Really? How'd she take it?"

Jasmine shrugged. "No big deal. She noticed some similarities between Wicca and Buddhism."

"Sure. The altar, the circle. Death, life, rebirth. Lots of shared truth." Bliss filched a chicken thinger from my plate.

"Yeah, though I'm not sure why it even matters to her, since she doesn't really practice Buddhism, either."

"It's a cultural thing," Bliss said, nodding wisely. "I respect that. But ultimately, you have to make up your own mind. Find your own truth. Religion isn't just something we should inherit from our parents or go along with, just to keep the peace." She turned to me. "No offense."

I didn't quite see what that had to do with me. I guess she assumed I was a Christian by default—just because my parents went to a certain church and we celebrated Easter and Christmas. And maybe I had been, but not anymore.

"Actually," I heard myself say, "Jesus said that He didn't come to bring peace, but a sword. And that he would turn a man against his father and a daughter against her mother... Stuff like that."

Where had that come from? I remembered hearing that verse before, but I didn't remember remembering it, if that makes any sense.

They both looked at me for a minute. Bliss took another piece of my chicken. Did anyone besides me remember that she was a vegan?

Jasmine said, "I really prefer less swords and more peace, honestly."

"Hey, check this out." Bliss reached under her collar and pulled out a silver chain. Dangling from the bottom was a pendant—a white stone. I blinked, stared harder. The same size as mine—and Sam's, Shayne's, Allie's, Jake's—with the same silver tag hanging behind it. I could even see that the tag was inscribed with lettering.

Bliss's brown sugar eyes watched me watching her. "Tam gave it to me. A Yule present. See?" She held it out. I looked but didn't touch.

"Let me see," Jasmine said. "Nice. I like the inscription: *Blessed Be*. Where'd she get it?"

"A great little jewelry boutique down the street from her shop. Hey, come with me to the shop today after school. You can help me unpack Tam's new shipment. She always lets me keep a few things."

"That'd be sweet."

I had lost my appetite. Good thing, since Bliss had eaten my lunch.

thirty-six

"That's it for me—I'm going in!" Shayne crab-walked across the frost-encrusted black shingles towards the dormer window.

"Hang on, I've almost got it," Sam said with white puffs of breath.

"Unh-uh. You can keep your Playdohies—"

"Pleiades."

"They're all yours. I'm freezing my Plee-a-dees off out here." She climbed back into the house with exclamations of sweet relief.

Jake pushed past me, not minding that I was frozen in place from equal parts fear and cold. "Lemme see." He put his eye to the viewer. "What? What am I looking at?"

"It's a star cluster."

"It's a blurry blob."

"No, look closer. You can see the—"

"Let's look at Mars again." But Sam boxed Jake's hand away before he could swing the telescope around.

"Hang on, I just spent ten minutes setting it up to see—"

"To see a blobby cluster. Come on, let's look at some planets. Which one's Saturn again? Hey, let go." They began wrestling and throwing punches and laughing, all of which I felt were seriously bad ideas up on a second-story rooftop. I dared to let go with one hand, scooped up some snow that had collected in the corner of the dormer, and flung it at them. Kind of like throwing water on fighting dogs.

Jake let out a holler. "That went right down my shirt!" He turned on me, searching for more snow—and revenge.

"Stop," Sam ordered. "You'll knock the telescope over."

"I'm wet and freezing, and she must pay."

"Suck it up. Or go inside and put on one of my shirts."

"As if they'll fit my hugely muscular physique," Jake said in his Eastern European Bodybuilder voice.

I almost commented on the possibility that it wasn't entirely muscle, thought better of it, and just kept a wary eye on him as he rapped on the window. Shayne opened it for him, and he climbed inside.

"You coming, Rory?" she asked, hugging herself against the blast of frigid air.

"In a minute."

"Aren't you freezing?"

"It's not that bad."

She shook her head and closed the window with a bang, making the 'cuckoo' sign at me.

Okay, yes, I was freezing. I was shivering so much that I was perfectly still, kind of the opposite of when you step into a hot shower and your body gets confused and gets goose bumps.

Sam gestured to the telescope. "Your turn."

In my fond imaginings, I confidently clambered over and peered into the viewer. Perhaps I would say something intelligent about star clusters. Ah, I love imagining.

In reality, my butt was frozen to the roof. Or it might as well have been. It was a sure bet that the moment I moved, I would go hurtling off the roof to my gruesome and agonizing death. I looked helplessly back at Sam. He gestured again.

"Um..."

"What's wrong?" he asked. "Are your pants frozen to the shingles?"

I laughed weakly.

"No, I'm serious. It happened to me a few days ago. Just pull hard."

"And go flying off the roof? No thanks."

"You won't fly. You'll just fall." He grinned, but at the same time I saw understanding glimmer in his eyes. "Afraid of heights?"

"How'd you guess?"

"I wondered why you didn't come over to see Mars before."

"I can see it just fine from here." I looked up. Mars, winking vaguely red, and Saturn, and the ring of stars Sam had called Auriga, and Taurus with its big orange eye. And a million others, some so bright I had an urge to reach up and pluck them like diamond plums. Others were almost invisibly faint; I had an impression that there were another million just outside my ability to see, outside my grasp, but I could feel them up there.

Sam looked up, too, quiet for a minute with me. "You could see even more before they put the streetlights across the field there. I wish you could've seen it then."

Funny, even with my body in an ice-cube state, my face was still warm. I have sub-zero resistant cheeks. I said, "It's still amazing."

"Well, come over here and see something even more amazing." When I didn't move, he slid towards me. "Look, I'll stay down here, so even if you slip—which you won't, it's not slippery at all—but if you did, I'd stop you."

"Or we'll both go toppling off together."

"Fine, and we'll land in those snowy bushes and have a good laugh."

I eyed him doubtfully.

"Come on. It's worth the risk." He held out his gloved hand.

I stretched out my mittened one. Before I could change my mind, he had me in a firm grip and I was hobbling over on my knees.

"Take a look."

I put my eye to the round black viewer and let out a frosty sigh. I straightened, looked up at the little fuzzy spot in the sky, then looked at it again through the lens. "I see four—no, six stars…maybe seven?"

"Yep." I could hear the smile in his voice. "The Seven Sisters. There's really over 250 stars in that cluster. Those are just the brightest. They're in a dust cloud. That's what causes that haziness, the dust reflecting their bluish light."

"Wow. Where'd you learn all that?"

He shrugged. "Books. Internet."

I remembered something from one of Ericson's evolution books. "I read about how, out of all the millions of galaxies and billions of solar systems, there's no sign that life as we know it could exist anywhere other than here, in this part of this type of galaxy, in this kind of solar system, on this type of planet, exactly this distance from this kind of sun."

"Yeah."

"And supposedly it just happened by chance."

He was silent for another minute. Sam was like his mom that way: easy to be quiet with. Then he said, "The Bible sometimes talks about angels as stars."

I had the sense that he wanted to talk about it. Had he dreamed another Gabby dream? I thought of my dream, the horrible cross that became the bearable yoke, and the strong but gentle and lowly One bearing the weight beside me. A rush of warmth flooded through me, raw, grateful love for that Helper, that Savior, and I wanted to tell Sam about it. But ironically, where the cold didn't make me shiver, the warmth did, and it shook me so hard I bumped the telescope. It swung around, then started to tip. *Oh no.* I grabbed for it, caught it. Started to slip towards the edge of the roof. Sam grabbed my coat. I grabbed his leg. There was a lot of grabbing.

This made it the perfect time for Shayne and Jake to open the window. And for a van to swing into the driveway to cast its bright beams on us in a spotlightish sort of way.

"Sorry to interrupt this...whatever this is," Jake said sweetly, "but your mama says playtime is over."

"What's going on?" Shayne leaned out, smiling.

"We're trying not to fall off the roof!" I panted. Sam said nothing. He was in what my dad used to call 'kinks of laughter'. "Sam!"

He couldn't talk.

"Crawl over here, Rory, we'll save you," Shayne said.

"Yeah, just scootch all the way over so we can do it from the warmth and safety of the indoors," Jake added.

I detached myself from the unhelpful Sam and was halfway through the window when a car door opened and shut down below. "Everyone okay up there?" a familiar voice called.

"Hey, it's Ericson," Shayne said brightly.

"I think he brought food." Jake took off for the stairs, Shayne right behind him. I tumbled the rest of the way into the dark room.

Sam's head poked through the window. "There's a lamp on the desk," he said. I found it, knocking a book off in the process, and we blinked against the incandescent glare. "Here, can you help me get this thing back in?" The legs of the telescope's tripod came poking inside, and I guided them to the floor. "Just set it on the bed." He jumped in and locked the window behind him, stamping his feet and rubbing his hands together. "I think we've suffered enough for one night," he said, whipping off his cap and gloves and scrubbing his hands through his now-shorter hair. It was still long enough for the curls to fall past the tops of his ears, but a change from the mop he'd been sporting since the fall.

I pulled off my knit hat and was rewarded with a static hair cloud.

"Nice," Sam said, though he couldn't actually see me. His glasses had fogged up.

"Was that really Ericson?" I asked. He nodded. "Does he come here a lot?"

He shrugged. "Sometimes I have my guitar lesson here, and he stays for dinner. And he's part of my mom's grievers' group." He polished his glasses, saw my puzzled look. "A support group for people who've lost someone close to them."

"Oh." I thought of my mom. "For adults?"

"Yeah." He hesitated. "They've invited your mom once or twice."

"Oh." My mom had talked to Sam's mom? She'd refused to come? Should I say thanks, or sorry? "Well, she works a lot...I guess maybe she's just not ready yet."

"They understand."

I picked up the book that I had knocked off his desk. Geometry. I set it with *Greek Myths* and *Latin Made Easy*, then noticed the illustration Sam had tacked to the wall above his desk. It was a traveler, maybe a knight, on a path that twisted and turned ahead of him, leading to a shining fortress at the horizon. *But seek ye first the kingdom of God, and his righteousness; and all these things shall be added unto you.*

He saw me looking. At the same time, we both glanced around as if we just noticed we were in Sam's bedroom. "I'd better go downstairs," I said quickly.

"Right. I'll be down in a minute. I have to pack up the telescope."

Ericson was at the bottom of the stairs. "I brought fried chicken and biscuits. Better hurry. Jake's already started."

"Thanks!" I flung my coat, hat and gloves on the pile by the front door and let him lead me into the kitchen.

"Shayne says Allie is sick," he said. "That's a shame. I hoped all five of you would be here."

"So what's she gonna miss, besides some extra spicy secret recipe Cajun chicken?" Jake asked, adding some more bones to the collection on his plate and licking his fingers.

"She's missing your exquisite display of table manners," Shayne said.

"You sound just like her," Jake complained.

"Just filling in."

Ericson gave Sam a clap on the back as he joined us at the table. Then he said, "I wanted to run an idea past you guys. Something Pastor d'Amico has been discussing for a while. We feel that Teen Scene is serving a good purpose, but that the large group setting doesn't meet the need for tight-knit, supportive small group connections."

Shayne was already drumming the table with excited fingers. "We're really going to form small groups? You guys, it's just like we've been talking about." Then she remembered, and she eased back a bit. "You mean, like what Kellie wanted to do?" she asked quietly.

Ericson nodded and smiled that certain way—his smile for Kellie. "I admit, I've resisted somewhat. It wasn't my idea. Don't get me wrong, I think it's a brilliant idea. I just never planned to do it without her." He let out a slow breath. We held ours. "But I know it's what she would want me to do."

We all shared hopeful glances. Sam asked, "How big will the groups be?"

"Pastor thinks four or five to start with. No more than, say, eight maximum per group. We're highly experimental at this stage."

"So we'll be your guinea pigs, is what you're saying," Jake observed.

"More or less. You guys are a natural place to start, since you've already got an unofficial small group thing going. You just need a little leadership."

"And that's you," Shayne said, doing a sitting victory dance in her chair. "So we'll call it—"

"The Jesus Machine. It's already got a name."

"I think I'll speak for Allie now," I said, "and tell you that it's time to put that one to rest."

"No problem. There's more where that came from. Let's see, Teen Scene small groups..." He snapped his fingers. "Eenie Weenie Teenie Scenies."

Ericson gazed heavenward, then dug into a small duffel bag and pulled out his Bible. "I was reading in First Peter today, praying about this. Truth be told, I was trying to see if God might have someone else in mind for it. Not someone more willing, because I am. Just someone more able. Then I read this passage. Can I share it?"

Of course we agreed. He read:

"'As you come to him, the living Stone—rejected by men but chosen by God and precious to him—you also, like living stones, are being built into a spiritual house to be a holy priesthood, offering spiritual sacrifices acceptable to God through Jesus Christ. For in Scripture it says:

> *See, I lay a stone in Zion,*
> *a chosen and precious cornerstone,*
> *and the one who trusts in him*
> *will never be put to shame.*

"'Now to you who believe, this stone is precious. But to those who do not believe,

> *The stone the builders rejected*
> *has become the capstone,* and,
> *A stone that causes men to stumble*
> *and a rock that makes them fall.*

"'They stumble because they disobey the message—which is also what they were destined for.'"

Ericson looked up at us, making sure he had our full attention before he continued, more slowly:

"'But you are a chosen people, a royal priesthood, a holy nation, a people belonging to God, that you may declare the praises of him who called you out of darkness into his wonderful light. Once you were not a people, but now you are the people of God; once you had not received mercy, but now you have received mercy.

"'Dear friends, I urge you, as aliens and strangers in the world, to abstain from sinful desires, which war against your soul. Live such good lives among the pagans that, though they accuse you of doing wrong, they may see your good deeds and glorify God on the day he visits us.'"

He tucked a slip of paper in the page and closed the Bible.

"That's us?" I asked softly. "A chosen people?" For some reason my eyes flicked up and met Mrs. Newman's. She was Jewish, one of the original chosen people. She nodded at me.

"A royal priesthood," Shayne said. "Coolness. People belonging to God." She smiled and pulled out her white stone. "Friends of God," she added.

"Aliens and strangers," Jake said. "Some of us more than others." He tilted his head and pointed at Shayne with his eyeballs.

"It's a great mission statement for the new group," Sam said.

"So what will we call ourselves?" Jake asked. "I vote for Alien Strangers."

"No, no." Shayne stood. "Chosen people—no, wait, that sounds too cliquish. Hey, how about Holy Nation?"

Sam laughed. "Sounds like a militant cult."

"Stranger Aliens, then," Jake tried.

"I don't think—" I started, then everyone looked at me. "I don't think we should name it after ourselves. It's not about us, you know?"

"She's right," Shayne said firmly, sitting down again.

"A suggestion, Rory?" Ericson asked.

"What was that part about those who put their trust in Him will never be put to shame?"

"'I lay a stone in Zion, a chosen and precious cornerstone—'"

I pointed. Sam nodded. Surprisingly, it was Jake who said it. "Cornerstone." He nodded. "Seems obvious now." He met our raised eyebrows with a steady gaze. "What? It's not as good as Alien Strangers. But it's pretty good."

All it took was a phone call to Allie—she approved the idea and the name somewhere between a sneeze and a coughing fit—and it was official. Mrs. Newman passed around mugs of cocoa with fat, melty marshmallows, and we toasted to Allie's health and to Cornerstone.

Ericson's toast was really a prayer. "Lord, may we seek always to build our lives on the Solid Rock of Jesus Christ."

"Amen."

Before we took our first sip, Shayne called out, "Marshmallow mustache contest!" We drank deeply and came up foamy.

"Tie between Sam and Jake," Ericson said.

"No fair." Shayne wiped her mouth with a napkin. "They have those little starter mustaches for the marshmallow to stick to."

"Little starter mustache?" Jake licked his lips clean. "This is the real deal, sister. I'm going to have to break down and shave it off, I suppose, before it interferes with my food."

"Really?" She leaned in. "Let me get my magnifying glass."

Sam ignored them and turned to Ericson. "Thanks for doing this."

"No problem. I love marshmallow mustaches." Ericson reflected Sam's grin. "Oh, you mean Cornerstone? Well, it's not just me. We met with the Pastor and the elders of the church, and everyone agreed that each small group should have two leaders, a man and a woman. For obvious reasons, I think."

"Really?" Shayne tuned in. "Who?" But her interest hit a glitch; a thought occurred to her that had also occurred to the rest of us. It should've been Kellie.

Ericson's expression didn't waver. "The person who's really been pushing for the small group idea for the past few months." He took a sip of cocoa and came up with a mustache. "Martina Thistlethwaite."

thirty-seven

"Welcome to the first official Cornerstone gathering," Martina said. A few weeks had passed since the actual first official Cornerstone gathering.

"It's technically the second," Jake drawled. "The first one was when I named it Cornerstone."

"You named it?" Allie challenged.

"You'd know that if you'd been here." He patted her hand.

She jerked it away. "I was sick. What else did I miss?"

"They elected me chairman," Jake said.

Martina clicked her violet-red fingernails on the Newman's kitchen table. "I missed it, too, Allie."

"Were you sick?"

"No. I had a manicure appointment I couldn't really cancel."

I met Shayne's glance. We were both thinking *oh, heaven forbid you miss a manicure!* Then Shayne's eyed darted away. Martina was watching us. Already we were off to a great start.

Ericson settled it. "This is our first technical and official meeting. Kingston, I'm glad you're joining us, too." That had been

Sam's idea. I felt kind of bad that it wasn't mine. "And thanks to the Newmans for letting us use their home."

"On behalf of the Newmans, you're welcome," said Sam. His parents had left us in privacy. And with chips and salsa.

"So," Martina said crisply, "two ways we can approach this. With a topical study guide like this one," and she held up a paperback booklet with photos of Average Teens Hanging Out under the title *Average Teens and Their Earthshattering Issues* or something like that. "This will keep us focused and moving forward in a purposeful direction. Or we can just gather and talk about the challenges and issues you guys are facing that week without any kind of structure, which could easily degenerate into a free-for-all."

"I vote for the free-for-all," Shayne said.

"I second that," Jake said.

Martina looked at Ericson. "Were we even calling for a vote?"

"I hope so, because I vote for the free-for-all, too." He smiled sheepishly. "No offense. I think the organized study format is done beautifully at the Scene. We need to give these guys a place to talk out whatever they're going through and support each other, like living stones."

"And eat," Sam said.

And that's what we did. Nothing earthshattering, but we all talked. I even shared a little bit about missing my dad, but I mostly felt myself holding back—I blamed it on the fact that Martina was there, and that I didn't feel easy with her. But even as I kept to the shallow end of my sadness, I privately began to see the deep, dark truth: the ragged hole in my life wasn't just going to slowly heal over. Something had to fill it, and I was searching for whatever that would be.

Maybe I knew they would say *God*, and maybe I knew they were right. But I didn't want to hear it. God seemed so far away sometimes. I desperately wanted something close enough to touch, something I could hold on to.

Funny, it was when I left to go upstairs for a bathroom break that I got the word in my ear I needed. I washed my hands, made sure my makeup wasn't smudgy and my hair wasn't frizzy and my white sweater wasn't salsa-y, then I stepped out into the hallway. There were Sam and Ben on the beach with their baby curls and big eyes with black lashes, watching me. Beneath that picture, hanging slightly askew, was a winter scene of just one of the boys, probably a year or two older. Sam alone.

I don't know how long I stood there, but eventually I felt Mrs. Newman behind me in one of the bedroom doorways. "What did you do?" I asked quietly, not turning, my hand resting on my chest. "To fill the empty place?"

"Nothing." She answered immediately, like she was expecting the question. "I tried to run from it. I sometimes still try." She came up beside me. "For me, it is more like a large crack in a jar. I want the Potter to patch it up, make me like new again. But He chooses to leave a crack. There are days when I think I am a useless thing, a leaky pot. But He uses even that. He keeps filling me, and my cracks let me pour Him out. Even in the suffering He has allowed me to help others."

I straightened the picture of Sam. "Helping others, I like. But suffering…"

She gently took my shoulder and turned me, pointing to the opposite wall. There was a small painting, a silhouette of a bowed head crowned with thorns. "We do not suffer alone," she said, then she looked closely at me. "You have words written on your face, *Yaroni*. You can say them."

"It's just, when I look at Jesus on the cross… Well, I feel like I don't have a right to complain or feel sorry for myself. No matter how bad I'm feeling, I'll never feel *that* bad."

"Ah." She smiled. "So the cross He bore trumps your own. Jesus is like that friend who, when you had a bad day, always had a worse day? You have a miserable cold, they have…pneumonia."

I twisted my mouth to one side. "When you put it like that…"

She took the little painting off the wall and ran her fingers over the texture of the brushstrokes. "You are wounded, child. One wounded creature recognizes another." She smiled faintly. "But do not think the Lord means for you always to be so. He will help your wound to heal, so it doesn't become the focus of your life, the filter through which you see and do everything. He does not want you always wounded. But broken… Broken is different. When we break, we stop trying to manage it all ourselves. We finally know our desperate need for God, and we press into Him."

I sighed. "Breaking still sounds painful."

She absently smoothed an escaped lock of my hair back into place, a mother's habit. "It is because He suffered so terribly that He can empathize with us. Even more, He suffers alongside us."

Alongside. That sounded familiar.

"And I think," she went on, "that I would rather suffer with Jesus than not suffer without Him."

It became my secret motto: *Suffering, but suffering with Jesus.* It actually helped. When the gaping wound of my life was especially raw—and it could happen any time, triggered by the silliest things: a TV show we used to watch together, a smell like his cologne, someone mentioning their own dad—I reminded myself that Jesus had carried the cross, and that He was sharing the yoke. I really felt some of the load lifted. Could it be a smidgen of that peace that passes understanding?

After a Sunday morning at the Believers' Church, where the message had been about Enjoying God's Peace, I even felt daring enough to talk about it. "I think I kind of understood some of what the Reverend was talking about today," I said, watching the cars splatter slushy snow as we drove home.

"Wonderful," Mom said.

"Wonderful," Sheelan echoed from the back seat. We had just dropped Jeph off at his house—and with him went both her reason for wanting to be there and her reason for being polite.

No one asked me what I'd understood. I cleared my throat, still kept my eyes out the window. "I mean, I know that there's always going to be painful stuff in life, but Jesus really can carry it for us." Had I said that out loud? Yes. And I was glad. For eight…nine…ten seconds.

Then Sheelan said, "The only problem with that is, people who keep throwing their baggage on Jesus never learn to deal with it themselves. Reality happens, and you have to handle it."

That couldn't be right. "But what about relying on God? You know, Him being strong when we're weak."

I could feel her eyes roll behind me. "Why do you think so many people see Christianity as a crutch?" she asked.

My mouth opened, but I had nothing. I looked at my mom. She gave a half-shrug. "Now, I can see what Rory means. Sometimes we need help that's bigger than ourselves. But Sheelan has a point, too. Doesn't the Bible say, 'God helps those who help themselves'?"

"Actually, it doesn't," Kingston told me later, from under our computer desk, fixing our internet connection.

"It doesn't?" I asked. "You mean that's not from the Bible?"

He crawled back out. "Nope. It's Benjamin Franklin. Here, I can show you now." He did an internet search for 'God helps those who help themselves', clicked on one of the results. "See? 1757 edition of the Poor Richard's Almanac. Don't feel bad. Most people think it's from the Bible. Here, check this out." He clicked another link. "I respect old Ben and all, but here are some verses that show the Bible teaches just the opposite of what he said."

I looked at the list.

Jeremiah 17:5—This is what the LORD says: 'Cursed is the one who trusts in man, who depends on flesh for his strength and whose heart turns away from the LORD.'

Proverbs 28:26—He who trusts in himself is a fool...

Romans 5:6—For while we were still helpless, at the right time Christ died for the ungodly.

"Maybe you should show these to whoever quoted that 'scripture'," he said.

"My mom?"

"Oh. Well, she probably just meant that we can't ask God to do everything for us—sit back, do nothing and wait for good things to happen. That's just laziness. When the Bible talks about God doing it all for us, it's usually talking about our salvation. We don't bring anything to that transaction. We're spiritually dead, He makes us alive."

"So you wouldn't call Jesus a crutch."

"What good is a crutch to a dead man?"

I wished Sheelan were around.

Kings tapped a few keys. "Everything's working now, but tell me if it starts acting squirrelly again. Here's your email... Yep, looks like a few days' worth of messages."

"I'd better check them. Probably junk, mostly. Oh, here's one from Shayne." Kings, who had turned to make his way back home, turned back again. I hid my smile. "She's talking about Cornerstone. Hey, she's asking for your email address. Should I send it to her?"

"She is?" He leaned in. "Well, okay."

"As you wish." I began typing *FisherKing@...* I felt him smiling behind me. "And it's off. She must want to send you something."

"I'd better go." He bolted for home. I never realized he could move so fast. My smile might've taken up long-term residence on my face, but as I scanned through my emails, a name leapt out at me.

Angelyte04@wiry.net

A zing raced through my body and ended up in a clench in my stomach. Angelica. She'd practically fallen off my mental radar. After so many days of hearing nothing from her, I'd assumed that either she'd received my very last InterFace message and tossed it in the scrap heap, or that for some reason she couldn't send an email. But I'd thought about her less with each passing week.

How could I do that, after what I'd seen in her photo?

That thought stopped my hand on the mouse. But what else could I do? I clicked.

Hi Rory, it's me. I hope it's still okay for me to write.

I'm not sure why I waited so long. I kept having these thoughts that you were really mad at me. Are you mad? I think I was kind of rude sometimes online. It's weird, that's just so not me. I think I'd be mad at me if I were you. Why did you leave InterFace all of a sudden? Your home page is gone, like you vanished. Freaky. I'm glad you gave me your email, though. Maybe we can email now. It's like I'm another person sometimes when I'm online. I'll be more me in an email I hope. -Angelica

P.S. You said we need to talk? If it's about my InterFace picture, don't worry, I changed it. That first one was lame.

I chewed my fingernails (yes, Gran Judy, I know all sorts of vile germs are hiding under my nails, but there must also be some fingernail nutrient that helps your brain function). Angelica did sound different in her email. A lot less sure of herself. I clicked 'reply', changed my mind and clicked over to the internet instead.

Just do it, Rory.

I looked her up on InterFace. I couldn't get to her homepage since I wasn't an official 'friend' anymore, but I could see a thumbnail picture. She was smiling—this time I thought I could see braces. A head and shoulders shot. Resting on one shoulder, a man's hand. It's all I could see of him.

Angelica,
I'm glad you wrote. No, I'm not mad, don't worry. InterFace was just getting too weird, I had to quit. I just looked at your new picture. Just a small version, but it looks good. Whose hand is on your shoulder? —Rory

I wondered how long before I would get a reply. Another month, probably.

How about five minutes?

"No way," I murmured. She was at her computer. It wasn't IM-fast, but it worked for me.

Hi! What do you mean about the hand on my shoulder? There's no hand.

I looked again, while a sensation like cold water ran under my skin.

I see a hand, Angelica, on your left shoulder. A boy's or man's hand.

I only had to wait two minutes this time.

Seriously? Rory, that is so absolutely freakin' sweet! You're never going to believe this. Remember how I told you that I'm into angels?

She had? I dug deep. Maybe she had. Like in our first IM chat. How could I have let that one slip by me? I mean, me of all people?

Well, I've been studying all I can find about them, and I found some information about how to contact your guardian angel. One of the signs said that my angel usually stayed near my LEFT side! Isn't that wild? Do you think it might be my angel? Do you believe in guardian angels? But I can't see anything in the picture. Do you have some psychic ability or something? You ought to find out if that runs in your family. I've heard of that happening. This is so SWEET!

I pulled a blanket around me and tried to keep it over my arms as I typed.

I know a little bit about angels, but not in a psychic way. From the Bible. And I do believe in guardian angels. I know they're real. But Angelica, you've got to know, there are fallen angels, too. Demons.

Remember your last InterFace photo? Was there anyone behind you when you took that picture?

I waited. Two minutes. Five minutes. I wrapped the blanket tighter. Had the furnace broken down? Why was it so cold in the house?

Ten minutes. I should've asked her for her phone number. This email thing was stupid. The IM-ing had been stupid. It made everything seem less real. I should've stayed on InterFace until I'd gotten through to her as soon as I'd seen that face in her picture. Why had I let it slide? What if someone had seen a demon face near me and just let it go?

Twenty minutes. An email popped into the mailbox.

Sorry. I had something to do. Let me guess, now you're going to say you saw a face behind me in my other picture? Look, the hand thing was impressive enough—you don't have to try so hard. Maybe I have a guardian angel, maybe I don't. Don't be like my ex-friend and use everything as an excuse to talk about religion. –AL-

I sat back. Will the real Angelica Lyte stand up?

I wrote:

I'm just concerned because of some things that happened to me last year.

What else to say? I remembered something Pastor Dan repeated a lot: 'speak the truth in love'. That way, if she got ticked off—more ticked off—because I spoke the truth, at least I'd know it wasn't because I didn't speak it the right way.

Bad things that I don't want to happen to you. It's not always crystal clear when something is good or evil. You have to know how to tell the difference. I learned the hard way. If you think you've had some kind of contact with angels, you'll know they're angels if they say the right things about Jesus. That he was crucified, and that he rose again. That he's their King and they serve and worship him. If they won't, or if they get slippery about all that, stay away. –RJ-

I clicked 'send' and waited. It was getting dark, and the screen was the only light in the room, grayish and cold. All the color and warmth seemed sucked out of the world. Then the reply came.

So you talk to angels? You never mentioned it before. Do you suppose we're both just schizo? Hey, guess what? I get to go to the big outlet mall that's not too far from you in a couple of weeks. Wouldn't it be great if we could meet? Gotta go. I'll write again soon. –AL-

I walked over to the thermostat and turned it up to eighty degrees. Sometimes it's just impossible to shake the cold.

thirty-eight

That was the last I heard from Angelica, until Valentine's Day.

I didn't see much of Bliss in that time, either, except in class. She claimed to spend a lot of her free time doing class president stuff, or in other words, planning her precious Earth Day celebration. Fine by me, since I'd started using my free time to read more for my *Fact vs. Faith* paper. That is, if I wasn't currently reading something fluffier and fictional. Or watching a favorite TV show. Or answering emails.

Technically Bliss still sat with me at lunch, on the days she even showed up in the cafeteria, but she spent most of the time talking to Jasmine. The plus side was that she nibbled on Jasmine's lunch instead of mine. (Which made more sense, since Jasmine was at least a vegetarian.)

Sometimes I was included in their conversations, but when they turned to matters spiritual, they tended to lean their heads in and lower their voices. Not so quiet that I couldn't hear every word, just enough to convey that my opinions weren't required.

I tried not to overhear these chats, or at least look as if I couldn't hear. But certain phrases would snag my attention like cleats on shag carpet. Such as Jasmine's "Will they let you do that? What about separation of church and state, all that?"

I couldn't help it, I looked up. "That's not actually a law," I said.

Jasmine sniffed. "It's in the Constitution."

"Nope." I sipped my milk.

"Hello? First amendment?"

I took another sip. Chocolate milk. Yum. "No, the first amendment says that Congress can't make any laws that establish a national religion or stop you from practicing your religion." The look Jasmine gave me was worth its weight—and oh my, was it a heavy look—in gold. Thank you, Sam Newman and Kingston Fisher.

They had ambushed me on the front steps on a Friday after school.

"You've gotta come in and eat cobbler," Kingston had said.

I eased my two-ton backpack off my shoulder. "What's the emergency?"

"It's rhubarb cobbler."

"So?" Rhubarb was like dynamite, nifty if handled with care.

"Hope made it. By herself, for the first time. If you eat some, too, our pieces will have to be smaller."

"We think she may have forgotten a key ingredient," Sam explained.

I shrugged, willing to overlook the fact that they were using me for rhubarb disposal. It sure smelled good. "I'm feeling lucky," I said.

The luck didn't last. Apparently the forgotten key ingredient was sweetness. We puckered our way through the cobbler, smiling/wincing while Hope scrutinized us, arms crossed. I think I saw a tear in Kingston's eye.

"It's not bad," I said. Relieved that for once I wasn't the humiliated party, I felt generous with my sympathy.

That made Hope generous with her cobbler. "Here, have some more."

"Oh, um... I really have to go and...work on my paper." Unfortunate choice of excuse. I wouldn't have minded hanging out for a while. Maybe moving in.

"It's the Paper That Ate Rory's Life," Sam said, his eyes connecting with mine for a second.

"Pretty much."

"Making progress?" Mrs. Fisher asked.

I sighed. "Well, I know what Mr. Hayes is looking for. He wants me to show that science deals with hard, testable facts, and religion depends on faith in what can't be tested and proven. But it's not always that clear-cut."

"You're sure right, it's not."

"I understand that he can't teach anything about God in science class, even if he did think it was scientific. The whole 'separation of church and state' thing."

Sam and Kingston exchanged a knowing look. "We've been learning about that," Kings said.

"And it doesn't mean what you think it means," Sam finished.

"So it doesn't mean what you think it means," I told Jasmine.

The black eyes narrowed. "So just where do we get that 'separation of church and state' idea, if not from the Constitution?"

I gave a knowledgeable shrug. Yes, I was enjoying myself immensely. Which should've been a big red flag. "Oh, it comes from a letter that Thomas Jefferson wrote to some Baptist church. You know, the first amendment was really meant to protect the churches from the government. If you know anything about the problems between the monarchy and the church in England—and the rest of Europe—you know why the founding fathers wanted the government to keep its nose out of the churches."

"That's crazy. They wanted to keep the church out of the government, so it would be fair for everyone, whatever their faith. Religious neutrality."

"If that's what the founders meant, why are there Bible verses and the Ten Commandments and references to God engraved all over the Capitol, the Supreme Court, the Liberty Bell, all those monuments?"

Before Jasmine could—or had to—come up with an answer to that, Bliss jumped in. "Did you say the first amendment protects our rights to practice our religion—keeps the government from interfering?"

"Basically, yeah."

"Perfect." She sat back with a smile. There was that red flag waving again. "Thanks, Rory."

It would be a couple of months before I saw those pridefully planted seeds grow and bear their nasty little fruits. But it was just a couple of days before Valentine's Day when Martina emailed:

How about a Cornerstone Valentine's Day excursion? We can go to the mall. (You know, what teenagers used to do back in the day—before online social networks and texting.) There's a chocolate shop inside the coffee shop inside the bookstore… How perfect is that? What do you say?
—Martina

We said yes because hanging out at the mall with your small group eating chocolate will always trump staying at home alone on Valentine's Day. Not that I think Valentine's Day is anything more than a red-satin-lined way to sell flowers and cards and candy and envy. A day to make a perfectly normal, never-felt-like-I-needed-a-boyfriend person feel like maybe she needed a boyfriend.

"I think maybe I need a boyfriend. Should I get one?" Shayne mused on the way to the mall, as if it were simply a matter of choosing one. For her it probably was that simple.

"No, you shouldn't," Martina said, smiling at us in the rearview mirror. Her sporty silver car had dark red velour seat covers that perfectly matched her fingernails. I wondered if she changed the seat covers every time she changed the nails.

"At least we won't be a pitiful band of lonely females roaming the mall," Allie said from shotgun position. "When are we meeting the others?"

"Which others?" Martina asked.

"The guys."

"Oh, they're doing laser tag or some such thing with Ericson. We thought it would be better. Didn't I mention that?"

We groaned.

"We won't look pitiful, I promise."

I sighed. "It's not as if walking around with Jake Dean would make us look any less pitiful."

"I thought you were sweet on him, Rory," she said.

I gaped. "According to Jake, everyone is sweet on him."

She winked. "Then we're safer outside his aura of irresistibility."

More groans.

I hadn't gone to the mall in ages. It wasn't so bad. There were some empty stores, and some were kind of shabby, but the bookstore was new and the chocolate shop was…well, it was the chocolate shop. We all decided on ice cream sundaes loaded with brownie chunks and smothered with hot fudge and nuts. We started pulling crumpled dollar bills out of our pockets, but Martina slipped a shiny plastic card from her little purse and said, "Your money's no good here."

"Really?" Shayne asked, concerned. "This one is a little bit ripped…Oh." She laughed as we pushed her towards a table by the front window. "Thanks, Martina."

"Are you sure we don't look pitiful?" Allie asked as we sat.

"I'm sure I don't care." Shayne shoved in a huge mouthful. "Who needs a boyfriend?" Fudge dribbled down her chin. We laughed.

Martina dabbed the corner of her mouth with a napkin. "Can I tell you something I've learned about romance? The version the world tries to sell is just a cheap, tarnished copy of something much bigger. It offers you a handful of diamonds, but when they're in your hand you realize they're just bits of broken glass."

"Happy Valentine's Day," Allie said, raising her sundae glass in a toast.

Martina raised an eyebrow but smiled. "Honestly, when I came to see Jesus, the Son of Man, as the hero that He really is, I was swept off my feet in a way far better than in movies and romance novels."

We all shoveled ice cream in our mouths and looked anywhere but at each other. I knew she didn't mean she was 'in love' with Jesus, but it came kind of close.

The silence was stretching on a smidge too long, which is probably why Shayne jumped in with, "Is that why you never got married?"

The eyebrow shot up again. "I'm twenty-eight, Shayne. I'm not sure that qualifies me as a spinster. No, relax, I know what you mean. In a way you're right. I've tried to put Jesus first in my life, and that has meant not pursuing the world's way of finding love, even though I hope that marriage and family is God's purpose for me. I've had to learn to be patient and turn to Him for comfort. Although I admit, in weaker moments I've been known to turn to chocolate."

We nodded. Our spoons glided through a dance from dish to mouth, dish to mouth. One confession inspires another, and I felt one coming on.

"Not too long ago I prayed that God would make me even hungrier for the Bible than I am for food," I said, my face barely higher than my ice cream dish.

"That's a good prayer, Rory. How was it answered?"

I noticed she didn't ask *if* it was answered. "Well, I've been reading it a bit more, but I still forget a lot. I *want* to want it more… I'm just not sure if God has answered the prayer yet."

Martina clicked her spoon against the rim of the glass while she searched for a thought in the air above her head. She came down with it. "I learned something a while back that really changed how I looked at God and how He works in my life. Do you realize that your desire to get into the Word is, itself, a gift from God? Even when you're not doing it, and you feel like there's nothing happening between you and Him—and you're possibly wondering if He even means to help you—the fact that you even *want* to come closer to Him at all, that's from Him. He places that into your heart, though His Spirit. It doesn't come from you."

I chewed on that while I chewed brownie. "So when I'm feeling bad for not reading the Bible more…"

"That's Him nudging you. Not condemning, just beckoning you to come and take a taste of the Bread of Life. I've heard it said that spiritual hunger is the opposite of physical hunger. With spiritual hunger, the more you feed it, the more it grows. So the way to get hungrier for the Word is to start reading it more."

"Kind of like Turkish Delight," Allie said.

"Only without the White Witch," Martina pointed out. "Or the evil." We laughed, which is maybe what encouraged her to push a bit further. "Another thing to consider. God's Word is like a royal banquet, prepared by the finest chefs, all of our favorite things, and we're invited to partake. But before we approach the table, we hork down a bag of cheese doodles, a box of dingle-dongs, and a bucket of soda. We fill up on garbage, so how can we enjoy the feast?"

Shayne and Allie nodded. Yeah, I understood her, too. She wasn't talking about nutritionally bankrupt food. She meant the spiritually bankrupt TV shows and books and music and internet time that kept me—I mean, us—from coming hungry to God's table. And maybe the cheese doodles, too.

I was still thinking about it when we left to stroll past the other stores. I pulled it, twisted it, examined it from all sides to see if I could find something wrong with what she said. But it withstood my poking and prodding. I had to admit it: Martina had shared something helpful. Something like wisdom.

I sneaked a look at her, to discover if I could see her with fresh eyes. Then she said, "Over there is where I always get my nails done."

Immediately my eyes wanted to roll, but I forced them to look the way she was pointing. It was only a kiosk in a rather deserted end of the mall, where the anchor department store had been closed for over a year (driven out of business by the Super Everything Store, some people said; others blamed the new outlet mall five miles away). It was a little shabby looking, too. The small woman sitting beside it seemed to be talking in a low voice, though no one else was nearby.

Allie and Shayne slowed their pace; I'd done the same. It's not like we were about to sit there and watch Martina get a manicure, even if she needed one. But she kept her brisk pace, and sure enough, the small kiosk woman spotted her.

"Ah, Thooey," she said with an accent, "good to see you. Back so soon? You chip a nail?"

"Hello, Syphay. No, my nails are perfect, you do such a good job."

Syphay smiled. She didn't seem especially old—her hair was all black—but she was missing two front teeth. "You bring me new customers, Thooey?"

"These are my friends. Allie, Shayne and Rory."

"Hello, girls. Let's see those nails. Oh, you need Syphay's magic. Who first?"

We mumbled, scrambling for a reply, but Martina cut in smoothly, "We won't have time for three manicures today, I'm afraid. I'll just have to bring them back one at a time."

Syphay had me by the hand now. She was strong for someone the size of an eight-year-old. She was also frowning. "No business today?"

Martina put a hand on my shoulder. "Just Rory, here. She could use a shaping and buffing."

"And cleaning," Syphay cackled. She pulled me down into a chair.

I looked up at Martina with my usual crisis expression: mouth open, nothing useful coming out of it.

"It won't take long," she told me. "Besides, I owe you twenty dollars."

Allie and Shayne exchanged puzzled smiles, but I knew exactly what she meant. The twenty dollar bill she had hidden in my Bible, to see if I was reading it—and taken away, to my public humiliation. She was apologizing, or giving me a pat on the back for progress. Or both.

Ten minutes later, I had clean, smooth, shiny fingernails and soft hands that smelled of plumeria, whatever that is. Syphay slipped her crisp twenty dollar bill into a little zipper case. It didn't have much company, just some loose change.

"Well?" Syphay asked. "You got anything else for me?"

Martina smiled. "I'm glad you asked. I have a surprise for you." She slipped a booklet from her coat pocket. Syphay grabbed it eagerly.

"Ooh, this is bigger than the other ones you give me. Look, it's not English!"

"It's the whole New Testament in the Lao common language."

"Your holy book?" Syphay asked, eyes wide. She shifted it in her hands like it was hot. "In my own language? I didn't know it was for my people."

"It's for all people, Syphay."

"Thank you for this gift, Thooey."

So, Martina's manicure fetish was actually about helping somebody else. I remembered a Bible verse from the Scene, something about pure religion and taking care of widows and orphans. Chalk up another jerk point for Rory.

At home, an email from Angelica waited for me.

Hey! Still want to meet at the new outlet mall? Let's pick a Saturday or Sunday to do it. I'm going to West Palm Beach for spring break, and I have to get a new bikini. Are you going anywhere? How 'bout some swimsuit shopping??? –AL-

On my List o' Fun, swimsuit shopping ranked right up there with removing splinters. What kind of person wanted to try on swimsuits with someone she'd never even met? But, in the spirit of trying not to continually misjudge people, I made my vague reply:

I'd like to check out the new mall sometime. I'll see if I can work it out. –RJ-

Not likely it would ever happen.

That night I dreamed that I roamed a vast labyrinth of steel and marble and glass with a group of people I knew to be friends, though not one of them had a familiar face. We moved from place to place, sunlight to shadow, urgently searching for something. I didn't know what. Then we came to a spacious indoor courtyard with people idly chatting and eating.

One man sat a little apart, his back to us. I knew I shouldn't let him see me. I didn't know why. I tried to duck out of sight, but I moved in slow motion. He also seemed to move in slow motion as his head turned, and turned, until it had turned an unnatural 180 degrees like an owl's, to stare straight at me. The eyes were all black.

thirty-nine

"Sheelan and I are going to the new outlet mall next Saturday if you guys want to tag along," Jeph said, seemingly unaware of Sheelan's eye daggers. Clearly he hadn't consulted her. "After the Scene."

"So you're actually coming to the Scene?" Shayne asked. This week Jeph was just dropping us off at the Front Street Temple, then going with Sheelan to the Believers' Youth Experience. Supposedly they were alternating Saturdays, but somehow more of the Saturdays seemed to fall in Sheelan's favor.

"We'll both be here next week. And Dad might let me take the van if anyone else wants to come to the outlet. Sam, Jake."

Sheelan's sigh said *this just keeps getting better and better.* "We'll be late, Jephry," she said with a soft smile and glittery-ice eyes. They drove off, and we all looked at each other.

"Did she just say *Jephry*?" Allie looked as if she'd smelled bad tuna salad.

"I'm afraid so," I said, feeling like I'd eaten the bad tuna salad.

"I know, it's disgusting, but he seems so happy," Shayne said. "Maybe a little too happy." Her eyes flicked over to me and then quickly away. I wondered what she meant by that. "But I'm still getting the chauffeur service, so hey, no complaints. Do you wanna catch a ride to the outlet with them?"

"Sure," Allie said. "There's a sporting goods store there. Maybe I can find the shoes I need for less than three months' allowance." They looked at me.

"Let me check with my social secretary," I said. The classic humor-as-a-stall tactic. "Or at least with my mom."

Lame excuse, since my sister was already going, but they didn't question it. I leapt on to the next excuse, the one I would give Angelica for going to the outlet mall without telling her. Or maybe I just wouldn't mention it at all. Maybe this was just one of those acquaintances that eventually trickled off into nothing. She wasn't exactly a positive influence—just one more distraction. A bag of cheese doodles that kept me from the banquet table.

Pastor Dan stood at the front of the gym with no screen, no laptop, no little remote. Like the neighbors' shaggy dog when he got shorn for the summer, sort of small and lost and forlorn. Not himself. "We'll be low-tech today," he said. "The equipment has gone on a weekend retreat with the women's ministry group. That's okay, because I want to use today to recap some of the things we've been discussing." He turned towards a noisy pocket of the audience and cleared his throat. "For some of you, it will be like hearing it for the first time."

"Who's hearing what, now?" came Jake's voice distinctly from the back. I huffed an exasperated breath and looked to see if Sam was giving him a hearty smack, but Jake was in a cluster of other boys. Sam, it turned out, was right behind me.

"Shirley," he said in greeting, straight-faced.

"Roger."

Nearby, Martina *ahem*ed and lifted an eyebrow at us. Cornerstone or no, she clearly had no plan to play favorites.

"So we've been talking about the dangers of worldliness," Pastor said, "and the need to avoid the shifting sands of our culture and to stand on the solid Rock. But I want to reiterate another point, and this is where the challenge lies. The tension, if you will."

He scrubbed his goatee. "We're called to be holy. Remember, that means set apart for God. But that doesn't mean set up on a shelf in the storage closet, like my wife's china. Those dishes sit up there for most of the year, and yes, they're awfully pretty when she takes them down for special occasions, and then we put them back up so they don't get damaged. But then we don't see them for months on end. We forget about them.

"Folks, it's the everyday dinnerware that serves our needs in our house. People are fed from those plates—not fancy-like, but fed. You and I need to be like those chipped and mismatched plates and cups in my kitchen cupboard. Real, not perfect, but ready to do God's work in the world. To serve, to be visible and present and make a difference in our own humble way.

"We need to be *in* the world, but first you need to learn how to keep from being *of* the world. You're called to be 'children of God without fault *in the midst* of a crooked and perverse generation, *among whom* you shine as lights in the world'. But you've got to get your shine on—and be plugged solidly into the King—before you can expect to bring His kingdom light to others."

I slumped a little, in one of those rare moments when I recognized that the message applied to me, not just that vague Somebody Else.

Okay, God. I'm sorry I compared Angelica to cheese doodles. She needs your light, just like I do. Help me get plugged into You. I know without You, I've got no shine.

"You're kind of quiet tonight," Allie said in the Svoboda's van on the way to the outlet mall the next week.

"And it's heavenly," Jake said. He and Sam were in the middle seat; us girls sat in the back.

"I'm good," I said, shooting a narrow-eyed look at him. There wasn't much chance to talk after that. Sheelan roamed through the pre-set radio stations and then picked one of her own, the kind of synthesized club music I despised. But Sam and Jake demonstrated some of their seatbelted dance moves and soon had us laughing. The drive was way too short.

Compared to our hometown mall, the outlet was sprawling, spanking-new clean, and surprisingly expensive.

"I must not understand the concept of 'outlet'," Allie said, looking at a pair of basketball shoes that cost more than a round-trip ticket to London.

"It's where obscenely overpriced goods are reduced to merely ridiculous prices," Sam explained.

"I'm beginning to see that." Then Allie saw something else. "Rory, that's like the fifth time you've looked at your watch. Got an appointment or something?"

Jake patted my head. "She turns back into a pumpkin at midnight."

I ignored him. "Hey, is that the food court over there?"

"No worries," Shayne said. "We've got over an hour before we have to meet Jeph and Sheelan."

"I think Rory is trying to tell us she's hungry," Jake said, kindergarten-style.

"Let's go get some ten-dollar french fries," Sam suggested.

We walked that way, though Shayne and Allie were distracted by several store windows along the way. "We didn't come for food," Shayne sniffed.

"I did," Jake said.

"I'm pretty much here for the food," Sam agreed.

"Well, we came to look," Shayne said, gesturing around at the well-lit shops, the gleaming marble floors.

"Look for what, exactly?" Sam asked.

"I don't know. That's why we need to look."

The guys exchanged a mystified glance.

By this point I could see the food court's main seating area. It was well-lit, bordered by brushed steel railings, and looked familiar in a foggy way, like a place I had seen years ago and forgotten, which of course didn't make sense. The place wasn't particularly crowded. Two groups were obviously families with younger children. There were some scattered adults and teenagers in twos and threes. I could only make out two people sitting alone. One was an older lady, the other a man with a laptop, his back to us. For some reason I half-expected him to turn his head and look at me.

It felt colder here, like the domed skylight way overhead was open to the black night sky. I pulled my coat a little tighter around me and peeked at my watch again. 7:44, and no Angelica.

I hadn't given up on her. But I had given up on good old-fashioned common sense. I'd gone ahead and told her about my planned trip to the outlet, and just as I predicted, she jumped at the chance to meet me there. Explaining this to my friends had proven too much for my feeble self. So I came up with the courageous solution of not mentioning it.

Angelica had promised to be at the food court at 7:30 that Saturday evening. I told her I'd look for her there—avoiding such words as *promise* or any specific arrival time. She planned to wear a bright red sweater. I may have mentioned that my coat was brown (if I wore that coat and not my new green one).

Angelica hadn't mentioned coming with anyone else. Then again, neither had I. As we meandered around the perimeter of the food court, I examined the groups of teens. No girls with dark blondish hair, no bright red sweaters. I relaxed a little. It was 7:48. She must've changed her mind.

My eyes still absently scanned the people. Then, though I'm not sure why, they snapped back to a single person. The man with the laptop open in front of him. But he wasn't looking at it; he was looking at me.

In a split second he looked away again, tapped casually at his keyboard. I jerked my eyes away, but I had to look again. The blond hair, expensive-looking clothes, the handsome face. No, it was a stranger's face. I hadn't seen it before. But for a second…

"Are you okay?" It was Sam's voice, beside my ear. I wondered why he was standing so close. Then I realized I must've swayed on my feet. "You're awfully pale, Rory."

"Oh my gosh, is she going to faint?" Allie asked. They made me sit on a nearby bench.

"I'm fine," I said.

"Overcome by the fragrance of fried food," Jake diagnosed.

"I said I'm fine. But it's cold in here." My voice sounded sharp in my own ears; they all watched me, not satisfied. "I just thought I saw someone I knew."

"You were looking for somebody." Sam wasn't asking. I avoided his watchful eyes.

"Really?" Allie asked. "Is someone else meeting us?"

I could clam up and be a jerk, or I could come clean. I considered the jerk option for a half a second. Then I said, "Angelica Lyte. She said she might be here tonight."

"Who? Oh—your internet friend? Really?" Shayne stood on tiptoe, scanning the crowd. "What does she look like? Did you see her?"

"I didn't see her. I thought I saw…someone else I know. But it wasn't."

Sam's eyebrows drew together, and his jaw went square and hard. "The man? I saw him look at you."

"What man?" Allie asked. "Who's Angelica? You guys lost me."

"Oh, I get it," Jake said. "You arranged a face-to-face with some friend you met online, but you wanted to check her out before you introduced us, in case she's got the mange or twelve toes or something."

"Who's the man, though?" Allie crossed her arms. Allie preferred to know what was going on at all times.

"That's easy. He would be the depraved lunatic who has been posing as Rory's teenage cyberpal."

"Be serious, Jake." Shayne shoved him.

"He is serious," Sam said.

"No, I'm not. Never ever, if I can help it."

"Well, I'm serious—"

"Almost always."

"How do we know it's not true?" Sam asked. "We talked about this. You never really know who you're talking to online, and after what you saw on InterFace…"

"What did you see? Allie asked.

I cut them off. "Look, I'm sorry. Next time I'll get your permission first."

"Ooh, sassy," Jake said. Sam went quiet.

"Let me get this straight," Shayne said. "You came here to meet that girl you know on InterFace, only there's some guy checking you out instead? Should we be getting the mall security or the police or something?"

"Just because a guy looked at me?" I asked. But it was more than that. I thought I saw Uri. Just for a second, like in the picture behind Angelica—if that was Angelica. What if it was some mentally warped predator? What if it was Uri? I felt an urgency, but it struggled as if under a soggy blanket, stuck in slow motion.

My eyes ventured back to the food court, but I couldn't see the man's table from where we were standing. He had looked a little bit like Uri, that was all. I'd had some momentary post-traumatic flashback because of the resemblance.

The others were talking, maybe to me, but I wasn't listening. Shoppers were passing, babies in strollers, people laughing, arguing. The massive glass-and-steel elevator dinged about thirty feet away. From the corner of my eye, I saw a red sweater.

"Rory. The guy's still there. Should we call security? Rory?"

I removed Shayne's hand from my arm, pointed. "That's her."

"Who? Where?"

"Angelica. Getting off the elevator."

"But I thought the guy was her, or she was the guy. Whatever."

"Apparently not." Angelica's eyes roved nervously over the food court, then beyond it right to our group and over us—and back again in a snap, landing on me. Her hand crept up in a half-wave, half-adjustment of her purse strap (cover, just in case I wasn't the right person). I waved back.

"Well, that's a relief," Allie said. "No scary internet stalker. But I still don't understand why you didn't tell us you were meeting her."

I was saved from having to explain by Angelica's arrival. A few inches shorter than me—but then who wasn't? to my dismay, I even seemed to be passing Sam by—dark blond hair, mild case of acne that hadn't shown in her photo. Braces with blue rubber bands. "Rory?" she asked.

"Angelica?"

"Hi. You look a lot different than your InterFace picture."

"Oh," Jake said sensitively, "you were hoping to meet the Jolly Green Giant, weren't you? This must be disappointing for you."

I shook my head, eyes closed. "This is Jake. And Shayne, Allie, and Sam."

"Hi," she said with a nervous giggle. "Oh, yeah. Hang on." She turned and looked at the upper level of the mall, where a gray-haired man stood leaning on the railing, looking down at us. She waved; he returned it. "My dad," she said. She pointed at me, and her dad waved to me, too. I waved back. He gave Angelica the thumbs-up and strolled towards a golfing store. "He wouldn't bring me unless he could watch and make sure I wasn't meeting any weirdoes."

"Don't worry, Jake," Allie said. "He probably can't tell from way up there."

"Ha ha."

"I guess that seems pretty lame, huh?" she asked.

"Not really," I said. She had stepped into my role as the self-conscious one, so there I was acting the part of the confidence-builder. Odd. "We were just having a little discussion about the perils of turning internet friends into real life friends. For a second I thought a guy looking at me in the food court was really you—I mean, that he'd been pretending to be you."

"Seriously? That's freaky. But hang on, how old was he?"

"Why?"

She looked up, but there was no sign of her dad. She leaned in anyway. "Because I really arranged to meet two people here. You're one. The other's a boy." Her voice had dropped to conspiracy-whisper level. "I was afraid you might be annoyed, but since you brought your friends, I guess it's cool, huh?"

I glanced at Sam, but he said nothing. Couldn't really blame him, after I'd shut him down before. "Is he here?" I asked. "Have you ever seen him before?"

"Just his picture online. Ohmygod, he's gorgeous. I can't believe he wants to meet me. But we've become really good friends, I mean, we talk all the time. So I know him really well."

"You know, that's not very safe," Allie said.

"Oh, I know all about internet safety and all that. My dad's always preaching about it. But it's like I said, I really know this guy. We've been talking for months and months. He knows so much about all the stuff I'm interested in. And he's really helping me find out who I am, and to see the world more clearly. He's always saying, he likes making the gray areas black and white."

I stopped. I wasn't going anywhere, but I stopped—stopped wandering in my thoughts, stopped breathing. Maybe my heart stopped for a beat. First Bliss, now Angelica... Could *he* be hanging around them because they were unfortunate enough to be associated with me?

Who *was* that man in the food court? "Angelica," I said, "peek around that plant. Do you see a guy with a laptop?"

"Yeah. Oh!" She ducked back. "He looked right at me."

"Is that the guy you came to meet?"

"Well...It almost looks like him, but too old. Lukes is just a little older than us."

"Ever hear of Photoshop?" Jake asked.

"Or he could've just used an old photo of himself," Shayne said.

"No." Angelica gaped. "Are you kidding? You think some thirty-year-old man was pretending to be eighteen? That's gross!" Then she shook her head. "No, it can't be. Lukes is definitely who he says he is."

"Did you ever talk about me with this Lucas?" I asked.

She ran her tongue over her braces, her eyes looking for somewhere safe to rest. "Not Lucas, Lukes. I think it's just a nickname for Luke. Anyway...yeah, we talked about you a few times. At least, I would tell him about some of the stuff we talked about, religion and stuff. Some of the things I said to you were really ideas I got from him."

"Did you tell Lukes you were trying to meet me here, too?"

"Yeah. Why?"

"Because that man out there looked at me before like he recognized me."

Her eyes got big. "You're starting to freak me out."

"I'm with her," Shayne said.

Sam's eyes narrowed dangerously. "We're going to have to walk out there, all of us, and just walk past him and see what he does. We'll know by his reaction if he's trouble."

"And then what?" Allie asked. "We all jump him at once?"

"Sounds like fun," Jake said, "but I think you guys weren't the only ones getting freaked out." He pointed.

The man was gone.

forty

The security guards had us repeat our story three times, but in the end there wasn't much they could do about a suspicious unidentified disappearing man. I personally think they chalked it up to overactive hormone-induced teenage imaginations.

Angelica's dad, however, took it quite seriously and informed her that she would be canceling her InterFace account, and all internet use and emailing would be done under his supervision. Our long-awaited meeting had lasted all of twenty minutes.

I decided not to mention the incident to Sheelan. Shayne, sadly, hadn't made the same decision regarding Jeph, so both of our siblings heard the whole story, complete with Jake Dean-esque embellishments, on the drive home. Sheelan turned several times to bestow upon me her withering look of disdain.

"You know, Rory," she said, "next time why don't you just listen to Sam? He's got way more sense than you." She smiled at him. His return smile was feeble. I suppose he knew an endorsement from Sheelan wouldn't exactly earn him any points with me.

When my mom heard about my internet-slash-outlet mall adventure, she got that silent, nostrils-flared look that made my soul shrivel. "No internet for a month," she said through a clenched jaw.

"What about my research paper?" I tried.

"Before the internet, we got information from books. Try it."

I gathered myself up for a sullen stomp upstairs to my bedroom, but suddenly Mom was there, pulling me into her arms. I didn't know what to do once I was there. I just kind of huddled.

"When I think of what might have…" She shook her head, like shaking the thoughts away. I knew they were thoughts of internet stalkers and not demonic ones, but I didn't know how much to tell her, because I didn't know which was true (maybe both). And I definitely didn't want her to call on Dr. McD to sort it out.

Mom finally released me. "No, this is it. This is it, I'm done."

I didn't know what 'this' was, or what 'it' was, or what was done. But I found out on our trip to Orlando.

"Say, 'Happy Birthday' to Rory!'" my mom ordered Dopey the Dwarf. He hugged me and she took a snapshot. He said nothing. Because he was Dopey.

Mom laughed and showed me the camera so I could view my humiliation in miniature. "No, thanks." If you've seen one mortifying picture of me, you've seen them all.

"So, what next? The teacups again? Or the mountain thing? Maybe the line's shorter now."

"How about another water ride?" I asked. Sheelan glared at me. She had made the mistake of wearing a white tank top and after the last big splash had been forced to buy the nearest gift shop shirt she could find for under fifteen dollars. It was a pink princess T-shirt.

"No way," she said.

"Aw, come on. It's my birthday," I said sweetly. Water rides were okay. Annoying Sheelan was better. I had to have a little fun on my fifteenth, even if I did have to spend it at the self-proclaimed Happiest Place in the Known Universe.

No, no, I'm not complaining, especially since it was warm, sunny, and a gift from Dad. But I wasn't technically there by choice—Mom had planned our itinerary. I hadn't even realized we were leaving for Florida the day before my birthday until the week before my birthday. Sheelan had been scandalized.

"We're going in eight days?" She huffed, tsked, huffed again. "I only have a week to pack? You do realize I have to find a new bathing suit?"

"Sorry," Mom said calmly. "I'm sure I'd told you guys when I booked the tickets last month." She looked at me. "We'll be there for your birthday."

"Oh." I'd been hoping to have the gang over for a 3-F evening: friends, food and films. I had already picked the films (comedies) and the food (Chinese), and I'd even asked my friends (the usual suspects). I guess I should've asked my mom first. Instead, I had to un-invite the gang.

"Bummer," Allie said.

"Can't we just do it the day before your birthday?" Shayne asked.

"That's the day we leave."

"How about the day before that?"

"It's an early flight, so I can't be up late the night before. It's okay, no big deal." Okay, it was a big deal, but I wasn't going to act like my birthday was a national holiday. "Maybe after I get back?"

"Yeah, I guess." Shayne shrugged, Pastor Dan called for our attention, and the subject was dropped. Kind of like a rock. On me.

I got a call from Mrs. Fisher that Wednesday, asking me to baby-sit the twins Friday night. I couldn't say no to some spending cash to bring to Orlando. So Friday I left Sheelan to her frantic last-minute swimsuit fitting frenzy and hopped over the railing to the Fisher's front door.

Before I could touch the doorbell, the door opened an inch. A brown eye peeped out at me.

"Hi," I said. "Cherry?"

"Tee-Tee."

"Hi, Tee-Tee. Can I come in?"

"Nope." The door opened a bit wider. Now I saw two brown eyes.

"Why not?"

"Because they're not done blowing up the balloons." Suddenly Tee-Tee disappeared, as if someone had yanked her away. Cherry stepped into her place.

"Who's blowing up balloons?" I asked.

"Kingston and your friends, but you're not supposed to know that." She scowled at Tee-Tee. "Pickle-wit."

"Hey! You're not 'sposed to call me that!" Tee-Tee charged Cherry, and they both ran off. I waited for a few seconds, then slipped in through the half-open door. The house had it usual yummy Friday smell. The living room was empty, so I walked to the kitchen. There on the table was the source of the smell, a rather lopsided but invitingly gooey chocolate cake.

Everyone was down in the family room—Shayne, Allie, Kings, Sam and Jake—gathering balloons and tying them together (or, in Jake's case, rubbing them on Kingston's head and sticking them to the ceiling). One drifted towards me on the steps, so I picked it up and handed it to Allie. "Thanks," she said, then looked at me and gave a little scream.

"Surprise," I said.

"I think that's our line," Sam said.

And so I'd had a friend party after all. But I still missed them a bit as I ate Chinese food in an Orlando restaurant with my mom and Sheelan the actual night of my birthday. My mom made up for it with her own cheerfulness.

"I sort of have a gift for you," she said between the egg drop soup and the barbequed pork.

"I already got my gifts." She'd let me pick out some souvenirs from the park.

"Well, it's more along the lines of good news," she said. "This past Friday was my last day at Rocky's."

"Well, we didn't think they'd make you drive all the way from Orlando to work," I said.

"Rory," Sheelan said, as if my name were another word for 'ultimate dweeb'. "She means she's not going to work at the restaurant anymore. You got the office manager position at Reinbolt's?" she asked.

"Yes, I did." I hadn't seen Mom this happy since… Hmm, I couldn't remember. Since I hit puberty, maybe. "So no more burning the midnight oil for me. It's 9-to-5 and then home, no nights, no weekends."

"Real dinners?" I asked.

"Leave it to you to make it about food," Sheelan said.

"Dinner together." She popped a whole wonton in her mouth.

I did, too. "Thd iz a gd brday prznt," I said.

It hadn't been my only unusual present. From Grandma Judy I had gotten the usual, the big bag of clothes and some money besides, brought over in time for me to pack some of it for the trip. From my friends, a less expected gift.

They gave it to me after the super-gooey cake, which turned out to be a Boston cream pie. Shayne handed me a tiny gift bag with a great big grin.

I suddenly found it hard to look anyone in the eye. "You guys didn't have to get me a gift."

"Trust me, we didn't," Jake said. Allie slugged him. "Shh," she said.

I removed a wad of tissue paper and fished out a digital music player. A loose one, not in a package—and it was just like the one Mom had given me for Christmas. I turned it over, saw a purple smiley face sticker on the back. It was the one my Mom had given me for Christmas.

"This is...mine," I said.

"Yes, it is," Sam said.

"Did you guys find it somewhere?"

"Did you think you'd lost it?" Allie asked.

"No. I mean, I haven't seen it for a few days—"

"Five days," Jake informed me.

"—but I figured it had crawled under my bed or something."

"Nope," Shayne said. "It crawled to us. Well, we asked Sheelan to find it and give it to us."

Allie couldn't stand my mystified look any longer. "A few weeks ago you said you hadn't been using it much, because you didn't know what songs to put on it."

That was true. I'd always been in the habit of turning on the radio to half-listen to whatever was popular at the time, but now that I actually listened to the lyrics and thought about them, I realized a lot of them were gross, or just stupid. All of a sudden, I lost my taste for it. Only I hadn't gotten around to finding something different.

"Well," Allie went on, "we took the liberty of putting a bunch of our favorite songs on there for you. Good music."

"We know you might not like all of it," Shayne said. "But this is a way to sample lots of different stuff and maybe find some new artists you do like."

I put one ear bud in and started the first song, then jumped through a few songs, listening to a bit of each. "Wow," I said. "It's Christian?"

"A lot of it. Not all, but I think it's all what you'd call 'clean'."

"Except for the selections of death metal that I added," Jake said.

"Ha ha."

I took the ear bud out. "Thanks, guys. This is great. I can't wait to listen on my trip. What a really cool idea."

"Thanks, it was mine." Jake ran a hand back through his shaggy hair.

"Was not," Shayne said. "It was Sam's."

"No," Sam said. "You thought of the music part, Shayne. I just thought of the stealing and sneaking part."

As I sat beside the pool in our timeshare condo complex, a whole new world of music opened up to me. I found myself trying to guess who had picked which songs. Jake's had to be the metal-driven, percussion-heavy ones with the lyrics that were hard to decipher through the general ruckus. The acoustic selections with more tuneful melodies or traditional hymn lyrics I attributed to Sam. And I could totally imagine Shayne in the upbeat, heartfelt hand-clappers, whereas I heard more of Allie in the thoughtful, hurt-but-healing songs. (I learned later that I had it backwards; it gave me a deeper glimpse into the hearts of my friends.)

I also had plenty of time to think about another birthday present—the strangest of all—from Bliss Hathaway. That same

Friday of my un-surprise party, Bliss had sat behind me in English class, as usual, but she ignored the usual group of friends who liked to chat before class and tapped my shoulder.

"I might have a birthday present for you," she said.

I wondered how she even knew my birthday was approaching; then I remembered—the 316 business. Ugh. "Don't worry about it," I said. I was still trying to figure out a tactful way to return her cell phone. It had been under my bed, turned off, for weeks.

"Not worried," she said breezily. "I'll know for sure after school."

Sure enough, she caught me at my locker after the final bell rang. "Well, I did it," she said. "It took some major sweet talking and heated negotiations," she flashed the dimples that had probably won it for her, "but I wore Mr. Hayes down. All you have to do is give a short presentation during my Earth Day assembly about ways to 'go green' and help the planet, and you're a free woman."

"What are you talking about?" I asked. Because I had no idea what she was talking about.

"Your evolution paper, *False Faith*, whatever it was supposed to be called. If you take part in my assembly, you'll get a grade credit in its place." I must've still had a blank face. "I got you out of your paper, Rory. Happy birthday."

forty-one

"So how was Orlando, Rory?"

Martina perched with perfect posture on the Newman's piano bench. For some reason I'd never paid any attention to the piano in the den.

"Good," I said. "Well, Sheelan got a sunburn and my mom says she gained five pounds, but I got to read books by the pool and listen to good music." I smiled at the others to say thanks. "Thanks for praying for our safe trip and...the other stuff." I hadn't divulged all my concerns about Bliss and Angelica, just enough so they could give me some spiritual back-up. I figured God knew the details.

"What books?" Allie asked. "I'm reading *Pride and Prejudice*. Have you read it? You have to read it."

"I love Jane Austen," Martina confessed with a sigh.

"No," I said, "actually it was non-fiction." A big change for me. I turned to Ericson. "Some of your evolution books. Sorry, I meant to bring them back today—it looks like I won't be needing them for that paper after all."

I told them about Bliss's 'birthday present'. Okay, I only told them I didn't have to do the paper if I took part in the Earth Day assembly, and left the Bliss part out.

Jake looked disgusted. "First you refuse to take a test, but you get a second chance to take it. You refuse again, and you get a third-chance paper to make up for it. Then you procrastinate like a knucklehead, but you get out of it totally."

"Hardly. I have to get up in front of the whole school and talk about saving the environment."

"I don't know," Ericson said, leaning back in the old recliner and crossing his arms. "I would've liked to have read that paper."

I smiled a *sorry...sort of* smile. "I did learn a lot from the books. It's bizarre how much of what's taught in school isn't totally accurate."

"Such as?" Allie asked.

"Well…" I thought about it. "Take the monkey-to-man chart."

"Yes, take it—away," Shayne said. "Disturbing."

"Don't worry, it's mostly imaginary," Kingston said.

I nodded. "When you look at that chart, you assume that all those middle stages between the ape and the man are based on fossil skeletons that have actually been discovered, but they're not. Paleontologists find, like, a few pieces of bone, and then they get all creative in the reconstruction. A lot of supposed 'missing links' have turned out to be just plain old apes. Some of them were even faked to look really old. And the hair on the ape-men in those pictures—and the slack-jawed yokel expression—how could they know how hairy or stupid something looked from a few broken pieces of bone?"

"The whole fossil record is a flop when it comes to showing how new species supposedly evolved from a common ancestor," Sam said, sounding way more intelligent than me. But he was backing me up, so it was all good.

Jake nodded wisely. "It's all so clear now: there's a vast conspiracy of evil scientists who want to convince us that we evolved from apes. Because...?"

"Well, that's kind of where I was going with my paper. Or where I would've gone, if I had to write it," I added. "The people who prevent anything other than Darwin's evolution from getting taught in schools say it's because the other ideas are just religion pretending to be science, and that Darwin is proven and true. But really, the whole theory and the way they're teaching it, it's more like religion than science."

"Well," Shayne asked, "if this Darwin stuff is really so full of mistakes and missing missing links and stuff, why wouldn't they tell us?"

"Right," Allie said. "Scientists just want to find the truth. If Darwinism is as weak as you make it sound, why aren't there other scientific ideas out there?"

"There's Intelligent Design," Kingston put in. "But evolutionists say that's just a creationist Trojan Horse." A few of us looked at him blankly.

Sam explained. "They say Christians are trying to sneak creationism into the classroom, disguised as science. You know, like the Greeks sneaked their soldiers into Troy inside the huge wooden horse."

"Not all of us have dads who are professors of ancient history," Shayne said, scruffing his hair.

Ericson stuck to the topic. "Some Intelligent Design advocates are Christians, but plenty aren't. The more we learn about the amazing intricacy of life at a microscopic level, the more scientists admit that randomness—even random mutations over billions of years—can't account for the complexity of even basic organisms. It points to a designer. And they're only some of the respected scientists who believe Darwinism, or naturalistic evolution, is a sinking ship."

"There's got to be a reason all the other scientists aren't exactly scrambling aboard the *S.S. Intelligent Design*," Jake said.

"Because it's not a *naturalistic* theory. Naturalism is the philosophy that everything arises from natural causes, and any supernatural or spiritual explanations don't count. That's their starting point."

Allie's forehead scrunched. "But that's basically saying their starting point is atheism."

Ericson nodded. "Science to them is godless by definition."

"So what happens if the honest, true and factual explanation for something is supernatural?" Allie asked.

"That doesn't compute. 'Scientifically impossible.' They search for another, naturalistic explanation. They've basically redefined 'science' to mean 'only naturalism'."

"So if the *S.S. Creation* or the *S.S. Intelligent Design* come alongside the sinking *S.S. Darwinism* and throw out life preservers..." Shayne said.

"The *Darwin* crew would rather go down with their ship," Sam finished.

Ericson said, "They'll cling to the wreckage and hope a different ship comes along. One with another godless paradigm, otherwise they won't abandon the wreckage of Darwinism." No one said anything for a minute, then he cleared his throat and cast an apologetic look at Martina. "But I think we've strayed off topic," he said.

She gave him a smile. "Not at all. We were going to talk about how we can dialogue with people who have different beliefs. It's vital to understand their faith, so we can speak Jesus into that worldview.

"Have any of you had to deal with criticism or teasing in the classroom because of your belief in the Bible?" she asked. Some scattered agreement. "How do you handle that?"

"Some people handle it by staying as far from classrooms as they can," Jake muttered, just loud enough to be heard. Sam looked at him, but Jake was too busy flipping a pen between his fingers to look back.

"Ah, do I detect an opinion about the homeschooling choice?" Martina asked.

"Hey." Jake held up his hands. "I'm no expert, but I don't see how you can be salt and light to the world when you hide at home."

"Okay, now we're getting into some meaty discussion," she said, uncrossing her long, blue-jeaned legs and then recrossing the opposite way. "Jake, how about it? Tell us about some opportunities you've had lately to share a little Biblical worldview at school. Oh, relax, I'm not trying to put you on the spot. Maybe you had a chance to but didn't do it? We understand. It's not always easy. But all the more reason to talk about it. This is how we learn and grow."

He crossed his arms. "We're not supposed to try to convert people to other religions at school. Some kind of school policy."

We couldn't help it; thinking of Kellie, all our eyes flicked over to Ericson. I felt a surprisingly painful stab of missing her. I could only imagine how he felt.

Martina pressed on. "What about before and after school? During lunch?"

"Still school property."

Martina turned to Kingston. "What about you? I don't suppose you get many opportunities to talk Jesus with people, hidden away there at home."

Kings shrugged in his amicable way. "My sisters already know Him. I'm not sure about the cat." Shayne laughed, and he beamed. Then his eyes got thoughtful. "But there was the lady outside the Shop 'n' Save. I was waiting for my mom, and this lady had a busted wheel on her shopping trolley, so I helped her.

We got to talking about God and stuff. Oh, and there's always the girls from Hope's gymnastics team who come over. Or when we go with my dad to the food pantry to unpack boxes. There's always people there to talk to."

Jake was examining the ceiling.

"And the playground," Kings added.

"Okay, we get the picture," Jake said.

"Library," Kings slipped in.

Martina smiled, a bit slyly, I thought. "So you might say that if we give God our willing hearts, He'll supply the opportunities. Rory, you look skeptical."

Was she always watching? She was as bad as Sam Notice-All Newman. "No," I said. "Well, maybe, but just as far as I'm concerned. I mean, talking to people, getting ideas across—it's not really my strong point."

"Really?" Jake asked, all astonishment. Martina's icy eyes shut him up.

"I'm new to a lot of this, so I don't think I'm really qualified to be out there talking to people about it. Convincing people."

"Good news, Cornerstonees," Ericson said. "It's not up to you to do any convincing. That's the job of the Holy Spirit. All you have to do is tell people about Jesus and what He's done—for you personally, for all who believe in Him. Like they say: one beggar telling another where to find bread." He leaned forward, resting his elbows on his knees and clasping his hands. "But that having been said, we have to face the fact that in the schools, more converting is happening in the opposite direction. Christian kids are being converted to a different sort of faith called secular humanism—where God doesn't really factor into the worldview, and human achievement is the pinnacle of existence.

"It takes a strong, spiritually-trained young person to navigate these waters and not be subtly won over to an unbiblical way of thinking. Frankly, not many kids your age have been getting that kind of spiritual education."

I looked at Kingston. Could that be the Fishers' whole philosophy—and now the Newmans'? Not so much to shelter their kids from the real world, but to prepare them for it *before* throwing them out into it? Kings looked at me and nodded, like he could read the question on my face.

"So, what—do we need some kind of diploma or credentials before we can be witnesses for Jesus?" Shayne asked.

"Sometimes I wish I had a degree in world religions and public speaking," Allie admitted. "I don't always feel really prepared to defend my faith."

Martina smiled sympathetically. "We live in a pluralistic society. Lots of people, lots of different ideas. But God doesn't necessarily expect you to address the multitudes. He may just want you to turn to the person next to you. Talk to them, ask them questions. Respect their freedom of conscience, their right to their beliefs. But be ready to give a reason for the hope within you."

"With meekness," Ericson added.

Jake made like he was deflating, balloon-style. "Why always the meekness and gentleness? It's hard to get respect when you have to be a sissy."

Ericson heaved a sigh of affectionate frustration. "You only say that because you don't understand the amount of strength it takes to be gentle. You also don't understand the term 'meekness'. It doesn't mean 'timid'. What would be the point of sharing the gospel timidly? Meekness refers to a certain calm temper of mind where you're not easily provoked. There's an element of humility and patience, even longsuffering."

"In other words," Allie said with a sniff towards Jake, "when you're meek, you're not always worried about 'getting respect'."

Martina was flipping through her Bible, scanning with a finger. For a half second, I was reminded of Gabby (though she never seemed to look at her Book, just read with her fingertip). "Here, and it's the LORD speaking: 'This is the one I esteem: he who is humble and contrite in spirit, and trembles at my word.'"

"Besides, the meek get to inherit the earth," Sam added. "I'd settle for a little island somewhere. I wouldn't need a whole planet, you know?"

Martina slipped a bookmark out of her Bible and tossed it into his lap. "You win an M. L. Thistlethwaite original bookmark for that example of meekness. But seriously, young people, when it comes to sharing your faith, meekness is key." She turned to me. "You may be a new Christian, Rory, but I bet you have a story to share about how that happened, and what it's meant."

I exchanged a quick glance with Sam. A story? No doubt. Was it one I could share with just anybody? So far I'd only found one person. But I supposed I could share the broad strokes, even if I didn't get into all the particulars (I tended to chat with angels).

My story. And His. "Yeah, I guess I do," I finally said.

"Nevermind that," Jake said. "Back up a minute. Did Ericson just call us Cornerstonies?"

There were two interesting emails when I got home that evening. (My internet ban didn't include emailing.)

Hey, Rory. Here's the poop: you get to do the "Go Green" presentation at the assembly, the more scientific part, anyway! "Positive Steps YOU can Take to Reduce Your Carbon Footprint", that sort of thing. Maybe a top-10 list. Work for you? Sure beats a 10-page paper...or was it 15? –Bliss

And the second one:

OMG! I can't believe I have to sit here and write with my dad watching. It's so degrading. I thought I should apologize about the whole mall thing. Talk about a big deal over nothing! But you know what stinks? I haven't had any messages from Lukes since that night. My dad left my InterFace active to see if he'd write. Also, he's been reading all of my past messages (lucky I deleted lots of them). Okay, he's about to read over my shoulder, so I'm going to click send. –AL

I wrote back.

Sounds fine. Top-10 list it is. How about I just do the research and you do the presentation?

And:

Angelica—do you think we can talk on the phone sometime soon? I have a story I think I need to tell you. Here's my number. Call whenever.

I got a reply almost immediately, but not from the person I'd hoped.

Hey, I wish you were still on InterFace! Emailing is sluggish and sad. And there is absolute madness and mayhem going on, it's great. Everyone's asking where you went. BUT I told them to mind their BEEZ. Rory has her mysterious ways.

About the presentation, nice try, but you have to do it, that was part of the Hayes Compromise. All you've got to do is read your list into a microphone. I'm taking care of the rest, so just relax.

And, stupidly, I did.

forty-two

April ambled in all innocent and lamb-like. I was fooled. Gentle Aprils will do that to you, after nasty Februaries and ornery Marches. The air feels like greenness and life when you breathe it in deep, and tastes faintly sweet when you let it go. Birdies twitter, squirrelies chitter. Heavy coats are forgotten in closets, their pockets full of interesting and needful items that won't be found again until next autumn.

"This is perfect," Bliss said outside the school on a particularly sunshine-and-dew-drenched morning. She hopped out of a car I didn't recognize as, dangerously close to tardiness, I hustled up to the front door. (I'd found my white school oxford shirt in the dryer, wet. I had time for about ten tumbles before I had to put it on and run.)

"Yeah. Nice," I said, damply, trying to hurry.

"It's supposed to be a gorgeous April," she said, not trying to hurry. "Not much rain. You know what that means?"

"No May flowers?"

"It means I can have the Earth Day celebration outside. Which is perfect. If it does rain, I'm going to take it very personally." She smiled, and the bell rang at the same moment.

I couldn't help watching the weather closely over the next few weeks.

"Anyone know if it's supposed to rain next week?" I asked after the Scene one Saturday while we waited for Jeph and Sheelan to pick us up. As usual, Jeph had gone to the Believers' Youth Experience, and as usual they were late getting back. Honestly, I wouldn't have minded the extra hang-out time at all—Sam and Jake always stayed as long as we did—but I picked up on some subtle annoyance vibes from Shayne and Allie, and in all fairness the blame could be squarely placed on Sheelan's shoulders.

"That's like the second or third time you've asked about the weather," Allie pointed out. "Why the sudden interest?"

"Do you need to ask?" Jake tossed me the ball with a smile. "Meteorology is the perfect nerdly hobby for Rory."

I gave him one of Sheelan's patented sweet but deadly smiles. "I'm just wondering if Bliss will get to have her Earth Day assembly outside. That's what she wants, and she always seems to get what she wants."

"You mean, where there's a will, Bliss hath a way?" Sam asked.

Jake narrowed his eyes and returned my smile. "Jealous?"

I narrowed my eyes back at him.

"Technically, wouldn't that be envy?" Sam asked. I looked at him. "Not that that's what—that you're—" He quickly took a shot at the basket. "Looky! Two points."

I couldn't help it, I laughed—a little. Enough to let him off the hook. "I guess it doesn't matter. Indoors or outdoors, I still have to get up there and read my little thing." I gave a theatrical shudder.

"You know," Sam said, "if it's outside, I might be able to watch." He saw my blank look. "If I go for a run. I sometimes take the trail around the school."

"I didn't know you liked to run."

He shrugged. "With my dad, early in the morning. Or, I stay in bed and just go on my own later, and listen to music." He brightened. "Do you run?"

I had to shake my head. "Maybe I should. I get tired of sitting around, and I feel like I just want to…" I flailed my arms.

"Escape? Burn off steam? Wear yourself out?"

"Yes, all that. I'm not really into school sports, with all the practices and games…besides the fact that coordination isn't exactly my strong point."

"Oh, we hadn't noticed," Jake said, throwing 'secret' knowing looks at the others. Allie tossed the basketball at his head. He ducked and then said, "You know, running is perfect for people who don't have any actual athletic talent. What? A 'sport' you can do while listening to your MP3? Imagine football players listening to music. Come on."

"Added any more tunes to your doo-mahickey?" Shayne asked me.

"I'm still listening to the stuff you guys put on there," I said. This launched a detailed quiz about specific songs and whether I didn't think they were the best ever. I played it safe and claimed to love it all equally. "Though the songs I've been listening to the most lately are just a guy and a guitar, kind of a quiet voice. But the songs are really powerful."

Sam rattled off a man's name. "Mostly he does old hymns."

"Maybe that's why I like them." I mentally high-fived myself. "I love his version of 'This is my Father's World'—oh, but there's another one that just gets me…"

"'My Song is Love Unknown'?" Sam guessed.

"Yes."

Jake winged the ball at me. "Can we please stop slobbering over love songs before I'm forced to gnaw off my own limbs?" His head turned at the distant sound of a car horn. "That's my dad. Gotta go. Sam, you're gonna have to catch a lift with someone. We're taking my sister back to the airport."

"No problem."

We watched the door close behind Jake, then I faced the others. "Jake has a sister?"

"Yep," Shayne said. "She's older. College, maybe."

"No, she's still a senior," Sam said. He recognized my puzzled expression, although it's hard to distinguish from my usual expression (I think they might be the same). "She lives with their mom."

"I can't believe I didn't know that," I said. I wondered what else I might not know about Jake Dean. Had I ever tried to get to know him? Not really. Did I plan to now?…Not really. My mistake, though I didn't think so for a while.

"What's up between you guys lately?" I asked Sam.

"I'm not sure," he said, his eyes still on Mr. Dean's gleaming red sports car. It peeled out of the drive with a roar.

In the spirit of not procrastinating on absolutely everything in life, I tackled my Top Ten Ways to Not Royally Mudge Up the Planet presentation that week. Or, I should say, I tackled it that Monday. More specifically, that Monday from six o'clock until seven. With a bathroom break and two snacks.

It was laughably easy. A quick internet search—my mom caved and let me go online just for school-related purposes—a few print-outs, and voila, I had something to read at the assembly. It took longer to change the printer cartridge than it did to find the information. Laughably easy. Really, I was literally laughing.

A rat in the maze called Rory's Life would've crept along carefully at this point, anticipating a nasty little electric shock. A chimp would be screeching and ducking for cover. But Rory Joyce just ran for the cheese, grabbed for the banana.

Earth Day dawned with all the sparkling brilliance of a fairy festival. Bliss had ordered her day with watery blue sky, popcorn clouds, tender green grass and perfumed blossoms unfurling on the trees. Mother Nature had delivered.

So the assembly was outside, color me all surprised. Bliss had chosen a prime spot to construct—or make others construct—a little stage: the two benches where once I and my friends had sat to read our notes from Kellie and receive our white stones. Now they were the main supports for a plywood platform, over which was draped a green cloth. A colorful banner hung across the front:

O mother earth, ocean-girdled and mountain-breasted, pardon me for trampling on you. —Sanskrit prayer

Interesting. I just hoped they didn't expect me to stand on that flimsy thing. It would be face-plant time for sure.

Behind the stage stretched the gentle gray limbs of Kellie's magnolia tree, conscripted into service as the backdrop. It was in full bloom, which usually didn't happen until May. Another Bliss Hath-a-way coup. For some reason I felt sorry for it.

Or maybe that was just the effect of the music—not a recording, actual musicians. A woman in a long dress sat with a small harp nestled against her, plucking out a slow melody. A man held a drum like a shield and tapped it with the short wooden stick in his other hand. A girl tootled a tin whistle. I was enough of a Joyce to recognize Irish music. (Perhaps they preferred 'Celtic'.) It actually wasn't bad, just sort of wistful. While they played, the classes filed out of the building and settled in a ragged half-circle facing the stage.

Bliss beckoned to me from 'backstage', or behind the tree. She had abandoned the old school uniform for one of her organic dresses, all clingy and flowy. Her hair swung around her shoulders, wavy like it had been braided, the warm brown streaked with gold, matching her eyes.

I was polyester and practical shoes. "Hey," I said.

"Your spot is towards the end of the program," she whispered. "After the little kids finish their dance."

The end? "I wouldn't say my stuff is actually 'grand finale' material," I said.

"I've got the finale covered," she said, her eyes roving the crowd. She lifted a hand and beckoned to someone else. "Got to get started," she said, breezing away.

And she did. Not on the little stage, but in front of it, she adjusted a microphone and nodded at the musicians, who finished their song. "Welcome all," Bliss said. "And a blessed Earth Day to you. Today we gather to learn about and to honor the Earth." She smiled at the youngest kids wiggling and squirming in front. "We have some special guests to help us do that. I'd like to introduce Ronnie Walking Cloud, who will lead us in an invocation."

An invocation. Sounds impressive, I thought. I'd heard the word before, but forgot what it meant.

An elderly man in blue jeans, a white buttoned shirt, and boots shuffled up to the microphone. He lifted his brown, weathered hands, then droned in a wavering voice.

> "To the four powers of Creation,
> To the Grandfather Sun,
> To the Grandmother Moon,
> To the Mother Earth,
> And to my ancestors.
>
> I pray for my relations in Nature,

All those who walk, crawl, fly, and swim,
Seen and unseen,
To the good spirits that exist
 in every part of Creation.

May there be good health
and healing for this Earth,
May there be Beauty above me,
May there be Beauty below me,
May there be Beauty in me,
May there be Beauty around me.
I ask that this world be filled
with Peace, Love and Beauty."

And he shuffled off again. I joined in the applause. He was sweet. You kind of wanted to hug him or give him coffee and a doughnut or something.

He was just the beginning. There was more music—a kind of eastern-sounding type—and to the kids' screeching delight, an animal handler with an endangered species of snake, some little hawkish bird, and a puffball of a chinchilla. The fuzzy fellow was particularly adored by the kindergarten set, who then launched into tears and fits when informed that naughty adults like to wear them as coats. "Animals are our brothers and sisters," the handler reminded them gently before making her exit. "And are often wiser than we."

Next was a woman who struck me as vaguely familiar. Her hair was braided like a crown around her head, and she wore a dress not unlike Bliss's except that she was considerably older and it clung in places she might not have intended. She spoke passionately about caring for the earth, and it struck me as a tad bit peculiar but mostly harmless when she invited the third grade class over to place their hands against the trunk of the magnolia tree.

"Isn't she beautiful?" the woman cooed. "Feel the life flowing through her. Close your eyes, and feel her spirit."

Huh? I stopped ripping up grass from the spot of ground where I sat cross-legged and looked around. I saw a couple of teachers exchange a certain look. They clearly thought this lady was a bona fide breakfast-cereal buffet: flaky, nutty, fruity and loopy. But I didn't hear anyone object to the whole tree spirit concept. Life, sure—as in sap. But 'her spirit'? Next she'd have us dancing in circles and chanting around the tree.

I hate when I'm right.

"I want you always to remember, children," the woman said, sweeping a hand to encompass earth and sky, "Mother Earth gives life. We came from the earth, and one day we will return to it—it is only right and natural. Just like the plants and other creatures. So we are all one."

That again? 'Death is a part of life' and all that rubbish? If death was so right and natural, why had my life been limping along ever since my dad was killed in the crash? Why was Mrs. Newman still 'cracked'? Why were Ericson's eyes about a mile deep with missing Kellie?

The woman finished and passed by me. I caught a wave of musky, earthy fragrance and instantly knew: I'd seen her in Tam's shop. She must've been one of her special sisterhood.

Bliss adjusted the microphone lower. "Now I would ask the classroom representatives to come forward and present their class gifts to Mother Earth."

One by one, a kid from each class walked up to the green-draped little stage, placed something on it, then turned to speak a few words.

"This is a baby tree," a kindergartener said, to widespread *ooh*s and *aww*s. "We're gonna plant it in the schoolyard."

The first grade representative followed. "This is our promise to recycle all our paper, plastic, and metals, and never let them get into the class wastebasket by mistake." He placed a paper with the promise and two dozen scrawling 'signatures' next to the baby tree.

And next: "Our class pledges to spend one Saturday afternoon each month picking up litter in the park."

And on it went, until, "We pledge to do whatever we can to reduce our impact on the planet," Jasmine Wee said as the representative of our class, though I didn't recall our class ever discussing it. Probably she and Bliss had discussed it, and that was enough. "Including reducing water and energy consumption, buying locally grown organic foods, reducing the amount of luxury items we buy, and most of all, telling our friends to do the same." She placed a piece of paper, rolled and tied like a scroll, onto the little stage.

That's when it finally hit me, that it wasn't a stage. No one had climbed up onto it. Everything had happened around it, in front of it, now things were being placed on top of it. Promises, pledges. Offerings.

It was an altar.

I'm sure my mouth was hanging open by this point. I searched the crowd again—other kids, teachers, anybody—for another face like mine. Mr. Hayes was yawning. Mrs. Palmer rubbed her temple, the other arm crossed over her chest. No one objected. It was just me, reading way too much into all of this.

Then the sweet music started, and the smiling kindergarteners made a circle around the altar and the magnolia tree, holding hands and moving with slow steps first one way, then the other. They sang, "Earth am I. Air am I. Water, fire and spirit am I. Ah wey ah hey, ah wey ah hey…"

Okay, I definitely wasn't reading too much into this.

The chanting ended. Bliss took the mike once again. "Thank you, Miss Leakey's Kindergarten class. That was inspiring. And thanks to all the classes for your thoughtful offerings. On the topic of reducing our negative impact on the planet, Rory Joyce from 8-C is going to offer up ten ways for us to honor Mother Earth, make her glad, and receive her blessing." She gestured to the mike with a 10-carat smile, while I froze on the grass. "Stand up, Rory."

For a second I didn't. I was digesting the words *offer up* and *make her glad* and *her blessing*. They gave me a stomach cramp. Heads began turning, searching for this Rory Joyce person who was holding up the show. I clambered to my feet, brushing off the many blades of grass sacrificed to my nervousness. Bliss stepped out of my way, still with that glitter in her eye, watching closely.

Along with a few hundred other people. I faced the audience, a restless faceless mass who seemed utterly unconcerned that this assembly had amounted to nothing more or less than an exercise in paganism. Now here I was, required to offer up my own personal sacrifice on the altar of Acceptable Public School Religion.

No big deal, said the voice in my head. *Read your piece. It's just about taking care of the world God made, and that's Biblical.* The fact that it was arriving in a outrageously un-Biblical package wasn't my fault. I'd just collected the ten ideas; I hadn't planned the whole Earth-goddess extravaganza.

Somebody from the sixth graders' territory shouted something I couldn't make out. Laughter sprinkled through the crowd. "Um," I said. The speakers screamed some feedback and everyone clutched their ears. There. It was a start.

Just read the dumb list, Rory.

My roaming eyes snagged on the face of Miss Jensen, the new art teacher. I thought of Kellie, suspended from teaching just because of a few tracts handed out in the parking lot and a few whispered words of Jesus-encouragement to me in the art room.

Yet here we were dancing around an altar, offering up our sacrifices to Mother Earth. So much for separation of church and state. Oh, yeah... That wasn't really a law. Just like I'd told Bliss.

I could just walk away. Mr. Hayes watched me from the edges of the crowd. The evil "I" for incomplete glowed like a red-hot brand in his eyes. Walk away...sure. Walk away from passing science, from graduating.

Then I saw Mrs. Palmer, also watching me closely. And, strangely, my eyes picked out Journey LeVey on the other side of the throng. And there, the dark piercing stare of Jasmine Wee. The surge of noise from the impatient crowd faded into a curious quiet. How long had I been standing there?

"Well?" a single voice called from towards the back. I was pretty sure I recognized Jake Dean's voice.

I opened my mouth, though it wasn't much use since I had no plan. Then, behind the assembled crowd, leaning just at the corner of the brick building, I spotted a lean figure in baggy shorts and a sweatshirt, a mess of black curls on top.

You'd better say a prayer for me, Sam.

Then I was talking.

"Um, I have a poem," I said, looking down at my paper, which had no poem on it.

A throat cleared behind me. "What about your list?" Bliss's voice whispered.

List, schmist. Half of it had already been 'pledged' by various classes. They already knew this stuff. How about something different? I swallowed hard.

> "This is my Mother's world,
> And to my listening ears
> All nature sings, and 'round me rings
> The music of the spheres.
> This is my Mother's world:

> I rest me in the thought
> Of rocks and trees, of skies and seas
> Her hand the wonders wrought."

Some politely listened. Most were distracted. Teachers shushed students—but not all of them. A few watched me closely. Mrs. Palmer lowered her temple-rubbing hand to her side.

> "This is my Mother's world.
> The birds their carols raise.
> The morning light, the lily white
> Declare Mother Nature's praise.
> This is my Mother's world:
> She shines in all that's fair;
> In the rustling grass I hear her pass,
> She speaks to me everywhere."

I stopped. Scattered claps swelled into applause of true appreciation—mostly because I was done. But the tree-hugging lady clapped with special enthusiasm and turned to Mrs. Knowles, the principal, asking, "Wasn't that just lovely?"

"Very nice," Mrs. Knowles said.

"Did you write that, Rory?" the other lady asked.

My eyes strayed out to the fringes of the crowd. Sam wasn't leaning against the wall anymore. He was standing straight and still.

Here we go, I thought, taking a breath and hoping my voice wouldn't shake. "No, I just changed it a little. The original goes like this: *This is my Father's world. / O let me ne'er forget / That though the wrong seems oft so strong, / God is the ruler yet. / This is my Father's world. / Why should my heart be sad? / The Lord is King; let the heavens ring! / God reigns; let the earth be—*"

"Well, thank you, Rory," Mrs. Knowles cut in, moving over to the microphone. "Now how about that list of ten ways to save the planet?"

"But I wasn't quite done."

"Oh, yes, you were," she said quietly, away from the mike.

To be honest, I was surprised to get as far as I did. "But it's the same song, just a couple of words changed."

"It's a hymn, Rory. A religious song." She accused me with a sharp brown eye.

"It was a hymn the first time I said it, too," I said, careful to keep my voice respectful and quiet. "I'm not sure I understand why it was okay to use the word 'Mother' but not 'Father'."

"Because one way just makes it a poem. The other makes it a Creationist hymn." She turned to Bliss. "Why don't you conclude the ceremonies, Miss Hathaway? I believe Rory is done here." She turned back to me. "Don't take it personally, honey. It's just a matter of what's legal and what's not."

Now, finally, my cheeks went supernova. In fact, I think I blushed all the way down to my toes. Apparently some adrenaline came with it, because words kept coming out of my face. "I don't mean any disrespect, but this whole program has been filled with religion. It doesn't make sense that we can praise the Mother Goddess but not the Heavenly Father."

Behind us, Bliss was waving to a group waiting to one side, and suddenly we were surrounded by people who looked like they'd just come from the Renaissance Fest, each carrying a drum. They ranged in front of the altar while Mrs. Knowles tried to steer me off to the side.

"'Mother Nature' is not a goddess—just a poetic way to refer to the earth."

"Then all the prayers and the invocation…" I remembered the word now; I'd seen it on the church bulletin. To invoke meant to summon something, like the presence of a spirit. "They were for the earth? So it's okay to worship the earth."

Mrs. Knowles gestured to Bliss to make the drummers start, took me rather firmly by the elbow and finally moved me to one side. Bliss stepped up to the microphone. "Thank you, Mrs. Knowles," she said. "And thanks, Rory, for that demonstration of the real meaning of 'separation of church and state'."

I couldn't say much. The air suddenly throbbed with the beat of drums, and I was being led, very firmly, to the school office.

forty-three

I sat in junior high purgatory, awaiting my fate. Elevator music played—suggesting I might already be descending to the gates of Doom—but I wasn't actually going anywhere. I was in the lobby of the school office. The scratchy upholstery and cold steel bars of my chair seemed to declare that comfort was but a distant memory.

Mrs. Knowles was in her office, the door closed, making phone calls. The secretary looked up from her keyboard occasionally to give me a certain unfathomable look. Disgust? Pity? Perhaps she already knew my fate.

Then the outer door swung open, and Journey LeVey wandered in and took a nearby seat. I stared at her.

"I was already here," she said blandly. "Just took an assembly break."

"Really."

She nodded, unconcerned.

"What're you here for?" I asked.

"I refused to participate in a social studies lesson."

"Oh."

Silence, except for elevator music and keyboard tapping.

"This is the best Earth Day ever," she finally said with a silvery flash in her eyes.

Ah, mockery. That's all that was missing. "So happy to entertain. My complete humiliation wasn't a total waste."

"Oh, I was entertained alright. But not because you were humiliated. Are you kidding? You're my hero."

I shot her a sidelong glance. There was definitely a laugh sneaking around her eyes and the corner of her mouth. "Is that right?" I asked.

"Bliss had you totally gulled. All my life I've watched her manipulate people into doing whatever she wants. Most of them just throw themselves at her feet and invite her to walk all over them, too. Sickening. But there you were, completely in her clutches, and to see you just flat-out refuse to play along... She finally came up against someone with actual deeply-held beliefs. I mean, it almost gives me something like hope."

I looked at her straight on now. Yes, she was cracking wise, but I detected an honesty behind it. So I returned the favor. "Thanks, but it's not like I was standing up for myself. It's just all that earth worship...I couldn't go along with that and still look myself in the eye—face myself in the mirror—oh, you know."

"Yeah, yeah. But it took guts."

I shrugged, kind of a *thanks, I guess, whatever*. I figured she'd stop talking then. I figured wrong.

"And then what you said," she continued.

What did this girl want from me? I had no brilliant ideas, so I just went with the truth (the only brilliant idea after all). "You know, that just sort of... Well, none of that was really me. I mean, I'm not the kind of person who just faces down the mob and speaks up for truth and all that. I'm basically a chicken."

"Yes." She cut me off with a slice of her hand through the air. "Don't you think I know that? That's the whole point."

"It is?" It was?

"Uh, yeah." She tucked her long black shield of bangs behind her ear, and for a few moments I got a rare unobstructed view of her eyes. After a slight hesitation, she said, "I know that wasn't just *you* up there. It was something else. The kind of something that makes a big chicken 'face the mob' and speak up."

I nodded, and waited.

"I just want to know what that something is."

And that's how she lobbed the ball smack-dab in the center of my court. Even I couldn't miss.

"Well, what are you doing this Saturday night?"

Just as if God had planned it, Sheelan came down with a slobbering head cold that Saturday, and she wouldn't let Jeph look at her let alone take her out in public. So there was an extra space in the car to bring Journey to the Scene with us. Groovy.

It also just so happened that Pastor Dan's talk was about 'How I Know Jesus is God'—how he demonstrated power over the spirits, over sin, and over death. I couldn't help but watch Journey, maybe cringing a little at the directness of the message. Too much too soon, I worried. I should've known that nothing worked better than directness on Journey LeVey. I probably shouldn't have been surprised that she and Martina hit if off instantly, either—in their own slightly sharp, sparring sort of way.

Still, I didn't quite relax until we were playing basketball afterwards. Once when Journey took a shot, her long sleeves crept up a couple of inches above her wrists. I saw those little pink scars again. She saw me seeing them, again. There was a faint challenge in her eyes, no embarrassment, but something else instead. Maybe something like hope.

"Checking out my wounds?" she asked me while the others dashed towards the other basket.

I shrugged. "I guess we've all got some. But I've been told that God doesn't leave us that way. Broken, maybe, but not wounded."

She had a hazy, thoughtful look. I think she might've said more, but the ball flew right at her. She caught it, flung it at the basket.

"You're hopeless," Jake told her after she missed by a mile.

"Yes," she said, then looked at me. "At basketball."

Soon we were crowded around the drinking fountains. "So tell me exactly what happened," Allie said for the second time, wiping her mouth. Jake had informed them of my performance at the assembly.

"Did you really tell everybody off?" Shayne asked.

"No. It wasn't like that." I felt my heart quicken, reliving it. Even so, I remembered it like it had been someone else—someone I was embarrassed for, like the goofus people on sitcoms, but not myself.

"She made a complete fool of herself," Jake said for the third time. He looked to Journey. "Didn't she?"

Journey shrugged. "You could say that."

I thanked her.

"That's awesome," Shayne said.

I thanked Shayne.

"Seriously. I mean, if you're going to make a fool of yourself, do it for Jesus, right?"

"That could be your personal motto, Rory," Jake said helpfully.

"You just wish it had been you," Allie accused him.

"Not likely."

"It's not a big deal, guys," I said, escaping for a second by taking another drink. "I'd rather just forget about it. It's not like I made an inspiring witness-stand speech. I mumbled a few words."

"Into a microphone," Journey added.

"I wasn't thinking about that at the time."

"You were there, Sam," Shayne said. "Did you hear it all?"

"Yep." He took a drink.

"So?"

He took off his glasses, dragged an arm across his forehead, then polished the glasses with his shirt. "Rory's braver than all of us," he said, inspecting the lenses carefully.

Allie, Shayne and Journey all turned to me with eyebrows raised at a *see? told ya* angle.

"Oh, stop it, you'll only encourage her," Jake said. "Who knows what she'll cook up for her next public escapade."

"No, thank you," I said sharply. "I'll gladly fade into oblivion. You won't get me up in front of a group again."

One day I'll learn not to make those kind of sweeping statements. My life has a certain pattern of contradicting them.

"So I'm guessing you didn't get the credit for science after all?" Allie asked.

Shayne clapped a hand over her mouth. "Rory," she gasped. "Does this mean you won't graduate?"

Now I relived that whole scene in my memory. "No. I can still do the paper."

Jake chuckled wickedly. "It's only fair. But I suppose you knew you had that to fall back on the whole time."

"No, she didn't." Journey shut him down. "For all she knew, she wasn't going to graduate unless she went along with Bliss's twisted ritual. All Bliss wanted to do was show that separation of church and state really only applied to Christianity—animism is fine, Wicca is grand. New Age spirituality, peachy. Even other religions like Islam are perfectly okay. I mean, I got in trouble for refusing to wear a head covering and playing a 'jihad' dice game during our Muslim unit in social studies. I got a detention for 'intolerance'—they wouldn't even listen when I told them it was about hypocrisy. I mean, can you imagine a unit about the teachings of Jesus? It's about time someone called them on it, and that's what Rory was doing. That's what Sam means about her being brave."

"Excuse me all to pieces," Jake said.

"But back to the paper," Allie said. "The good news is you get a second chance—wait, a third chance?"

"I think this would be the fifth," Shayne said. "The test re-take was the second chance, and the paper was the second second chance, so really the third. And the assembly was the fourth chance, so that makes this—"

"As I was saying, that's the good news."

"Hooray for good news," I said flatly. "The bad news is, I've got less than two weeks to get it done."

"But that's the better news," Allie said. "Because we're going to help—for real this time. I'm good at organizing. Footnotes, bibliography, all that."

"I like proofreading," Shayne said.

"I guess I can nag you when you're procrastinating," Journey put in.

"Wait, I want the nag position," Sam said.

"And I'll deliver it to Mr. Hayes dressed in my Hermes Messenger of the Gods costume, with a brass band playing in your honor," said Jake.

"Wouldn't that basically be a little skirt and a pair of winged booties?" Sam asked.

"A winged helmet, too."

"Oh, good. Wouldn't want you to catch cold."

I laughed, probably more than their humor deserved. It was fueled by relief. "Thanks, guys."

"Don't thank them yet," Shayne said. "You realize they're just coming over to eat all your snack food."

I hadn't exactly conveyed to my mom the seriousness of my incomplete grade in science, but maybe she knew more than I thought. The sheer quantity of snack food in the house the afternoon my friends came over suggested a certain desperate appreciation. Ordinarily this would've been a superb act on her part, but I found the selection—particularly the pseudo-baked goodies—unexpectedly embarrassing. Since my mom was right there in the kitchen (also slightly embarrassing, but kind of nice, too, having her home more), I couldn't hide them.

Jake and Sam dove into the box of Twinkle Cakes as soon as my mom offered it. Sam thanked her.

"Not exactly sufganiyot," I said, apologetically.

"Are you kidding? I love these things, but my mom refuses to get them." Sam bit half of one, then popped the rest in his mouth. Jake did the same only without biting it in half first.

"Let's get to the task at hand," Allie called from downstairs.

"Allie Taskmaster speaks," Jake said around his second Twinkle.

"Are you sure this is allowed?" my mom asked, setting out some milk and juice bottles. "Collaborating like this on a paper that's meant for one person?"

"Don't worry, Mrs. Joyce," Allie said. "Rory has to do all the hard stuff. I'm just here to help her organize it, and Shayne's going to proofread it. Jake can handle the graphics—he and Kings can do the technical stuff."

"And I'm here to keep her focused," Sam said. "And eat Twinkle Cakes."

I'm not sure how much focusing Sam would help me do now, but Allie was surprised to see how much I had already done. I was, too. Whenever I'd read a good article online ('good' = I understood it), I would save the link and then write a little summary in my own words. I'd done the same on little slips of paper tucked into strategic chapters of Ericson's books. Allie and Sam looked them over, and he said, "Looks to me like this paper is mostly written."

"Sam's right," Allie said. Tack on an introduction, a conclusion, and the charts and illustrations, and you've pretty much got yourself fifteen pages."

It was a good thing, too, because not long after that, the phone rang. My mom came around the corner holding the phone out to me. "It's someone named Angelica," she said.

Everyone's eyes snapped to me. "Finally," I said, though what I meant was, *now what do I do?*

I took the phone and walked towards the living room. Sam gave me a little thumbs-up signal. I gave him a *here goes nothing* half-shrug and rounded the corner.

"Hello?"

"Rory? It's Angelica. Hi. Wasn't I supposed to call you?"

"I was hoping you would."

"You said you had a story to tell me. What's that all about?"

I hesitated. Which girl had called me, the slightly unbalanced, approval-seeking Angelica or the hard-edged, easy-to-tick-off Angelyte? "It's something I should've talked to you about a long time ago," I started, "but I wasn't sure how much to say. It's about angels."

"Really?" She sounded more like the eager Angelica now. "That's cool. I think it's sweet that we're both into that. I want to hear all about your experiences. Maybe you can help me get in touch with my own angels."

"Well, that's just it. I think you already have—at least a little bit."

"You mean the ones you saw in my photographs? I guess because I couldn't see them, they didn't seem real to me. Are you ever able to see yours?"

I sucked in a slow breath. The others were downstairs, waiting for me to work on the paper. I had every excuse to put this off. But who knew when I'd have another chance—or what could happen in Angelica's life in the meantime? I knew what my friends would tell me to do.

I thought about Jesus, and the possibility that this might have something to do with the obedience that would grow my roots down deeper into him.

"Do you have a little time?" I finally asked. "Because it's kind of a long story, and I want to tell you all of it. It's not all good."

"Seriously? What could be 'not good' about angels? Aren't they, like, good by definition?"

"That's what we need to talk about."

forty-four

And we did talk, for almost half an hour. I told her everything. I even included the part where I'd tried to use my angel experiences to score points with Bliss and her family, and what a spectacularly ungreat idea that had been.

I told her about Uri.

The more I told her, the quieter she got. The quieter she got, the drier my mouth seemed to get. But I plunged ahead, and I didn't stop when I got to the part about Jesus, the Commander-in-Chief of the angel armies. I kept on plunging.

Eventually I did stop, mainly because I wasn't sure she was still there. She was.

"Honestly," she said, a little quiet, a bit flat, "I think it's a lot simpler to stick with just the angels, and not get too mixed up in all the traditional religious stuff."

"I know what you mean," I said. "But that's my whole point: angels are messengers and helpers. Any angel who doesn't come announcing who sent them, and why, is hiding something. That can't be from God."

Quiet for a few, excruciatingly long seconds. "You said something before about my InterFace friend, Lukes, and that strange man at the outlet mall. You really think there's some connection between them—and that Uri you talked about?"

"I do. I think you need to be really careful. He came after me, and now you're the second friend I think he's tried to get to." I hadn't exactly forgotten the séance and Bliss.

"Well, don't even worry about that. I haven't had a message from Lukes since that day, and even if he tried, my dad would get it first. And I don't think I'll be allowed to go back to the outlet mall until I'm eighteen."

I felt the muscles in my shoulders slowly unclench. "Your dad just wants to protect you. Be thankful you've got him."

"Yeah, thankful. Right." Silence again. "Listen, I've got to go."

"You'll think about what I said?"

"Sure I will. I'll be in touch, 'kay?"

"Okay, good. Thanks for calling, Angelica."

"Bye, Rory."

"Bye."

When I hung up, I didn't have a lot of hope that I'd hear from her again. But hope that maybe I'd said enough to make a difference.

This raises the question: how much is enough said? And how do you ever really know if you made a difference?

Such deep thoughts were not going through my head when the day came to turn in *Fact vs. Faith*. I was merely wondering whether I'd said enough to make a difference in my science grade.

Mrs. Palmer was watching me with those owlish eyes when I came into homeroom that morning. In answer to her unspoken question, I held up my paper in its shiny protective report cover.

"Do I have your permission to make a copy of it for myself?" she asked me. "I would be very interested in reading it."

"Sure." I couldn't exactly say no.

She slipped off to the copy room before class started and returned with a small stack. "Here's your report back. Nicely formatted, by the way. Good use of graphics."

Thanks, Jake, I said silently. Hard words to say out loud.

"Oh, and here." She handed me a stiff stack of clear sheets. "I forgot to check the copier before I started, and I accidentally printed your paper on transparencies. They're kind of expensive, so I didn't want to just throw them out. You may as well keep them."

"Yeah, okay." Whatever. I slipped them into my science folder.

"Thank you," she said, tucking her own paper copy into her desk drawer. "I look forward to reading this over lunch."

I thought it might make a better naptime story, but I kept that to myself.

It was a warm day, and Mr. Hayes had taken off his oxford shirt to reveal the T-shirt underneath, one of his favorites. It bore the black-and-white image of a bearded man—a man I now knew all too well. Charles Darwin.

Mr. Hayes noticed me noticing. He smiled as we all took our seats, then said, "Rory Joyce, I believe you have something for me."

No brass band, no Jake in his Hermes Messenger of the Gods costume. I just passed the report into Mr. Hayes's outstretched hand. I might've seen Jasmine roll her eyes in my peripheral vision. Jake mouthed *yippee* with a look of deadly boredom. Bliss observed it all without any expression whatsoever.

Mr. Hayes walked to his desk, set the paper down. Then he got a thoughtful look and ran a hand through his thick, sandy hair. I watched, alarmed but not knowing why, as his hand settled back onto the paper and picked it up again.

"You know," he said, "more than one of you have expressed a genuine interest in what Rory uncovered in her months of research. What do you say to coming up here and making this an oral report, Rory?"

What do you say was an interesting choice of words, because of course I had absolutely nothing to say. Talking isn't an option when your brain-to-mouth connection short-circuits. Though there were plenty of words careening through my head: *What is he doing?! He's getting the last laugh, that's what. Or he's checking to see if you know the material and didn't just grab it from the internet. Or he hates you. Or Bliss gave him this idea. Yes, that had to be it. Revenge.*

"Here, you can use your paper for reference—I won't make you do it from memory." Mr. Hayes extended the report to me. Somehow I was out of my chair, up at the front of the class, feeling every whisper and snicker like biting ants that crawl under your clothes. I searched the faces and saw suspicion, boredom, scorn, but not a hint of encouragement. A hostile audience.

"Go ahead," Mr. Hayes said. "We know you can speak to a crowd when you're inspired." Ah, a reference to the assembly. And the package of my utter despair was complete.

But then, strangely enough, I remembered Mrs. Palmer's words. *What I see isn't a girl who can't do it—I see a girl who doesn't want to try and fail in front of everyone. Could this thing you're trying to pass off as humility really be pride in disguise?*

I hadn't grasped her meaning back then. But now I almost heard the *ding* of getting it. Pride, me? Well, what was holding me back now? The fear of looking stupid? Of not being able to prove Mr. Hayes wrong? Did that even matter? Why not just stand up there and share what I'd learned with some kids who might be hearing it for the first—possibly only—time?

Mrs. Palmer butted into my thoughts again. *I accidentally printed your paper on transparencies...*

No way.

I turned to Mr. Hayes. "Can I use the overhead projector?"

"The overhead?" He watched me pull the transparencies from my folder, utterly mystified. "Uh, sure."

My thoughts tumbled over themselves. Had Mrs. Palmer somehow...? No, she couldn't have. Could she?

I cleared my throat.

"Hi," I said.

Two yawns. Three eye rollings. Off to a great start.

"Okay, um..." I slid the first transparency onto the projector. "I guess I won't just read all this to you," or, in other words, *you might run me out of town if I just read all this to you,* "so I'll sum up. I was supposed to compare fact and faith as far as the science of evolution goes. But first I had to figure out where to start. So I boiled it down to what most people would think of when they hear 'faith'—a Biblical view—and what they might think of as 'fact', the evolutionary view.

"Basically, the Biblical view says that God created all creatures 'after their kind'—"

"And Noah managed to squeeze millions of them onto one boat, right?" a voice muttered from the back. I didn't have to look to know it was Kevin Sebeck. I'd gone practically all school year without any trouble from him, so I suppose he was overdue.

"Not exactly," I said. "'After their kind' is sort of a basic starting point for each type of animal. We learned about variation and adaptation in this class, and that's what caused these basic types to change over time—I think Mr. Hayes uses the word 'diversify'—but the changes happened *within* the 'kind'. That's not the same as Darwin's evolution."

"Change over time? It sounds the same," Jasmine pointed out.

"Well," and I flipped to the next page, "see here? Darwin's theory says that all creatures descended from the same ancestor." I pointed to the branching diagram. "In other words, from one kind came all the other kinds—all the oodles of species emerged over oodles of time, but they all supposedly came from the same great-great-great granddaddy one-celled swamp sludgie."

"We've seen this before," Jake whispered loudly, ever-so-helpfully pointing out the same diagram in our science textbook.

"Yeah, I know." Now wasn't the time to pulverize Jake. Had to move on. "The question is, so what?"

"Good question," someone said under their breath. I preferred to believe it wasn't Jake.

"What I mean is, what's the next logical step? If you believe the Bible, that God created things all living things—all the 'kinds'—basically at the same time, then you would expect there to be a bunch of new fossils all appearing at the same time. Then there's Darwinism, which says that species evolved over gazillions of years, so then you would expect to find lots of transitional fossils—the in-between creatures as one species changed gradually into another."

They just looked at me with their *yeah, so?* looks. "But the evidence is pretty sketchy when it comes to in-between fossils." I couldn't see, but I sensed Mr. Hayes lean forward at his desk behind me. He didn't have to say anything.

"What about all the examples in our science book?" Tiffany asked for him. She hadn't asked a single question in science that I could recall, not since Mr. Hayes had gone on a rant about her calling evolution a 'theory'. But maybe this was her chance to redeem herself. Stepping on me in the process. Oh well.

"You mean like this one?" I changed transparencies again. "This supposedly shows how the whale evolved from a land mammal to an ocean mammal. There seems to be a gradual but obvious change, feet to flippers and all that. But I read more about his, and now that scientists can actually look at the molecules, the DNA and all that, they've actually decided there's no reason to think that these fossils had any relation to each other at all, or that this one could've even descended from that one."

The skeptical, hostile looks were mostly gone now, replaced by fuzzy *you're losing us* looks. I pressed on. "The whole thing about interpreting fossils is, well, it can be pretty hard. I've got a great example here." New transparency. "Check out these skulls. What does it look like to you?"

"Like the transition from an ape to a human skull," Bliss said. "See how in each picture the facial bones gradually get flatter, but the cranium gets larger? And the brow bone juts out less and less. Just like the Evolution of Man chart."

I nodded. "I found this in an article by an evolutionist, not a creationist. She wanted to show how, whether we realize it or not, we take the ideas we already have and find the evidence that fits them. In other words, someone could look at this series of 'fossils' and decide that they show the evolution of apes into humans. Another person might look at them and just see the skull of a baboon," and I pointed to one of the pictures, "and a gorilla. A chimp, a squirrel monkey…oh, and a fake 'missing link'." I pointed to the skull next to the last, human skull. "This was called Piltdown Man, and it got everyone excited for a while since it seemed to finally give fossil proof of a primate between apes and humans. Turns out someone patched it together to fool scientists."

"Well, you can't blame the scientists for that," someone said. It came from the vicinity of Ronnie Plowman.

"For what? Looking for evidence to support their beliefs?" I asked this quietly, sensing that sheer loudness wasn't going to win the day here. "Science is supposed to work the other way: follow the evidence wherever it leads. Or do we decide that we know the truth, then judge the evidence based on whether it fits our truth?"

I glanced through the next page, but nothing leapt off it to inspire me. But my mouth didn't seem to mind. "You know, sometimes people who believe the Bible are criticized for having faith—for believing that it's from God and it's true, even when 'evidence' supposedly contradicts it. But somehow it's okay to believe strongly in a scientific idea, and when any discovery contradicts it, to assume the new evidence is wrong or get suspicious about the person who discovered it."

Silence. I might have been imagining it, but it didn't seem as hostile. I can't say it seemed 100% interested, but I had the attention of some of them.

Again, Ronnie Plowman. "So what about the Biblical view? You said Darwinism calls for lots of transitional fossils that aren't there, but what about all the fossils a creationist would expect to find?"

Glad you asked, I didn't say. "Right, it's sort of the opposite. A sudden appearance of lots of the major groups of animals in a short geological time—with no fossil evidence of any common ancestors."

"But that never happened," Jasmine said.

Mr. Hayes saved me from having to contradict Jasmine. "It did, as far as we can tell. It's called the Cambrian Explosion."

Black ice: not just for winter highways anymore. Jasmine's eyes froze over. Getting corrected by Mr. Hayes apparently wasn't a comforting substitute for being corrected by me. "I don't remember reading about that," she muttered, scanning the index of our science book.

"They can't fit everything into a general overview," Mr. Hayes said.

Bliss leaned forward at her desk, and everyone locked onto her. Her eyes locked onto me. "So what you're saying is that Biblical creationism isn't just based on faith, and Darwinian evolution isn't just based on science."

For once I didn't mind that she phrased things as statements and not questions. "I remember reading something that said it like this," I began. "Faith is what we add on to the evidence we've got in order to reach a certain conclusion. There's a lot of science out there about all this," I said, "but the facts don't fit together into the perfect, orderly picture some of these books want us to believe—what the authors seem to want to believe. They're convinced that when all the real 'facts' come in, they will support this one theory. I'm no expert, but it seems to me that's a kind of faith."

I waited, but there were no more challenges. I wished I had a glass of water, more oxygen, an irresistible charisma that would convince everyone. Nope. I'd just have to wing it, Rory-style.

"I learned a lot by doing this paper," I said. "Now that it's done, I'm kind of glad I had to do it. I've got to admit, at first I mostly just wanted to prove that I was right and that our science book was wrong. Now I know it's a hugely complicated thing.

"But…" and I took a steadying breath, "what I learned is that it's not unscientific to believe in the Bible. So much of what is being discovered—stuff they had no idea about back in Charles Darwin's time—points to something bigger than his idea.

"And I learned that belief in Darwinism, or naturalistic evolution, isn't purely scientific. To say that evolution is random and godless and purposeless—that's a philosophical statement, not a scientific one. Somehow the definition of 'science' has been changed to mean 'naturalism', that nature is all that exists. That's definitely a philosophy, and it takes faith to believe it."

I hesitated. Maybe I thought Mr. Hayes was going to jump in and splatter my conclusion all over the wall like a blob of Play Putty. But he just leaned back in his chair, his hands templed under his chin, watching me with those snapping blue eyes.

I lifted the last page of my report, cleared my throat. "Here's something Congress announced not too long ago: *'…a quality science education should prepare students to distinguish the data and testable theories of science from religious or philosophical claims that are made in the name of science. Where topics are taught that may generate controversy (such as biological evolution), the curriculum should help students to understand the full range of scientific views that exist, why such topics may generate controversy, and how scientific discoveries can profoundly affect society.'"*

I dared a quick glance at Mr. Hayes, who still leaned back in his chair, hands now templed in front of his mouth. I went on, "In other words, teachers shouldn't be punished if they point out the deeper meaning behind the science, or the other theories that are out there. They should be encouraged to do it. And students need to learn how to separate the philosophy from the science, because one way or another, it's always there."

So now it wasn't Rory vs. Mr. Hayes anymore, and my fellow students picked up on that. I think this made it less interesting for some of them. But some others suddenly seemed more ready to forgive me, since I was taking his side, in a way. Probably not a bad time to wrap things up.

"I ended my paper with a quote that came from the guy who got the distinguished job of writing the introduction to a new edition of *Origin of the Species*—you know, Darwin's book. Here's what he said:

'…evolution is the backbone of biology and biology is thus in the peculiar position of being a science founded on unproven theory. Is it then a science or a faith? Belief in the theory of evolution is thus exactly parallel to belief in special creation. Both are concepts which the believers know to be true, but neither, up to the present, has been capable of proof.'"

I tensed, praying that Mr. Hayes wouldn't spring like a hunting lion. After all, I'd just said evolution was an unproven theory. But hey, they weren't my words. "And he also said that the theory of evolution *'forms a satisfactory faith'*," and I paused to let that last word sink in, "'*on which to base our interpretation of nature.'* In other words, the belief comes first, and the search for evidence follows.

"Well, that's about it. Thanks for listening." I took my seat to the thunderous sound of…no applause.

Mr. Hayes slowly disengaged from his chair and took his place at the front of the class. He uncapped his rainbow of dry erase markers, each with a distinct little squeak, and lined them up on the tray, unhurried. Then he spoke.

"Thank you, Rory. Since you fielded questions during your presentation, we'll forego a Q&A and just jump back into our current lesson on photosynthesis."

And he did, just like that. Back to work.

forty-five

But the rebuttal had to come eventually. Mr. Hayes couldn't miss a chance to tear apart my puny stab at science with his vastly superior knowledge...right? Wasn't that the whole point of putting me up there in front of the class?

But that day passed, and several more, with nothing. Now and then I would feel his eyes on me. It was almost as if something had surprised him. Maybe it was what I said, but I kind of doubted that. I had a vague feeling that it had more to do with the way I said it.

I would find out soon enough, when I got the paper back, complete with grade and comments.

> *While I take issue with some of your science, I'm impressed by your thoughtful handling of the philosophy behind it. Keep Thinking Deeply and never abandon your quest for truth.*

Even as I finished reading it, my heart taking a mighty leap, its arms stretched heavenwards, my eyes moved to the grade written underneath, which slapped that old heart right back down to the ground: **C**.

He gave me a C? After I'd thoughtfully handled the philosophy, practiced deep thinking, quested for truth? A big fat C?

Okay, I'd take it. Because C is for Craduation.

Graduation (as it's more commonly spelled). Mere weeks—even days—away. Now that I knew it would be days and not years, my entire being yearned for it. To leave behind forever the blue cinderblock walls, the cramped lockers, the plaid skirts and polyester shirts, the Specials of the Day… It couldn't happen too soon.

It couldn't happen at all for Bliss Hathaway, or so rumor had it. It was the latest, juiciest bit of gossip to travel the halls of Whitestone Elementary. It traveled very quietly, because Bliss always seemed to be at school these days. Just another sign that the rumor was true, the rumormongers said. Because it was due to her many absences that Bliss supposedly wouldn't be allowed graduate.

Like the seventeen-year-old-boyfriend rumor, this one turned out to be true. Journey confirmed it over lunch one day.

"Yeah, it's a real shame," she said with total blandness. "I guess someone was keeping tabs on those attendance charts after all."

I glanced uneasily down the table, but Bliss and Jasmine had taken to sitting a safe distance from us, and there were people in between. "Isn't she upset?" I asked. Because she didn't look like a girl with a major problem. No stress-induced pimples, no hair twined into dread-locks (locks caused by dread). No cowering behind a mountain of french fries.

"Oh, she's miffed. But you know Bliss." Journey sipped lemonade through a straw. "She'll manage. Just wait."

Happily, not much waiting was required. June was just around the corner. But first things first: the eighth grade field trip. No uniforms, no cafeteria lunches, no books or desks whatsoever. Just a couple of buses, a few teachers, and a cargo of sugared-and-caffeinated kids headed for roller coasters.

But education just wouldn't go down without a fight. I learned three things at the amusement park: one, sunblock never lasts as long as it claims, especially after water rides and sweating; two, cotton candy and centrifugal force (spin and barf) rides don't mix; and three, I didn't really have any good friends at school. I usually had someone to ride with or talk to in line, but I mostly thought about my Cornerstone friends and wished they were there to share a joke or survive a devastating coaster with me.

It was probably social suicide (who cared, with graduation days away?), but I sat with Mrs. Palmer on the bus ride home. Her ponytail was decidedly looser today, and although her sunglasses were huge and black, the sleeveless shirt and capris looked so everyday normal, I was forced to confront the shocking truth: teachers are real people with lives outside of school.

"Enjoy your day?" she asked.

"It was good," I said. "Aside from the cotton candy." Then I had a revelation. I could ask her the same thing. "How about you?"

"I had a good day, too, thanks. If I can get through the evening without a migraine, I'll be golden." She saw my uncertain reaction. "The glare of the sun can trigger some pretty nasty headaches for me."

"Yeah, I've heard migraines can be pretty bad."

"I've been managing them for years—since I wasn't much older than you. But sometimes it's just impossible to function." Her voice faded out a little at the end. I tried to imagine controlling a room of twenty-eight teenagers, all with a blinding headache. Oh, and then actually teaching them something.

I changed the subject. "I probably should've told you before, but I got my paper back from Mr. Hayes." He was towards the back of the bus with the coolest kids, so I knew it was safe to talk. "I only got a C on it, though." I felt like I owed her better than that.

"Oh, he would never give you anything higher. It's the principle of the thing," she said. "Besides, the grade is meaningless. Its only value is in allowing you to graduate. What matters is what you accomplished."

I chewed on that. "Well, I learned a lot. But I don't think I accomplished much more than that."

"I wouldn't be so sure, Rory." She looked at me over the top of her sunglasses. "You got up there and shared something priceless. Not just the information you'd gathered, but the desire to go out and find it. I think it was the Irish poet, W.B. Yeats, who said that education isn't filling a bucket, it's lighting a fire. Who knows what little sparks you might have struck? And you got out of your own way to do it—it wasn't about you. Mr. Hayes can't help but respect that."

I remembered that when I received my final report card from Whitestone Elementary. Science, B-. I'd take it. Because B- is for B-raduation.

After a giddy half-day of returning textbooks, cleaning desks, cleaning out lockers, and smiling warmly and wistfully at teachers we could now imagine missing when we were gone...we were gone.

Only to return the next evening, bedecked in our dignified caps and gowns (if you think slithery, shapeless and obnoxiously blue is dignified). Underneath mine I wore a dress my mom had helped me choose, of a certain shade of green that supposedly brought out the green in my eyes-of-indeterminate-color. It was also of a style that made my mom do a double-take in the Reinbolt's dressing room.

"What?" I asked. In a dressing room, *What?* translates into *You think it makes me look like a rhinoceros, don't you?*

"Oh, nothing," she had answered, her eyes half-focused. "You just looked like a young woman for a second, there."

So the dress was mine, complete with necklace, earrings, and my first pair of heels—if you call an inch-and-a-half a heel. I didn't need the added height, but Mom assured me they looked more elegant than flats (which meant they didn't make my feet look as big). Most of the ensemble was hidden beneath the electric blue draperies we were required to wear. Not that any of it mattered, because it's not like I was out to impress anyone.

The teachers lined us up outside the gymnasium doors; I peered inside to see if I could pick out any familiar faces in the crowd. It was a milling mass of faceless humanity. The music began. We were made to walk in a stately but brisk fashion—try it sometime; it's harder than it sounds—past the countless watching eyes. I took each step carefully, almost without a single wobble. A person might not be out to impress, but you could never tell who was watching.

We filed into our designated rows and at the end of the song—Jake still insisted it was the "Pom-Pom Circle Dance"—all sat with a mighty rustle of polyester. I crossed my legs, ever-so-ladylike, and felt the heel of my pump snag on my pantyhose. I sighed deeply on the inside.

On my left, Tiffany Klipfel fidgeted and cleared her throat as if she were preparing to make a big speech. But that honor went to the valedictorian, who to everyone's surprise (I think maybe even the teachers'), turned out to be Ronnie Plowman. Apparently his sleeplike state in class had been a covert method of absorbing enormous amounts of information. He had undeliberately edged out Jasmine Wee for the highest grade point average by a hundredth of a point.

As Ronnie gave his unsurprisingly brief speech about life and dreams that lulled me into a strangely dreamlike state, I couldn't see Jasmine, way back in the WXYZ row. But somehow I could feel her cold black eyes shooting their invisible darts at the podium.

The seat on my right—H for Hathaway—was empty. Only temporarily, though. Bliss was next to take the podium as student council president. Her speech was more eloquent, but it was hard to concentrate with the extreme fidgeting happening on my left. I believe I heard Tiffany reciting her own speech under her breath, probably one she had written for just this occasion back in the fourth grade. Alas, the occasion now belonged to Bliss. Tiffany's last, desperate hope had shattered when Bliss agreed to a solution to her absentee problem: summer school. Her condition: that she still be granted her diploma on graduation day.

The applause still lingered as Bliss took her seat beside mine. She smiled at me and crossed her legs (no pantyhose snag), saw me noticing her own pumps (three-and-a-half inches to my one).

"Nico bought them for me," she whispered. "They're Italian." She turned toward the audience, blew a little kiss.

"He's here?"

She nodded, hugely satisfied. "My mom flew him in two days ago for my birthday. And for this, of course."

I hadn't known about her birthday. "Oh. Well, happy birthday," I whispered. "So you're..."

"Fifteen."

I still could hardly believe she wasn't eighteen. But it was nice to not be the only fifteen-year-old graduating.

At this point the awarding of the diplomas began. This was it: the slippery, floppy robes, the rickety stairs, the dangerous shoes, the handshake confusion. Only one thing missing—an Applause-o-Meter.

We may as well admit it: we compare the volume and duration of the clapping after each person's name is called. Who gets shouts and whistles, who (oh, the horror) gets the sound of one hand clapping. All of this despite the principal's request that all applause be held until the end of the ceremony.

One by one, the rows ahead of us emptied, until it was our turn to file out and line up by the stairs. I enjoyed a moment of distraction when Jake prepared for his moment in the spotlight. Mrs. Knowles read his name.

"Jacob Leslie Elwood Dean."

The words were met by applause and—did I imagine it?—a brief laugh that sounded like Sam Newman's. Jake took his diploma with less of a production than might be expected. I suspected his request for *Jake Elwood Dean* had been disregarded by the school.

The distraction was too short. This was a time of reflection, and my brain helpfully offered up a feast of memories from my days at Whitestone High—each of them a tasty morsel of degradation, fear or shame. From the time I got lost between the bathroom and my first grade classroom to the balance beam incident in sixth-grade P.E. class, I relived them all. Then came junior high, an encyclopedia of embarrassment unto itself.

Why, there was the very spot I'd had my first public seizure, where now the makeshift stage ended with its second set of wobbly steps. That patch of beige rubber floor I knew so well. Destiny seemed to be calling out to me.

Bliss's name was next. Then it would be me. My chance to hear three people clapping (Mom and Grandma Judy, plus Sheelan if the mood struck her). But hold on…that was a best-case scenario. What if someone booed? Someone who hadn't appreciated my, for lack of a better phrase, deeply-held beliefs? Or what if everyone laughed when I fell...*if*. IF I fell. Oh, crud.

Get over yourself, Rory.

I looked around. No one had said it. It was just my own voice in my head, though it sounded a little like Gabby and—strangely—a bit like Sam, too.

"Rory Erin Joyce."

It's not about me.

I stepped carefully up—not too wobbly, but a tiny bit slippery—and moved towards the school district superintendent, Mr. Anton, who held out my diploma. Disappointingly, a faux leather little folder, not the ribbon-tied scroll you see in cartoons. And I heard clapping, scattered, but coming mostly from two small pockets of people, as far as I could tell. Someone whistled—the good kind. Wow. Not that it mattered.

As my hand reached out to take the diploma (left hand, keep right hand free for handshake), a sharp movement pulled my eyes away.

Bliss, descending the opposite stairs, suddenly disappeared. There was a small murmuring gasp from the part of the crowd nearest that corner of the stage. In what was probably only a few seconds but felt like forever, no one moved, no one hopped up to help her.

I pulled my diploma from Mr. Anton's hand and hurried down the steps. By now the janitor, who had been behind the stage and closest to the steps, was beside Bliss. But she looked at me.

I held out my hand. "You okay?"

She took it. "Never better."

I let the sarcasm slide; I knew it wasn't for me. "Hey, I've been flat on my back in that same spot. You did it more gracefully, though."

By now Mr. Hayes had come up alongside us. I half expected Bliss to abandon my help for his, but she hung onto my arm. She wobbled when she tried to stand straight.

"Twist your ankle?" Mr. Hayes asked.

She didn't answer, just looked down at her right shoe. The three-and-a-half-inch heel had snapped off completely.

"I have some epoxy that will take care of that," the janitor said. "Just come backstage here for a few minutes, and we'll have you fixed right up." She followed him without saying a word. But I had a feeling Nico would hear plenty about this.

Mr. Hayes gestured for me to make my way back to my seat. Before I stepped away, he gave me a light pat on the back and said, "Good job, Rory."

I puzzled over which job he might mean. Since no one appeared to be injured, the ceremony resumed behind me as I walked away. Mr. Anton spoke the next name. "Tiffany Amber-Lynn Klipfel."

Only as I took my seat did an unexpected laugh bubble up and almost burst out. Tiffany Amber-Lynn Klipfel: T.A.L.K.

"Well, next year should be better," I observed after the ceremony was over and the crowd was milling around on the gymnasium floor. I had been searching for my family when Journey LeVey found me. She seemed very somber—more than usual. Especially considering what had just happened to her sister. "You'll be in eighth grade, and Bliss will be at Whitestone High," I added.

Journey shook her head. "No."

"No? Is she going to private school?"

"I don't know. But it won't be here. We're moving."

But they'd just got here. "Really?"

"The 'numbers are leading us onward'," she quoted—obviously her mom—with rolling eyes.

"What about Tam, her shop and everything?"

"Oh, she goes wherever my mom goes. Really wherever Bliss goes." Journey's disgust had clearly reached unplumbed depths.

Follow your Bliss, I thought. Bizarre. Suddenly I had two strong, competing reactions. First, and I wasn't proud of it, relief — Bliss wouldn't be at Whitestone High, and I wouldn't have to constantly be on my guard against her, against slipping under her influence. Second, regret. I would miss Journey.

"I don't suppose you could stay," I half-joked.

I saw a flash of gray as she scrutinized me briefly for sincerity. She seemed satisfied. "Wouldn't that be dandy? But I go where they go. My fate is all tangled up with Bliss's."

A tricky fate. But I thought I saw something in her face that went beyond the usual scorn for her older sister. I was right. "You know," she went on, "I used to just look at her, and it would make me plain sick. But now…I don't know. I mean, she still makes me sick, but it feels more like sad than sick."

That's when I had a rare flash of what you might call insight (and therefore it's unlikely that it came from me). "I think I know what you mean. It's getting harder for me to look at people the same way I used to — even Sheelan." That didn't come out easily, but it did come out. "It's kind of like, I used to see what everyone else was doing wrong. Now I see myself in them. Almost as if — "

"As if we're all sick," she finished.

I thought about that, then nodded.

"But you think you've got the cure." Did she say it like an accusation, or more of a question?

"Me? No." Well, yes. Jesus was the only cure. A lot of people didn't like that, that there was only one cure, not a Super Everything Store aisle full of choices. But the Only Cure was offered free to anyone who would take it, and you could hardly argue with that. "I mean, it doesn't come *from* me. But I have it now. I mean, I've come to know — "

She waved her hand in *yeah, yeah, I get it* style and cut me off. "Well, there they are," she said, her eyes on Bliss, Tam and Sylvie, who were across the gymnasium, making their way to the doors. Nico trailed several steps behind. "Looks like I have to go."

"I wish you didn't have to." I risked honesty. It could be the last time I'd see her.

"But I think I do, don't you?" She tucked her hair behind her ears, looked at me straight on. "Those people." She tilted her head towards her odd little family. "They're blown around, here and there, everywhere, like shifting sand. They need something solid in their lives."

My eyes snapped onto hers. She didn't flinch. "You mean," I began, "like a...cornerstone?"

The corner of her mouth crept upwards, just for a second before she brought it under control. "Yeah. Like a Cornerstone." She looked back at them. "They just don't know they need it. Yet."

My mouth was hanging open at this point (I really have to work on that). Journey turned back to me, observed, and laughed, despite herself. "And now I exit stage left," she said. But all of a sudden she wrapped an arm around me and gave me a quick hug. It was over in a half-second, felt like mostly chins and elbows—and I didn't even have time to respond—but it was a hug. "Thanks, Rory."

And she slipped into the milling crowd and was gone.

I stood there, staring after her, seeing nothing for a while. Then someone was at my elbow.

"Wake up, Rory." It was Allie. "Couldn't you hear us calling?"

Shayne came up alongside her. "Did I just see Journey LeVey hug you?"

"Yeah. I think you did."

"What was that all about?"

I shook off my stupor and turned around. Jake and Sam were there, too. And there, beside Sam, was Tali. I fumbled for words. "Oh, um. She was saying goodbye. They're moving."

Jake scoffed. "As if. They haven't even been here a year. Besides, I would've known before you." But he must've seen the truth in my face, because his own face went like a storm cloud. Clearly this wasn't Jacob Leslie Elwood Dean's day.

"Too bad Journey's leaving," Sam said. He held a small gift bag in his hand, crinkling it a bit without seeming to know it. "She'd just started coming to the Scene." He saw a smile creep over my face. "What?"

"Oh, it's just... I think it was enough."

His eyebrows shot up. "Really? You mean..."

I nodded.

"What?" Allie pounced on the unspoken words. "Are you saying that Journey—"

"Is now planning to infiltrate the enemy camp," I finished.

Shayne clapped her hands together. "Sweet! That's fantastic. Who knew?"

"Oh, Bliss is going to love that," Jake said. "Leave it to Journey to become a Christian just to annoy her sister."

I had the urge to pummel him, but this is such a common reaction to Jake, resisting it had become second nature. "I don't think it's like that at all." My eyes shifted to Tali, who was watching our exchange with a mysteriously bland face. It was impossible to tell if she was following along or not. She caught me looking at her, smiled, and signed something at Sam. His hands seem to clutch the little gift bag tighter, but he didn't have a chance to respond.

"So, who's coming to my party?" Jake demanded, obviously expecting all of us and not waiting for a reply. "I'm going home to get things started. Come whenever." He swaggered off, swinging his robe for effect.

Allie turned to me. "What about you, Rory? Is your mom planning something?"

"She offered to, but I figured Jake's party was enough."

"He certainly thinks so."

"So," Shayne said, "will we all go over together?"

"My grandma wants to take the family out to dinner first," I told her. "Then she'll drop me off."

"I guess we'll see you over there. Congratulations, Rory!"

forty-six

The pseudo-Irish restaurant wasn't so bad that evening. In fact, I'd chosen it. There wasn't a solid reason for it, but it reminded me a little of my dad, just not in a direct way that would make me miss him even more than usual.

"You did great tonight, honey," Gran Judy said.

Sheelan paused in mid-sip of her diet cola. "Yes, the way she walked up, grabbed her diploma, and ran off—it was inspiring."

"She was rushing to help a fallen comrade," Mom put in. "And that was very nice of you, Rory. You were a good friend."

I took a giant bite of fudge volcano cake to avoid responding. I wasn't so sure that I'd been good for Bliss in any sort of way. If I could go back and do it all over... Alas, no. No replays, no do-overs.

"I have something for you," Grandma said suddenly, delving into her state-of-Texas-sized purse and coming out with a small box.

"But you already gave me my gift, Gran." It had been the same as my mom's gift: a card with a check inside. The gift that keeps on giving.

"Well, this is more of a memento. I came across it when I was cleaning out the old bureau. It smells like the cedar, it's been in there so long."

I accepted the box, surprised to find that it was wood. It opened on squeaky hinges. Inside on a silver chain hung a silver pocket watch, its face no bigger than a quarter. "Wow," I said. "It's really nice."

"I know it's a man's watch, but it's a small one. And I'm sure your grandfather would be delighted for you to have it—seeing as you're his namesake and all." She saw my puzzled look. "Flip it over."

On the smooth back side of the watch, the words *Roy Aaron Blankenship* were engraved, with a date underneath.

"Hey, it's today's date," I said. "Only...what, like fifty years ago."

"That grade school education is really paying off," Sheelan said lightly.

Gran ignored Sheelan (one of a thousand reasons to love Gran). "Yes, it was the day your grandpa graduated from grammar school. Funny, isn't it? Same date, almost the same name."

I looked at his name again. I'd always known my grandpa's name was Roy, but I didn't remember ever hearing his middle name. "You mean...?"

"You knew you were named after your grandpa, Rory," Grandma told me. She turned to my mom. "She's always known that, right?"

"Oh, we told her all the time when she was little."

"I don't remember," I defended myself. "So Rory Erin is from Roy Aaron?"

"Well, you were supposed to be a boy," Mom laughed. Sheelan, amazingly, kept her mouth shut. "When you weren't, your father found a suitably Irish version of the name that almost matched."

I was named after someone. How cool was that?

That night was all about names, it turned out. They dropped me off at Jake's on the way home, and I had to admit, it was an impressive spectacle. The house was all lit up, but most of the party was outside, with tiki torches and music, and tables packed with food. I regretted the volcano cake.

"You know the rules," Mom reminded me.

"Yeah, yeah. Nothing illegal, immoral, or..."

"Idiotic," Sheelan helped.

"And now that you have a new watch," Mom said, "you can be sure to be home on time."

"Mom, it's already eight o'clo—"

"Home by eleven."

I snapped my mouth shut. I was expecting ten. "Okay."

"Call for a ride if you can't tag along with a friend."

"Okay. Thanks, everyone." I leaned forward and kissed Mom and Grandma in the front seat, then, on a quirk, pretended I was going to kiss Sheelan next to me. She pulled back like I was the plague on fire.

"Funny," she said. "By the way, you have a huge run in your hose. You may as well just take them off."

So I did.

"Not here! I meant you should go to the bathroom or something." She shook her head. "Twisted."

I hopped out, my shoes in my hand. It was a beautiful night, and I wasn't about to try walking on a lawn in heels. "See you later."

The grass was a plush carpet luxury on my newly-liberated feet. I extracted the claw clip from my hair, not caring if it all fell in a mess around my face and shoulders. I was ready to...well, let my hair down.

There seemed to be a lot of people I didn't know in the backyard, but mixed in were the faces of classmates and, eventually, Jake Dean himself. "Hey, Rory. This is my dad." He jabbed a thumb towards a broad-shouldered, thick-middled man in slacks and a sport jacket. The man grinned at me with square, white teeth.

"Call me Les," he insisted.

"Um, okay. Hi," I said. Then he was gone, telling other people to call him Les, to eat more food, to try a drink served out of a pineapple or a coconut. Which left me with Jake, but he was watching Bliss's house. It looked back with dark, empty eyes.

"Is she coming?" I asked.

"Doesn't matter to me," he said breezily. "Well, enjoy yourself, Jolly Green." He sauntered into the crowd.

I plucked at my dress. Maybe the green had been a mistake. At least I wasn't as giant-ish with my shoes off. And no one had heard him.

"Did he just call you 'Jolly Green'?" Shayne's voice said behind me.

Allie was beside her. "That's just because you look beautiful and he doesn't know how to handle it. Right, Sam?" Her smile was slightly wicked.

Sam's froze on his face. I saved him from having to answer, grabbing at anything to say. "Is Tali here?"

He nodded, pointing across the lawn to where the speakers were pumping out music. I saw her, golden in the torchlight, dancing. Sam saw my mystified look. "She can feel the bass," he said. "She loves to dance."

Of course she did. All part of her exotic charm. But when I turned back to Sam, he wasn't looking at her. He pulled his eyes away from me quickly.

"So, did I miss much?" I asked.

They all shared a look. "Just Mr. Dean's big 'surprise' for Jake," Shayne said.

"What, a legal name change?" I asked. Sam laughed.

"Nope," Allie said. "His dad pulled strings—and I suppose paid lots of money—to get Jake accepted into Miles Harrington Preparatory School." She said the name with a pompous British accent.

I'd heard of Miles Prep, and as far as I knew it wasn't run by the British, but it did have a reputation for being 'the best of the best for the cream of the crop'—or at least the crop that grew in our no-name part of the world. I'd never known anyone who went there. "Isn't that like a boarding school?" I asked.

"More or less. Very prestigious."

"So Jake's head is inflated to quadruple its normal size, I take it?"

Sam shook his head, trying to find Jake in the crowd. "I think he's pretty upset. He's been talking about playing football for Whitestone High ever since third grade."

"Poor Jake," I said. "First Bliss moving, and now this."

Shayne snorted, thinking I was joking. "Oh, the trials and tribulations of being a rich kid."

Tali bounced up beside Sam, slightly flushed and perspiring from her dancing interlude. Of course it gave her a lovely glow. "Hi," she said to me with a wave. Then she signed at Sam.

"Not yet," he said. She signed some more. "I won't forget. No. Yeah, okay. I'll get it." He said to the rest of us, "My mom sent a little gift for Rory, but it's in the house." He brightened a little. "You want to just come and get it?"

I was pretty sure the question was meant only for me, but Shayne jumped on it. "Yeah, come on. We all want to see." So everyone followed Sam. He walked in a slightly hunched way, hands in pockets, eyes ahead.

Jake's house had that manly style of interior decorating, gray with lots of glass and metal and edges. There were mostly adults inside, sipping drinks from tinkling glasses full of ice, scanning us and looking away without pausing in their conversations. They had the feel of business associates.

Sam headed for a table full of presents and cards and pulled out his small gift bag from the back. "Here it is," he said, holding it out to me, only now noticing that it was crumpled like he'd wrung it out to dry. "It's kind of...hmm. Sorry." He shrugged with a faint, crooked smile.

"It's okay. Thanks." I kept my face cool by sheer force of will and pried the top of the bag open. There was a little white envelope inside, with *Yaroni* handwritten on the front.

Shayne spotted it. "Yaroni? Oh, yeah...I've heard Mrs. Newman call you that, right?"

"Yeah. I think it's easier to say."

"But what does it mean?" Allie asked Sam.

He shrugged again. "I'm not sure." But Tali laughed beside him and made a few gestures. He shook his head, not understanding. She tried something else. Finally he said, "It means 'to sing'."

Tali repeated a gesture, moving her hand sharply away from her mouth.

Sam said, a bit reluctantly, "To shout and sing."

"Perfect." Jake had appeared, naturally, in time to hear it all. "Obviously Mrs. Newman has heard your shout-singing."

Tali pushed past Jake and waved a hand and shook her head. She cleared her throat and said slowly, "'She will rejoice'."

Shayne gave one loud clap. "It is perfect—for your name, and your verse." She tapped her white stone. I smiled and put a hand over mine. *She will rejoice.* I suddenly wanted to do something really nice for Mrs. Newman, give her chocolates or mop her floors or hug her or something.

"That's what I'm saying," Jake said. "Her verse is all about shouting and singing, remember?"

"Oh, speaking of names, I have to show you something," Allie said. "Hang on, I'll be right back."

While they puzzled over what Allie was up to, I peeked at the card. I felt Sam watching. *Congratulations on your graduation,* it read. *Please accept this small thing, I think it is meant for you to have. Sincerely, Elena Newman.*

Beneath a piece of tissue paper, my hand cupped around something smooth and rounded and cool to the touch. I pulled out a small ceramic pot with delicate handles, glazed with strokes of blues and greens. I turned it in my hand, and as I did I felt the flaw. Down one side, a jagged crack, hardly more than a whisker's width but enough to let any liquid leak out. A cracked pot.

Tali signed at Sam.

"No, I didn't drop it. It must've been like that…" His voice trailed off, and his eyes darkened, if that was possible.

"It was," I told him. "She meant to give it like this. It's okay. I understand what she means." He let me catch his gaze, and I gave him a nod and a smile. His shoulders relaxed and his head came back up.

"Good," he said quietly. "I wasn't sure. She's a little…off today. Today's the day—" He stopped because Allie returned with a smile, holding a plaque out for us to see.

"Oh, goody," Jake said. "Let's look at Allie's latest awards."

"It's not that, Snerdly."

"Well, let's see: *Outstanding Freshman Award*. No, you're right. How snerdly of me to think it was an award."

"I brought it to show you the name, genius."

We all read the engraved aluminum. *Alessandra Ughi,* it said.

"Hey," I said. "You did it. You took your Grammy's name."

"Yep, and proud to do it."

"Allie-Oogie!" Shayne cheered and pulled me into a three-way hug with Allie. Jake grabbed Tali and Sam and made it a tangled, jostling six-way, then added the chaotic element of jumping up and down.

"Okay, okay, give me some air," Allie said, panting.

"Good idea. Let's go back outside," Shayne said, grabbing Tali and Allie by the arms and promenading them out. Jake pranced after them, walking girly-style. Sam and I were just a step or two behind.

Sam's steps, I noticed, were decidedly slower than theirs. I had already guessed why. "Were you going to say that today is the day Ben died?" I asked quietly.

"Yeah."

I'm sorry, I almost said. But I'd heard those words so many times after my dad had died, I hated to turn around and use them on someone else. There really weren't words.

But there were always elbows. I reached out and nudged his with mine. "You okay?"

"I guess. Mostly I worry about my mom. But then it sneaks up on me." He looked up at the night sky, searching for constellations out of force of habit. The glow of the tiki lanterns and house lights erased all but the brightest stars. "I lost something, too, not just my folks. Then I think, maybe I lost more—he was my twin brother, after all. And I start resenting it all: my mom barely functioning sometimes, my dad's silence about the whole thing. I mean, I'm still here, right? I have to figure out how to deal with it, too." He raked a hand through his hair. "Then I realize I'm being a selfish ass and I feel worse."

I nodded. "Selfish Ass Syndrome strikes me all the time. Usually just makes things worse." He almost smiled. "Honestly, though, I don't know if you're being selfish. God must understand our mixed-up feelings. We just need His help so that we don't turn them against other people."

"So," he began, giving careful thought to what I'd said, which was dangerous for obvious reasons. "The mixed-up feelings aren't selfish unless we turn them into selfish actions?"

"I don't know. I'm just a dumb eighth-grader."

"Freshman."

"Oh, yeah."

A few moments of quiet. "Kind of like love," he said, out of the blue.

I stubbed my bare toe in the grass. "What is?"

"Selfishness. No. I mean—" He grappled for words. "The whole feeling-versus-action thing. Most people think love is a feeling, but it's really a way of treating people. It's what you do, not how they make you feel."

"Okay. Yeah." Why did I have a flashback of Sam pulling me out of Bliss Hathaway's house? Why was talking to Sam so easy and so confusing at the same time?

Had he asked me something? Because he was not-looking at me so intensely it felt like he was waiting for an answer.

Tali breezed up and saved the day. Hooray. She made a gesture, a face. *Why so glum?* I understood her to say. Sam tilted his head vaguely, and she signed three hand motions that I recognized as fingerspelling, though I didn't know the letters.

"Yeah, we were talking about him. And my mom." The others were joining us by now.

"What is she saying?" Shayne asked.

"Um, I think she's just reminding me that my Aunt Sabra is there with my mom." He watched her, then nodded. "And it looks like she'll be around whenever my mom needs her."

"Really?" Allie spoke directly to Tali. "What about Tel Aviv?"

Tali shook her head, signed. Sam translated (though I think he already knew what she was saying, so he didn't really have to decode her flurry of signs), "Her mom got a job an hour from here.

They're only going home to pack their things. They'll be back for school in the fall."

"Seriously?" Shayne asked. "Sweet! Tali's here for keeps."

forty-seven

"Aren't you going to swim, Martina?"

It was the sort of July day when the patches in the road got sticky and smelled of tar and you would test the old fry-an-egg-on-the-sidewalk experiment if you could be bothered to try. But we were sitting pretty—not that I had any intention of sitting, and at 92 degrees, pretty wasn't a huge concern, either. Martina's apartment building had an outdoor pool, and she'd swooped in with her great big movie star sunglasses and little silver car to save the day.

Poolside, I threw my towel over the deck chair and kicked off my flip-flops, ready for the shocking embrace of cold water. Martina was still in a shirt and shorts.

"This is my swimsuit, Shayne," Martina answered seriously. But there was a laugh in her sky blue eyes.

"Honestly?" Shayne fingered the fabric. "Yeah, I guess it could be. But it just looks like regular clothes."

"Trust me, it's meant for swimming. I prefer a more modest style."

"But you're like a model. You could wear anything and look good."

Martina smiled. "I think you're missing the point of modesty."

I risked a glance down at myself—a maneuver it's usually best to avoid while in a swimsuit. Mine hadn't been chosen with modesty in mind so much as extreme self-consciousness. A one-piece with a little skirt, I'd found it by sheer luck, a needle in the haystack of strings and tiny triangles that were the hot style in swimwear these days. Or maybe it was more like the haystack in a pile of needles?

"Is mine modest?" Shayne asked, suddenly concerned. Her tankini had a longer top, but there were a couple of tight, tan tummy inches between it and the bottom. Shayne, of course, effortlessly achieved the even, glowing bronze usually seen only in airbrushed magazine ads. "Do you think it is?" she asked again.

"The important question is," Allie said, whipping off her cover-up and revealing an athletic one-piece, "can it stand up to this?" She ran to the edge of the pool, dove in head-first, came up with a gasp and slicked her blond hair back. "The water's great! Too bad the guys are missing out."

"Yeah, why didn't they come?" Shayne asked.

"Because I didn't invite them." Martina looked at us over her sunglasses. "You understand."

I did. For whatever reason, it was considered perfectly normal to parade around in what often amounted to less than your underwear, so long as it was called 'swimwear'. But it still felt a lot like parading around in your underwear—especially with boys around.

"It's girl time," Shayne said. "I get it."

I jogged to the edge of the pool. Time to stop sweating and start splashing. I jumped just as Shayne spoke: "Still, it would've been nice to hang out with Sam before he goes away."

The water closed over my head in a bubble of cool silence. Sam go away?

The summer, so far, had been (to use my dad's favorite adjective) brilliant. The separate-school thing was behind us—school itself was behind us, for a couple of shining months—and we had already spent all kinds of time together. I liked the fact that Shayne or Allie or both would just show up at my front door some days, and we would find something silly to do. Or just do nothing.

"Next summer we'll probably be working actual jobs," Allie pointed out.

"And driving." Shayne turned an imaginary steering wheel and tooted a pretend horn in a sort of victory dance.

"So we may as well enjoy a summer of nothing, one last time."

Enjoy it I had. It didn't hurt that Sam came to the Fishers at least two or three times a week, now that he and Kings were good friends on top of being schoolmates. There were days when I guiltily remembered my once-upon-a-time best friend, Jenna, and how betrayed I'd felt by the 8-year-old Kingston who moved in to take her place. Now I could hardly resist rubbing his fuzzy black head and feeding him chocolate-covered marshmallows in appreciation.

So Sam and I had talked plenty. (Of all my friends, he had become the one I could really *talk* with. Mostly I treasured it. Sometimes I wished I had clicked on that level with Shayne or Allie. In a lot of ways it would be so much simpler.)

We'd even had one more Cornerstone gathering before Jake went to spend the summer in California with his mom. So in all this getting together, why hadn't I heard a single mention of Sam going away? Or hadn't I been listening?

Come to think of it, I'd done more of the talking at Cornerstone. But you could hardly blame me, after I picked up the Martina-made bookmark that had fallen out of Sam's Bible. I looked at it, then at Sam with narrowed eyes.

"What? What'd I do?" he asked.

But I had already turned to Martina. "Could I ask you a question? These bookmarks of yours—why does every one I see have Proverbs 4:23 on it?"

She slipped one from her own Bible, displaying it. "Because that's the verse I chose."

"Not for mine. Who else got the one with my verse on it?"

"What do you mean?"

"I have a different verse."

She shook her head. "That can't be. I only did the one."

"I'm telling you, mine is different. I even know the verse—Proverbs 27:12. I don't remember it exactly…" I grabbed my Bible. "But here, I'll show you."

Martina was frowning. "I don't know that verse offhand."

"I have it," Allie said, flipping pages.

"Of course you do," Jake muttered.

She read, "'A prudent person foresees the danger ahead and takes precautions. The simpleton goes blindly on and suffers the consequences.'"

"That's it," I said.

Martina laughed, but her forehead was scrunched, too. "I don't think so, Rory. Show me the bookmark."

"I can't find it," I had to admit. Hadn't it just been in there last night?

"That's okay," Jake said. "It's much more mysterious this way. We all know Rory loves to shroud herself in mystery."

"God Himself is a mystery," Ericson reminded him. "Maybe He had something to tell Rory at a crucial time."

Sam raised his eyebrows at me. I said, "I don't know if it did much good. I went blindly on anyway. My friends had to take the precautions for me."

"That's why God meant us to be a community," Ericson said. "Lone wolf Christians are in a dangerous position. Remember, we're 'living stones, being built into a spiritual house to be a holy priesthood'. One stone on its own doesn't make much of a house." He grabbed his guitar and chugged some uplifting chords. "Don't worry, Rory. You'll have plenty of opportunities to be a firm stone for your friends when they're shifting. Let's just be sure that at the foundation we've always got the Chief Cornerstone."

We all walked home from the Newman's after the meeting, and Sam came along for company. Our first stop was Jake's house, then Allie's and Shayne's.

"Want to come in and say hi to my dad?" she asked Sam. "He hasn't had a chance to show off his latest games to you in, like, forever."

Sam hesitated. "Can we do it next time?" he asked. "I was already planning to hang out with Kings."

"Sure. Guess we know who you love best," Shayne said, with an unconvincing pout.

"Tell your dad hello, though."

"Gotcha. Bye, guys. See you next time."

We walked on.

"Wow," Kings finally said.

"What?" Sam asked.

"You picked me over her?" By now it was pretty obvious that Kings would find it hard to choose anyone over Shayne Svoboda.

Sam's cheeks seemed to get a little warm. "It was a prior commitment. Today's Friday, right?"

"Yeah…"

"So your mom's sure to be baking something."

Kings chuckled, but he shook his head. "Too warm. Today she's making ice cream with Cherry and Tee-Tee."

"Even better."

Within a half an hour we were sitting on the Fisher's back porch eating homemade ice cream—not cherry or tee-tee flavored, just strawberry—out of mismatched bowls. When Kings went back in for seconds, Sam looked at me sidelong.

"So, what's it like?" he asked.

I licked my spoon. "Heavenly."

He grinned. "No, I mean, what's it like getting special messages from God?"

"Oh." I set the spoon down. "You mean the bookmark." He nodded. "So, you believe me, that my verse was different?"

"Why would you make that up?"

"Because I love to shroud myself in mystery."

He waved Jake's words aside like a pesky fly. "You seem to me like someone who would just love some normalness, but mystery keeps butting in. As a person who lives in Plain Old Normal, I just wonder what that's like."

I was already shaking my head. "Uh-uh. Remember, you moved to Strangeville months ago? I believe we've met—I'm the mayor?" He laughed, but I could see he wasn't satisfied. "You want to know the truth? Mostly I feel like an idiot, because God has to hit me over the head with something before I get it."

"Yeah, but to get to talk to angels? And have dreams that aren't just sock drawer dreams, but actual visions?" He wasn't looking at me. "It's got to make a person feel pretty special sometimes."

I plunked my empty vintage Super Sugar Crunch cereal bowl down on the concrete and leaned back in the chaise lounge, shielding my face from the white glare of the sun with my arm. Closing my eyes made it a little easier to talk about this.

"Special...sure," I said. "Come to think of it, it's right about the time I started wanting to feel 'special' and impress Bliss that I got into trouble. I made it all about me. Remember what Pastor Dan said? When we start worshipping ourselves, bad company is sure to show up. Then the good messengers couldn't even get through. Tam said that someone or something was blocking my dreams, and in a way she was right. I think it was me. My heart took a wrong turn. The only one who showed up then--well, you know which one it was. I practically invited him, and maybe even put Bliss and then Angelica in danger."

"But the good messengers did get through, Rory," Sam said solemnly, reminding me of what I never could forget, that he'd been my substitute dreamer.

I nodded. We said nothing for a while. Finally he asked, "Had any lately?"

"Not recently." I sighed a little. "You?"

Those dark eyes flicked up to mine for a second, then away again. "Not since that couple of weeks." More quiet. "I don't think you really put Bliss and Angelica in danger," he added suddenly.

"No? Wasn't it because of me that *he* went after them?"

His eyebrows drew together like two blackbirds fighting over the same crumb. "Yes and no. I mean, it might have been because of you, and I'm sure it would please him to lead them astray even more than they were. But why would he bother to 'go after' them?" He pointed at me. "Remember the first day your sister came to the Scene?'

"No. I paid a lot of money for a memory wipe of that incident."

He smiled crookedly. "Sorry to undo it, but I remember Pastor talked about how the enemy doesn't have to go full-frontal assault on unbelievers, since they're unfortunately already moving in the direction he wants."

"Okay, yeah..."

"Well, there would be no real reason to attack Bliss or Angelica."

I fixed him with a look. "So," I began slowly, "you're saying that *he* was just using them to...try to get at me?" He winced a little, apologetically. I sat back, wondering how it was that I had blundered through all of it, scarcely aware of the danger. And if I was out of danger now. Or if I ever would be, in this world. "Thanks, very comforting," I sighed.

"Take comfort in the fact that you're well defended."

"Yeah. I do, believe me. Another thing God has had to hit me over the head with to see."

"But you actually got to *see*." His face was wistful.

I fumbled for the right words. "Sometimes I wish..." I tried. Then, "I'd love for God to talk to me the way He talks to you." Sam shot me a quizzical look. "Like just now. The way you seem to *get* stuff. How you see the battles where I just see science tests and assemblies and stuff. How you understand the Bible and...stuff." Yes, a career in public speaking was clearly my destiny.

"Hardly," he said, but he sat a little straighter. "That's just a matter of time and exposure. And stuff."

I scowled at the mischief in his eye. Not a very convincing scowl. "I have a feeling it's more than that," I said. "But I suppose time and exposure is a good place to start." And we were quiet for a little while, which is just fine with Sam, but there it was, all kinds of opportunity for him to, oh, I don't know, maybe mention the fact that he was going away for over a month? But no. I had to find out a week later from Shayne at Martina's pool.

"Let's go by Sam's and say goodbye," Shayne suggested as we piled into Martina's car after our swim.

"Sure, I guess," Allie said.

I reached up to feel what the chlorinated water had done to my hair. What I found wasn't encouraging.

"Oh, you look fine," Allie said. "Windswept and sunkissed."

Martina gave me a certain knowing look in the rearview mirror. "I can drop you ladies off at the Newmans', but I won't be able to stay. I have an appointment."

"Let me guess. Manicure?" Shayne asked.

She shrugged but couldn't deny it. "If I don't come once a month, I hear about it," she admitted. If I didn't know better, I'd say I detected a smidge of embarrassment. But by now I knew it wasn't about the fingernails.

"Just one question, though," I said. "Why does she call you Phooey?"

Martina laughed. "Thooey. It's an affectionate term where she comes from. I think it means 'Chubby'. Syphay's a funny lady."

Mrs. Newman answered the door with a smile, but I thought she looked tired. "Samuel is not here," she told us. "He went to the Fisher house for the afternoon. I think he was hoping to see you." She meant all of us, but she just happened to be looking at me when she said the last bit. I felt the pink creep into my cheeks.

So Martina dropped us off at my house and zipped off to see Syphay the funny fingernail lady. "Want to come in and change?" I asked the others.

"Nah. I'm practically dry." Shayne wore one of her dad's T-shirts over her swimsuit like a dress. Allie had thrown her shorts over hers. "I'm good, too," she said.

"Well, I'll be back out in a minute." I wasn't going to flounce around in my suit any longer than I had to (plus there was the matter of my hair). "Meet you over there?"

"Sure."

When I returned five minutes later, no one answered my tap at the Fisher's door. I tried the bell. Nothing. I walked around the Fisher half of the duplex to the backyard.

I should've cut through my house. I had just rounded the shrubbery and caught sight of everyone on the back patio when the ground suddenly disappeared beneath my right foot and I went down like a moose with a tranquilizer dart in his behind.

The twins were there almost instantly. "Mama!" Tee-Tee shouted. "Rory got herself stuck in a hole again!"

Ah, yes. The *again*—Tee-Tee's special touch.

I managed to get my foot out of the only hole *I* recalled getting stuck in—it was only about a foot deep—but my flip-flop remained wedged until I pried it out. By this time everyone had gathered around to help.

"Kingston Zedekiah Fisher," Mrs. Fisher said, voice snapping. "What did I tell you about digging holes in the yard?"

"Sorry, Mama. I thought I filled them all."

"How's your ankle, baby girl?"

"Oh, I'm fine. Trying to catch 'possums, Kings?"

"Naw. Just wanted to see what I'd find down there."

"Dirt, I think."

"And Rories," Cherry said. She giggled and ran off with her sister.

Mrs. Fisher sat me down on the patio with some sweet tea in a glass that was sweating even more than me. Shayne said, "Sam was just telling us about his trip. He's going to England."

"I'm so jealous." Allie glared at him, in a friendly way.

"Just for two weeks," Sam said quickly. "My dad's going over to do some research. He said I could come if I paid for my plane ticket. I've been doing odd jobs since Christmas to pay for it."

So he'd known since Christmas? This got better and better. Maybe it was my turn to say something, because for a few moments there was only the clicking of summer bugs and the squeals of kids running through a sprinkler five yards down. Finally Sam went on. "Then I have to spend a few weeks with my grandma and Aunt Bekah in New York."

"Man, I'll be lucky if I get to go to the lake a couple of times this summer," Shayne groused.

I doubted I'd do even that. But I wasn't jealous of Sam. He was the sort of friend who, when he got to do cool stuff, it was almost as good as if it were me. Maybe that's the reason it chafed that he hadn't even mentioned it. I would've been happy for him.

"Think you can send us some pictures while you're there?" Kings asked.

"Yeah, sure. I can post them online."

"Sweet!" Shayne said. And the conversation veered off into randomness, which I only half heard.

Eventually Sam looked at his watch. "I have to go," he said. "I promised my mom I'd start packing tonight."

"Start? Aren't you leaving tomorrow?" Allie asked.

"Yeah, but she won't let me pack in the morning."

She gazed heavenwards. "Guys. Unbelievable."

Kings cleared his throat. "How about we pray for Sam?"

"Great idea," Shayne said, grabbing Kingston's arm. "Come on, circle 'round, Cornerstonees. Jake's missing, but let's just say he's here in spirit."

"If we must," Allie whispered. But it was with a smile.

When we drew together, I ended up with Kings on one side and Sam on the other. We assumed the position we'd started using in our Cornerstone gatherings, with our right hand on the shoulder of the person beside us—closing the circle without the awkwardness of hand-holding. I felt the dampness of perspiration under Kings' shirt, and I imagined the hand he placed on Shayne's shoulder was just as damp. Sam's hand came to rest lightly on my shoulder.

Kings started the prayer, and Shayne put in some of her own, mostly about safe travel and meaningful time with family. When Allie added more about Sam learning and appreciating the world,

I realized I would be the only one who didn't have something to contribute.

Unless I did. After a pause that probably wasn't as long as it felt, I said, "And keep your angels around him. And Mr.—Dr. Newman." I felt Sam's fingers tighten, just slightly, on my shoulder.

"In Jesus' name," Kings prompted, "all His Kingdom kids said…"

"Amen!"

"Group hug," Shayne declared.

A five-way hug isn't a hug as much as a tangle of arms, and an occasional conking of skulls. But it provided some comic relief. I smelled lemons and chlorine and sweat—and eucalyptus and rosemary? Sam's head beside mine, close enough that I could smell his shampoo. (The same as my dad's. I knew it too well.) That fragrance tapped a deep well of emotion, like smells sometimes do, but I pushed it down. A sudden burst of tears at this point would be totally misunderstood.

All of that in about three seconds' time, then we were pulling back again. But Sam's face turned, and for a moment his mouth brushed over my hair, beside my ear. I think I felt the tickle of his breath for about a month afterwards.

"IM?" he murmured. The others, laughing, couldn't hear.

What could I say? Two-letter questions had to get two-letter answers.

"OK."

forty-eight

My next five-and-a-half weeks were unexpectedly unawful. First of all, they were busy. Freshman orientation at Whitestone High pounced upon me—not so much like the lion on the gazelle, more like the queen hen on the lowly, unsuspecting chicken, pointless and a little bit sad but maybe also sort of funny. Take the concept of 'orientation'. A couple of hours wandering the labyrinth of halls and meeting the leaders of all the school clubs who adore your older sister and assume you'll be her genetic clone... Surely it was a typo; they meant 'disorientation'. But it wasn't all bad: my ID photo turned out halfway decent (no glaring blemishes).

Then there was Gran Judy, who felt we hadn't been spending nearly enough time together and therefore drafted me into gardening service in her yard. "You're in training. By next spring you'll be ready to tackle your own yard," she said. When I wasn't weeding, watering, weeding, pruning or weeding, she would take me along on some of her church's Feed My Sheep meal deliveries for shut-ins. Shut-ins, it turns out, are perfectly nice people who it just so happens can't get out to shop and stuff. They tend to want you to eat cookies and talk with them. This I can manage.

On top of all this, something new: back-to-school clothes shopping with Mom and Sheelan. Of course I'd seen the two of them do this for a few years now, usually with envy (not for the particular clothes Sheelan chose, just the freedom from school uniforms). Now I gained a glimmer of wisdom, a glimpse of the goodness of the dreaded uniform. It had made things so much *simpler*.

Multiple days and endless hours of trudging through malls, department stores, and discount emporiums (minus Sheelan, of course, at the discount joints) saw me with a semi-decent, Mom-and-Sheelan-approved fall wardrobe. I had no clue whether it reflected my own sense of style since I wasn't sure I had one. Unless comfortable is a sense of style.

During all of this, I never failed to make a daily visit to the website where Sam would post his latest shots of England, then New York (not the city, like I'd pictured…apparently there was much more to NY than NYC). We could leave comments, which is how we ended up also keeping in touch with Jake over the rest of the summer. There was always a running commentary, even on the days when Sam hadn't posted anything new.

But whether he posted photos or not, I could almost always count on hearing a *ding* from the computer sometime in the afternoon (while he was in England) or evening (New York). I made it a point to be within earshot of the computer after dinner. Sheelan seemed to find this inconvenient or slightly annoying, and my mom, maybe a bit amusing, but she didn't say much. For the most part, they even gave me some privacy.

I can't say there was anything private going on in our messaging. It was 75% everyday stuff and about 20% sheer silliness, but with an unpredictable 5% Deep Conversation scattered throughout. I had to admit, the easiness of talking to

Sam was made that much easier when he was far away. Somehow I just seemed to relax and my brain worked better.

"You've been chatting quite a bit with that boy friend of yours," Mom said in passing one night.

"He's not my boyfriend, Mom."

"I didn't say boyfriend," she said, all innocent and twinkly-eyed.

I resisted the urge to proclaim up and down that Samuel Solomon Newman was definitely not my boyfriend. Somehow I had the sense to realize that protesting would only make it look like I was trying to hide the truth. The truth was, he wasn't anything like that. Somewhere in all those IM conversations, I'd realized, almost against my will, that Sam had become my best friend. Only I couldn't just call him that, claim him like that, so I wondered if it really counted.

I began knowing another Friend better, too. Of all my visitations, visions, dreams, and whatever other names you might give my experiences in the last eighteen months or so, one in particular had left the deepest imprint on me—like a thumbprint pressed into my soul, so the deepest parts of me flowed along its curving, bending pathways. It was the dream of the condemning voice and the horrible weight on my back, a weight suddenly lifted that became a yoke, shared by a Friend, gentle and lowly of heart, who offered rest for my soul. (The day I found Matthew 11:28-30, I had one of those soul-singing, life-coming-together-with-a-great-big-satisfying-click moments. Martina had been right: the more I ate at this Banquet, the hungrier I got.)

So, perched on the verge of some big changes in my life, I had a surprising calmness. I knew better than to think I had it all together, but the pieces of my life were at least starting to gravitate towards each other instead of the usual random scatter. Mom was home more, and the days had a rhythm because of it. My friends had pulled together into the unit I'd always hoped we could be—

and some parts of it were even better than I'd hoped. I had started to draw nearer to God, and what do you know, proving Himself faithful to His promises yet again, there He was, drawing near to me. No doubt, there were still holes and cracks in my life, but they weren't hurting as much.

So late in August, the night before we expected Sam to return from his trip and mere days before the start of school, when I had the dream, I welcomed it. The timing just seemed right, a period at the end of a sentence. I walked the dream path before me, steady-footed and looking ahead patiently but eagerly.

I saw her sitting beside the path, her back to me. She seemed intent on something—the Book in her lap, I guessed. I walked towards her, ready for the Word she would read to me with the tip of her finger.

But she turned and stood, and the thing in her hands was not a Book, but a sheathed Sword. It was her but not her: some familiarity of feature, but chased with a fierce light, as if it were a façade barely covering the truth beneath it. Beautiful, but not even necessarily female. I had the barest glimpse of what this creature really was, and it was enough to turn my legs to jelly.

She (he? it?) ran a hand along the length of the scabbard; it gleamed with the letters of some otherworldly alphabet. Somehow for an instant I could read them: *Thy Kingdom Come.* She observed me with eyes like cut emerald cups holding yellow flame. I looked down at myself and saw that I wore some Armor. Not heavy or clunky, not even what you would call solid, unless water and fire can be solid. Sleek and perfectly made for me...but not firmly strapped on, the pieces not all there. I looked back up at that almost unbearable face and found, to my relief, that there was still a gentleness there.

She didn't speak, but a thought was conveyed to me as clearly as if she had. *You didn't think this was over, did you?*

Over? Of course not.

Well, maybe I thought I was in a straightaway. A smooth stretch. A time out, even. "No," I answered.

Good. Because it's time you learned to wield this. With a song of steel, a swift flash of light, she dragged the Sword from its scabbard.

I woke suddenly in the pearl-grayness before dawn to the sounds of birds and the soft quick thudding of my own heart. I had that feeling you might feel on the morning you were leaving for a big trip. And not a trip as in tripping down the stairs—a life-changing, who knows when you'll get back and if you'll even be the same person when you do kind of trip.

That wasn't exactly what happened next. Then again, it sort of exactly was.

Made in the USA
Lexington, KY
27 June 2013